OUT OF CONTROL

OUT OF CONTROL

Assessing the General Theory of Crime

EDITED BY ERICH GOODE

STANFORD SOCIAL SCIENCES
An imprint of Stanford University Press
Stanford, California

Stanford University Press
Stanford, California

Printed in the United States of America on acid-free, archival-quality paper.

Library of Congress Cataloging-in-Publication Data

Out of control : assessing the general theory of crime / edited by Erich Goode.
    p. cm.
 Includes bibliographical references and index.
 ISBN 978-0-8047-5819-2 (cloth : alk. paper) — ISBN 978-0-8047-5820-8 (pbk. : alk. paper)
 1. Criminology—Methodology. 2. Criminal behavior. 3. Self-control. 4. Gottfredson, Michael R. General theory of crime. I. Goode, Erich.
 HV6018.O87 2008
 364.01—dc22

                        2008005789

Typeset by Bruce Lundquist in 10/13.5 Minion

crime is an artifact of age, sex, and race and whether this basic correlation is sustained after these key variables are held constant or controlled. In Chapter 4 Sally Simpson and Gilbert Geis expand on the concept of opportunity in Gottfredson and Hirschi's self-control theory. Francis Cullen, James Unnever, John Paul Wright, and Kevin Beaver discuss in Chapter 5 the link that Gottfredson and Hirschi draw between poor, inadequate child rearing and low self-control—the linchpin of their general theory.

Part II covers how various criminological theories fare under the onslaught of Gottfredson and Hirschi's critiques. In Chapter 6 Ronald Akers treats the question of whether social learning theory might actually subsume self-control theory, that is, whether the general theory might be a *subset* of Akers's learning theory of deviance. In Chapter 7 Richard Rosenfeld and Steven Messner share their views on the relationship between the general theory of crime and the anomie approach. In Chapter 8 Ross Matsueda argues that Gottfredson and Hirschi have overly constricted the general theory of crime; their framework must be expanded to be compatible with social disorganization theory. And last for this part, in Chapter 9 LeeAnn Iovanni and Susan Miller challenge the general theory with omissions and distortions with respect to the role of gender in crime causation and victimization.

Part III is devoted to a discussion of the impact of the general theory on types of crime. Chapter 10, by David Friedrichs and Martin Schwartz, focuses on white-collar crime; in Chapter 11, by Richard Felson and Wayne Osgood, violent crime makes its appearance; Marc Swatt and Robert Meier's Chapter 12 covers property crime; and my contribution, Chapter 13, treats drug use.

Part IV offers the reader some concluding thoughts: Chapter 14, by Gilbert Geis, gives us a "hypercritical assessment"; and in Chapter 15, responding to the critics of *A General Theory of Crime*, Travis Hirschi and Michael Gottfredson have the last word on the subject of the validity of self-control theory.

I take this opportunity to thank the contributors to this volume for their outstanding essays on the general theory of crime, an approach that has become perhaps the most compelling perspective in the field of criminological theory. I feel especially grateful to Travis Hirschi and Michael Gottfredson for their willingness to cooperate with this project, one that exposes their precious intellectual offspring to the rough, rude, inconsistent hands of unbelievers, skeptics, and supporters alike. But this book, as others and I explain, provides testimony to both their brilliance and the importance of their theory's central place in criminology—more than fair exchange for the critical assessment collected here.

Erich Goode
Greenwich Village
October 2007

recognition of this contradiction in substantive positivism was worth the price of admission. In any case, it earned my respect and piqued my interest.

The second feature that intrigued me about Gottfredson and Hirschi's general theory of crime was their stress on situational factors, or "opportunity." They argue that the substantive positivist's failure to address the process that translates a *general tendency* into a *specific act* is a critical flaw of positivist criminology. When I was in graduate school, Albert K. Cohen published an article in the *American Sociological Review* titled "The Sociology of the Deviant Act" (1965). In it Cohen raised a number of points that remain with me when I think about the relationship between deviant behavior and social interaction. Addressing Merton's anomie theory, Cohen asks, given anomie, "what will a person do about it?" A major portion of industrial society experiences the generic force Merton refers to as "strain." But how does strain translate into the deviant behaviors that are sketched out in Merton's "Social Structure and Anomie" (1938)? What is the connection between a factor and an act? Cohen locates this intermediary step in the "micro-sociology of the deviant act."

Gottfredson and Hirschi raise much the same point as Cohen did, but they supply a radically different answer. They distinguish "criminality," that is, the tendency or *predisposition* to engage in criminal behavior, from "crime," that is, the enactment of the criminal *event* in a particular situation at a particular time. For them, opportunity, not social interaction, bridges this gap. Gottfredson and Hirschi recognize that predispositions do not automatically translate into behavior. A particular tendency expresses itself only if the appropriate conditions—that is, opportunities—present themselves. This recognition and the discussion that followed it attracted me to *A General Theory of Crime*. I wish the authors had accorded the role of opportunity as much detail and space as they gave self-control, the other half of their crime equation, but they open the door to such a discussion, should other researchers wish to accept their invitation. I found, interestingly, their discussion of opportunity to be consonant with an aspect of Albert Cohen's interactionism, even though the substance of the two theories is worlds apart.

I came to this project, therefore, with the utmost respect for Michael Gottfredson and Travis Hirschi as criminologists and sociologists and for their self-control explanation of deviance and crime, as spelled out in *A General Theory of Crime*. As controversial as the general theory is, it has not received a book-length assessment by a range of scholars who weigh in, variously, on its merits. This book attempts to undertake precisely that mission.

THE BOOK

Out of Control offers the first detailed, book-length assessment by a range of scholars of the pros and cons of Gottfredson and Hirschi's *General Theory of Crime* for the field of criminology and deviance studies.

Part I is devoted to the considerations raised by the general theory of crime. In Chapter 1, the introduction, I summarize the general theory of crime and the central issues it raises. In Chapter 2 Alex Piquero discusses the fundamental issue of how Gottfredson and Hirschi measure the relevant variables, especially self-control. In Chapter 3 David Greenberg focuses on the matter of whether and to what extent the relationship between self-control and

CONTENTS

the topic and the approach of these theorists are worlds removed from, even antagonistic to, my own. This assessment is inaccurate. For me two major features made a detailed exploration of *A General Theory of Crime* a compelling and rewarding experience.

The first feature of Gottfredson and Hirschi's general theory of crime that intrigued me was the authors' brilliant solution to a problem that had puzzled me for decades. Some thirty-odd years ago, Hirschi (1973) took me, among others, to task for my constructionist approach to deviance, crime, and delinquency. What interested me back then was the paradox of and seeming contradiction between how violating norms and laws—socially constructed phenomena—could be caused by essentialistic, materially real forces, such as social structure, neighborhood disorganization, individual background factors, childhood experiences, and genetic predisposition, that are *independent* of this construction process. If positivist criminology—and, by extension, explanations of deviance—bases its definition of crime on the law or the norms, both socially constructed, how can any theory it devises posit the causal influence of stable, universal factors that are constant in a range of social settings? This is clearly a contradiction. How can one explain a variable with a constant? How can one explain the violation of socially constructed phenomena with factors that are independent of these phenomena, defined not by the state but by the scientist? Such an exercise seemed to me (as it does to Gottfredson and Hirschi) to violate one of the most fundamental rules of causality. At the time the mission of positivism seemed to be in jeopardy; all explanatory schemes, those in the social sciences at least, seemed in peril. In 1975 I wrote a paper on the subject and delivered it, at the invitation of David Peterson, as a lecture at Georgia State University, but I lacked the confidence to shape it into publishable form; its manuscript has been lost through the cracks in my many moves since that time.

It wasn't until I read Gottfredson and Hirschi's *General Theory of Crime* fifteen years later that I came upon a resolution of this dilemma. Gottfredson and Hirschi brilliantly recognize this dilemma as a fatal flaw of positivism—at least, the brand of positivism they refer to as "substantive" positivism. Positivist criminology's flaw, they say, lies in its *legalism*, that is, in passively accepting the state's definition of what a crime is. Clearly legalism is a form of constructionism: It deems that the *law* defines a crime, not the scientist. Laws vary from one jurisdiction to another. Basing one's definition of what a crime is on what the state says it is fogs up the issue of what the basic, essential nature of crime is. In so doing, the criminologist passively complies with the action of a social body that is *separate from and independent of* the dynamics that produce a certain type of human behavior. Why should there be any connection between the actions of a legislature and what causes the behavior we wish to explain? The legalistic definition of crime is artificial because it has nothing to do with the actions it attempts to explain; what it *does* address is what legislators do. Hence any explanatory theory based on it must of necessity ring hollow.

Rather than define crime as a social construct, Gottfredson and Hirschi adopt a materialist or *essentialist* definition. Crime exists—*as crime*—regardless of what a legislature says it is, they argue. Their definition makes the claim that crime is the same everywhere, in all societies at all times, a universal—and, in a sense, an absolute in organized human life: It is force or fraud in pursuit of self-interest. The criminologist must adopt a definition that is true to, reflects, and is consistent with the phenomenon itself. For me, Gottfredson and Hirschi's

PREFACE

More than forty years ago, in the preface to his "discussion and critique" of Robert K. Merton's anomie theory of deviance, Marshall Clinard wrote, "Few sociological formulations have provoked greater interest and discussion than anomie" (1964, p. v). Today, following the eclipse and partial resurrection of anomie theory, the same "greater interest and discussion" description applies to Michael Gottfredson and Travis Hirschi's *General Theory of Crime*, published in 1990. No book in the field of criminology is quoted, commented on, and critiqued as much as *General Theory*, and none has been both widely praised and damned as much. Although Merton's formulation argued that "deviant behavior such as crime, delinquency, mental disorder, alcoholism, and suicide arises, in large part, from inadequacies in the social structure" (Clinard, 1964, p. v), Gottfredson and Hirschi *reconstituted* the relevant dependent and independent variables, arguing that deviant behaviors such as crime—including white-collar and property crime, delinquency, violence, illicit drug use, smoking and alcohol abuse, sexual irresponsibility, reckless driving, poor school performance, and laziness—arise in large part from inadequacies in parenting.

This is an astonishing claim, and for several reasons. For one thing, in our era of specialization it makes a bold, broad, and sweeping claim, seemingly explaining a major swath of human misbehavior. No, a different explanation for a different crime, much of the field argues; each theory should explain a segment of the picture, says common wisdom. Gottfredson and Hirschi reject such qualifications, storming the fortress of criminological theory with a consistent, coherent, and unified theory. Moreover, these investigators offer an empirical, material, eminently generalizable explanation—surely the measure of a *positivist* theory—in the context of their *critique* of positivism. And in an age of ever more sophisticated statistical elaborations, Gottfredson and Hirschi's argument is eminently accessible to the nonquantitative reader.

What led me, a constructionist and symbolic interactionist of deviance and drug use, to become sufficiently interested in Gottfredson and Hirschi's general—and *positivist*—theory of crime as to be moved to edit a collection of original essays on the topic? It would seem that

CONTRIBUTORS

RONALD L. AKERS is a professor of criminology and sociology in the Department of Criminology, Law, and Society at the University of Florida. He is the author or coauthor of *Deviant Behavior, Criminological Theories,* and *Social Learning and Social Structure* as well as more than 100 book chapters and articles in sociology and criminology journals such as *Social Forces,* the *Journal of Research in Crime and Delinquency,* and *Criminology.* He is a past president of the American Society of Criminology.

KEVIN M. BEAVER is an assistant professor in the College of Criminology and Criminal Justice at Florida State University and the coauthor of two dozen articles and chapters in social science and criminology books and journals.

FRANCIS T. CULLEN is Distinguished Research Professor of Criminal Justice and Sociology at the University of Cincinnati and the author or coauthor of a half-dozen books, including *Criminological Theory, Rethinking Crime and Deviance Theory,* and *Combating Corporate Crime.* He also has published articles in such journals as *Criminology,* the *American Sociological Review,* and *Social Problems.* Cullen is a past president of the American Society of Criminology.

RICHARD B. FELSON is a professor of crime, law, and justice and sociology at Pennsylvania State University. He is the author of *Violence and Gender Reexamined,* coauthor of *Violence, Aggression, and Coercive Actions,* and coeditor of *Aggression and Violence.* In addition, he is the author of dozens of articles in the social science and criminological literature.

DAVID O. FRIEDRICHS is a professor of sociology and criminal justice and Distinguished University Fellow at the University of Scranton. He is the author of *Trusted Criminals: White Collar Crime in Contemporary Society* and *Law in Our Lives* and editor of *State Crime.* In addition, he has contributed more than 100 articles, book chapters, and entries in encyclopedias.

GILBERT GEIS is professor emeritus in the Department of Criminology, Law, and Society at the University of California, Irvine, and the author or coauthor of two dozen books, including *White Collar and Corporate Crime, Criminal Justice and Moral Issues,* and *Not the Law's Business: An Examination of Homosexuality, Abortion, Prostitution, Narcotics, and*

Gambling in the United States. Gilbert Geis is a past president of the American Society of Criminology.

ERICH GOODE is professor emeritus of sociology at the State University of New York at Stony Brook and is currently a visiting scholar at New York University. He is the editor of a half-dozen anthologies, most recently, *Extreme Deviance*, and the author of ten books, including *Drugs in American Society, Deviant Behavior, Between Politics and Reason: The Drug Legalization Debate*, and *Deviance in Everyday Life*.

MICHAEL R. GOTTFREDSON is a professor of criminology, law, and society and sociology and the executive vice-chancellor and provost at the University of California, Irvine. He has published numerous articles, chapters, and books, including *Control Theories of Crime and Delinquency, The Generality of Deviance*, and most notably, *A General Theory of Crime*.

DAVID F. GREENBERG is a professor of sociology at New York University and the author, coauthor, or editor of *The University of Chicago Graduate Problems in Physics, with Solutions, Struggle for Justice, Mathematical Criminology, Crime and Capitalism, Linear Path Analysis*, and *The Construction of Homosexuality*.

TRAVIS HIRSCHI is a regents professor emeritus in the Department of Sociology at the University of Arizona. He is the author of *The Craft of Criminology* and *Causes of Delinquency* and coauthor of *Delinquency Research* and of the subject of this volume, *A General Theory of Crime*. Travis Hirschi is a past president of the American Society of Criminology.

LEEANN IOVANNI is a lecturer in the Department of Sociology, Social Work, and Organization at Aalborg University in Denmark. She has published extensively in the areas of labeling theory, deterrence, social control theories of juvenile delinquency and dating violence, and criminal justice responses to violence against women.

ROSS L. MATSUEDA is a professor of sociology at the University of Washington. He has contributed dozens of articles and chapters to the criminological literature and is a coauthor of two chapters that appeared in *The Many Colors of Crime*.

ROBERT F. MEIER is a professor of criminal justice at the University of Nebraska, Omaha, and the coauthor of *Sociology of Deviant Behavior, Criminal Justice and Moral Issues, Crime and Its Social Context*, and *Victimless Crime? Prostitution, Drugs, Homosexuality, and Abortion*. In addition, he has published numerous articles in criminology and criminal justice journals.

STEVEN F. MESSNER is a distinguished teaching professor of sociology at the State University of New York at Albany. He is coeditor of *Theoretical Integration in the Study of Deviance and Crime* and the coauthor of *Crime and the American Dream* and has contributed dozens of articles to the literature.

SUSAN L. MILLER is a professor of sociology and criminal justice at the University of Delaware and the author of *Victims as Offenders: The Paradox of Women's Violence in Relationships* and *Gender and Community Policing*. She is editor or coeditor of a number of books of readings, including *Crime Control and Women* and *Criminal Justice and Diversity*.

D. WAYNE OSGOOD is a professor in the Crime, Law, and Justice Program in the Department of Sociology at Pennsylvania State University. He edited *On Your Own Without a Net:*

The Transition to Adulthood for Vulnerable Populations and has written more than sixty journal articles and book chapters.

ALEX R. PIQUERO is a professor of criminology, law, and society at the John Jay College of Criminal Justice at the City University of New York. He is the author or coauthor of more than 150 academic articles and book chapters as well as coauthor of three books: *Rational Choice and Criminal Behavior*, *Key Issues in Criminal Career Research*, and *Police Integrity*.

RICHARD ROSENFELD is a professor of criminology and criminal justice at the University of Missouri, St. Louis, the coauthor of *Crime and the American Dream*, and the editor of *Crime and Social Institutions*.

MARTIN D. SCHWARTZ is a professor of sociology and a Presidential Research Scholar at Ohio University. He is the author, coauthor, or coeditor of fourteen books, including *Professing Humanist Sociology*, *Race, Gender, and Class in Criminology*, *Under Siege*, and *Sexual Assault on the College Campus*. He has also published more than 100 articles and book and encyclopedia chapters and entries.

SALLY S. SIMPSON is professor and chair of the Department of Criminology and Criminal Justice at the University of Maryland, the editor of *Of Crime and Criminality*, author of *Corporate Crime, Law, and Social Control*, and author or coauthor of dozens of articles in such professional journals as the *American Sociological Review* and *Criminology*.

MARC L. SWATT is an assistant professor of criminal justice at Northeastern University. He has collaborated on articles on subjects as diverse as sex differences in criminal homicide, research methods in criminology, crime victimization, and urban crime patterns.

JAMES D. UNNEVER is an associate professor of criminology at the University of South Florida, Sarasota, and author of *Understanding Crime* and a score of articles published in the professional literature.

JOHN PAUL WRIGHT is an associate professor of criminal justice at the University of Cincinnati. He is the coeditor of *Taking Stock: The Status of Criminological Theory* and has published more than fifty academic articles across a range of scientific journals.

OUT OF CONTROL

I GENERAL CONSIDERATIONS

1

OUT OF CONTROL?

AN INTRODUCTION TO THE

GENERAL THEORY OF CRIME

Erich Goode

Theories that explain a broad range of phenomena are powerful. The broader the range of phenomena a theory explains, the more powerful it is. The aim of any theorist is to account not simply for this or that particular phenomenon but for entire *classes* of phenomena. The ambitious criminologist aims to explain not merely, say, the theft of sterling silver but theft in general; not merely theft but all crime; and, perhaps most ambitiously, not merely crime but wrongdoing or deviance in general. Still, every theorist encounters exceptions to the rule. Perhaps thieves who specialize in stealing silver are so rare as to be exceptional, uncharacteristic of thieves in general. If the theft of silver is rare, atypical, and exceptional, then no theory that explains crime in general but fails to account for such theft can be regarded as deficient. But if such theft does have a common thread with crime in general, then an explanation that accounts for crime in general will explain it and hence will satisfy our defining criterion of a powerful theory.

In this book the contributors and I look at and evaluate an explanation of crime—the general theory of crime, also referred to as self-control theory—that is perhaps the most ambitious theory criminologists have yet devised. This theory is the brainchild of criminologists Michael Gottfredson and Travis Hirschi; the title of their book that spells out the theory expresses the ambitiousness of their scope: *A General Theory of Crime* (1990). As Gottfredson and Hirschi boldly state in the preface to their book, no other explanation in the field of criminology "seems to have the ring of truth" (1990, xiii). All other theories of crime, they argue, collapse when confronted by the evidence, because such theories do not take into account the fundamental nature of crime. All other explanations that came before, Gottfredson and Hirschi say, are laid to waste by their general theory of crime. Only theirs, they assert, possesses that ring of truth.

In *A General Theory of Crime* Gottfredson and Hirschi argue that low self-control is *the* explanation for criminal behavior in general. (To be precise, low self-control is half the criminal equation, a point I'll return to shortly.) In other words, Gottfredson and Hirschi claim that their theory has broad, sweeping, and general application—as we saw, the hallmark of a powerful theory.

Even crimes not customarily associated with low impulse control are swept into the theory's orbit. White-collar crime, say Gottfredson and Hirschi, is not the patient, high-level, planned-out, organized, future-oriented behavior most criminologists think it is. The bulk of white-collar crime, they argue, is made up of petty, sordid, low-level, impulsive, boiler-room enterprises run by poorly educated, underfunded operators who are caught because they have no idea what they are doing. Drug use? There's no need to explain the relationship between crime and drug use because they are two aspects of exactly the same behavior—two sides of the same coin. Explain one and you have explained the other. Specialization in a particular type of crime? There is virtually no such thing; criminality is a general tendency, and the reasons that certain people engage in it are generalizable to all crime. In fact, their theory is so sweeping, Gottfredson and Hirschi say, that it explains behavior that is not even criminal, such as getting into accidents, being unemployed, experiencing marital discord, smoking, drinking, and engaging in teenage sex. In short, criminals are *versatile*; they engage in a wide range of criminal acts and analogous behavior. Gottfredson and Hirschi do not believe that specific theories need or should be invoked to explain specific types of crime. Specific crimes should not have their "own theory" (Gottfredson and Hirschi, 1990, xvi). Following the rule of parsimony, one theory ought to explain all crimes. Theories addressing narrow classes of phenomena are *weak* explanations; theories accounting for broad classes of phenomena—the broader, the better—are, as we saw, *powerful* explanations.

Plausible theories of any general class of phenomena—explanations whose creators convince a substantial number of practitioners in a given discipline or field that their explanation is true and valid—are extremely difficult to devise. Theories that capture the imagination of those practitioners and stimulate a substantial number of researchers to pursue new lines of investigation come along perhaps once every generation or so. The boldness of Gottfredson and Hirschi's claims and the persuasiveness of their arguments have inspired a virtual Niagara of research, references, citations, books, and scholarly articles. A recent citation count of articles appearing in the twenty most prominent and widely read criminology journals revealed that no other work was cited with greater frequency than Gottfredson and Hirschi's *General Theory of Crime* in the five years following its publication (Cohn and Farrington, 1999). From the volume's first to its third year in print, the number of citations to it in the literature, as measured by the *Social Sciences Citation Index*, tripled. All criminology textbooks devote a major discussion to self-control theory. It is one of the leading two or three theoretical perspectives adopted by graduate students conducting their research; it has inspired dozens of theses and dissertations. And members of the field talk about it—in the classroom, in their publications, in informal groups. Clearly, self-control theory is an explanation of crime that is of *interest* and *importance* to the entire field. Its place in criminology is unique. The general theory of crime cries out for a lengthy, detailed evaluation by a range of observers. That is precisely what we intend to achieve in this book.

GOTTFREDSON AND HIRSCHI'S DEFINITION OF CRIME

All explanatory or ethological theories have the same logical structure. They posit an *independent* variable and a *dependent* variable. The independent variable is the factor that *causes* something, and the dependent variable is *that which is caused*. In all explanatory theories of crime, the dependent variable is *crime*, or criminal behavior, and the independent variable is the central mechanism, factor, or variable named by the theory. A biogenetic theory of crime argues that certain configurations of genes (the independent variable) cause criminal behavior (the dependent variable). Social disorganization theory argues that living in a socially and geographically unstable neighborhood (the independent variable) causes crime and delinquency (the dependent variable). What is Gottfredson and Hirschi's dependent variable? The answer is much more complex—and much more interesting—than "criminal behavior."

The question "What causes crime?" puts the cart before the horse, Gottfredson and Hirschi argue; it necessitates a prior and more fundamental question: What is crime? Gottfredson and Hirschi intend to define crime's "essential nature" before they attempt to explain what causes it (1990, xv). Other, competing theories do not ask what it is specifically about crime that forges a causal link between it and their variable or factor—whether a biological defect, peer or gang influence, or economic deprivation. Gottfredson and Hirschi's general theory of crime is almost unique in the extent to which it offers an explicit and detailed definition of criminal behavior. As we will see, this is an absolutely crucial point because Gottfredson and Hirschi demonstrate how *their theory* of criminal behavior articulates with *their definition* of crime.

Nearly all explanatory or positivistic theories of crime adopt a *legalistic* definition of crime: A crime is an act that violates a criminal statute or law. But laws are the creation of legislatures, courts or legal precedents, or, in earlier times, edicts issued by a monarch. In other words, if criminologists adopt the legalistic definition of a crime, they are acting in "passive compliance" with the action of a social body that is separate from and independent of the structure, logic, and dynamics that produce a certain type of human behavior (Gottfredson and Hirschi, 1990, 3). What connection could there possibly be between what a legislature says is against the law and what causes the behavior we wish to explain? The law does not call forth behavior of a certain sort. The legalistic definition of crime is artificial, the violation of a social construct, and hence cannot serve as our dependent variable. Therefore any explanatory theory based on it must, by its nature, be misleading. No other theory of crime asks the fundamental question, What is it about the legalistic definition of crime that causes a particular theory's independent variable to cause the behaviors named by it? The fact is, there is no inevitable connection between the legal construct and any conceivable material cause. It is this defect that Gottfredson and Hirschi address.

Instead of a definition based on a social construct—that is, the decisions of the representatives of one or more government institutions—Gottfredson and Hirschi adopt a materialist or *essentialist* definition. Crime is a materially real phenomenon in the material world—a reality separate from and independent of what social bodies decide "is" a crime. Crime exists—*as crime*—regardless of what the powers that be think or say it is. Gottfredson and Hirschi's definition makes the claim that crime is the same everywhere, in all societies, at all times, a universal—and, in a sense, an absolute in organized human life. Rather than chase after a whimsical, chimerical, ever-changing social creation, criminologists should adopt a *scientific* definition of crime, one that is true to, reflects, and is "consistent with the phenomenon itself" (Gottfredson and Hirschi, 1990, 3).

Gottfredson and Hirschi (1990) define crime as "acts of force or fraud undertaken in pursuit of self-interest" (p. 15). This includes theft (which provides "money without work"), rape ("sex without courtship"), violence ("revenge without court delays"), and a thousand and one actions we all recognize as criminal. According to this definition, the vast majority of such acts—crimes—"provide *immediate* gratification of desires" or provide "*easy or simple* gratification of desires"; they are "*exciting, risky, or thrilling*"; they "provide *few or meager* long-term benefits*" for the offender, "require *little skill or planning*," and "often result in *pain or discomfort for the victim*" (Gottfredson and Hirschi, 1990, 89). The "risky" aspect of this formulation is crucial because such acts are highly likely to result in injury to the victim as well as possible injury and arrest for the perpetrator. Hence the rewards that such acts reap are short-term; in the long run the actor loses more than he or she gains. Nearly all crimes are "mundane, simple, trivial, easy acts aimed at satisfying desires of the moment" (Gottfredson and Hirschi, 1990, xv). *These* are the essential qualities of crime, Gottfredson and Hirschi argue; any attempt to account for crime, they say, must be true to these qualities, and any explanation of crime that seeks to achieve that "ring of truth" must also define crime in this way.

Harnessing an explanation of crime to a legalistic definition *cannot* achieve its goal, because legalism reflects the social and cultural vagaries of legislative bodies. Any definition of crime as an act that requires the enterprise of a "diabolical genius" or an "ambitious seeker of the American dream" (Gottfredson and Hirschi, 1990, xv) must be false, because it cannot comport with the qualities detailed earlier. Only a theory based on a definition of crime that reflects the central character of crime—its petty, self-serving, mean-spirited, shortsighted, impulsive, hedonistic, and ultimately self-destructive nature—can ring true and be verified by scientific research.

Gottfredson and Hirschi open the door to the possibility that certain acts may be crimes, according to their definition, but are *not* shortsighted, impulsive, hedonistic, or, over the long run, self-destructive. For instance, consider extremely low risk, potentially high-payoff corporate crimes. From the strictly business perspective such crimes may make a great deal of sense—they would be economically rational—but they also qualify as acts of "force or fraud undertaken in pursuit of self-interest." (This assumes, of course, that the interests of the corporate actors and the interests of the corporation they work for are the same, or that, in achieving corporate ends, individual corporate actors achieve their own personal ends.) We will have more to say about the implications of white-collar and corporate crime in Chapter 10.

In proffering their own definition of crime, Gottfredson and Hirschi open a second door as well: the possibility that certain acts will be crimes according to the *legalistic* definition but not according to *theirs.* Consider the many "public order," "victimless," or "vice" crimes, such as prostitution, illicit drug possession and sale, public intoxication, and unauthorized gambling. All these actions violate one or more legal statutes but entail neither force nor fraud and have no clear-cut, nonconsensual, predatory victim. In Gottfredson and Hirschi's scheme of things, they qualify as "deviance" but not "crime."

Consider also crimes—*legalistic* crimes—much in the news following the events of September 11, 2001: terrorism. According to Gottfredson and Hirschi's definition, terrorism, a crime from the legal standpoint, is *not* a "crime" because it is not an act that is undertaken in pursuit of a self-interested goal. "Terrorist acts," Gottfredson and Hirschi state, "are excluded from self-control theory because they are assumed to reflect commitment to a political cause or organization. Terrorists do not act without regard for the broad or long-term consequences of their acts" (Hirschi and Gottfredson, 2001, 94). Therefore terrorism is not a crime—at least as Gottfredson and Hirschi have defined the term—and is not illuminated by their theory. Of course, terrorism is still a *state-defined* criminal act, they would say—it is just not explained by a lack of self-control.

As we saw, Gottfredson and Hirschi make an assertion that is even more daring than the claim that they intend to explain "all crime": Their theory also applies to the vice crimes, many of which are only technically illegal. In fact, crime as they have conceptualized it is but a *subset* of a much larger class of actions that is generally referred to as deviant behavior. These behaviors, or allied actions, include, in addition to the public order crimes I just mentioned, "accidents, victimizations, truancies from home, school, and work . . . , family problems, and disease," along with a swarming host of cognate or parallel behaviors, such as getting tattooed, smoking, drinking to excess, being lazy, being a couch potato, not exercising, eating unhealthful foods, having precocious sex, engaging in unprotected sex or sex with multiple partners, being sexually unfaithful to one's marital or domestic partner, cutting corners, slacking off a task, quitting, cheating, lying, and getting into angry arguments. Again, although none of these acts entail force or fraud—and hence, they are not crimes—they *do* share with Gottfredson and Hirschi's criminal behavior the qualities of being immediately gratifying, shortsighted, impulsive, and/or risky. Hence they too can be accounted for by the theory spelled out in *A General Theory of Crime.*

In sum, then, Gottfredson and Hirschi's theory attempts to explain most—but not all—acts that are defined as crimes both by the state and by their definition (e.g., burglary, robbery). Their theory also attempts to explain many acts that are not crimes according to both their and the state's definitions (e.g., alcoholism, sexual promiscuity, smoking). It also attempts to explain some acts that are defined as crimes by their definition but not by the state's (e.g., lying). It does *not* attempt to explain some acts that are defined as crimes by the state but are not so defined by their definition (e.g., terrorism). Of course, many acts that are products of low self-control—and hence acts that are explained by Gottfredson and Hirschi's theory—may technically be crimes in some jurisdictions but not others (e.g., adultery, gambling, the distribution and possession of pornography). In evaluating their theory, it is crucial to know that Gottfredson and Hirschi's definition of a crime overlaps with but is *not* identical to the legalistic or state-sanctioned definition.

Note that it is only because Gottfredson and Hirschi have discarded a constructionist definition of deviance and crime that they can argue that this class of behavior is explained by a lack of self-control. If we define deviance and crime by the violation of norms or laws, we face a much trickier and more daunting—indeed, in all likelihood, impossible—explanatory task. For instance, from a constructionist perspective homosexuality is clearly (although decliningly) a form of deviance: It violates the norm of heterosexuality. But it is *not* a consequence of the lack of self-control; its causal roots lie elsewhere. Hence homosexuality receives no illumination whatsoever in Gottfredson and Hirschi's general theory of crime. The same is true of a great many sexual variations—such as swinging and sado-masochism—that require, as does homosexuality, consent and/or an organized community. Likewise, most deviant beliefs—for instance, religious heterodoxy, belief in paranormal powers, or the belief that extraterrestrials are real—do not grow out of low self-control and hence remain outside the scope of Gottfredson and Hirschi's explanatory ambit. In addition, aberrant mental conditions, disorders, and illnesses remain unilluminated by self-control theory. And likewise, physical conditions, which violate the norms of acceptable appearance or performance—Goffman's "abominations of the body" (1963, 4 and elsewhere)—cannot be explained by the general theory of crime. Most generally, these behaviors, beliefs, and conditions do *not* flow from a lack of self-control, and, more specifically, they are *not* crimes (or even deviance) by the lights of Gottfredson and Hirschi's definition because they do not entail "force or fraud undertaken in pursuit of self-interest."

Nonetheless, the claim of *A General Theory of Crime* is bold. It underscores the point that general theories are powerful theories. Self-control theory is above all—as the title of the book that conveys it announces—a *general* theory of crime, and much more as well. It denies that specific crimes have different, particular, and specific explanations. As we saw, the aim of the theory is "to explain all crime at all times, and, for that matter, many forms of behavior that are not sanctioned by the state" (Gottfredson and Hirschi, 1990, 117). Gottfredson and Hirschi are contemptuous of the criminological practice of devising one theory for white-collar crime and a different one for street crime; one theory for serious crimes and one for petty offenses; one for property offenses and one for violent offenses; one for victimless, public order, or vice crimes and one for predatory crimes, that is, those that victimize others; and, for that matter, one theory for burglars who specialize in stealing silver and a different one for those who do not specialize at all. "All of these distinctions are without import," they say, and "such distinctions mislead more than they inform." Pursuing separate and particular explanations for varieties of crime, they argue, "is a waste of time" (Gottfredson and Hirschi, 1990, 22). Gottfredson and Hirschi are adamantly opposed to "typologizing" or creating typologies, "empirical clusters," of different *kinds* of crimes, a different explanation for each type or cluster (1990, 50). They seek an explanation that is grounded in "a general theory of behavior" (1990, 49). It is to that theory we now turn our attention.

To repeat, it is important to emphasize that Gottfredson and Hirschi's definition of crime is an *essentialist* or materialist definition, not a constructionist one. Their position has enormous implications not only for the actions they seek to explain, as I just pointed out, but also for the conceptual territory they stake out. Their mission is exclusively explanatory. By this I mean that they have no interest whatsoever in exploring the construction of the social norms or the criminal laws. The whys and wherefores of social control are outside the scope of their theory. How certain norms came into being and are enforced, the dynamics of stigmatizing and labeling miscreants, how actors come to acquire a deviant or criminal identity, how they live with it—all these issues are excluded from Gottfredson and Hirschi's explanatory goal, as they are for all explanatory theories (except insofar as they might bear on explanations of wrongdoing). This is a limitation imposed by Gottfredson and Hirschi themselves, not a defect. Why do some of us commit crime? Why *don't* some of us commit crime? These are the guiding questions of the writers of *A General Theory of Crime*. The issues that constructionist sociologists of deviance are interested in, for example, are outside the scope of the concerns of Gottfredson and Hirschi.

WHAT IS THE GENERAL THEORY OF CRIME?

Two intellectual traditions spawned criminology: the "classical" or free will perspective; and positivism, that is, the natural science model (i.e., studying human behavior by adopting the same materialistic, cause-and-effect model that natural scientists use when they study rocks, stars, and frogs).

The classical perspective is the product of utilitarian thinkers such as Césare Beccaria (1738–1794) and Jeremy Bentham (1748–1832), who argued that human behavior is the outcome of a rational, self-interested calculation of how much pleasure will be derived or pain averted by engaging in or avoiding a given action. Actors, the free will theorists argue, attempt to maximize pleasure and minimize pain. Crime, this perspective claims, is no different in this respect from any other action. The classical school argues that citizens are "free to choose their course of conduct, whether it be legal or illegal" (Gottfredson and Hirschi, 1990, 5). Hence, proponents of the classical perspective argue, the state should inflict only so much pain on offenders as to avert the crime, that is, pain sufficient to offset the pleasure enjoyed by committing the offense. When citizens contemplate committing an offense, they weigh the immediate and potential pleasure they are likely to derive against the pain of punishment in the event of apprehension. If punishment is highly likely, reasonably swift, and sufficiently severe, most of us will decide not to offend. Nonetheless, as a result of inadequate or insufficient information, some misguided citizens may continue to make bad choices and offend anyway. Still, such citizens must be punished humanely. Above all, the classical school is a *legalistic* theory: Its fulcrum of attention is centered on the law and violations of the law. And it all but ignores individual differences. "In pure classical theory, people committing crimes had no special propensities. They merely followed the universal tendency to enhance their own pleasure. If they differed from noncriminals, it was with respect to their location in or comprehension of relevant sanction systems" (Gottfredson and Hirschi, 1990, 85).

The natural science model that emerged a century later was very different indeed and in many ways was contradictory with the classical theory. The first fully developed positivist studies of crime were undertaken by Adolphe Quételet (1796–1874), a Belgian mathematician who noticed that criminal offending varied from one social category to another and from one region to another. Even though Quételet always accepted some assumptions of free will theory, he believed in the natural science model to study human behavior, seeking the patterning of criminal behavior in lawlike regularities. However, it was not until the publication of *L'uomo delinquente* (*The Criminal Man*) in 1876, written by Italian physician Césare Lombroso (1835–1909), that criminology became fully clothed in the mantel of the natural science approach to the study of crime. Initially, Lombroso argued that crime was caused by biological defects or "atavisms"—genetic throwbacks to a more primitive form of humanity—that compelled some people to engage in crime. (In later editions of his work,

Lombroso modified his theory to encompass an increasing number of factors that caused criminal behavior.) His theory provided the foundation for the thinking of a cadre of researchers who make up the Positive school. Its most well-known American representative is Earnest A. Hooton (1939a, 1939b; Rafter, 2004).

Lombroso's brand of positivism contained the following elements. First, Lombroso rejected the "free will" assumption of classical criminology by arguing that some people are not rational. Indeed, he said, they are compelled to engage in antisocial behavior as a result of reasons they do not fully understand.

Second, Lombroso and his colleagues shifted the criminologist's focus away from crime as defined by the law to the characteristics of the actor. In fact, their theory differed markedly even from Quételet's more sociological, although decidedly positivistic, approach, which stressed the influence of social context and location. In contrast, Lombroso saw the relevant criminogenic factor as being located within the individual actor. In contrast, Quételet argued that variability among the population in the tendency to commit crime was the key explanatory variable here.

Third, the biological characteristic that marked criminals represented a defect or abnormality. The criminal was not only "different" from the rest of us normal folk, he was medically defective.

Fourth, for Lombroso and his followers, the concept of crime was not intellectually problematic. Indeed, they passively accepted the definition provided by the state. Gina Ferraro, Lombroso's daughter, said, "A criminal is a man who violates laws decreed by the State to regulate the relations between its citizens" (in Gottfredson and Hirschi, 1990, 49).

And last, because he realized that biological defect clearly could not explain *all* crime, Lombroso increasingly fell into the trap of creating ever-more elaborate classifications of different *kinds* of criminals, which included the "born" criminal, the "insane" criminal, the "epileptic" criminal, and the "occasional" criminal.

Despite the defects of his theory, however, Lombroso may well have been the most important criminologist who ever lived. The Positive school should not be remembered exclusively for being wrong about the importance of the biological factor in the genesis of crime, which the vast majority of criminologists, Gottfredson and Hirschi included, now reject. The work of Lombroso and his followers should be remembered because it firmly fixed in the intellectual community's mind the notion that criminology could be a scientific discipline. The legacy of the Positive school is that crime is caused by mechanisms that can be identified and explicated by the criminologist. This, not its biogenic focus, is its enduring legacy. And it is a legacy that Gottfredson and Hirschi share with Lombroso and his followers.

But for contemporary criminology there is a second legacy of the Positive school, one that the general theory of crime does *not* share. This legacy can be summed up in the following phrase: Study the *tendency* to commit crime and you have explained the *genesis* of crime. It is this track that Gottfredson and Hirschi most emphatically reject. They argue that criminality—the propensity to commit crime—must be married to the classical school's emphasis on the rational actor.

In the field of criminology the perspective spelled out in *A General Theory of Crime* is referred to as both self-control theory and the general theory of crime. In practice, the two terms are used interchangeably, and this book will follow that tradition. In principle, however, the theory is composed of two interlocking elements, only one of which concerns itself with self-control. Hence the term *self-control theory* is misleading because it identifies the part with the whole. The same is true of several other perspectives as well. For instance, labeling theory is only partly about deviance labeling; at least two proponents of the supposed theory have rejected this term for the perspective, preferring the term "interactionism" or "the interactionist approach" (Becker, 1973, 181, 183; Kitsuse, 1972, 235). But labeling theory is a catchy title, so it has stuck. And this applies to self-control theory as well.

What are the two foundational elements of the general theory? They are *criminality*, or the relative tendency or propensity to commit crime, and *crime*, or the actual commission of criminal behavior—which, following the self-interest component of the classical school, is contingent on the opportunity to commit crime. Criminality and opportunity are analytically separate and distinct components. The criminally inclined do *not* commit crime under any and all circumstances; they commit crime only after assessing their odds of success and failure, and that assessment takes place within the context of opportunity. As we saw, with the shrewd corporate executive the opposite side of the coin is that, under ideal conditions—circumstances with little risk of apprehension—individuals with high self-control are highly likely to commit criminal acts. Indeed, given that Gottfredson and Hirschi see humans as self-interested, certain risk-free opportunities to engage in force or fraud can be said to be *criminogenic*—that is, extremely likely to call forth criminal behavior for nearly all actors.

Indeed, Gottfredson and Hirschi are clear that an absence of self-control alone does not produce criminal behavior; it must be harnessed to opportunity. The lack of self-control "does not require crime and can be counteracted by situational conditions" (Gottfredson and Hirschi, 1990, 89). This makes their theory different from the "kinds of people" theories that argue that because criminals are different from the rest of us, they naturally, routinely, and inevitably commit crime. Whether or not they commit crime, Gottfredson and Hirschi argue, depends on the circumstances in which they are implicated. Hence both criminality and opportunity contribute to committing offenses and both must be investigated. By itself, a *propensity* to commit crime does not *automatically* produce criminal behavior. Taken separately, these two perspectives cannot fully explain crime; the combination of the two together, Gottfredson and Hirschi argue, provides the only empirically valid explanation of crime.

Gottfredson and Hirschi reject the notion that explaining the tendency to commit crime explains criminal behavior. Still, criminality is half the equation. What explains the tendency or propensity to commit crime? As the name *self-control theory* suggests, low self-control causes crime. Note that Gottfredson and Hirschi clearly feel uncomfortable using the word *cause*. Sometimes, when they do use it, they put it in quotation marks. What they mean by this is that self-control is not the only causal factor in determining criminal behavior. In fact, it is only half the equation. Obviously, opportunity plays a crucial role as well. The explanatory or positivist theories that Gottfredson and Hirschi critique seem to be missing the opportunity element of the crime equation; the authors object to the fact that people with low self-control commit crime under any and all circumstances. For Gottfredson and Hirschi's theory self-control is the positivist or explanatory component of their theory. People with low levels of self-control are more likely to engage in criminal behavior—holding opportunity constant—than those with higher levels of self-control. For Gottfredson and Hirschi's self-control theory of crime, low self-control defines—that is, constitutes—criminality.

Actors are characterized by low self-control to the extent that they are "vulnerable to the temptations of the moment" (Gottfredson and Hirschi, 1990, 87). And the explanatory or positivist theories that Gottfredson and Hirschi critique are missing the opportunity element of the equation. Hence, by implication, these theories seem to imply that, in being "vulnerable to the temptations of the moment," the actors are under the compunction to engage in criminal behavior under any and all circumstances, because much of what is tempting at a particular moment is crime. It provides the "*immediate* gratification of desires" (Gottfredson and Hirschi, 1990, 89). It is simpler and easier, quicker and more efficient, to grab what one wants illegally rather than obtain it through legitimate means. Obtaining and working at a legal job to pay for a watch, fashionable clothes, and a car take much more time and effort than stealing does. Enjoying the pleasure of getting drunk or high is immediate, visceral, and hedonistic, an experience available to anyone. In contrast, turning down that joint, those drinks, that pipe or line, may—or may not—yield health benefits ten or twenty (or more) years from now and involves giving up what is intrinsically pleasurable *right now*. Speeding down the highway at 120 is thrilling, exciting, and risky; traveling within the speed limit is boring and safe. For the violent, impulsive, and foolhardy, hitting someone who disses you over the head with a baseball bat exacts revenge. In contrast, figuring out a verbal way of retaliating with the use of wit, charm, or logic takes restraint, intelligence, and skill. "In sum, people who lack self-control will tend to be impulsive, insensitive, physical (as opposed to mental), risk-taking, short-sighted, and non-verbal, and they will tend therefore to engage in criminal and analogous acts" (Gottfredson and Hirschi, 1990, 90).

Gottfredson and Hirschi claim that manifesting low self-control is intellectually non-problematic. It is the natural thing to do, what humans would do in the absence of restraints. It is doing what comes naturally. It is what we would do in a feral condition. What needs to be explained, they say, is not low self-control but high self-control. Low self-control is not produced or inculcated in us by any positive processes, "not produced by training, tutelage, or socialization" (Gottfredson and Hirschi, 1990, 94–95). It is not learned; indeed, it does not *have* to be learned. Its causes are negative, not positive, that is, produced in the *absence* rather than the *presence* of something. No effort is required to produce it. The tendency to engage in crime is not "a product of socialization, culture, or positive learning of any sort" (Gottfredson and Hirschi, 1990, 96). In other words, their theory is *not* a theory of motivation (Gottfredson and Hirschi, 2003, 7). Indeed, no motivation to commit crime or deviance is necessary. All theories that claim that people need to be motivated to commit illicit acts are wrong, Gottfredson and Hirschi aver. What we need to learn, they say, is *not* to commit illicit acts.

Most social scientists would formulate self-control as a continuum, picturing a linear relationship between self-control (our independent variable) and criminal behavior (the dependent variable), taking into account, of course, the second of Gottfredson and Hirschi's independent variables—opportunity. Accordingly, we could plot this relationship in the form of a straight-line graph, with self-control as the x axis and crime as the y axis. Curiously, Gottfredson and Hirschi do not formulate their argument in probabilistic terms. Indeed, "the authors seem to de-emphasize the continuous qualities of a self-control trait, choosing instead to characterize it as a dichotomy. They typically refer to high or low self-control as if these were distinct categories" (Tittle, 1995, 60–61). Given everything we know about human behavior, it is inconceivable that self-control is a dichotomy, and it is not clear what purchase Gottfredson and Hirschi gain by conceiving it as much.

What produces low self-control? In a nutshell, "ineffective child-rearing" (Gottfredson and Hirschi, 1990, 97). Overwhelmingly, "discipline, supervision, and affection tend to be missing in the homes of delinquents" (p. 97). And the key to poor parenting is the failure to emotionally care for the children in their charge and to monitor, recognize, and sanction these children's untoward behavior. Indeed, "many parents do not even recognize the *criminal* behavior in their children, let alone minor forms of deviance whose punishment is necessary for effective childrearing" (p. 101). Once again, this is not a conscious process; parents do not choose or aim to produce asocial, feral children with low self-control who engage in delinquency and crime. Yet, by not caring for the child emotionally, by not having the time or energy to monitor the child's behavior, by not recognizing that certain harmful behavior is wrong, or by being unable or unwilling to punish the child, this is precisely what happens.

Note that poor parenting does not consist entirely of a laissez-faire or hands-off policy of child rearing. Indeed, harsh, misguided, ill-informed, and cruel punishment typically produces the same result (Gottfredson and Hirschi, 1990, 100; Hirschi and Gottfredson, 2003, 157–159). Gottfredson and Hirschi also argue that correlative to, in conjunction with, and in tandem with inadequate parenting are the nature of the emotional bond between parent and child, parental criminality, family size (the greater the number of children in a family, the less able a parent is to supervise the behavior of any specific child), living in a single-parent household (a single parent is less capable of supervising children than is true of two parents), and having a mother who works outside the home (a frequently absent mother is less able to monitor and control the behavior of her children than is one whose primary responsibility is child rearing). Each of these factors is related to bad parenting, Gottfredson and Hirschi write, and hence are likely to produce children with low self-control.

Do child-rearing practices constitute the only cause of criminality and hence of crime? Of course not, Gottfredson and Hirschi state (1990, 101n). In any given case any number of factors could contribute to deviant, delinquent, and criminal behavior. But exceptions aside, Gottfredson and Hirschi argue, low self-control is the preeminent cause of crime, and poor and inadequate parenting is the preeminent cause of low self-control (taking into account, as I explained, opportunity). In fact, another major institution is responsible for the supervision of the child's behavior at an early age: the school. To the extent that representatives of the school are unable or unwilling to maintain order and discipline and control disruptive behavior, they may contribute to the engenderment of their ward's lack of self-control and hence enable delinquent and criminal behavior. In principle, schools should impose restraint, inhibit the "unfettered pursuit of self-interest," and require and encourage accomplishment (Gottfredson and Hirschi, 1990, 107). In other words, the school is a "potentially successful training ground for the development of self-control" (p. 107). When schools fail to accomplish their mission, they contribute further to the growing child's criminal tendencies. In fact, Gottfredson and Hirschi regard the child's inability to perform in school—truancy, getting poor grades, school-related delinquencies, and dropping out before graduation—as one of the best predictors of later criminal behavior (Gottfredson and Hirschi, 1990, 162–163).

THE ROLE OF OPPORTUNITY IN THE GENERAL THEORY OF CRIME

Criminality alone, emphasize Gottfredson and Hirschi, does not explain the commission of criminal behavior; it does not demand or require crime. In a given instance someone with low self-control and hence strong criminal tendencies may refrain from committing a specific crime. In another instance someone with high self-control and hence a weak tendency to commit crime *may* commit a specific crime. A theory of criminal tendencies is the identification of a *distal* cause—a factor that lies in an actor's past. What a complete theory of crime needs, argue Gottfredson and Hirschi, is harnessing criminality to factors *proximate* to the criminal act. And those factors are addressed, the theorists say, by the classical or free will tradition.

As we saw, the classical school is based on the assumption that all humans tend to act to maximize pleasure (one component of which is the pleasure derived from the benefits of crime) and minimize pain (one component of which is punishment, including arrest and imprisonment). In short, this theoretical tradition assumes a *rational* actor. Of course, there are sanctions other than and in addition to being punished by the criminal justice system. The criminal act itself may be difficult or dangerous ("natural" sanctions); being caught or known as an offender may entail attracting social stigma ("social" sanctions); if one is religious, having committed a sin enters into the equation ("moral" and "supernatural" sanctions). In any case the classical school argues that the risk of arrest—or the actor's *perception* of the risk of arrest—enters into the "hedonistic calculus." To offend or not to offend? That is the question. Actors consider the answer to this question, the classical school argues, by using the same considerations that enter into contemplating any action. In this respect crime is no different from contemplating making a purchase, getting married, or choosing to go or not to go to college.

In classical theory's formulation punishment of offenders that is characterized by swiftness, certainty, and severity is effective in deterring crime; punishment that is slow, uncertain, and mild is unlikely to work. Here is one point, however, at which Gottfredson and Hirschi part company with classical theory. They do not believe that any criminal justice system—at least, none in a currently constituted, liberal, Western democracy—can deter crime. This is because the characteristics of the offender and the operation of any realistic criminal justice system are incompatible. No such system can impose punishment that is sufficiently swift, certain, or severe as to deter crime among individuals with low self-control. Such individuals do not consider the long-run perspective, that is, that which is outside the immediate situation of the offense itself. Hence they do not take the workings of the criminal justice system into account when contemplating whether or not to commit a crime. "Criminal justice penalties are typically too far removed in time for individuals low on self-control to incorporate them into their decision-making" (Gottfredson and Hirschi, 2003, 13).

Two actors could agree that by burglarizing a given house, the odds of getting caught and punished are one in ten. But someone with a high level of self-control would say that those odds are not worth it, whereas a low self-control person might feel that receiving pleasure from the stolen items *right now* is worth that chance. This is because, even in the unlikely eventuality of getting caught, apprehension may take place in, say, a day or a week, and being incarcerated may happen months from now. As it is currently constituted, the criminal justice system cannot administer justice immediately, and hence punishment can be eliminated as a possible restriction on the actions of offenders. Quite obviously, however, swiftness may be *so* swift as to represent the limiting case—say, a police officer around the corner who administers immediate "nightstick" or "curbstone" justice to the perpetrator. Hence even individuals low on self-control "will tend to be intimidated by the prospects of rapid reaction by the criminal justice system" (Gottfredson and Hirschi, 2003, 13). Of course, the visible, obtrusive presence of the police, like the visible presence of locks, private guards, dogs, or bystanders, will most decidedly deter crime because, again, this is a factor in the immediate criminal situation. In addition, offender perception of *certain* punishment will produce some inhibition in offending. What does *not* produce a deterrent effect is the severity of the penalty, whose effect is nearly zero.

Individuals with low self-control act most decidedly in the here and now, considering only the factors in their immediate surroundings. They are impulsive and act as a result of the contingencies of the moment, that is, as a result of the opportunities that present themselves in their day-to-day, minute-to-minute lives. "Self-control theory sees crime as split-second events" (Gottfredson and Hirschi, 2003, 7). Rather than taking the initiative, actively seeking out opportunities, most criminals do not make special efforts or possess sophisticated skills that would enable them to commit difficult crimes, nor do they tend to create opportunities where they do not exist. They usually commit crimes that are close to their daily rounds instead of figuring out which crimes are most lucrative and going to the locales where they might commit them. "No special skill or preparation and no planning are required to snatch a purse, throw a rock through a car window, open an unlocked door or cash drawer, or fire a gun at a stranger" (Gottfredson and Hirschi, 2003, 6–7).

Ordinary barriers to crime close down opportunities for committing crime: a locked door, a large, barking dog, a guard, a burglar alarm, a safe. What these barriers have in common is that they deter unsophisticated potential offenders; only the more skilled offender can circumvent them—and that eliminates most offenders. What does *not* much deter crime, say Gottfredson and Hirschi, is the fear of being apprehended and punished *beyond* the confines of the immediate criminal situation. Criminal opportunities also present themselves in the form of access to the paraphernalia that facilitate certain kinds of crime. Hence if teenagers (a high-crime category in the population) have unlimited access to cars, guns, and alcohol, their likelihood of committing crimes increases. Contrarily, if teenagers find it difficult to get their hands on such crime-facilitating paraphernalia, offending will correspondingly be made more difficult (Hirschi and Gottfredson, 2001, 93).

In short, according to Gottfredson and Hirschi, self-control alone does not explain or account for offending. Circumstances in the immediate context of a decision whether or not to offend (opportunities) may deter even individuals with extremely low self-control. Likewise, other circumstances may be so rife with the promise of lush reward and so barren of potential sanction that nearly all actors will decide to offend. Indeed, such a formulation is *required* by Gottfredson and Hirschi's adherence to rational choice theory. But what is relevant is not such limiting cases but the day-to-day, moment-to-moment perception of opportunities that are seized by the person characterized by low self-control and bypassed by those with high self-control. What Gottfredson and Hirschi have done is attempt to marry the radically different traditions of positivism, which focuses on criminality, and classical theory, which focuses on crime. Whether and to what extent this marriage is successful has preoccupied the field of criminology for the past two decades.

Schulz (2006) argues that Gottfredson and Hirschi do not develop their concept of opportunity in a sufficiently detailed or systematic fashion. In fact, Gottfredson and Hirschi do not address two crucial aspects of opportunity: First, opportunity has a subjective (or perceived) as well as an objective dimension; and second, opportunity may vary systematically by self-control, that is, individuals who can be characterized by low self-control may seek out opportunities for offending.

Gottfredson and Hirschi (1990) state that "under some conditions, people with low self-control may have few opportunities to commit crimes, and under other conditions people with high self-control may have many opportunities to commit them" (p. 220). Crime takes place, according to the formulation spelled out in *A General Theory of Crime*, when a person with low self-control is located in a high-opportunity situation, that is, in a situation in which the pleasure to be derived from exercising force or fraud is maximized and the immediate pain to the actor (mainly risk of apprehension) is low.

But this formulation raises a question: How did the actor come to be located in a high-opportunity situation? In real life, how are social control and opportunity related? Are they independent, more or less randomly related? Does the lifestyle of individuals of low versus high self-control open up more criminal opportunities? Contrarily, are people with low self-control more likely to seek out opportunities to commit crime? And if so, does this introduce the factor that Gottfredson and Hirschi have striven so mightily to exclude from their theory, namely, motivation? Moreover, in their attempt to construct a formulation that will be taken seriously by positivist criminologists, Gottfredson and Hirschi have sidestepped a crucial issue: the perception of opportunity. Is it possible that individuals with low self-control are more likely to perceive opportunities where high self-control persons do not? In other words, are Gottfredson and Hirschi guilty of leaving totally undeveloped what should be a major aspect of their theory (see Chapter 4 of this volume)? Gottfredson and Hirschi pay little attention to the independence versus the interdependence of these two factors and seem to take no interest in addressing the relevance of their interpenetration for the general theory of crime.

Writing before Gottfredson and Hirschi's theory was fully articulated, James W. Coleman (1987) argued that "an opportunity requires a symbolic construction making that particular behavioral option psychologically available to individual actors" (p. 424). Far from opportunity being an objective quality that either exists or does not exist in a given situation (Reed and Yeager, 1996, 375), opportunity should be regarded as "unattractive or attractive *from the standpoint of a particular actor*" (J. W. Coleman, 1987, 424; italics mine). In other words, opportunity is both an objective and a subjective quality that is likely to vary systematically by self-control. According to Zager (1993), "Opportunity effects may be found in both the act and the actor. . . . An individual's perception of opportunity . . . involves both the extent to which the situation lends itself to engaging in these behaviors and the extent to which the individual perceives that the situation lends itself to such behavior" (pp. 31, 42). The sensitive analyst of theories of crime is likely to raise the issue of the degree to which these two extents are related to one another and wonder why Gottfredson and Hirschi did not address this issue.

As we have seen, for Gottfredson and Hirschi determinism does not imply strict causality. In fact, all criminal actors pick and choose the time and place to engage in crime. There is, as Gottfredson and Hirschi say, a world of difference between criminality, or the propensity to commit crime, and crime, or the concrete enactment of criminal behavior. Positivism, including all the most prominent sociological theories of crime, tends to focus on criminality, assuming that it and it alone drives crime. In contrast, theories that focus on situational factors—routine activities theory, rational choice theory, opportunity theory—tend to ignore criminality, assuming that there are plenty of motivated offenders around to do the deed. Gottfredson and Hirschi believe that they have created the ideal combination of these two factors to explain all criminal behavior.

But is there anything distinctive or unique about self-control theory, with its roots in positivism, that lends itself to a marriage with a perspective that stresses situational factors or opportunity? Can this same dovetailing with classical theory be accomplished with all the other causal theories?

Albert K. Cohen (1965) argues that the strict determinism implicit in anomie theory, as it is spelled out by Robert Merton (1938), can be transcended by asking, "Now, *given strain*, what will a person do about it?" (p. 7). In other words, how do we take the step from criminality to crime? We can ask the same question of all the criminogenic or explanatory factors "causing" deviance and crime. Cohen's answer is that deviant action is "part of a collaborative social activity" (p. 7). People almost never enact illicit or illegal behavior simply because of impulses from within or broad, general influences from without. Instead, says Cohen, deviant acts emerge out of a rich, complex, and distinct interactional matrix involving gestures and countergestures, offers and responses, action and reaction. People are not impelled or compelled to do something regardless of what others around them think or do, irrespective of the social cost to themselves. All human action—whether deviant or conventional—"is something that typically develops and grows in a tentative, groping, advancing, backtracking, sounding-out process. People taste and feel their way along. They begin an act and do not complete it. They start doing one thing and end up by doing another. They extricate themselves from progressive involvement or become further involved to the point of commitment" (A. K. Cohen, 1965, 9). The development of an act is a feedback or interaction process. "The antecedents of the act are an unfolding sequence of acts contributed by a set of actors." In the case of deviance, "A makes a move, possibly in a deviant direction;

B responds; A responds to B's responses, etc. In the course of this interaction, movement in a deviant direction may become more explicit, elaborated, definitive—or it may not" (A. K. Cohen, 1965, 9–10).

Cohen is just as insistent as Gottfredson and Hirschi that the reactions of others may open up or close off illegitimate opportunities and open up or close off legitimate opportunities. The presence of a patrol officer may discourage a burglary, whereas his or her absence may invite a burglary; locking a door may result in no theft, but leaving it unlocked may invite one. An invitation to a party may result in a burglary averted. But Gottfredson and Hirschi's solutions to the "given criminality, what then?" question is radically different from Cohen's. Cohen's analysis sees deviant actors as distinctly social, whereas Gottfredson and Hirschi's deviant actors are distinctly asocial. Cohen stresses, as Gottfredson and Hirschi do not, the possibility that opening up and closing off legitimate opportunities may influence the enactment of deviant behavior. Cohen argues that the positivist tradition can be extended by incorporating opportunity into each determinist model, whereas Gottfredson and Hirschi use opportunity to critique positivist theories. Cohen focuses pretty much on the action-reaction-interaction as a determinant of deviant opportunities, whereas Gottfredson and Hirschi reach considerably beyond social interaction to include any and all opportunities, interactional, physical, and otherwise. But Gottfredson and Hirschi *agree* with Cohen that positivist theories usually err by narrowing their focus on criminality, or the tendency to commit crime. All need to be supplemented by a consideration of opportunity.

But the fact is, and as I have mentioned, considering Gottfredson and Hirschi's claim that the general theory of crime has married the classical with the positivist tradition, opportunity is a surprisingly underdeveloped aspect of their book (Schulz, 2006; Chapter 4 of this volume). Moreover, in the same way that Gottfredson and Hirschi have done with self-control theory, opportunity could be incorporated into any of the other positivist explanations of crime with no loss of theoretical integrity. The fact is, with respect to the factor of opportunity, there is no inherent relationship between self-control theory and any other explanatory theory of crime. All explanatory theories could graft opportunity onto their causal logic and take it into account. Self-control theory attempts to account for criminality, not crime, as do anomie, learning, social control, social disorganization, and other explanatory theories. A major difference, however, is that Gottfredson and Hirschi thought of doing it for the general theory, whereas the other theorists did not do so for theirs. But note: Both social control theory and social disorganization theory are inherently and by their very nature explanations of both criminality and crime, because by implication both consider the relative absence of surveillance and sanction as well as the presence of criminal opportunity in their logical structure. Although Gottfredson and Hirschi are successful in conceptualizing the distinction between crime and criminality, they have not paid sufficient attention to the precise articulation between these elements in their theory. Unfortunately, their rival theorists have paid virtually no attention to this issue at all, which is one of the reasons that *A General Theory of Crime* deserves the attention it has received.

Gottfredson and Hirschi argue that their perspective is compatible with, indeed *necessitates*, opportunity explanations of crime. The most often cited and discussed of all the contemporary free will, rationality, or opportunity theories is referred to as *routine activi-*

ties theory. Routine activities theory argues that criminal behavior will take place when and where there is a conjunction of three elements or factors: the motivated offender, a suitable target, and the absence of a capable guardian (L. E. Cohen and Felson, 1979). The most remarkable feature of this theory is that it makes a radical break with nearly all other rationality theories in that it dispenses with criminal motivation. The motivated offender is very much in the background, a given—simply *assumed* by the theory. There will always be plenty of people who are motivated to break the law if that is profitable to them. Criminal behavior, the theory argues, is a purposive and rational means of attaining an end—that is, acquiring money more efficiently than by any other method. People tend to act according to the utility that the outcome of their actions has for them, this theory argues. Other things being equal, if homeowners leave a house unoccupied and a door unlocked, their house is more likely to be burglarized than if they stayed in the house, locked the doors, installed burglar alarms, and kept a large guard dog. Many—no doubt most—people will not burglarize the house because their utility is not maximized by the burglary; that is, the likelihood that they will be caught and punished and that they will not be able to steal anything of value to them is increased by an occupied house, decreased if it is unoccupied.

Routine activities theory focuses mainly on opportunities for committing crime—and by extension, a great deal of deviant behavior as well. (In contrast, the theory does not address deviant beliefs or conditions at all.) A suitable target could be money, property, even the opportunity to engage in a certain activity that might be deemed desirable by a motivated offender. And the absence of a capable guardian would refer to the fact that formal or informal agents of social control are not operative in a particular situation. Hence, for instance, if a potential rapist encounters a woman, alone, in a physical setting in which she could be threatened or overpowered, the likelihood that a rape will take place is greater than if she were accompanied. To the extent that corporate behavior is not monitored by or accountable to government or any other social control agencies, corporate crime is more likely to take place than if these control systems are operative. The theory would predict that unrestricted access to illicit drugs would result in vastly higher rates of use than is currently the case; in the absence of video cameras, store guards, and the prying eye of sales clerks, shoplifting would be much more common than it is now; and cheating on exams would be more likely in the absence of watchful professors, teaching assistants, and honest fellow students. In other words, many more of us would engage in nonnormative—or deviant—behavior if capable guardians were not watching over and able to sanction our potential wrongdoing.

Rationalistic theories do not so much attempt to explain deviance and crime as take the motivated offender for granted and focus on the conditions that bring him or her out of the woodwork. Although rationality certainly enters into the crime and deviance equation, the fact that jails, prisons, and reform schools are full of young and not-so-young men (and women) who committed crimes impulsively, without planning, and got caught as a consequence, indicates that at the very least their calculation of whether one or more capable guardians were in the picture is flawed. The free will factor alone is not a totally viable explanation. The fact is, most individuals who commit crimes to make money could have earned more, in the long run, by working at a low-paying drudge job. Clearly, some other explanation is necessary; apparently, the thrill, excitement, and self-righteousness that much criminal behavior entails is at least as powerfully motivating as the rational acquisition of money or the engaging in self-evidently satisfying acts (Katz, 1988).

At the same time—even for irrational actors who seek more than a concrete goal, such as money—opportunity is related to the enactment of deviance. For all actors and all activities, the greater the perceived payoff and the lower the likelihood of apprehension and punishment, the greater the likelihood that deviance will be enacted.

In sum, to the extent that opportunity makes up half the equation of the general theory of crime, routine activities theory is compatible with Gottfredson and Hirschi's explanation of crime. But to the extent that self-control theory relies on motivation—and Gottfredson and Hirschi say that it is *not* dependent on the mechanism of motivation, whereas their critics argue that it is smuggled into the theory, so to speak—routine activities theory and self-control are incompatible.

THE GENERAL THEORY OF CRIME: CONTROVERSY AND DEBATE

The impact of Gottfredson and Hirschi's general theory of crime leads us to a paradox. Despite the spectacular success of self-control theory, it remains extremely controversial. It has been critiqued, attacked, even dismissed. Charles Tittle writes that *A General Theory of Crime* "will almost convince a reader that black is white" (1991, 1610). Gottfredson and Hirschi's polemical style of argumentation, Tittle adds, amounts to a "confrontational approach" (p. 1611). Contrarily, Tittle also says that in his opinion, "Travis Hirschi is a genius" and the general theory of crime "is extraordinary and admirable." But in addition, he also says that the theory is "another instance of old wine in new bottles" that "does not fully meet" the field's theoretical needs. It illustrates the "inherent, counterproductive tendency toward defensiveness by those who purport to invent theory" (Tittle, 1995, 55). Ronald Akers (1991) takes Gottfredson and Hirschi to task for their "oppositional strategy" (p. 206). Geis (2000) refers to the "gaping holes" in Gottfredson and Hirschi's analysis of white-collar crime (p. 44). Susan L. Miller and Burack (1993) focus on Gottfredson and Hirschi's inability to account for the role of gender in crime, referring to their "fake gender neutrality" (p. 120). Polk (1991) asserts that Gottfredson and Hirschi display a "tendency to ignore inconvenient evidence" (p. 576). Schulz (2006) argues that it is questionable that self-control theory can claim to be a general theory of crime. After reading such a whirlwind of positive and negative assessments—sometimes both by the same observer—the reader hardly knows what to believe about the general theory of crime.

It is not unusual for a theorist to be acclaimed by one observer and reviled by another. Consider the fact that the works of Charles Darwin (1809–1882), Karl Marx (1818–1883), and Sigmund Freud (1856–1939) were greeted with both glowing praise and utter damnation. To be innovative, scientific and literary work must be bold, it must make large claims—and *A General Theory of Crime* is nothing if not bold. Gottfredson and Hirschi say it plainly: "Modesty per se is not a virtue of a theory." And their theory is far from modest, they admit. It intends to explain "all crime, at all times." Indeed, they add, it is also meant to explain "many forms of behavior that are not sanctioned by the state" (Gottfredson and

Hirschi, 1990, 117). This is an intoxicating claim, very likely to be infuriating to scholars who defend the theoretical edifices that Gottfredson and Hirschi attempt to tear down. Clearly, in making their sweeping proclamations, Gottfredson and Hirschi gore the intellectual oxen of many a scholar and researcher, challenge formulations on which many a career and reputation have been built, and undermine perspectives that many a criminologist has long believed in and accepted as true.

Such an attribution raises the question, What if Gottfredson and Hirschi's self-control theory is wrong? What if their critics are right? And how would we decide? Modesty is no virtue, it is true, but by itself boldness is not sufficient to prevail in intellectual debate. With the hindsight of history most scholars now consider most of the central tenets of Marx's and Freud's theories empirically wrong, and Darwin's theory of natural selection continues to attract critical assaults. What of the general theory of crime? Would a serious assessment resolve the paradox of self-control theory's Janus-faced reception—its spectacular success and heated denunciation? This book is dedicated to understanding the theory, undertaking that assessment, and attempting to resolve this paradox.

THE GENERAL THEORY'S CRITIQUE OF POSITIVISM

As we have seen, Gottfredson and Hirschi argue that *A General Theory of Crime* annihilates all rival theories of crime and deviance: cultural and social learning theories, anomie and strain theories, labeling theory, even Hirschi's social control theory. One critique the student or researcher finds in the book might prove to be puzzling, however: Gottfredson and Hirschi's attack on positivism. What is self-control theory but a positivistic attempt to explain or account for criminal behavior? We might think that Gottfredson and Hirschi would enthusiastically *support* positivism, not critique it. Hence the theorists' particular understanding of positivism demands an explanation.

As we have seen, Gottfredson and Hirschi reject the nineteenth-century version of positivism that was promulgated by Césare Lombroso and his followers. The idea that biological defect is the—or even a—major cause of crime has been soundly rejected in the field of criminology since the 1920s. Since the 1960s a small band of biologically oriented researchers has attempted to reinsert physical defect into the mainstream of the field, without a great deal of success. The vast majority of criminologists are social scientists, and nearly all of them believe that life experiences are the major reason that some people commit crime—not congenital impulses or tendencies present at or even before birth.

However, readers of *A General Theory of Crime* may be puzzled to find Gottfredson and Hirschi attacking not just the nineteenth-century Positive school specifically, or even the more contemporary version of biological defect theory, but, seemingly, positivism in general. Dictionaries define positivism as the school of thought whose proponents reject metaphysics and theism as explanations for human phenomena, arguing instead that propositions must be "scientifically verified and falsified." (Here, I rely on the *New Shorter Oxford English Dictionary*.) Pretty much all the theory chapters of all the textbooks on deviance and crime place self-control theory squarely *within* the ranks of positivism. For instance, my own text (Goode, 2008, 23–27) identifies positivism as an approach based on empiricism (a reliance on the data conveyed by the five senses), objectivism (the belief that phenomena in the world are objectively real, pregiven entities), and cause-and-effect determinism—all qualities most emphatically shared by Gottfredson and Hirschi's self-control theory. How can Gottfredson and Hirschi reject positivism if their theory is a prime example of it?

The answer to this question hinges on Gottfredson and Hirschi's distinction between methodological and substantive positivism. Methodological positivism—which I just spelled out—is an approach that Hirschi and Gottfredson say they "accept" (1994b, 267n). They have no argument with empiricism, objectivism, or determinism. Their objection rests with a particular version of positivism, which they refer to as "substantive" positivism. Rather than a "method of knowing," as it should be, positivism has turned into "*a substantive perspective*" (1994b, 263). The specific version of positivism they reject, they say, is composed of several particulars, which I outline in the following paragraphs; their objections to these particulars are similar to but far from identical with their objections to Lombroso's Positive school.

The first particular is the reliance on a state-sanctioned definition of crime. Substantive positivism runs into a contradiction between objectivism, which says that explanations must be about real or objective phenomena in the material world, and constructivism, which says that social phenomena are socially created or constructed at a particular time and place. Criminal laws—as we know, a social construction—vary from society to society and come and go over time, but "force and fraud in the pursuit of self-interest is everywhere condemned" (Gottfredson and Hirschi, 1990, 257). Criminological positivism, that is, substantive positivism, cannot resolve this contradiction. Gottfredson and Hirschi have solved the problem, as I pointed out, by junking the state-sanctioned or constructivist definition and defining crime essentialistically, objectively, as a materially real phenomenon in the material world.

The second, and related, particular is the tendency to reverse the order of causality. Positivists take criminality—the characteristics of the offender—as the focus of their attention; for them the nature of crime is something of an afterthought. Gottfredson and Hirschi reverse the order of these two factors and take the nature of crime as the focus of attention. Low self-control is not exactly an afterthought in their theory, but it follows from the nature of crime. *Given* that crime is defined as "force and fraud in pursuit of self-interest," that is, acts that are shortsighted, hedonistic, self-interested, and ultimately, self-destructive, it almost inevitably follows that individuals with low self-control would be more likely to commit them. The general theory of crime hinges primarily on the nature of crime, not criminality. In contrast, by focusing on the characteristics of the offender, the positivist fails to understand what it is about crime that leads people of a certain type to engage in it. How do we link up the dependent variable with the independent variable? According to Gottfredson and Hirschi, substantive positivists have no adequate answer to that question. In contrast, although it seems strange to put the matter this way, Gottfredson and Hirschi "start with the dependent variable," that is, with the phenomenon they wish to explain (1990, 255), and deduce from that the characteristics of the independent or explanatory variable. It is the focus on the criminal rather than on the crime that dooms positivist reasoning, Gottfredson and Hirschi say.

Third is an overly deterministic view of causality. As I said earlier, Gottfredson and

Hirschi's theory does not "dispute the idea of causation." They agree that "it is possible to find factors reliably related to the decision to choose crime rather than some alternative behavior" (Gottfredson and Hirschi, 1990, 260). What they reject is the notion that "people in the clutches of the causes of crime must commit criminal acts . . . regardless of their own assessment of the consequences" (p. 260). In other words, what Gottfredson and Hirschi reject is the idea that factors *compel* certain people to commit crime under any and all circumstances. For them it is the notion of force or compulsion that is the sticking point of causality. By wedding self-control (their independent variable) to the classical school's emphasis on free will or choice, Gottfredson and Hirschi have sidestepped the compulsive force of substantive positivism's explanations of criminal behavior. Criminals choose to commit crime—they are not forced to do so. Of course, to be fair and accurate, none of the theories that Gottfredson and Hirschi identify as positivistic sees the criminal as forced or compelled to commit crime; all concede that other factors are at work, some, to dissuade the criminally inclined away from illegal acts. But Gottfredson and Hirschi are correct in pointing out that these theories fail to explain the circumstances under which actors choose crime over law-abiding behavior.

The fourth particular is the tendency to typologize. As we have seen, Gottfredson and Hirschi reject the notion that different crimes have different explanations. One of substantive positivism's major failings, they say, is its proponents' inability to account for all crime with a single explanation. All positivistic theoretical schools, they say, spin out increasingly specialized explanations for increasingly narrow crime categories based on meaningless distinctions. This exercise "begs the issue, treating as discrete, independent events acts that are . . . conceptually identical and empirically strongly correlated with one another" (Gottfredson and Hirschi, 1990, 263). What criminology needs, they say, is a single, powerful theory for what amounts to a single and consistent, although broad, phenomenon. Gottfredson and Hirschi say they have devised such an explanation, because the way they have defined crime unites all behaviors for which all criminologists seek, or should seek, an explanation.

And fifth, Gottfredson and Hirschi dislike in substantive positivism the tendency to argue that crime is motivated behavior. Once again, "force and fraud in pursuit of self-interest" does not have to be explained. Crime is not behavior that is positively motivated—it is behavior that has to be restrained. Theirs is a restraint or control theory, not a motivational explanation of crime. By turning the equation around—by rejecting the "Why do they do it?" and reformulating it into the "Why *don't* they do it?" question—Gottfredson and Hirschi believe they have sidestepped the dilemma that comes with attempting to account for behavior that is expected and unproblematic. If one is left unrestrained since childhood, crime is simply "doing what comes naturally"; it does not require an explanation. What has to be explained, Gottfredson and Hirschi say, is why people do *not* seek immediate gratification. It may or may not be the case that actors do not have to be motivated to engage in criminal behavior, but the fact is, Gottfredson and Hirschi's focus is actually on criminality, or the tendency to *violate* the law—not, as they claim, the tendency to *obey* the law. As Akers says (1991, 208), self-control theory is clearly an explanation of criminal behavior, not conformity, and Gottfredson and Hirschi's relevant independent variable is low, not high, self-control.

In short, Gottfredson and Hirschi have no quarrel with positivism as a method of conducting research, or even as a mode of thinking about cause and effect. They themselves adopt the natural science model for studying criminal behavior and the cause-and-effect model of how it comes about. In that sense they are positivists—methodological positivists. But as we have seen, they argue that what has come to be called positivism is a particular subtype of the scientific model—substantive positivism, with all its flaws and limitations. Because of these flaws, this brand of positivism cannot adequately explain crime and must be abandoned. It is only by giving up these five particulars—a state-sanctioned definition of crime (and beginning our investigation with the true nature of crime), the tendency to reverse the order of causality, an overly deterministic model of crime causation, the tendency to typologize different types and hence different explanations of crime in favor of a single type of crime and a single explanation, and the notion that crime is motivated—that we can explain this hugely important sector of human behavior. But the fact is, matters of emphasis aside, self-control theory is no less positivistic a theory than any of the other perspectives in criminology (Akers, 1991, 208; Schulz, 2006). In reality, as we will see throughout this volume, Gottfredson and Hirschi really are engaged in a "Why do they do it?" enterprise. It is an explanatory or positivistic theory with a codicil attached.

CONCLUDING NOTE

Gottfredson and Hirschi define crime as acts of force or fraud undertaken in pursuit of self-interest. What sort of person engages in such actions? The theorists argue that the criminal is characterized by impulsivity, insensitivity to the feelings of others, shortsightedness, poor judgment, and a prioritizing of immediate gratification over delaying pleasure to obtain long-term rewards. Not only is most crime mundane and ordinary, requiring little or no skill, but also most criminals are versatile in that low self-control characterizes enactors of all criminal and cognate behavior, including illicit drug use, heavy alcohol consumption, and risky sex. Gottfredson and Hirschi base their general theory of crime on two components: (1) criminality, the propensity to commit crime, or low self-control, an individual trait caused largely by poor parenting during the first eight years of life, and (2) opportunity, a structural factor external to the offender. The conjunction of these two components produces criminal behavior, or crime.

Hirschi and Gottfredson (1994b) and Britt and Gottfredson (2003) have gathered together research findings from researchers sympathetic to their own views. What of the field in general? Pratt and Cullen (2000) conducted a meta-analysis of more than twenty empirical studies of the relationship between self-control and crime and cognate behaviors—the central thesis of *A General Theory of Crime*—and concluded that, regardless of the measure used or the sample drawn, self-control is a robust and significant predictor of criminal and deviant behavior. Still, Pratt and Cullen argue, longitudinal studies, that is, those that follow samples over time, show weaker results than the general theory's claim would predict; in addition, despite Gottfredson and Hirschi's insistence, most studies verify the influence of social learning on crime, deviance, and delinquency.

In assessing the general theory of crime, we must make a distinction between Gottfredson and Hirschi's principal generalization (the relationship between low self-control and crime) and the explanation of or theory accounting for that generalization. Support for the first is overwhelming; that for the second is mixed. Several studies (e.g., Grasmick et al., 1993; Dugan et al., 2001; J. J. Gibbs and Giever, 1995) have demonstrated somewhat weak support for Gottfredson and Hirschi's chief explanation, but for the most part the field has verified its principal components more often than it has undermined them. Still, qualification is the rule more than refutation.

J. P. Wright and Cullen (2001) found that poor "parental efficacy" exerts a substantial effect on adolescent delinquency across varying age groups. Hay and Forrest (2006) agreed that low self-control significantly influences crime and that self-control is stable between the ages of 7 and 15, but in a minority of their nationally representative sample, parental socialization continued to exert an influence after the age of 10 and well into adolescence. Tittle and Botchkovar (2005) verified that low self-control predicts crime in Russia—indicating that Gottfredson and Hirschi's theory is not culture-bound—but they argued that it is not fear of punishment that deters crime but motivation, a factor that Gottfredson and Hirschi explicitly deny applies to their explanation. Lussier et al. (2005) showed that Gottfredson and Hirschi's general criminal propensity to offend more powerfully predicts male sexual aggression against women than the specific factors of high sexual drive and deviant sexual interests.

Burt et al. (2006) demonstrated that among a sample of young African Americans, low self-control is indeed positively associated with involvement in delinquency but that self-control "only partly attenuates" the negative effect of parental efficacy on delinquency; moreover, additional social relationship factors (improvements in parenting over time, attachment to teachers, association with prosocial peers, and association with deviant peers) "explain a substantial portion of the changes in self-control." J. P. Wright and Beaver (2005) agreed that parents matter but argued that Gottfredson and Hirschi have left genetic factors, especially attention-deficit/hyperactivity disorder (ADHD) out of the picture. Chernkovich and Giordano (2001) argued, as Gottfredson and Hirschi do, that the antisocial behavior of *serious* offenders is more stable and resistant to change than is that of more typical and less serious offenders. Ousey and Wilcox (2007) argued that "anti-social propensity" to commit delinquent behavior is less amenable to measurement than Gottfredson and Hirschi claim. Sullivan et al. (2006) see criminal specialization as greater than the general theory of crime would have it. Morselli and Tremblay (2004) even argue that, ironically, offenders with low self-control earn more money at crime than offenders with higher self-control. And of course, whether and to what extent self-control theory can explain white-collar crime specifically remains a vigorously contested issue in the field of criminology (Benson and Moore, 1992; Simpson and Piquero, 2002).

Reflecting the criminological literature, the researchers who have contributed to this volume represent a range of views on the general theory of crime: Some support it, with qualifications, whereas others mount a critique against it. How do Hirschi and Gottfredson launch a critique of their critics? Their reply can be found in Chapter 15. In this book they have the final word.

2 | MEASURING SELF-CONTROL

Alex R. Piquero

There is no mistaking the contribution that Gottfredson and Hirschi's (1990) general theory of crime has made to criminology. Published at a time when criminological theory was said to be paralyzed (Wellford, 1989), the theory forced researchers in the field to think carefully and critically about the causes of crime and the relationship between crime and key demographic factors such as age, sex, and race. In addition, by denying the relevance of these factors, the general theory demanded that criminologists demonstrate the need for longitudinal studies and the feasibility of their recommendations for a policy response to crime. Whether or not one agrees with the validity and reach of Gottfredson and Hirschi's theory, it is the key reading in the field and will likely be so for years to come.

That said, the most pressing and continually unresolved issue concerning Gottfredson and Hirschi's theory is the measurement of its principal theoretical variable: self-control. My purpose in this chapter is to provide an overview of the measurement issues surrounding self-control, including an overview of the attitudinal and behavioral issues, a discussion of some unresolved issues that self-control has raised, and an outline of several promising directions for measuring self-control.

MEASUREMENT OF SELF-CONTROL
AS A KEY AND CONTENTIOUS ISSUE

In the original statement of the general theory, Gottfredson and Hirschi stated that self-control, defined as the tendency to pursue immediate gratification to the neglect of its long-term negative consequences, is mainly composed of six elements: temper, risk taking, self-centeredness, impulsivity, preference for simple solutions to problems, and preference for physical activity over those that are more sophisticated, such as verbal persuasion. Gottfredson and Hirschi believe that self-control develops by the end of the first decade of life as a result of inadequate parenting and is relatively stable across individuals over the life course and largely impervious to change. Gottfredson and Hirschi did not suggest how these six elements could be measured, which forced researchers to interpret the concept of self-control in their own manner, provide further clarity on the concept, and come up with their own measures of self-control. Here, I review the main self-control measurement strategies that researchers have suggested and summarize the debate that such strategies have spawned.

THE ATTITUDINAL-BEHAVIORAL DEBATE

Which measures self-control better: attitudes or behavior? The debate emerged with the publication of three articles in a 1993 issue of the *Journal of Research in Crime and Delinquency*. In the first paper Grasmick et al. (1993) developed a twenty-four-item scale, designed to tap into the six facets of self-control that Gottfredson and Hirschi outlined. Using data from several hundred respondents from the Oklahoma City Survey, their respondent-driven self-report scale, developed largely from questions from the California Personality Inventory (CPI), was a strong measure with a high-reliability coefficient, indicating good internal consistency. Grasmick's group then proceeded to assess the relationship between their attitudinal measure of self-control and measures of crimes of force and fraud.

Several key findings emerged from their study. First, the main effect for low self-control was significant on crimes of fraud but not on crimes of force, and a measure of crime opportunity was significantly associated with both types of crime. Second, when Grasmick's group examined the interaction of low self-control and a measure of opportunity, they found the expected effect that low self-control, combined with opportunity, was significantly associated with both crimes. Third, they noted that a substantial proportion of variance in crime was left unexplained by self-control and opportunity.

In the same journal issue as the Grasmick et al. study, Keane et al. (1993) measured self-control in a behavioral—not attitudinal—fashion and used data from the 1986 Ontario Survey of Nighttime Drivers, which contained several measures associated with elements of self-control. To measure risk taking, Keane's group employed an item about whether drivers used seat belts. To measure impulsiveness, they used responses to the item "Did anyone try to discourage you from driving tonight?" Finally, they included a variable that could be viewed as reflective of a particular lifestyle; this survey item asked respondents to report the number of alcoholic drinks they had consumed in the previous seven days. Keane's group then examined how these items related to an objective measure of level of alcohol in the bloodstream while driving as well as the respondents' self-report of their degree of intoxication. The results strongly confirmed that for both males and females the behavioral self-control items were linked to driving under the influence.

These two studies were followed by an insightful commentary by Hirschi and Gottfredson (1993), in which they put a stake in the ground with regard to measuring self-control. Although the theorists noted that multiple measures of self-control were desirable, "behavioral measures of self-control seem preferable to self-reports" (p. 48). They went on to argue that the problem with respondent-driven self-reports of self-control (and the potential modest results that come along with them) is due to the low validity of survey methods, especially because individuals with low self-control may be unwilling or unable to participate in surveys and because their responses will likely restrict the range of both independent and dependent variables. Hirschi and Gottfredson further pointed out that behavioral measures of self-control "counter the tendency to translate the control concept at the core of our theory into a personality concept" or "an enduring criminal predisposition" (p. 49). Paying respect to classic accounts of control theory, the theorists deny the existence of personality traits as a measure of self-control.

In an effort to push forward the behavioral self-control strategy, Hirschi and Gottfredson have attempted to better delineate behavioral indicators of self-control. Two of their examples are worth highlighting. First, Hirschi and Gottfredson (1994a) argue that logically independent measures of self-control include "whining, pushing, and shoving (as a child); smoking and drinking and excessive television watching and accident frequency (as a teenager); [and] difficulties in interpersonal relations, employment instability, automobile accidents, drinking, and smoking (as an adult)" (p. 9). Second and more generally, Hirschi and Gottfredson (1995, 134) claim that "the best available operational measure of the propensity to offend is a count of the number of distinct problem behaviors engaged in by a youth" (Hindelang et al. 1981; Robins and Ratcliff, 1978).

Two important studies that sought to directly address the use of attitudinal or behavioral self-control measures were carried out by Tittle et al. (2003b) and Marcus (2003). Tittle's group used data from the 1994 Oklahoma City Survey, which included the same attitudinal items as those used by Grasmick's group. Their behavioral self-control measure consisted of two forms: a factor-based scale that contained items such as alcohol use, cigarette smoking, marital status, seat belt use, debt problems, and medication use, and an alternative Guttman scale behavioral measure that included items related to education completion, involvement in a retirement savings plan, seat belt use, medication use, blackout during drinking, and accident or injury involvement. Tittle's group used self-reported survey data to compare the two main approaches to measuring self-control in their ability to predict eight measures of crime and deviance.

Several key findings emerged from the Tittle et al. (2003b) study. First, although Tittle's group found that both measurement strategies provided supportive evidence—self-control relates to crime—the behavioral measures did not operate any better in terms of prediction than the attitudinal or cognitive measures. Second, and unlike the attitudinal measures, different types of crime-analogous imprudent behaviors were not highly interrelated, a finding that runs against the general theory's expectation that all sorts of behaviors are interrelated. Along similar lines a recent study of public high school students by Brenda (2005) found that a behavioral measure of self-control was a stronger predictor of delinquency than a cognitive measure.

In a second study comparing attitudinal and behavioral self-control measurements, Marcus (2003) developed an alternative self-control measure, the Retrospective Behavioral Self-Control (RBS) Scale, which is based on a count of sixty-seven different behavioral acts with long-term negative consequences committed by an individual during childhood, adolescence, and adulthood. Marcus found that such a measure passed the test of reliability and construct validity in three different samples, whereas the self-control scale devised by Grasmick's group did not.

One problem with the use of behavioral measures of self-control deals with tautology, because several of the behavioral items used by previous researchers to assess self-control also tap actually illegal behavior. This may, in the words of Tittle et al. (2003b, 339), "provide a tautological advantage to the behavioral measure" and may be one reason that Hirschi and Gottfredson (1993) prefer such measures; this has to be the case, they argue, because it is how they constructed the theory in the first place.

The larger issue of tautology with respect to self-control was first raised by Akers (1991). He claimed that "it would appear to be tautological to explain the propensity to commit crime by low self-control. They are one and the same, and such assertions about them are true by definition. The assertion means that low self-control causes low self-control" (p. 204). Similarly, Akers adds, "Since no operational definition of self-control is given, we cannot know that a person has low self-control (stable propensity to commit crime) unless he or she commits crimes or analogous behavior. The statement that low self-control is a cause of crime, then, is also tautological" (p. 204).

Hirschi and Gottfredson (1993), however, view the claim of tautology as a compliment, because, they say, they "followed the path of logic in producing an internally consistent result" (p. 52). That is, they started with the conception of crime, examined what crimes had in common—the tendency to pursue immediate gratification—and from it developed a conception of the offender. The theorists claim that they do not recognize a propensity to commit crime but rather see self-control "as the barrier that stands between the actor and the obvious momentary benefits crime provides. We explicitly propose that the link between self-control and crime is *not* deterministic, but probabilistic, affected by opportunities and other constraints" (p. 53). It seems that, to the extent that behavioral measures are viewed as problematic when it comes to measuring self-control, an easy way around the problem of tautology is simply to refrain from using crime-type measures as items in a self-control scale, behavioral or otherwise. Hirschi and Gottfredson (1993, 53) and others thereafter have made such a recommendation.

Regardless of one's preference for attitudinal or behavioral measures of self-control, the use of either method, although yielding substantively similar effects on criminal activity, has led to the identification of five issues that plague the measurement issue and that have yet to be resolved. I outline these in detail in the next section.

UNRESOLVED ISSUES

Five unresolved methodological issues currently surround the measurement of self-control within the context of the general theory: factor structure, group invariance, survey response, conceptual overlap between self-control and other personal factors, and social desirability.

With regard to factor structure, our first unresolved issue, the problem once again can be traced back to Gottfredson and Hirschi, who argued that self-control, as a general cause of crime, is linked to crime in the same way across all demographic groups and cultures. This, of course, implies that the measure of self-control is similarly structured and has similar scale properties across all demographic groups. Unfortunately, issues related to factor structure and scale invariance and reliability have not been as frequently assessed as studies that link self-control to crime. However, some research does exist on this score.

Longshore et al. (1996) were the first to assess the unidimensionality of a modified version of Grasmick et al.'s (1993) self-control scale using a sample of offenders. Specifically, Longshore's group examined whether the self-control scale could adequately be summarized by one factor and the degree to which the individual items in the scale were invariant (or the same) across demographic subgroups (ethnicity, sex, and age). Results from factor analysis of offender data indicated that a one-factor solution, as reported by several other researchers using general population samples, did not appear to be valid. Instead, after allowing for correlated error residuals and the deletion of some items, Longshore's group found that a five-factor solution provided an adequate fit to the data, with those scoring lower on the self-control measure more likely to be involved in crimes of force and fraud. More important, however, the five-factor solution did not hold well among females, and the scale was not a better predictor than some of its subscales.

Alex R. Piquero and Rosay (1998) reanalyzed Longshore et al.'s data in large part because they were concerned with the use of correlated error terms, which tend to improve the fit a model provides to the data, absent strong theoretical rationales. Their reanalysis led to a different set of conclusions than those reached by the Longshore group. In particular Piquero and Rosay found that the Grasmick et al. scale conformed to a one-factor solution, was equally reliable and valid across sex, and was related to crimes of force and fraud as well as to the more complex five-factor solution advanced by the Longshore group. In a response Longshore et al. (1998) disagreed with some of the specific methodological and statistical decisions (e.g., goodness-of-fit statistics, the use of principal components analysis, the exclusion of correlated error residuals) made by Piquero and Rosay and concluded that regardless of the reanalysis, their main conclusions—that the Grasmick et al. self-control scale does not provide a sound measure of self-control among women and that the lower order components of the self-control scale are just as, if not more, predictive than the overall self-control scale—remained intact.

Higgins (2004) examined the distribution differences across sexes in key measures from self-control theory among college students. His results showed that all measures were different across sexes (e.g., parents apply parental management tasks differently to male and female offspring, males and females have different mean levels of self-control and participation in deviance) but that the central model for males and females was similar, supporting Gottfredson and Hirschi's view that a general, central model is useful for both male and female deviance. Higgins and Tewksbury's (2006) structural equation modeling analysis on a cross-section of juveniles found that Gottfredson and Hirschi's causal model held for males and females but that multiple-group modeling findings supported the theory that differences in the measures and causal model hold for both sexes.

The issue of obtaining the same findings regardless of how variables are measured is important because Gottfredson and Hirschi are insistent that their theory is invariant from one society to another. In an important set of multination comparative studies, Vazsonyi and colleagues examined the hypothesis of the invariance of the self-control hypothesis across cultures (2001) and whether the theory holds among Japanese adolescents (2004). In their first study Vazsonyi's group used adolescent samples from Hungary, the Netherlands, Switzerland, and the United States to examine how self-control related to deviance. The findings indicated that the self-control measure did not conform to a one-factor solution and was multidimensional, was tenable across demographic groups (sex, age, country), and was related to deviance similarly across cultures, thereby providing support for Gottfredson and Hirschi's culture-free hypothesis. In their second study Vazsonyi et al. (2004) examined the measurement of low self-control (using the Grasmick et al. attitudinal measure) and the low self-control/deviance relationship among Japanese adolescents and found that the measure was a valid and reliable indicator of low self-control, was valid and reliable across sexes, and was multidimensional. In addition, their results indicated that low self-control was related to a diverse array of deviance measures, and in a comparison between Japanese and United States adolescents it was invariant across all measures of deviance except alcohol use.

Several other studies have also examined the dimensionality issue across cultures and the relationship between self-control and crime and deviance in those cultures. For example, Romero et al. (2003) found support for multidimensionality of the self-control construct using data on Spanish youth. Wang et al. (2002) found no direct link between impulsivity and measures of social control, substance use, and deviant behaviors in a sample of youth from southern China. Killias and Rabasa (1997) used data from a sample of Swiss adolescent males and found that a single-item measure of low self-control was related to some but not all measures of violence. Morris et al. (2006) found that self-control influenced all forms of substance use when controlling for race and in race-specific analyses, but self-control was a stronger predictor of marijuana and serious drug use among Native Americans. And Hwang and Akers (2003) found that six single-item indicators of self-control related to tobacco and alcohol use in a sample of Korean adolescents. In short, the different findings and summary statements with respect to the uni- versus multidimensionality issue may be based on different interpretations of Gottfredson and Hirschi (Arneklev et al. 1999).

DeLisi et al. (2003) further examined the dimensionality of the Grasmick et al. self-control scale using a sample of male parolees residing in work-release facilities. Using several analytic approaches, they found that the scale was not unidimensional. Specifically, they tested a series of models, including a six-factor model (in which each of the twenty-four items were grouped into the six factors outlined by Gottfredson and Hirschi), a second-order model with seven factors, and a model in which all twenty-four items loaded on one factor. They found that the six-factor model provided the best fit to the data and that the other two models provided poor fits to the data. Their final analysis, which predicted self-reported delinquency and adult prison offending, showed that the six factors had differential predictive powers and that the "losing one's temper" dimension was the strongest predictor of delinquency.

A third unresolved issue is critical with respect to Hirschi and Gottfredson's stance against attitudinal measures of self-control: the extent to which a person's self-control will affect survey response. One study that examined this issue was undertaken by Alex Piquero et al. (2000). Piquero's group applied item response theory (IRT) analysis, which focuses on the interaction between the human subject and survey items and the extent to which cumulative scales fail to provide fundamental measurement. Their application of IRT to the Grasmick et al. self-control attitudinal scale indicated that, although conventional factor analytic techniques yielded similar results to those reported by others (Grasmick et al., 1993), the IRT analysis indicated that individuals' level of self-control influenced their self-report response, a finding consistent with Hirschi and Gottfredson's (1993) concern with respect to self-report attitudinal measures of self-control.

A fourth unresolved issue concerns the relationships and overlap between self-control and other personality characteristics. A key relationship here is that between low self-control and psychopathy. Wiebe (2003) focused on whether their separation was theoretically or empirically justifiable and whether their common or unique content better accounts for delinquency. After presenting a comparison of common or unique elements of psychopathy and low self-control (the Grasmick et al. version), Wiebe used data from a sample of university students and found that (1) antisociality should be considered a separate construct from self-direction (which is composed of elements of self-control and psychopathy); (2) the models that proposed a unitary self-control or psychopathy construct fitted the data poorly; (3) the effects of self-direction on delinquency were indirect, working through antisociality; (4) antisociality and self-direction may be manifestations of a higher-order construct; and (5) variation in offending was better explained by models that integrated self-control and psychopathy as opposed to models that included self-control only.

Cauffman et al. (2005) assessed whether, in addition to self-control, psychological, neuropsychological, and physiological correlates distinguished between serious (or incarcerated) and nonserious (high school) juvenile offenders in California. Their analysis indicated that although self-control was able to distinguish between the two groups, so too did neuropsychological and biological factors, a result that simultaneously supports and refutes Gottfredson and Hirschi's hypothesis that self-control is the sole personal characteristic implicated in crime. Moreover, when examining minor delinquency among the nonserious offenders, Cauffman's group found that although self-control was related to delinquency, neuropsychological and biological factors were not.

A final issue that has only recently emerged concerns that of social desirability, a problem that is specific to self-reported self-control responses, regardless of whether they are attitudinal or behavioral. In particular, social desirability response bias reflects the tendency exhibited by some respondents to provide survey responses that are biased toward presenting an especially favorable self-impression, and it is clear how this could influence attitudinal or cognitive measures of self-control that ask individuals to make assertions about their personality and preferences.

To investigate this issue, MacDonald et al. (2008) examined the extent to which socially desirable responding accounts for the relationship between self-control and crime. MacDonald's group used a five-item social desirability response set (SDRS-5), which asked respondents to indicate (1) their level of courteousness to disagreeable people, (2) occasions when they have taken advantage of someone, (3) attempts to get even rather than to forgive and forget, (4) feelings of resentment when they do not get their way, and (5) the extent to which they are good listeners. MacDonald's group found that social desirability was significantly associated with criminal activity. However, the findings indicated that accounting for social desirability only marginally reduced the relationship between the Grasmick et al. scale and crime and did not eliminate the effect of behavioral self-control measures, thus only partly confirming Gottfredson and Hirschi's speculations.

Along with the measurement directions afforded by Gottfredson and Hirschi in their original work, the findings from the attitudinal and behavioral studies, and the recognition without resolution of the unresolved issues just outlined, several promising directions have recently been outlined for the measurement of self-control. In the final section I review these specific measurement strategies.

NEW AND PROMISING DIRECTIONS

Fortunately for self-control researchers, the measurement-oriented research has further refined the delineation and operationalization of self-control measures. In addition, this line of work has led to a number of new and promising directions for conceptualizing self-control. In this section I outline these new directions and then close with a recommendation for considering self-control within the context of a more developmentally based approach to thinking about crime.

The first elaboration of self-control outlines a conceptual distinction between capability for self-control and the desire to exercise it and thus opens the door for contingency-based hypotheses within the general theory of crime. Tittle et al. (2004) argue that Gottfredson and Hirschi's theory can be improved by recognizing that individuals' capacity for self-control is distinct from their interest in restraining themselves, that the two are important, and that they vary with crime independently. As Tittle's group surmises, "Some people may have a strong capacity for self-control but may not always want to exercise it, while others may have weak self-control ability but have such a keen interest in controlling their deviant impulses that they end up conforming" (p. 146). Specifically, Tittle's group assesses the following expectations: "Those who can control themselves may not always want to do so; instead, they may sometimes deliberately choose to commit criminal acts, while those who lack the capacity for strong self-control may nevertheless so fervently want to control themselves that they refrain from criminal acts" (p. 146). And, as these researchers add, "People who simultaneously lack the capacity for strong self-control and who possess little desire to control themselves may be especially prone to criminal conduct, while those with strong capability for self-control and with great interest in exercising self-control may be especially unlikely to offend. Logically, then, self-control ability and interest in exercising self-control should interact in producing misbehaviors" (p. 146). To assess their hypotheses, Tittle and his research team used data from the Oklahoma City Survey and measured both self-control capability and the desire to practice self-control. Self-control capability was measured using the Grasmick et al. self-control scale, and the desire to practice self-control was measured through items tapping various theories, including social learning, social control, social bond, and rational choice.

Several key findings emerged from Tittle et al.'s (2004) study. First, both the capacity and the desire to exercise self-control exhibited independent, cumulative, and interactive relationships with each other. Second, depending on the measure of crime and deviance, self-control capability was stronger when the individual's interest in exercising self-control was low, but its effect was reduced when desire to exercise self-control was high. Third, combinations of capacity and desire to exercise self-control were particularly important; for example, the magnitude of the coefficient for self-control ability decreased as the magnitude of self-control desire increased, and the coefficient for self-control ability became smaller (less negative), moving from low scores on self-control desire to higher scores, even becoming more significant for some crime indexes at the higher level of self-control desire (Tittle et al., 2004, 163–164).

In short, the effect of self-control ability on crime and deviance depends on the individual's interest in self-regulation: "Ability to exercise self-control appears to be most relevant in inhibiting deviance when an individual's desire to control his or her actions is weak. Under that condition, ability appears to 'stand alone' as a major contributor to misbehavior" Tittle et al. (2004, 163–164). However, Tittle's group adds, "When the desire to control one's behavior is strong, the ability to do so becomes much less relevant in predicting offending. Strong desire to exercise self-control, therefore, may help 'override' the potential influence of weak self-control ability in leading to misbehavior" (pp. 164–165). Clearly, the Tittle team has opened up an important avenue for subsequent theoretical and empirical work that will help researchers understand the conditions under which self-control relates (or does not relate) to criminal and deviant behavior.

A second new development with regard to the measurement of self-control is likely to be viewed with some controversy and skepticism, but it is an important one to highlight. Recently, Hirschi (2004) has taken the view that the original statement of the general theory with respect to the measurement of self-control may have led to more confusion than clarity. He now argues that the list of six self-control elements and the measures based on it may have "muddied the waters" (p. 542). In particular, Hirschi has identified four major problems that have plagued this line of research. First, both the original list of six self-control elements and the measures suggest differences among offenders in motives for crime, contrary to explicit assumptions of the general theory that motives do not matter. Second, the list and the measures contradict the assertion that personality traits do not hold value for the explanation of crime. Third, both fail to explain how self-control operates; instead, "both suggest that offenders act as they do because they are what they are (impulsive, hot-headed, selfish, physical risk takers), whereas nonoffenders are, well, none of these" (p. 542). Fourth, "this exercise fails to produce a measure of self-control in which more is better than less, in which the effects of the individual traits on criminal behavior are cumulative" (p. 542). Hirschi then proposes a new measure of self-control that would include a count of the number of different acts that have long-term negative consequences for the individual committing them and that contains elements of both cognizance and rational choice (p. 542).

More specifically, Hirschi (2004) defines self-control as the "set of inhibitions one carries with one wherever one happens to go" (p. 543), a definition that clearly combines both elements of cognizance and rational choice and recognizes that the offender considers the full range of potential costs and not necessarily and solely the long-term implications of the act. The "tendency to consider" under Hirschi's redefinition of self-control is now broader and more contemporaneous than previous conceptualizations. Following rational choice models of crime, Hirschi indicates that these inhibitions, or factors, "vary in number and salience" (p. 545).

Alex Piquero and Bouffard (2007) collected data from several hundred young adults who responded to two hypothetical vignettes (drunk driving and sexual coercion) designed to measure Hirschi's redefined and reconceptualized self-control concept and compared its predictive ability to the Grasmick et al. attitudinal self-control scale. Their findings indicate that Hirschi's redefined self-control concept and their measurement of it are significantly and negatively associated with both acts and eliminate the direct effect of the Grasmick et al. self-control measure.[1] Piquero and Bouffard conclude by outlining a theoretical extension in which they argue for the utility of conceiving of self-control as a situational construct. Although it is too early to tell whether this new measurement will yield any further clarity or introduce more ambiguity, it seems apparent that Hirschi's redefinition of self-control may be worthwhile.

A third promising direction for self-control measurement comes from a team of researchers who have developed the notion of self-control depletion, which functions as a muscle that can be depleted by use (Muraven et al., 2005, 2006). In this example individuals have a reserve of "self-control strength" (measured in the same fashion as the Grasmick et al. scale), which diminishes as self-control is exerted throughout the day as the person faces various "self-control demands." Individuals may have less self-control to use at any given moment in time, and they may also have differing levels of self-control strength in stock more generally. Under this conceptualization individuals who experience more self-control demands should be lower in self-control strength than individuals who experience fewer self-control demands. In two related studies Muraven and his colleagues found that self-control demands and self-control depletion were important correlates of drinking in one study and of cheating in another. They also reported that individuals high in trait self-control were less affected by self-control demands than individuals lower in trait self-control, suggesting that "individuals high in trait self-control may have a larger pool of resources at their disposal and therefore are less affected by self-control demands than individuals lower in trait self-control" (Muraven et al., 2005, 145).

In a recently proposed alternative conception of self-control and its role in crime causation, Wikstrom and Treiber (2007) propose that self-control is best viewed as a situational concept (a factor in the process of choice) as opposed to the personal, individual trait expressed by Gottfredson and Hirschi. Here, self-control is part of the process of choice, not an individual trait, and self-control becomes something that "we do—'exercises of self-control oppose something in support of something else rather than something we are'" (p. 243). This view of situational self-control, which is influenced by an individual trait of executive capability, is relevant only in situations where an individual considers (deliberates) whether or not to engage in crime. When individuals act out of habit and/or believe that the (criminal) act in question is not in violation of a moral proscription or is not seen as a viable alternative, then self-control is believed to be an unimportant factor. Importantly, Wikstrom and Treiber view morality as a stronger determinant of criminal behavior and reserve the influence of self-control for only certain conditions restricted to particular circumstances.

Thus Wikstrom and Treiber's conception of self-control as a situational characteristic and not a trait stands in contrast to Gottfredson and Hirschi. This is not to mean that they do not offer traits as an important part of the theoretical process; they do. However, the trait (executive capability) functions as the influence of an individual's ability to exercise self-control and the exercising of self-control (as part of the process of choice).

In short, when the Piquero and Bouffard, Muraven et al., and Wikstrom and Treiber efforts are considered together, they underscore the importance of considering self-control in a situational manner, and they move the research away from considering self-control as an enduring personal characteristic that is fixed and stable over the life course—and importantly—across situations. The totality of the evidence from these efforts suggests that consideration of trait and situational self-control may be a useful distinction in subsequent research.

CONCLUSION

There is no denying the impact and importance of Gottfredson and Hirschi's theory; yet much controversy and criticism exist with respect to measurement of their key and underdeveloped causal variable, self-control. In this chapter I set out to provide an overview of the measurement issues, relevant research, unresolved issues, and new and promising directions with respect to operationalizing and measuring self-control. Although many of these directions will undoubtedly yield an important array of findings, the extent to which they will collectively help to clarify matters with respect to the general theory is an open, empirical question.

When considering these new directions, it will be useful to bear in mind two more general points with respect to conceptualizing and measuring self-control across time and populations. These two points have not been given adequate research attention but both are central to matters at hand.

The first point concerns the issue of whether self-control is relevant for understanding crime across all samples and populations, as Hirschi and Gottfredson (2000) claim is the case. Several discussions in the white-collar/corporate crime literature argue that self-control is not a relevant causal factor in the decision-making process. Simpson and Piquero (2002) in particular failed to find an effect for a behavioral measure of self-control on corporate crime. It may be instead that although personal or individual characteristics matter for all offenders, only certain ones matter for specific samples, such as corporate managers—for instance, the desire for control or the general wish to be in control of everyday events (N. Piquero et al., 2005). In fact, in an interesting comparison between low self-control and desire for control as causal agents in corporate decision-making, Nicole Piquero et al. (2008) found no effect for low self-control, whereas the effect of desire for control was significant in predicting corporate offending. In short, the role of self-control may not be as general (with regard to all offenders and crime types) as originally envisioned by Gottfredson and Hirschi.

The second point considers self-control within a developmental context, one that examines how individuals change in an orderly way over the life course. Although antagonistic toward developmental and typological theories, Hirschi and Gottfredson (1995) take a developmental approach toward the formation of self-control (changing throughout the first decade of life in response to parental socialization efforts). To this end, consider the case of a longitudinal study, where people change over time. In this context it must be remembered to assess how the construct of self-control changes over time—attitudinally, behaviorally, and situationally (Turner and Piquero, 2002; Mitchell and MacKenzie, 2006). Recently, Alex Piquero et al. (2007) used data from the Dunedin Health and Multidisciplinary Human Development Study to link two measures of self-control (childhood and adolescence) with various criminal career dimensions and found that both measures related equally well to persistence and desistance. Researchers need to examine in more rigorous detail how the self-control concept and the items and constructs used to measure it change over the life course and how such changes relate to changes in crime and key substantive conclusions.

NOTE

1. It is important to describe the Piquero and Bouffard self-control measure. After reading each vignette, participants were presented with seven blank lines for which they were asked to develop a list of up to seven "bad things" (costs) that might occur if they engaged in the offending behavior depicted in each scenario. This follows Hirschi's suggestion that the number of consequences to which an individual attends when making decisions to offend is related to that individual's self-control. To measure the salience of the consequences that the individual considers, Piquero and Bouffard developed an approach that allowed individuals to provide data on the salience of potential inhibiting factors associated with criminal activity. After listing relevant costs, participants were asked to indicate "*How important* each one of these things would be *when making your decision* whether or not to (offense behavior) under the circumstances in the story." These items were rated using a scale from 0% (Not Important) to 100% (Very Important). Piquero and Bouffard obtained Hirschi's redefined self-control measure by taking the number of costs generated by the respondents and multiplying it by the average salience applied to these groups of costs (i.e., all costs). This provided a measure of self-control that focused on the inhibiting/cost factors (i.e., where higher scores are indicative of higher self-control), which can be quite broad (depending on the respondent's nomination) and which certainly are contemporaneous because the data were obtained immediately after the individual was asked to rate the likelihood of engaging in the hypothetical criminal act.

3 | AGE, SEX, AND RACIAL DISTRIBUTIONS OF CRIME

David F. Greenberg

In this chapter I ask whether the empirical relationships between crime on the one hand, and age, sex, and race on the other are those posited by Gottfredson and Hirschi. I begin with age and then turn to sex and race.

AGE

Arrest statistics suggest that involvement in crime rises during childhood, peaks in adolescence or early adulthood, and then declines (Greenberg, 1977b, 1985; Farrington, 1986). Before they formulated their self-control theory, Hirschi and Gottfredson (1983) argued that this pattern holds for all offenses, at all times and in all places and for all races and both sexes. They insisted that no variables known to criminology could explain it. After formulating self-control theory, they acknowledged that this theory could not explain the pattern either. Rather, they attributed the decline to "the inexorable aging of the organism" (Gottfredson and Hirschi, 1990, 141). Critics, however, contend that the age distribution of crime varies by offense, race, country, and historical period and that it can be explained, at least in part, by criminological theory (Greenberg, 1985; Farrington, 1986; Steffensmeier, 1989).

To evaluate Hirschi and Gottfredson's position, let's consider evidence regarding the age distribution of crime. Is it the same for all offenses, places, and time periods? What can legitimately be inferred from cross-sectional aggregate data? Does the pattern extend to behaviors that are not illegal but just imprudent? What patterns emerge when studying individual life-course trajectories? Is it true that the age distribution cannot be explained by strain or learning theories? What about the social bonding theory that Hirschi enunciated in 1969? Could the age distribution be explained by self-control theory if we dropped the assumption that self-control does not change over the life span? Several different kinds of evidence can be used to answer these questions. I first consider research on aggregate patterns, then studies on individual patterns, and then the role of social integration for individuals.

Observed Aggregate Patterns

In an early assessment Steffensmeier et al. (1989) examined the age curves for several different offenses in individual years. When distributions in a given year are used to draw inferences about the age distribution, there is a risk of confusing age differences with cohort differences (Greenberg, 1985; Greenberg and Larkin, 1985). Like most researchers studying this issue (including Hirschi and Gottfredson), Steffensmeier ignores this problem. Comparing burglary, fraud, and gambling, he finds appreciable differences in the shapes of the curves for different offenses in a given year. Rates of self-reported domestic violence (not studied by Steffensmeier) are virtually independent of age (Center for Injury and Violence Prevention, 2004, 40), unlike most other offenses. These findings are inconsistent with the claim of universality.

Researchers have also conducted studies of imprudent, risky behavior. Deaths from automobile accidents, which can result from unsafe driving practices, decline with age but then rise slightly starting around age 60 (probably because of age-related impairments), whereas arrests are still declining at that age (National Highway Traffic Safety Administration, 1991; Sorensen, 1994). Self-reported cigarette use shows no clear downward trend with age in daily smoking or smoking more than half a pack a day. Heavy drinking declines with age, but daily drinking (which, in moderation, is not imprudent) does not. The use of marijuana, amphetamines, powder cocaine, hallucinogens, barbiturate tranquilizers, MDMA (Ecstasy), and crystal methamphetamine all drop with age. However, use of crack cocaine, steroids, and heroin does not. Alcohol use declines only slightly up to age 45 (L. D. Johnston et al., 2004, 88–108). Visits to hospital emergency rooms for drug overdoses peak at ages 35–44 and are almost as frequent at ages 45–54 as for the teen years (my analysis of Drug Abuse Warning Network data for 1997). Deaths from drug overdoses are higher in the 35–54-year-old age bracket than in younger age groups (Office of Applied Statistics, 2004, 109–122). Seat belt use depends only weakly on age. The same is true for drinking and driving and having smoke detectors at home (Center for Injury and Violence Prevention, 2004). Keeping a firearm at home increases with age, declining only for ages 65 and older. Some of these patterns fit the Hirschi-Gottfredson paradigm; others do not.

Some of the patterns are race specific. In 1998 the prevalence of smoking tobacco cigarettes in the past month among non-Hispanic whites was slightly higher among those who were 35 or older than at younger ages; for Hispanics the prevalence almost doubled, and for non-Hispanic blacks it more than doubled (National Institute on Drug Abuse, 2003, 51).

Steffensmeier et al. (1989) looked for evidence of historical variability by comparing the age distributions for 1940 and 1960 with those in 1980; they found some change for most offenses. Further change is evident when data from the two decades since Steffensmeier's study are considered. Gottfredson and Hirschi (1990, 133) call these changes trivial, and it is true that some of the differences between offenses and between years are not great. However, some of them are substantial. During the 1980s arrests of youths younger than 24 for homicide rose sharply, probably because of the crack cocaine epidemic, and rates for older offenders held steady. In 1980 the arrest rate for 16-year-olds was lower than for all other age brackets. By 1993 the arrest rate had almost tripled, surpassing the rates for 25–29-year-olds, and was virtually the same as for 22-year-olds. By 2001 it was again lower than for all the older age brackets up to ages 25–29 (Blumstein, 1995; Blumstein and Rosenfeld, 1998). When arrest rates increase for one age bracket but not for other age brackets, the age distribution of arrests necessarily changes. In this instance the change was temporary. After a few years homicide arrests for youths began to drop, restoring the earlier distribution.

A similar shift in the age-crime relationship occurred in Japan after 1970. In just a decade arrest rates of 14–15-year-old larceny offenders increased by a factor of 2.5. They almost doubled for ages 16 and 17 but did not rise at all for older offenders. Arrest rates for violent offenses tripled for 14–15-year-olds in the years after 1980 but declined at older ages (Harada, 1988). In Finland homicide rates of teenagers and young adults dropped throughout the twentieth century much more than the homicide rates of older people did. As a result, the peak age bracket for homicide has risen from 20–29 to 30–39. The downward slope is now much shallower than it was early in the twentieth century, so much so that the homicide rate for 40–44-year-old individuals is about the same as that for 20–24-year-olds. In the years 1924–1939 the homicide rate was less than one-sixth of the rate for 20–24-year-olds (Lehti, 2004a, 2004b).

In nineteenth-century New York homicide rates were essentially flat up through the mid-50s age bracket, unlike the distribution in modern New York, which begins sloping downward at a much earlier age (Monkonnen, 2001). The pattern in nineteenth-century Columbus, Ohio, was similar (Monkonnen, 1975). In eighteenth-century France rates of violent crime were lower in the teenage years than they were for older adults (Ruff, 1984, 90–91). These are substantial changes; they refute claims that the age-crime curve is a transhistorical universal. The changes point to social influences that act differentially according to age. It follows that the age-crime curve cannot be due exclusively to physiological aging, although that may contribute.

The cross-national invariance of the age-crime distribution has also been tested through a study of Israeli arrests. Shavit and Rattner (1988) found that the number of Jewish offenders and the number of offenses at each age between 18 and 26 (the oldest age they were able to study) were constant. By contrast, in the United States in 2001 the number of arrests for index offenses in the 25–29-year-old age bracket was only a little more than one-third the number at the peak age of 18. The Israel pattern is not a trivial departure from universality.

Studies of Individuals

A given aggregate age-crime curve can be generated by a wide range of individual age-crime curves. Consequently, a full test of the universality of the age-crime distribution requires data for individuals. Several researchers who have studied individual criminal trajectories have found that the probability of someone recidivating after a conviction diminishes with age (Kruttschnitt et al., 2000; Laub and Sampson, 2003, 260–261; Ezell and Cohen, 2005). These studies have also found that a young age at first arrest predicts a criminal career that tends to extend over a longer period and has a higher frequency of offenses (Loeber and LeBlanc, 1990, 1998). Hirschi and Gottfredson (1993) see nothing of etiological importance in these observations beyond an underlying "criminality." As they see it, those who display higher criminality have weaker self-control, start committing crimes at an earlier age, and commit them more often and for a longer period of time.

A number of researchers (e.g., Nagin and Land, 1993; Sampson and Laub, 1993; Laub and Sampson, 2003, 260–261; Ezell and Cohen, 2005) have analyzed arrest records to determine whether all offenders have the same age-crime profile. If Hirschi and Gottfredson are correct, these studies should reveal that some individuals are persistently more criminal than others, but the intensity of their involvement should follow a uniform temporal pattern in which illegal activities peak early and decline with age in exactly the same way, so that the relative rankings of criminal behavior stay the same over time. These studies and others show that offender criminal histories do not all conform to the same temporal pattern. They find three to six distinct groups, each with its own trajectory. In each group criminal activity declines with age, but some offenders change groups, so that the rank ordering of criminal intensity changes.

Most of these studies fail to examine crime-specific trajectories. However, several studies have found that there are some offense-specific patterns; the age-crime curve is not identical for all offenses (Wikström, 1990; Bachman et al., 2002; Massoglia, 2006). These results also are inconsistent with the Hirschi-Gottfredson model.

Social Integration

Hirschi and Gottfredson emphasize the resistance of criminality to change after childhood. In their view life circumstances could affect criminal activity by changing the opportunities that prospective offenders confront, but not in other ways. This claim entails an implicit repudiation of the version of control theory that Hirschi (1969) advanced in a study of juvenile delinquents in Oakland, California. There he argued that social bonds tend to inhibit crime. Children who have close relationships with parents, teachers, and friends and who are involved in legitimate institutions, he maintained, would tend to avoid crime to avoid social disapproval and loss of future prospects. Such involvement is likely to vary with age, bringing about changes in criminal behavior.

Numerous studies, including those that follow subjects over the life course, have confirmed that social bonds are associated with lower rates of criminal law violation. Social bonds established after childhood, such as marriage or attachment to spouse, employment, and enlistment in the army, reduce involvement in crime (Uggen, 2000; Sampson et al., 2006). These findings challenge self-control theory and suggest that participation in legitimate institutions in adulthood alters either motivations to commit crime or willingness to act on those motivations or both. Although the explanatory power of social bond theory is weak (Greenberg, 1999), it is no worse than for other sociological theories of crime. For this reason we should be reluctant to abandon the theory without a compelling reason.

Gottfredson and Hirschi (1990), however, propose an alternative interpretation of these findings: that the relationship between crime on the one hand and work, marriage, and military service on the other is spurious. According to this view, low self-control not only causes crime but also reduces the likelihood that someone will marry and, once married, will stay married. Low self-control reduces the likelihood that someone will seek a job, get one, and keep it. Poor health, which could be the consequence of a dissolute lifestyle followed by individuals lacking self-control, could also result in inability to marry or get a job. Consequently, crime, being unmarried, and being unemployed could all be the result of low self-control. If this is so, marriage and employment will not reduce criminal behavior. Only aging and reduced opportunities could do that.

The research findings are not consistent with this explanation. By examining changes in criminality for a given individual over a span of time during which marital status, employment status, and military status change, the supposedly stable attribute of self-control is controlled, that is, held constant statistically. Consequently, institutional integration (being part of a family, having a job) influences levels of involvement in crime. Warr (2002, 91–114) suggests that marriage does this by influencing the peers with whom someone associates. After young men marry, they typically spend less time with delinquent and criminal friends and more time with their wives and children. This shift in patterns of peer association reduces crime. The impact of this shift is magnified by the greater influence that peer pressures have during adolescence than at other ages (Greenberg, 1977b; Gardner and Steinberg, 2005). Other research confirms the influence of delinquent peer associations on an individual's delinquency, controlling for stable individual traits (Nagin and Paternoster, 1991; Paternoster and Brame, 1997; McCarthy et al., 2004).

It is also possible that institutional involvement alters motivations to commit crime or affects criminal conduct by changing the schedule of costs and rewards that a rational decision maker would take into account (deterrence) or by strengthening social bonds. We could dismiss these possibilities only if we were certain that the self-control theory is correct in its insistence that none of these factors distinguishes those who conform to legal requirements from those who do not. Yet there is evidence that motivational factors and deterrence do influence illegality and alter the shape of individuals' criminal careers (Greenberg, 2004; Tittle and Botchkovar, 2005). Consequently, these possibilities cannot be dismissed.

Apart from the influence of marriage and lawful employment, criminal behavior can also be influenced by government responses to an individual's criminal activity (e.g., imprisonment or placement in a rehabilitation program). In the early 1970s several surveys of the effectiveness of correctional programs found that most evaluations failed to show rigorously that the programs reduced recidivism (Lipton et al., 1975; Greenberg, 1977a). It would be an exaggeration to say that these studies found that "nothing works," but this is how many have understood them. This oversimplification is presumably the basis for Gottfredson and Hirschi's assertion that treatment programs consistently fail.

The proposition that rehabilitation programs do nothing to prevent further crime is now out of date. Evaluations show that some programs do reduce return to crime for some juvenile and adult law violators (Gendreau and Ross, 1986; Izzo and Ross, 1990; Lipsey, 1992; Lösel, 1995; Dowden and Andrews, 1999). They also compel a modification of the position that criminality cannot be influenced after childhood. Criminal behavior can be reduced by making appropriate, effective programs available. Consequently, these interventions can alter the shape of criminal career trajectories. They do so independently of opportunities to commit crimes. If this is so, then criminal careers cannot all be uniform in shape, and they can be influenced by social processes.

Aging and the Age Curve

To assess the claim that the biological aging of the human body explains the decline of crime with years, we must consider the precise mechanism that makes aging relevant. Possibly aging reduces crime by weakening the strength and agility of potential perpetrators. Perhaps robbers abandon mugging because they are no longer confident of being able to overpower their victims or escape pursuers. Burglars may lose the ability to climb into second-story windows when they get older (Farrington, 1986). On its face, this explanation is plausible. Most people are less fit as they get older and might well take this into account in deciding whether or not to commit a crime.

As a complete explanation of the decline, however, the explanation seems flawed. The decline in crimes of violence is slower than the decline in property crimes, which is not what one would expect if physiological aging accounts for the drop in crime. It is not plausible that large numbers of auto thieves slow down or abandon stealing cars by age 18 because they are much less fit than 15-year-olds. Moreover, physical decline is not one of the explanations that former criminals themselves commonly give to explain their abandonment of crime (Adler, 1985; Shover, 1985, 1996; Baskin and Sommers, 1998).

The age distribution of white-collar crime provides another test. The existence of white-collar crimes is a challenge to self-control theory (Steffensmeier, 1989; Benson and Moore, 1992; Reed and Yeager, 1996). White-collar crimes are often committed by business executives who would never be in their positions if their lifestyles were typical of individuals with little self-control. Indeed, many (although not all) of the defendants convicted of white-collar crimes in federal court and studied by Weisburd et al. (2001) and by Benson (2002) led lives that were, to all appearances, sterling—apart from their crimes. Hirschi and Gottfredson, however, insist that their theory applies to white-collar offenders as well (Hirschi and Gottfredson, 1987, 959–960; Gottfredson and Hirschi, 1990, 200).

In the sample studied by Weisburd's group the mean age of the defendants ranged from 30 for bank embezzlement to 50 for antitrust violations. For the sample as a whole the mean age was 38.5; in the Benson study it was 41. This age is higher than the mean age of 29.2 for those arrested for violent crimes in 2000.[1] The average age at which the first arrest occurred was high compared to the average age of "common crime offenders," whose first arrest typically occurred in the teen years. The mean age at last recorded arrest was in the low 40s. The careers of all offenders who had at least two offenses lasted, on average, fourteen years, with some extending a quarter of a century (Weisburd et al., 2001, 33, 39). In a different study, based on self-reports among Oklahoma City residents, Tittle and Grasmick (1998) found that cheating on taxes peaked in the age bracket 35–54, much higher than for other kinds of theft or crimes involving force.

In part, these high mean ages reflect opportunities. Teenagers would rarely be in a position to commit antitrust violations. It is not so clear that the comparatively short durations of involvement in many common crimes can be explained by reduced opportunities in adulthood. Middle-aged people would seem to have just as many opportunities to commit burglary, rape, and murder as youngsters.

In a statistical analysis of recidivism in their sample, Weisburd et al. (2001, 124–125) found that age has no predictive value whatsoever. Because physical prowess is not needed for white-collar crimes, this is what one would expect if deterioration of the body explains desistance. At the same time the finding is also contrary to the Hirschi-Gottfredson claim that the age distribution of crime is universal.

The physiological aging hypothesis can also be tested with motor vehicle violations, because these do not require exceptional strength. In a study of drinking and driving among Canadian motorists, blood alcohol concentration, as determined with Breathalyzer tests in random motor stops, for men was higher at ages older than 24 than at ages 16–24. For women the levels began to decline with age only at age 40 (Keane et al., 1993). This pattern is quite different from what is seen for property crime and crimes of violence.

Although physiological aging would seemingly be most plausible as an explanation for crimes of interpersonal violence, even this can be doubted. A typical middle-aged or older man or woman has enough muscle strength to pull the trigger of a gun or to slit a throat. If people do this less often when they have passed their 20s, it is probably for other reasons than the deterioration of their bodies.

Another possible physiological explanation involves declining levels of androgens such as testosterone (Gove, 1985). In popular belief testosterone is positively related to dominance and aggression and thus could be a cause of crime. However, studies of the relationship between testosterone and crime are not conclusive. Levels of free testosterone do decline with age in both sexes (Zumoff et al., 1995; Labrie et al., 1997; Davison et al., 2005) but probably too slowly to explain the decline in crime fully.

Recent research in neuropsychology shows that the human brain continues to develop through the second decade of life and suggests that changes in brain structure that occur in late adolescence improve the capacity to manage emotions, curb impulsivity, and take the long-term consequences of actions into account (Beckman, 2004).

A parsimonious explanation of the decline in crime with age—an explanation that Hirschi and Gottfredson reject—would posit that self-control tends to become stronger with age. People may learn to manage anger or greed in ways that are less likely to bring them into conflict with the law. Several studies have found that self-control, as measured with survey instruments, tends to increase with age (Tittle and Grasmick, 1997; Tittle et al., 2003a). Tittle et al. (2003a) found that self-control increases with age, explains various kinds of illegal and deviant behavior, and contributes significantly to the age-crime relationship. This finding confirms the importance of self-control in the explanation of illegality (as have numerous other studies) but challenges the Hirschi-Gottfredson understanding of the age-crime relationship.

Survey research shows that older Germans tend to be more risk aversive. The age dependence of risk aversion is quite similar to that of self-reported crime, suggesting another mechanism by which aging could reduce crime apart from physiological aging (Dohmen et al., 2005).

SEX

Arrest rates, self-report surveys, and victimization studies indicate that males are considerably more likely than females to commit almost all kinds of crime. The only exceptions in the contemporary United States are embezzlement, probably reflecting the large number of women who are sales clerks; prostitution, no doubt a result of greater demand; and running away from home, probably because daughters evoke greater parental concern when they run away (Hindelang, 1979; D. A. Smith and Visher, 1980; Steffensmeier and Allen, 1991). Similar patterns are found in other countries.

Boys are also more likely than girls to be victims of accidents (Junger, 1994; Gottfredson and Hirschi, 1990, 130; Zager, 1994). Male Americans between the ages of 19 and 30 are more likely than females to use alcohol and illicit drugs daily and to drink heavily, although the differences in cigarette smoking are minuscule (Gibbs and Giever, 1995; L. D. Johnston et al., 2004, 88). There is also little difference between the sexes in driving after drinking too much alcohol (Center for Injury and Violence Prevention, 2004). Women are more risk averse than men in financial decision making (Jianakoplos and Bernasek, 1998) and are more likely to take preventive health care measures, such as dental flossing and checking blood pressure (Hersch, 1996). On the other hand, women are no more likely than men to engage in binge eating (Reagan and Hersch, 2005). A meta-analysis of 150 studies found that in many contexts women are more cautious than men, but when caution is measured behaviorally, the differences for some types of behavior are small. For some behaviors they have the "wrong" sign (Byrnes et al., 1999).

Gottfredson and Hirschi (1990, 144–149) suggest that sex differences in criminality are unlikely to be due entirely to differences in opportunity. Although they acknowledge that differences in social control may contribute, they tentatively suggest that the sex differences could be primarily due to differences in self-control, especially for juveniles. This is a reasonable suggestion. Parents supervise young daughters more closely than they do young sons, and they allow sons greater independence (Simmons and Blyth, 1987, 73–79). This strategy may be more successful in instilling powers of self-control in daughters than in sons; it may also increase the strength of girls' bonding to parents. Of course, it is also possible that parents, schools, and the mass media socialize boys and girls differently. Consequently, a predominance of males for many criminal and deviant activities, although consistent with self-control theory, does not fully establish it.

If self-control alone explains sex differences in crime, then the sex ratio should be the same for all offense categories. Yet there are differences (Zager, 1994): 63.5 percent of those arrested in 2001 for larceny were male, compared to 86 percent for burglary, 90 percent for robbery, and 90 percent for homicide (Pastore and Maguire, 2002, 359). In a number of European countries women are less likely than men to consider corruption and tax evasion justifiable (Torgler and Valev, 2006), suggesting that learned moral beliefs may also help to explain the sex difference.

The Hirschi-Gottfredson explanation of the sex differences can be tested statistically by seeing whether females have more self-control than boys, whether self-control reduces crime and imprudent behaviors in both sexes, and whether the relationship between sex and crime is explained partly or fully by self-control. A meta-analysis of studies of sex differences in personality concluded that there are no large sex differences in self-control (Feingold, 1994). On the other hand, a more recent study found that this conclusion depends on how self-control is assessed. When self-control is measured with an attitudinal scale, there are no significant differences between males and females. However, when self-control was measured by participation in imprudent behaviors (e.g., drinking alcohol, smoking tobacco, using a seat belt while driving, getting into debt, taking medicine for a minor illness) and by the variety of those behaviors, Oklahoma City females were more self-controlled (Tittle et al., 2003b). However, this study measured self-control in a manner that could be considered tautological. Imprudent behaviors are supposed to be what self-control explains. Only if we accept the explanation can the behaviors be considered a measure of self-control. In a study of Canadian high school students LaGrange and Silverman (1999) found the expected sex differences for several different measures of self-control (impulsivity, risk taking, and present orientation) but not for temper and carelessness. Sex differences in smoking were small and not statistically significant. In another study female undergraduate college students drank less alcohol than male undergraduates, even when self-control was taken into account (Gibbs and Giever, 1995).

Looking at the effect of self-control measures on delinquency, LaGrange and Silverman (1999) found that self-control consistently reduced general delinquency and property offenses (except that impulsivity did not significantly affect property crimes) but did not consistently influence involvement in crimes of violence or drug offenses. Sex differences in general delinquency, property crimes, and violent crimes were partly but not fully explained by self-control and opportunities; however, self-control and opportunity fully explained the (smaller) sex differences in drug offenses. In the Tittle et al. (2003b) study each of several measures of self-control reduced crime deviance, and the behavioral measures reduced the effect of sex by roughly 50 percent, rendering it statistically nonsignificant. In still another study Burton et al. (1998) found that when self-control and opportunities are taken into account, the relationship between sex and crime is reduced by 50 percent and becomes nonsignificant statistically. The age effect, however, is only partly explained by these variables. Moreover, for women (but not men) there is evidence that having criminal friends is criminogenic, contrary to the claim of self-control theory. Love (2006) found lower levels of self-reported crime and some forms of what Love considered illicit or deviant sexual activity among female college students than among males but no significant differences in the number of sexual partners before starting college (another measure of low self-control). The sex difference in delinquency persists even after self-control and opportunities are controlled. McMullen (1999) found that sex differences in criminal, deviant, and risk-taking activities carried out by Virginia college students persisted when measures of self-control were taken into account. Finally, in a statistical analysis of juvenile delinquency in a national sample, Zager (1994) found that social control differences do not fully explain the sex difference in delinquency. These studies, then, find some merit in the Gottfredson-Hirschi contention, but it is not the whole story. Sex differences in socialization and subjection to social control may also be relevant.

RACE

When Gottfredson and Hirschi discuss race and crime, they limit their discussion to differences between blacks and whites. Although blacks make up 12 percent of the U.S. population, in 2000 they were, according to arrest statistics, 18 percent of the arsonists, 25 percent of the burglars, 28 percent of the drug law violators, 35 percent of the rapists, 50 percent of the killers, 56 percent of the robbers, and 86 percent of the gamblers arrested (Pastore and Maguire, 2002, 357). These percentages imply extremely high disproportionalities. For example, the homicide and robbery rates for blacks exceed those for whites by factors of 7.33 and 9.33, respectively.

We know that these disproportionalities are not primarily the product of differential law enforcement practices because they have been confirmed by surveys in which crime victims report the race of their attackers. For the more serious predatory crimes disproportionality has also been confirmed from studies of self-reported delinquency, although not for non-predatory crimes such as truancy and drug violations (Elliott and Ageton, 1980). Blacks are slightly less likely than whites to wear seat belts when driving (Center for Injury and Violence Prevention, 2004; Schichor et al., 1990); they are underrepresented, however, among those arrested for driving under the influence of alcohol and for liquor law violations. For drunkenness they are represented roughly in proportion to their presence in the population (U.S. Department of Justice, Federal Bureau of Investigation, 2001).

Gottfredson and Hirschi (1990) tentatively suggest that race differences in crime could be due to racial differences in self-control. If self-control theory is right, blacks should also be overrepresented in various imprudent behaviors. Studies of deaths of motor vehicle occupants as a result of accidents find that blacks are overrepresented by 11 percent, quite a bit less than for many criminal offenses (S. P. Baker et al., 1998). Blacks are more likely than whites to have gonorrhea or syphilis, by a factor of 30 to 1. They are also more likely to have hepatitis B and genital herpes (Centers for Disease Control, 2000). They are disproportionately HIV-positive. For non-Hispanic white males the number of cases in 2003 is estimated to be 18 per 100,000; for non-Hispanic black males, it is 127 per 100,000, seven times higher. The comparable figures for white and black females are 3 per 100,000 and 66 per 100,000, respectively (Centers for Disease Control, 2005); the black rate is twenty-two times higher than the white rate. Blacks are less likely than whites to take precautionary health measures, although some of these differences lose statistical significance or reverse once other individual characteristics are taken into account (Hersch, 1996).

These results are consistent with the Gottfredson-Hirschi proposal. However, until recently, blacks were less likely than whites to smoke tobacco cigarettes and were about as likely to use marijuana, contrary to Gottfredson and Hirschi's theory. Among high school students blacks are also less likely than whites to use some drugs—alcohol, inhalants, LSD and other hallucinogens, Ecstasy, amphetamines, tranquilizers, and noncrack cocaine. They are also less likely to engage in heavy drinking (L. D. Johnston et al., 2004, 25–27; National Institute on Drug Abuse, 2003, 51) or binge eating (Reagan and Hersch, 2005). These findings are inconsistent with self-control theory and are not plausibly due to differential opportunities (unless the availability of discretionary funds is an opportunity). One suspects, therefore, that something other than self-control or opportunity is responsible.

If race differences in crime are due to differences in self-control, then the effect of race on crime should disappear when self-control is controlled statistically. In a study of delinquency in a sample of Alabama students in grades 9 through 12, Vazsonyi and Crosswhite (2004) found delinquency to be higher among those with low self-control. This was true for African Americans and Caucasians and for males and females. Vazsonyi informed me in a private communication that the introduction of self-control has little effect on the race-delinquency relationship. Love (2006) also found that black overrepresentation in delinquency survives the introduction of controls for self-control, age, sex, and parental income. Although the findings of these studies are consistent with self-control theory, it appears that racial differences in delinquency are not entirely due to self-control. These findings point to the need for supplementing the self-control theory with insights from other theoretical traditions.

SUMMARY

A strict interpretation of Hirschi and Gottfredson's claim that the age-crime distribution is universal cannot be sustained. The distribution varies by place and time, at times substantially. It varies with offense and from one individual to another. There is evidence that increasing levels of self-control contribute to the decline of crime with age, but other factors contribute as well, including social bonds—which constitute a form of social control distinct from self-control.

Sex and race differences may be, in part, a product of differences in levels of self-control, but other factors are likely to contribute as well. When considering differences among individuals who are demographically similar in the same place at the same time, it may be sufficient to supplement the self-control theory with insights from other social-psychological theories, such as learning theory. However, when considering group differences, such as those associated with sex and race, it will be necessary to extend the theoretical framework beyond the individual person or the family. One can hardly hope to understand sex and race differences in crime and other forms of deviance without considering the culture of sex, gender, and race and the institutional practices that sustain an age-graded, gendered, and racialized social order. That the gap between males and females in propensity to undertake risk has been declining (Byrnes et al., 1999) is most plausibly explained by the sweeping changes in the gendering of American social life in the past few decades. That racial disproportionality in arrests has also been declining points to changes in the American racial order. Consequently, a full explanation of group differences in crime cannot be confined to the realm of individual psychology.

NOTES

I am grateful to Shirley Witcher of the U.S. Bureau of the Census for providing census data, to Walter Gove, Arthur Lurvey, Allan Mazur, and Alan Block for helpful discussions, and to Erich Goode for editorial suggestions.

1. If we restrict the category to individuals age 18 or older (to make the computation comparable to the sample prosecuted in criminal court), the mean age rises to 31.8, still appreciably lower than in the Weisburd et al. sample.

4 THE UNDEVELOPED CONCEPT OF OPPORTUNITY

Sally S. Simpson and Gilbert Geis

In a brief vignette in *The Great Gatsby*, Nick Carroway, the book's first-person narrator, asks Gatsby about Meyer Wolfsheim (a character based on the notorious gangster Arnold Rothstein), a man Gatsby had brought with him to a lunch meeting. "Who is he, anyhow, an actor?" Nick wants to know after Wolfsheim departs. "No, he's a gambler," Gatsby answers and then adds that Wolfsheim had been involved with Chicago White Sox players in fixing the 1919 World Series (later notoriously derogated as the "Black Sox" scandal). "How did he happen to do that?" Carroway asks. "He just saw the opportunity" is Gatsby's answer (Fitzgerald, 1925, 74).

The facts were a good deal more complicated than Gatsby's truncated explanation. For one thing a similar opportunity was offered to a pitcher on the Cincinnati team (Horace "Hod" Eller), which was opposing the heavily favored White Sox. Acting on rumors, the Cincinnati manager asked Eller if he had been offered a bribe. "After breakfast this morning a guy got on the elevator with me, and got off at the same floor I did. He showed me five thousand-dollar bills, and said they were mine if I'd lose the game today," Eller reported. "What did you say?" the manager asked. "I said if he didn't get damn far away from me real quick he wouldn't know what hit him. And the same went if I ever saw him again" (Ritter, 1966, 203). Eller validated his statement by beating Chicago that day and then again in the fifth game of the series (Asinof, 1963; see also Rathgeber, 1982).

Fitzgerald's account can serve as a precursor to our exploration of the use of the concept of opportunity as a crucial element in the explanation of criminal acts and the roster of maladaptive (or as one set of writers has labeled them, "imprudent") behaviors (Arneklev et al., 1999) listed in Michael Gottfredson and Travis Hirschi's *General Theory of Crime* (1990). The theory argues that a particular human condition—the absence of sufficient self-control—is the key factor that explains illegal and correlative behaviors. It couples low self-control with opportunity as the two conditions that underlie such behavior.

Gottfredson and Hirschi (1990) write that the absence of self-control "is meant to explain all crime, at all times, and for that matter, many forms of behavior that are not sanctioned by the state" (p. 117). Five years later, in a modified statement, Hirschi and Gottfredson

(1995) suggest that "although we argue that self-control is a general cause of crime, we do not argue that it is the sole cause of crime" (p. 140). It is not clear how one distinguishes a "general" cause from a "sole" cause, although the theorists add a further explication, saying that their theory "takes the social and economic conditions of offenders as a reflection of their tendency to offend, not a cause of offending" (Gottfredson and Hirschi, 1990, 81). One could argue that self-control itself is also only a tendency because it is acted out only when appropriate opportunities are in place.

Self-control theory has produced a considerable number of tests that attempt to determine how much of crime and deviance it can explain (Tittle et al., 2003b). Results from these studies are varied and controversial. Our purpose in this chapter is to deal with a largely unexplored element of the theory: the underdeveloped concept of opportunity. Certainly it is true, as commentators have observed, that "the role of . . . opportunity is unclear in self-control theory" (Higgins and Ricketts, 2004, 77) and that it remains "conspicuously untested" (T. R. Smith, 2004, 542).

Although Gottfredson and Hirschi emphasize self-control as lying at the heart of their theory, they also indicate, as we have noted, that the behaviors they are interested in interpreting can be carried out only when adequate opportunity exists (see also Grasmick et al., 1993). For example, a sharecropping farmer in Alabama would have difficulty engaging in insider trading or an antitrust violation. At the same time the opportunity for some of the behaviors Gottfredson and Hirschi examine are ubiquitous: Anybody with suitable accoutrements could commit murder or steal something of value most any time they might be so inclined. Katz (1988) argues that acts may ultimately be committed only after the perpetrator has bypassed the same opportunity on innumerable occasions, pointing out that a person may walk by a jewelry store window for months on end before deciding one day to break the window and grab the watches and bracelets on display.

In a footnote Gottfredson and Hirschi (1990) maintain that the "assertion that crimes are a product of the criminality of the actor and assertions that environmental conditions are necessary for crimes to occur are not necessarily inconsistent" (p. 2). The "not necessarily" is one of those qualifiers that often make self-control theory difficult to pin down. There clearly are times when environmental conditions preclude criminality. But the more basic question is, Are there real or hypothetical situations when two individuals with equivalent low levels of self-control respond differently to precisely similar environmental conditions—that is, one commits a crime and the other does not? We argue that such situations exist. Consider the White Sox baseball scandal. Two players might have shared low self-control attributes, but one might have needed the bribe money much more than the other, say, for debts or because of a family crisis. If so, it is not the absence of self-control that presumably determined the two players' discrepant responses to an offer of a bribe but rather the environmental profiles that characterized the two people. The same would appear to be true of the striking differences in levels of crime between nations. It seems not to be either self-control or opportunity that often bears so pervasively on crime but rather poverty, discrimination, and other structural and cultural conditions.

Gottfredson and Hirschi (1990) maintain that "there is every reason to believe that the necessary conditions strategy of opportunity theory is compatible with the idea of criminality, although the connection between the two is far from straightforward" (p. 23). To this statement they add that the connection "has been largely neglected" by classical and positivist traditions (p. 23). Like the rest of the field, Gottfredson and Hirschi have neglected the role of opportunity. They claim that their approach "allows us to judge the validity of theories of criminality based on the consistency between their notions of criminality and opportunity theories of crime" (pp. 23–24), but although they chronically criticize approaches that compete with theirs, they fall short in applying the same kind of critical standards to their own theory.

What exactly do Gottfredson and Hirschi mean by opportunity? They describe it as one of a "set of necessary conditions (e.g., activity, opportunity, adversaries, victims, goods)" and tie it to crimes per se, which are said to be "short-term, circumscribed events" prompted by the leitmotif of inadequate self-control. Self-control is defined as a "relatively" stable individual difference "in the propensity to commit criminal (or equivalent) acts" (Gottfredson and Hirschi, 1990, 125). The word *relatively* is bothersome in a theory that claims universal predictive accuracy. Certainly, "victims" and "goods" supply opportunities, although "activity" seems to lack standing relative to those items and it is difficult to comprehend how opportunity, postulated as the second integral prong of the theory, becomes equated with adversaries and the other items on the definitional roster.

The term *opportunity* and its plural do not appear often in *A General Theory of Crime*. By our count the two words can be found sixty-four times in a book with slightly more than 274 pages. The uses of *self-control* obviously are much greater in number than those for *opportunity*. At times *opportunity* is used in a commonplace way that has nothing to do with the elements of self-control theory. For instance, Gottfredson and Hirschi (1990) write, "A major attraction of the contemporary call for longitudinal research is that it offers the opportunity to distinguish clearly between ordinary offenders and career criminals—in other words, the opportunity to study 'the dimensions of active criminal careers'" (p. 240; Blumstein et al., 1986, 55).

The word *opportunity* also surfaces when Gottfredson and Hirschi note the title of the classic study, *Delinquency and Opportunity*, by Richard Cloward and Lloyd Ohlin (1960). They indicate that Cloward and Ohlin's formulation is "ironically, one of the etiological theories most *in*compatible [their emphasis] with opportunity explanations of crime" (Gottfredson and Hirschi, 1990, 24). Because Cloward and Ohlin were suggesting an opportunity theory, as Cook (1986, 2) points out, it is difficult to understand how what they offered could be incompatible with this type of theory, unless they ignored an orthodoxy that seemingly did not exist then or, for that matter, does not exist now. Cloward and Ohlin maintained that young recruits do not freely select their forms of deviance; rather, those who practice and control the deviance select from the pool of possible newcomers, so that it is the nature of the deviant activity, not personality proclivities such as self-control, that is paramount in the process. Their levels of self-control notwithstanding, not all wannabes share the opportunity to participate in an organized crime syndicate because a particular slate of traits is required to qualify for recruitment. For Gottfredson and Hirschi the crucial point here—although they do not directly address their concerns about this form of opportunity theory—is that it really does not matter what criminal, deviant, or destructive outlet is selected by those with minimal self-control, only that such persons act in these ways because of the absence of adequate self-control. For our part we would note that if slum youngsters are selectively incorporated into organized crime, one of the criteria that often will be used will be the presence rather than the absence of self-control.

Gottfredson and Hirschi favor the criminal opportunity views advanced by Lawrence Cohen and Marcus Felson (1979). They begin with the observation that "we take the conditions necessary for crime in general as commonly stated in opportunity theory" (Gottfredson and Hirschi, 1990, 24) and then declare that the Cohen-Felson formulation requires a motivated offender, the absence of a capable guardian, and a suitable target. Consistent with the framers of this opportunity theory, Gottfredson and Hirschi assume a motivated offender and then construct the picture of the offender post hoc (after first understanding the role of guardian and targets). They suggest that the offender created by this approach "does not resemble the picture painted by current theories of criminality" (Gottfredson and Hirschi, 1990, 24).

Gottfredson and Hirschi explicate their position regarding opportunity by referring to Michael Hough's 1987 study of burglary in England. In this study Hough determined that offenders judge the suitability of targets in terms of proximity, accessibility, and reward. Burglars, Hough reports (and Gottfredson and Hirschi agree), prefer easily available targets that offer prospects for success. Gottfredson and Hirschi (1990) then add, "Extension of this insight leads directly to difficulty for some theories of criminality, since many would require burglary by people who tend toward criminality regardless of their assessment of the target" (p. 24). The disconnect between this observation and the formulation of self-control theory in regard to opportunity is important because Gottfredson and Hirschi prioritize the absence of self-control. Yet assessment of the suitability of burglary targets would appear to indicate the possible dominance of opportunity appraisals over the absence of self-control. In truth, of course, plenty of burglars plan carefully and go far afield to thieve because they presume that residences in elite neighborhoods possess more loot (R. T. Wright and Decker, 1994). Hochstetler (2001) discusses how antecedent events, potential co-offenders, and interactional dynamics shift perceptions of illicit opportunities and ultimately of offending decisions. Simply put, the conjunction of opportunity and absence of self-control may provide some helpful hints about some burglaries but hardly about all or perhaps most burglaries.

Gottfredson and Hirschi (1990) make an observation that "burglary can be prevented by putting sufficient restraints on people who encounter attractive opportunities for burglary" (p. 27). We assume the theorists consider such restraints as counterweights against the hardening of burglary targets; that is, it is meant as a focus on the offender and not the situation. But we find it difficult to understand what Gottfredson and Hirschi have in mind. What sort of sufficient restraints will deter a determined burglar who comes across an unlocked door in an unoccupied house in a wealthy neighborhood? The authors do not specify what they mean by their statement.

Gottfredson and Hirschi seem not to take into account the empirical fact that Cohen and Felson (1979, 598) supported their ideas with evidence that the crime rate had escalated from the 1960s to 1979. But there has been a significant decline during recent times in the amount of crime in the United States that has occurred, notwithstanding an apparent decrease in the number of "capable guardians" (i.e., more women working and leaving homes unguarded) and an increase in the number of "suitable targets" (i.e., more durable goods to steal). Notably, too, the rate of homicide has dropped considerably, despite no obvious changes in the level of self-control in the populace or the availability of potential victims. Gottfredson and Hirschi (1990) are aware of this development, but they deal with it in what we find to be a perplexing manner: "Of course, it is always possible that the apparent variation in opportunity is in fact variation in the availability of offenders. Television sets may be getting lighter at the same time people are becoming more interested in stealing them; people may be leaving houses at the same time other people are becoming more interested in its contents. To study the effects of opportunity in crime we should therefore make some effort to 'control' the propensities of individuals" (pp. 218–219). The use of *apparent* in the first sentence of the quote seems questionable because the remainder of the quote grants variations in opportunity. Nor do Gottfredson and Hirschi explicitly explain why people would be "becoming more interested" in stealing television sets unless it was because they were more easily transportable.

The powerful role that opportunity can play in criminal behavior and its explication in self-control theory is conveyed in the following brief observation by Gottfredson and Hirschi (1990): "In our theory, crimes have minimal elements over and above their benefits to the individual: for example, they require goods, services, victims, and opportunity, elements that do vary from time to time and place to place and therefore do much to account for cross-national differences in the rate at which crimes are committed" (p. 177). There is a contradiction, of course, between the idea that opportunity and the other denominated conditions are "minimal elements" in criminal activity and the next point that they "do much" to explain variations in criminal rates. The message would appear to be that such extrinsic elements can significantly trump whatever impetus an absence of self-control might provide for undesirable behavior. If so, policymakers might be well advised to manipulate such matters as opportunity rather than trying to focus on training child rearers to recognize and reverse episodes of poor self-control in the young.

Gottfredson and Hirschi indicate that in societies with limited opportunities for lawbreaking, those who do break the law will be the individuals with the lesser amounts of self-control. Ignoring concerns with tautology, we would maintain that, even if this assertion is true (and what we know indicates that it would be true only to a certain extent), the theory should still be required to incorporate the influences of extrinsic considerations on illegal and related forms of behavior. Self-control may seem to Gottfredson and Hirschi to be a (fixed) personality trait, but so too may be those traits that put actual opportunities into perceptual frameworks. As Matsueda (1988) has pointed out, "Opportunity is a complex concept, since the crucial element is perceived rather than objective opportunity" (p. 283). Further on in their monograph Gottfredson and Hirschi admit as much. They write: "Our theory sees crime as a consequence of relatively stable characteristics of people and the predictable situations and opportunities they experience" (Gottfredson and Hirschi, 1990, 249). Surely no one is capable of accurately predicting the opportunities and situations a human being will experience in the course of a lifetime.

The most comprehensive discussion of opportunity occurs within four pages of the conclusion of the Hirschi-Gottfredson monograph. Here the theorists for the first time clearly tell us that self-control is not the lone essential element of their general theory but that opportunity can play havoc with regard to situations in which individuals with low self-control are involved. They maintain that "criminal acts are problematically related to the self-control of the actor: under some conditions people with low self-control may have few opportunities to commit crimes and under other conditions people with high self-control may have many opportunities to commit them" (Gottfredson and Hirschi, 1990, 219–220). This statement conflicts with the earlier declaration that opportunities for crime are ubiquitous and with the iteration of the point that offenders do not confine themselves to one form of lawbreaking or misconduct but are ecumenical in their choice of illegal and self-defeating behavior. We interpret these passages as recognition that opportunity confounds the predictive power of self-control.

Gottfredson and Hirschi seek to resolve this dilemma in the subsequent paragraphs, which contain six of the sixty-four uses of the word *opportunity* in their monograph. As Gottfredson and Hirschi themselves say: "One solution to this problem is to attempt to measure criminal tendencies independent of opportunity" to commit criminal acts (1990, 220). This may be done in several ways. For example, tendencies may be assessed before crime is possible; that the measure of criminality is constructed from information available in the pre-adolescent years (and validated by its ability to predict subsequent behavior). Opportunity may also be held constant through an assignment to conditions of varying opportunity, by natural variation, restricting attention to people sharing identical crime-relevant characteristics. Differences in criminal activity can then be ascribed to differences in tendency, since there are no differences in opportunity.

"Of course, the best way to distinguish crime from self-control is through experimentation where the researcher controls the assignment of individuals to conditions and is able to vary the level of opportunity and to measure self-control independent of opportunity" (Gottfredson and Hirschi, 1990, 220). There is a mixture of wisdom, wishful thinking, and intellectual waywardness in this call for research to determine the relative significance of opportunity and self-control. Most of all it undercuts the persistent claim throughout the book (and the one accepted by most of those who address the theory) that it is self-control itself that singularly determines crime and the other misconduct denominated and not a panoply of "crime-relevant tendencies."

In this passage Gottfredson and Hirschi treat opportunity as though it were a factual condition equivalently perceived by those confronted by it, and those with lesser amounts of self-control will more often grab at such opportunity. The truth is far more complex. One person's opportunity need not be seen that way by another person, even if their levels of self-control are similar. One may be in dire need, the other affluent; one may be more clever at evaluating opportunity as a good chance, the other less likely to do so. Those with the greater desire to succeed may grab at an illegal opportunity; those more content or cowardly may restrain themselves when offered the same opportunity. So although opportunity itself may be an objective situation, a considerable variety of other considerations will intrude on whatever self-control may promote or inhibit action.

Gottfredson and Hirschi suggest how opportunity might be assessed in terms of their theory. They advocate that "tendencies" toward stipulated misconduct could be measured in preadolescent years and then compared to subsequent behavior. This is a surprising recommendation from the authors, given their strong objections to longitudinal research. Besides, a discomforting historical record of such efforts shows that these efforts typically are focused on the introduction of allegedly remedial interventions at an early age before predicted problems surface. What is most characteristic of such work is the high level of false-positives.

One long-ago experiment dovetails with the Gottfredson and Hirschi proposed research strategy. Hartshorne and May (1929), the experimenters, did not look at the possible influence of self-control but offered some clues to how conditions other than self-control might bear on errant behavior. The criterion for opportunity in the experiment was that "the test situation and the response should be of such a nature as to allow all subjects equal opportunity to exhibit the behavior which is being tested. That is, there should be nothing about the test itself which would prevent anyone who desired to deceive from doing so" (Hartshorne and May, 1929, 47). A typical experimental tactic allowed classroom teachers to obtain information about students' test performance before the students graded their own papers. This could be accomplished by timing the test to conclude when the class was dismissed, gathering up the papers, grading them secretly, and then returning the unmarked papers the next day for self-grading. It was found that "the most common extraneous motive [for cheating] is a desire to do well in class"; that is, the pressure to succeed and to get ahead turned out to be the most compelling force (Hartshorne and May, 1929, 394). Students whose parents and who were themselves pressing for outstanding performance were the ones who did the most cheating; those less motivated did not bother. It is not unlikely that the pupils pressing for achievement were better socialized into the self-control ethic than their less competitive peers.

THE ROLE OF OPPORTUNITY IN SELF-CONTROL RESEARCH

In one of the most sophisticated and well-reasoned examinations of self-control theory Grasmick et al. (1993) emphasize that Gottfredson and Hirschi have paid altogether too little attention to opportunity, despite the fact that it is an essential element of the theoretical postulation. "Unfortunately, compared to their discussion of self-control, Gottfredson and Hirschi say relatively little about crime opportunity" offering only "a meager discussion" (Grasmick et al., 1993, 19). Grasmick's group operationalizes opportunity in terms of three criteria: (1) the ease with which individuals would be able to commit the kind of act that self-control theory is said to explain, or what other writers call "the convenience" of the act (Forde and Kennedy, 1997, 265); (2) the gratification of the moment that the act can provide; and (3) the absence of much chance that someone who might do something about the behavior would quickly learn of it. They point out that there is a certain inconsistency between the observations in Gottfredson and Hirschi's book that lack of self-control is marked by risk taking and that taking advantage of opportunities is marked by a low risk of detection. Grasmick et al. (1993, 21) found that opportunity alone is a more effective predictor of crimes of fraud and force than is the direct effect of self-control or the interaction (opportunity × self-control) predicted by the theory. It might be that a general theory of crime and imprudence could be constructed based on opportunism. A study of drug users in Amsterdam, for instance, showed them to be individuals "alert and ready to seize any opportunity, especially as far as acquisitive crime is concerned" (Grapendaal et al., 1995, 194). Major targets in that study were the omnipresent bicycles and the contents of automobiles.

The findings of the Grasmick et al. (1993) study on opportunity were troubling to the researchers, "given the relative lack of attention devoted to this variable" (p. 22). Gottfredson and Hirschi, disagreeing with the critics, suggested that self-control and opportunity are conceptualized to operate independently *or* in interaction. Thus the theory can be measured and assessed "without undue concern for differences in opportunities to commit criminal, deviant, or reckless acts" (Gottfredson and Hirschi, 2003, 9).

Most evaluations of self-control theory pay little or no attention to opportunity. In some cases the word *opportunity* never appears, nor is its absence remarked on (Hagan, 1989; Hagan et al., 1990; Blackwell and Piquero, 2005; Evans et al., 1997). A recent meta-analysis of the self-control literature noted that opportunity did not work well as a moderating variable but was a successful predictor as an independent variable (Pratt and Cullen, 2000). Pratt and Cullen give hesitant support to self-control theory—because they found that low self-control is associated with increases in criminal and analogous behavior—but they indicate that "on a relative level, it is unlikely that the theory can claim the exalted status of being the general theory of crime" (Pratt and Cullen, 2000, 953). In the five-page discussion of their results they do not refer to opportunity.

A handful or so of contributions do attend to opportunity in one way or another. One approach focused on the number of evenings during a week that the respondent went out for recreation (Burton et al., 1994, 1998, 1999; Evans et al., 1997; Longshore, 1998), an interesting but hardly adequate proxy for opportunity. The subject might well have been going to a basketball game or to a movie.

A pair of researchers opted for the amount of parental or other adult supervision to determine opportunity. LaGrange and Silverman (1999) used eight questions administered to secondary school students to operationalize opportunity. Four questions concerned the parents' knowledge of where youths were during the day and whom they were with; two concerned whether they had a curfew, and the remaining two dealt with time spent with other youngsters without adults present. In this last category one inquiry read, "How often do you and a friend get together where no adults are present?" and a second asked, "How often do you and a friend drive around in a car with nowhere special to go?" (LaGrange and Silverman, 1999, 53). There is no question that adult supervision can reduce the opportunity for undesirable behavior, but there can be no question either that individuals with high levels of parental supervision can and do readily locate suitable opportunities to get into trouble if they are so inclined. Of course, asking for a yes, no, or "don't know" answer with regard to curfew tells us little about the time limits attached to such arrangements. There is a considerable difference between a midnight curfew and one set at 9 p.m. And numerous youth activities outside the presence of adults can be quite benign. Besides, these limitations may reflect not a portrait of adult supervision per se but a possible response to parental estimations of the risk of wrongdoing by their adolescents. Simply put, this measure, like the others, possibly taps an ingredient of opportunity but hardly encompasses it.

Less persuasive is a tabulation of the number of credit hours that sociology students are taking as a stand-in for lesser or greater amounts of opportunity to stray from middle-class standards of conformity (Cochran et al., 1998). Cochran and colleagues themselves appreciate the shortcomings of the definitional platform on which they are perched and adopt a plaintive defense: "We are uneasy about the face validity of this [opportunity] measure. Nevertheless, we find our measure is as strong as (or as weak as) those used by others" (Cochran et al., 1998, 253). They add that they found it difficult to construct a suitable measure because of the lack of clarity in the Gottfredson and Hirschi formulation.

Nor is consideration of the amount of association with criminal friends (Longshore, Turner, and Stein, 1996; Longshore and Turner, 1998) quite what the idea of opportunity would seem to indicate. This, however, is an improvement on a study of self-control among drug users with a long history of criminal involvement by the same scholars. In that work the two major constructs in the Gottfredson and Hirschi theory are self-control and "opportunity, a function of structural or situational circumstances encountered by the person" (Longshore, Turner, and Stein, 1996, 209). Longshore's group thereafter pay no heed to opportunity because it is beyond the reach of their data. They observe that, had they been able to look at opportunity, it might have had special importance in connection with gender and self-control and further note that most of the drug offenders in the study "may have had ample opportunity to commit other sorts of crime as well. Perhaps this is why self-control was significantly related to crime in our sample despite our not having directly tested the interaction between self-control and opportunity" (Longshore et al., 1996, 224).

In a particularly informative early study seeking to understand why heroin users stopped using, Schasre (1966) found that their families and/or they themselves had moved to another geographic location and the cessation of drug use was tied to an opportunity factor: The users had not been able to locate sources from whom they might obtain heroin. Opportunity apparently ruled supreme in that situation.

One approach has jettisoned the word *opportunity* and looked at what were labeled "situational characteristics" in seeking to assess self-control theory in a sample of undergraduates. A. R. Piquero and Tibbetts (1996) used what are labeled "realistic scenarios" about shoplifting and drunk driving to tap into likely respondent behavior if confronted with the conditions set out in the vignettes. Using a similar technique, Simpson and Piquero (2002) evaluated the claims of self-control theory as they apply to corporate crime. They found little support for the theory, but they also fudge on the opportunity measures. They suggest that formal and informal sanction risk and criminogenesis in the corporate environment are proxy measures of opportunity. Unfortunately, these measures are also consistent with social control, deterrence, and socialization constructs.

MOTIVATION AND OPPORTUNITY

A few years before Gottfredson and Hirschi set forth their general theory, criminologist James W. Coleman (1987) explored a theoretical pathway similar to in many ways but interestingly different from that of Gottfredson and Hirschi. That Coleman did not present his views in a monograph or with the verve that marked *A General Theory of Crime* likely accounts for its relative neglect. Also, by focusing on motivation rather than on self-control in tandem with opportunity, Coleman favored a variable that is much more difficult than self-control to operationalize. Coleman highlighted two conditions that he said offered theoretical insight into white-collar crime: appropriate motivation and opportunity. Like all such theories, the confluence of the two conditions could, without much tweaking, be declared to "explain" all human behavior, a conclusion that no social scientist is likely to take seriously. For Coleman motivation for white-collar crime is associated with the social structure of industrial capitalism and the culture of competition to which it has given rise. Coleman points out that in preindustrial times there was not enough surplus wealth to breed competitive behavior. He defines motivation as "a set of symbolic constructions, defining certain kinds of goals and activities as appropriate and desirable and others as lacking those qualities" (Coleman, 1987, 409). Although motivation so defined might be determined after an act, it is at best arguable how well it could serve as an attempt to predict that act, except in the sense that, for instance, someone who believes that smoking pot is perfectly appropriate and desirable can reasonably be presumed to be more likely than someone with the opposite view to smoke marijuana. The same shortcoming in terms of scientific demonstration is true of Coleman's definition of opportunity, which is said to be a circumstance regarded as attractive or unattractive from the standpoint of a particular individual. Coleman's version of opportunity has four components. The first is the actor's perception of how great a gain he or she might expect to reap from the opportunity. Second is the perception of potential risks, such as the likelihood that the criminal will be detected and the severity of the sanctions that would be invoked if detection occurs. The third factor is the compatibility of the opportunity with the ideas, rationalizations, and beliefs that the individual actor possesses. Finally, evaluation of an illicit opportunity is made in comparison with the other opportunities of which the actor is aware (Coleman, 1987, 424).

Coleman's broad interpretive sweep is useful in calling attention to ingredients that particularly seem to characterize white-collar crime, but his theorizing lacks the parsimonious neatness that is a desirable characteristic of sophisticated theoretical statements. It also suffers from an absence of a catchy title. Labels help considerably to promote theories in the competitive marketplace of intellectual ideas.

DISCUSSION

In our view, except for their endorsement of the Cohen-Felson work on opportunity and crime, Gottfredson and Hirschi fail to inform readers in any comprehensive manner of what they mean by opportunity, and only rarely have those who have addressed the theory in their own research come to grips with the concept. Opportunity is a more complex concept than writings about self-control theory suggest. The best known social scientific usage is found in the term *opportunity costs*, an idea, said in a blurb for a book on the subject, to have been in circulation for more than 200 years but one still not fully understood today with regard to decision making (Heymann and Bloom, 1990). By itself, the word *opportunity* does not convey its full meaning, but its presence calls attention to what is involved in any chosen opportunity. The concept seeks to attend to alternatives that are forgone when any course of action is selected. The simplest, but by no means simple, task has been to calculate gains and losses from actions in monetary terms. When it comes to less concrete measures, the theory moves into analytical territory that its advocates acknowledge can be highly challenging, a conclusion that self-control theory fails to appreciate adequately.

The quest for a general theory to explain so diverse a panorama of human behavior as criminal acts, not to mention a variety of behaviors said to be analogous to them, is much like the hunt for nirvana. It is, perhaps, a stimulating but ultimately feckless enterprise, one that might be compared to an attempt to locate a single cause of illness and disease. "Strict and pure causation works nowhere and never," physicist and philosopher Mario Bunge (1959, 337–338) has written. "Causation works approximately in certain processes limited both in space and time—and even so, only in particular respects." Then there is the debunking observation of Norwood Hanson (1972, 135): "Causes certainly are connected with effects; but this is because theories connect them, not because the world is held together by cosmic glue." When it comes to opportunity, that key ingredient in self-control theory, researchers have figuratively thrown up their hands.

It is axiomatic that you cannot falsify a tautological theory. Self-control theory renders itself vulnerable because it applies, not to all crime and analogous behavior—as its blueprint declares it does—but most particularly to acts that are by definition marked by a failure to exercise sufficient self-control. The general theory does not embrace inchoate offenses or many strict liability crimes. In essence, self-control theory is not a taut tautology. Its inclusion of opportunity as part of its formula allows it to escape "explaining" facts that are inexplicable within its specified interpretive formula. In that regard it can join much headier concepts such as Freud's latent homosexuality and Marx's false consciousness as resting on an explanatory escape hatch.

CONCLUSION

The precise part to be played by opportunity in the general theory proposed by Gottfredson and Hirschi remains uncertain; nor are its ingredients satisfactorily precise. A cadre of scholars have been seeking to factor opportunity into their assessments of self-control theory, although others ignore the concept. The published research reports are replete with terms such as "mixed results," "partial support," and similar evaluative statements. With regard to opportunity, part of the problem is that opportunity is a wickedly difficult construct to operationalize. Take the crime of murder. About 16,000 individuals kill someone else each year in the United States with malice aforethought. Most of them are readily apprehended, which would suggest that the likelihood of being caught, often considered a negative aspect of opportunity, did not figure prominently in their plans, however driven by an absence of self-control their behavior might have been.

It seems to us that at this stage it behooves the progenitors of self-control theory to carefully examine the mixed-results research and respond helpfully to the issues that rather persistently are raised about flaws in their conception. A recent chapter by Gottfredson and Hirschi (2003, 10), titled "Self-Control and Opportunity," raises hope that the concept will be theorized more fully. Unfortunately, the theorists suggest only that the job is too complex to undertake because opportunities for crime can be affected by various situational and individual level factors "other than self control." Further, we are told that such theorizing is quite possibly unnecessary—at least in terms of crime-prevention strategies. "Perhaps it would be of value to consider particular settings in which self-control theory might contribute to practical crime prevention and to compare its recommendations to those stemming from other perspectives, especially environmental criminology" (Gottfredson and Hirschi, 2003, 11).

We would recommend as background the remarks of Ronald Dworkin, a preeminent legal philosopher, at a memorial service for Herbert Hart, an Oxford University colleague: "He never became, as so many other philosophers have, a janitor or press flak for his own theories, patching up leaks and working tirelessly for more domination. He seemed almost embarrassed when he had not been persuaded to change his mind, and it gave him great pleasure when he had been" (Hart, 1998, 214). On a more upbeat and promising observation, the opening paragraph of a review of the work of Karl Lewin (Berscheid, 2003) sets forth the trials and tribulations that any theoretical framework, such as that of Gottfredson and Hirschi, must overcome if it is to persevere.

> Great works are great because they cause people to see the world differently than before. As original and creative constructions of the world, they challenge accepted views, often those deeply held and cherished by powerful people in entrenched religious, political, financial, and academic establishments. For a new vision of the world to have an impact, it first must capture people's attention, including the attention of the people it threatens and those who have every incentive to ignore it. If a work is successful in securing widespread attention, including the attention of hostile forces, both the work and its creator must then survive the soul-withering fires they often ignite. A work that cannot emerge whole from the furnace of fair—and even unfair—criticism will have no impact, and its creator will be buried in the crowded tomb of the "Unknown Great Scientist." (Berscheid, 2003, 109)

Ellen Berscheid, a well-known social psychologist, adds that if a work is original and groundbreaking, the creator's part has only begun. "To make a great contribution to knowledge, successfully completing the task of assuring the impact of an idea is as important as the idea's originality. Successfully selling the idea is perhaps even more important than the idea's originality because there are few entirely original ideas" (Berscheid, 2003, 110). This point is supported by the observation that Edward Jenner was not the first to inoculate people with cowpox to protect them against smallpox, that William Harvey was not the first to postulate the circulation of blood, and that Charles Darwin was by no means the first person to suggest evolution (Beveridge, 1950, 49–50).

Self-control (and opportunity) theory has taken long strides on the path to success—the existence of the present book alone vouches for that. How much farther it will go and its ultimate fate remain unclear. Much depends on how the originators of the theory put into play their own self-control and use it to take advantage of the opportunity to redesign their theory in light of research conclusions and other recommendations that could prove helpful.

NOTE

We would like to thank Katherine Martinez for her helpful assistance on this chapter.

5 | PARENTING AND SELF-CONTROL

*Francis T. Cullen, James D. Unnever, John Paul Wright,
and Kevin M. Beaver*

Gottfredson and Hirschi propose that low self-control regulates both criminal involvement and social failure across the life course and that the causal relationships identified by socio-logical theories of crime—including social class, social learning, anomie, and labeling—are spurious (Hirschi and Gottfredson, 1995). Within the context of this antisociological the-ory, however, they retain one fundamentally sociological thesis: that the level of self-control is due to the degree of effectiveness of the parenting that a child receives. According to Gott-fredson and Hirschi, parents who care about their children will monitor them, recognize misbehavior, and punish that deviance when it occurs. By exercising social control, parents create self-control in their children; in contrast, low self-control lies in ineffective or poor parental management of the child-rearing process.

In this essay we attempt to assess Gottfredson and Hirschi's *parental management thesis*. Gottfredson and Hirschi boldly predict that with few unimportant exceptions, parenting alone is responsible for establishing, early in childhood, differential levels of self-control that persist throughout the life course. They also contend that parenting fully mediates the effects of all other family and parental factors on self-control and thus participation in wayward conduct. We call this the *parental mediation thesis*.

This essay is divided into three sections. The first details the parental management thesis. In so doing, we highlight the differences in the role of parenting in Hirschi's two theories of crime: social bond theory and self-control theory. In the second section, we evaluate the parental management thesis, with a special emphasis on the existing empirical literature. And in the third section, we discuss the theoretical implications of the parental manage-ment thesis in view of the assessment we have provided.

THE PARENTAL MANAGEMENT THESIS

Hirschi (1979, 1989, 2002b; Laub, 2002) has long argued that good theorizing requires that the components of a theory be internally consistent. The goal of internal consistency forces scholars both to sharpen the logic of their theory and to clarify how their model's core assumptions and predictions differ from alternative perspectives. In this context we first discuss the parental management thesis, showing how Gottfredson and Hirschi's emphasis on the importance of parenting is consistent with their views of the nature of low self-control (or "criminality") and of the stability of individual differences in self-control across the life course. We then show that the quest for theoretical consistency also leads Gottfredson and Hirschi to argue that parenting mediates the effects of other family structural and dispositional factors on self-control. Finally, we discuss how the internal logic of self-control theory necessitates a vision of parenting that departs from that articulated previously by Hirschi (1969) in his social bond theory.

Parenting and Self-Control

Gottfredson and Hirschi discuss the "causes of self-control" in several places (Gottfredson and Hirschi, 1989, 1990, 2003; Hirschi, 1994; Hirschi and Gottfredson, 2001, 2003). Although we can detect minor discrepancies in these accounts, a common explanation arises: Self-control is instilled early in life as a result of parents who care enough about their children to make the effort to effectively discipline them. This is a strong proposition because it asserts that self-control has no other major sources. Other institutions, such as the school, might have a minor influence, but this is the exception and not the rule. Further, if self-control is due to effective child rearing—and virtually nothing else—this means that level of self-control is calibrated in childhood and not thereafter. We return to these themes shortly.

Importantly, Gottfredson and Hirschi see self-control as natural and universal. Individuals are born with the desire for easy and immediate gratification, which leads them to engage in acts—such as crime and analogous behaviors—that provide such gratification. Crime and self-control (or "criminality") thus share the same general characteristics. Indeed, "self-control theory assumes that the nature of the offender may be inferred from the nature of criminal acts, and vice versa" (Gottfredson and Hirschi, 2003, 6). As Hirschi (1969, 34) pointed out in his earlier *Causes of Delinquency*, the motivation to offend need not be explained; everyone has it. The question is not "Why do they do it?" but rather "Why don't they do it?" Seen in this light, low self-control is the universal motivation to offend—that is, to engage in acts, including crimes, that offer gratification.

There is thus no initial variation in a birth cohort in the motivation or propensity to offend. As a result, biology presumably is the cause of low self-control, because humans as a species are born into the world seeking gratification. But biology has little to do with *variation* in self-control, because, again, low self-control—that is, the absence of control—is universal at birth. Gottfredson and Hirschi (1990) do admit that biological factors might affect the ability to acquire self-control in the socialization process. But this is a passing insight that is not integrated into their theory in any meaningful way. In fact, they observe that "effective socialization . . . is always possible whatever the configuration of traits" (Gottfredson and Hirschi, 1990, 96). So much for biology.

This view of low self-control allows Gottfredson and Hirschi to reject cultural deviance or social learning theories that see the motivation to offend as learned. Consistent with the views expressed in *Causes of Delinquency*, the propensity to offend—that is, low self-control—requires no positive learning. "One thing is . . . clear," observe Gottfredson and Hirschi, "low self-control is not produced by training, tutelage, or socialization" (1990,

94–95). Something that exists naturally and universally requires no social causation or, for criminologists, no explanation.

What does require causation and explanation, however, is the *presence* of self-control. For individuals, self-control is not natural but must be internalized. It is a form of personal capital: the ability to resist immediate, easy gratifications that produce short-term benefits but long-term social failure. As Gottfredson and Hirschi (1990) state, "There will be little variability among people to see the pleasures of crime" (p. 95). However, "there will be considerable variability in their ability to calculate potential pains. . . . Everyone appreciates money; not everyone dreads parental anger or disappointment upon learning that the money was stolen."

But where will self-control come from? Clearly, individuals are not naturally equipped to acquire it on their own. In fact, Gottfredson and Hirschi's logic suggests that people will be resistant to forfeiting the pleasures that seem right within reach. After all, Gottfredson and Hirschi (1990, 2003) maintain that opportunities to offend are ubiquitous. Accordingly, someone is going to have to make the concerted effort to instill in people the self-control needed to resist their natural impulses.

Still, who in their right mind will take on this daunting and likely unrewarding task? For Gottfredson and Hirschi, such an investment will be made only by someone who cares deeply for an individual's current and future welfare: *parents*. Not all parents, however, care equally about their children. This lack of parental attachment to one's child is thus an initial source of variation in self-control.

Caring for a child, however, does not ensure that parents will do their job effectively. But what is effective parenting? Here, Gottfredson and Hirschi do not become warm and fuzzy. For them, cuddling, nurturing, and loving your kid has no direct effect on self-control. Caring about your child matters only to the extent that it is a motivator to parents to do what really matters: exercising direct social control over their child. Good parental managers of children instill self-control; poor parental managers do not.

Gottfredson and Hirschi are clear that effective parental management in socializing children entails three interrelated steps that must all be present for self-control to be internalized. As Hirschi revealed in an interview with Laub (2002), this insight "came from the Gluecks and the family process literature. Actually it came from [Gerald] Patterson, but since it was virtually identical to what the Gluecks had said it was very easy to accept" (p. xxxvi).

The components of direct control that produce self-control are as follows. First, parents must monitor or watch their child. Second, parents must recognize deviant or inappropriate conduct when it occurs. Third, parents must punish such misconduct. This seems like a simple recipe for effective child rearing. But as Gottfredson and Hirschi (1990) caution, "What may appear at first glance to be nonproblematic turns out to be problematic indeed. Many things can go wrong" (p. 98). Indeed, the research literature suggests that parental management is a challenging task. "Not all caretakers punish effectively," note Gottfredson and Hirschi (1990, 100). "In fact, some are too harsh and some are too lenient." Further, it is not sufficient to reinforce correct conduct. "Given our model," assert Gottfredson and Hirschi (1990), "rewarding good behavior cannot compensate for failure to correct deviant behavior" (p. 100). Unpunished deviant behavior will continue because it is inherently gratifying; as Gottfredson and Hirschi remind us, "Deviant acts carry with them their own rewards" (p. 100).

We should note that in a recent version of the theory, Hirschi and Gottfredson (2003) incorporate an additional factor into their model of effective parenting: the attachment of the child to the parent or caregiver. As we will revisit in detail later, attachment is a major social bond and a source of control identified by Hirschi (1969) in *Causes of Delinquency*. In Gottfredson and Hirschi's general theory, however, a child's attachment is reduced to a condition that is "requisite to successful socialization" (Hirschi and Gottfredson, 2003, 157). That is, "affection or at least respect for the caregiver" is salient because it makes the child more receptive to the discipline of the parent. Interestingly, Hirschi and Gottfredson (2003) suggest that because effective child rearing is contingent on or made easier by the child's attachment, parents may limit their use of severe punishments. Thus "excessive punishments would destroy the relationship and vitiate their effectiveness" (Hirschi and Gottfredson, 2003, 157). "Corporal punishment is apparently in this respect risky. It may sometimes exceed the tolerance level of the child and destroy attachment to its source" (p. 157).

The parental management thesis also is central to Gottfredson and Hirschi's (1990) efforts to explain the stability of differences in offending over the life course. By logic, a person's level of self-control has to emerge in childhood because individual differences in behavior start then and are firmly established once and for all early in life, by ages 8 to 10. Of course, parents have primary responsibility for children at this time of life and are most influential in the nature and quality of child rearing that occurs. As Hirschi and Gottfredson (2001) explain: "The differences observed at ages eight to 10 tend to persist from then on. Good children remain good. Not so good children remain a source of concern to their parents, teachers, and eventually to the criminal justice system. These facts lead to the conclusion that low self-control is natural and that *self-control* is *acquired* in the early years of life" (p. 90).

In short, Gottfredson and Hirschi's view of the emergence and nature of low self-control—and their rejection of biological explanations—led them to a conclusion that was internally consistent with their paradigm: the parental management thesis. We are thus able to state this thesis as follows:

> Because low self-control is natural and universal, self-control must be acquired. The main source of self-control is effective child-rearing, which occurs when parents who are attached to their child care enough to monitor the child's behavior and are able to recognize and punish deviant behavior when it occurs. Ineffective or poor parenting results in lower levels of self-control. Individual differences in self-control or "criminality" are established by age 10 and persist across the life course.

The Parental Mediation Thesis

From their research on parenting, Gottfredson and Hirschi are knowledgeable that other family factors are related to offending. How can these relationships be explained? Never inclined to be theoretically modest, Gottfredson and Hirschi (1990) argue that these empirical findings present no difficulty because of the "consistency of the child-rearing model with our general theory" (p. 100). In fact, they assert that "this child-rearing model goes a long way toward explaining all of the major family factors in crime: neglect, abuse, single parents, large number of children, parental criminality" (Hirschi and Gottfredson, 2001, 90–91; see also Gottfredson and Hirschi, 1990, 100–105).

Again, Gottfredson and Hirschi's theorizing is internally consistent: These family factors are implicated in crime and other wayward conduct because they all influence either "the extent of parental concern for the child or are conditions that affect the ability of the parent to monitor and correct the child's behavior" (Hirschi and Gottfredson, 2001, 91). For example, the positive relationship between family size and delinquency is "perfectly explicable from a child-rearing model" because, assert Gottfredson and Hirschi (1990), parents have less time to spend with their offspring and less energy to monitor the children and "to enforce their edicts" (pp. 102–103). And to take one other example, parental criminality is related children's offending. The connection is not because these parents pass on crime-related genetic traits or positively socialize their kids to be criminals, because "our theory does not allow transmission of criminality, genetic or otherwise" (Gottfredson and Hirschi, 1990, 100). Instead, criminal parents—in part because they too are likely to lack self-control—do not have the traits that incline them to care about their children and, even when they do, to parent them effectively. Criminal parents are less likely to recognize behavior as deviant when it occurs. Further, they discipline in ways that reflect their own low self-control, using punishment that "tends to be easy, short-term, and insensitive—that is, yelling and screaming, slapping and hitting, with threats that are not carried out" (Gottfredson and Hirschi, 1990, 101).

The broader implication of this discussion is that for any factor—whether family, community, or societal—to influence self-control and thus offending and analogous behaviors, it must have an impact on the effectiveness of the parenting that occurs early in life. Notably, this insight allows Gottfredson and Hirschi to supply much needed theoretical guidance in an area in which the empirical correlates are well known but not coherently explained. As Farrington (2002) notes, "It is difficult to determine what are the precise causal mechanisms linking family factors—such as parental criminality, young mothers, family size, parental supervision, child abuse, and disrupted families—to the delinquency of children" (p. 143). The general theory, with its emphasis on features of parental management, provides an understanding of what these causal mechanisms are. And in this context we can state Gottfredson and Hirschi's parental mediation thesis: Parental management mediates the impact of family factors and all other factors on self-control, which then leads to crime and analogous behaviors. These factors have no other direct effects on self-control or crime, and their effects on self-control are not mediated by any other intervening variable.

Parenting, Self-Control, and the Social Bond

Hirschi's conversion from a social control theorist to a self-control theorist was facilitated by, among other things, his reconsideration of the "age effect" (Laub, 2002). Social bond theory was devised in part to explain "maturational reform" (Matza, 1964), or why adolescents involved in crime eventually stop offending as they move into adulthood. As Hirschi (1969) recognized, maturational reform was a problem for both strain and cultural deviance theories, because they link crime to relatively permanent conditions: denial of opportunity for those trapped in the lower class and positive learning for those ensconced in a subculture approving of crime. But social bond theory had the theoretical advantage of being more flexible.

For Hirschi, the strength of social bonds is variable because it is determined by ties to conventional others and institutions that can tighten or loosen as individuals travel through life. In *A General Theory of Crime*, however, Gottfredson and Hirschi dismiss the idea that individual change in offending is influenced by change in social bonds. Indeed, this is why they reject the age-graded social bond theory of Sampson and Laub (1993, 1995). Instead, they argue that the age-crime curve—offending rising into the teenage years and declining thereafter—is invariant: It affects everyone. What does not change, however, is self-control or criminality. Relative to others, individual differences in self-control established in childhood persist throughout life.

Each theory's view of parenting flows from this understanding of offending. In social bond theory, a major source of social control is a child's attachment to parents, which is presumably fostered by parents' attachment to their child. Because a child's attachment may vary over time, it helps to explain variation in behavior. In fact, Hirschi (1969) explicitly rejects the idea of internal or "personal" control because it "creates difficulties in explaining variations in delinquent activity over time. If the conscience is a relative constant built into the child at an early age, how do we explain the increase in delinquent activity in early adolescence and the decline in late adolescence?" (p. 87). In other words, permanent self-control would be theoretically inconsistent with maturational reform. Again, this is a position Hirschi would abandon in *A General Theory of Crime*.

Theory of Crime

Why, then, does attachment to parents produce control? Hirschi (1969) argues that "direct control"—face-to-face supervision—"is not . . . of much substantive or theoretical importance" (p. 88). Youths might refrain from misconduct when parents are present. But, anticipating his later views on opportunity (Gottfredson and Hirschi, 1990, 2003), Hirschi (1969) observes that "delinquent acts require little time" and that "most adolescents are frequently exposed to situations potentially definable as opportunities for delinquency" (p. 88). Instead, what matters is not *direct* control but *indirect* control or the parents' "virtual supervision" of the child (p. 89).

"The important consideration," argues Hirschi (1969), "is whether the parent is psychologically present when temptation to commit a crime appears" (p. 88). Children who are attached to their parents—who have "affectional identification, love, and respect" for them—in turn care about what their parents will think of them and how their parents will be affected by their misconduct (p. 91). Those with weak ties to parents, however, have nothing to restrain their pursuit of easy gratification through the ubiquitous opportunities for delinquency they encounter. As Hirschi (1969) states, "If, in the situation of temptation, no thought is given to parental reaction, the child is to this extent free to commit the act" (p. 88). Alternatively, attached children will worry that their parents will disapprove of and, if disclosed, be embarrassed by their waywardness. Because their parents matter to them, they will be socially controlled. Again, the significant point is that this control is exerted even though parents are physically separated from their children; their psychological presence is sufficient to deliver restraint.

In Laub's (2002) interview with him, Hirschi suggests one way of reconciling his social control and self-control theories in this area: "I'd say that the supervision described in *Causes* is nothing other than self-control. The child supervises himself" (p. xxvi). Gottfredson (2006) echoes this view of "variation in the strength of the social bond" (p. 87). He notes that "children with high self-control have a long-term concern for their parents and behave accordingly." He adds that "affectionate parents create self-control by establishing a reciprocal bond between parent and child. Once self-control is present, it may be witnessed by—even described by—elements of the social bond" (p. 88).

This effort to link indirect control to self-control might be theoretically promising, but it also faces difficulty. In *Causes of Delinquency*, Hirschi is careful to reject internal controls and, instead, to place the source of control in the quality of the social bond. This is why Hirschi (1969) states "that the psychological presence of the parent depends very much on the extent to which the child interacts with the parent on a personal basis" (p. 94). But the quality of social bonds can change over time and can account for variation in criminal involvement. This insight informs Sampson and Laub's (1993, 1995) use of social bond theory to explain not only continuity but also change in offending across the life course.

Indeed, short of theoretical integration, reconciling Hirschi's two theories of parenting and delinquency seems a daunting, if not impossible enterprise. Thus, as seen in Table 5.1, self-control theory gives considerable causal influence to direct parental control; social bond theory does not. Self-control theory proposes that the child's attachment to parents increases receptivity to direct control; social bond theory sees the child's attachment as central to indirect control. In self-control theory the attachment of parents to children is what motivates the parents' willingness to impose direct control over their offspring; social bond theory suggests that parental attachment helps to create—or has a direct effect on—children's attachment to parents. In self-control theory the nature of control is internal, takes

TABLE 5.1
Comparison of self-control and social bond theory in the conceptualization of parenting

Dimension	Self-control theory	Social bond theory
Direct control by parents	Main source of self-control	Unimportant
Attachment to parents by child	Not part of the original theory; later seen as increasing a child's receptivity to direct control	Major social bond and source of control
Attachment to child by parents	Fosters parents' willingness to exert direct control over child, which then produces self-control	Fosters child's attachment to parents
Nature of social control	Internal or "self"	Indirect (psychological presence of the parent)
Stability of causal factor	After childhood, stable individual differences persist; explains continuity in offending	Variable, because control resides in the quality of the social bond; explains continuity and change in offending

the form of an individual difference, and is stable over the life course; by contrast, social bond theory depicts control as indirect, as residing in the social bond, and as potentially variable over the life course.

EVALUATING THE PARENTAL MANAGEMENT THESIS

Empirical Tests of the Parental Management Thesis

Research focusing specifically on Gottfredson and Hirschi's parenting ideas has lagged behind investigations of the effects of measures of self-control on offending and analogous behaviors (Gottfredson, 2006; Pratt and Cullen, 2000). Even so, we were able to uncover thirteen studies that assess the parental management thesis. Several of these studies also provide evidence regarding the parental mediation thesis. The extant research is summarized in chronological order of publication in Table 5.2.

First, across the studies, the pattern of results is generally consistent with Gottfredson and Hirschi's parental management thesis: Various measures of effective parenting tend to be related to levels of self-control. It would appear, therefore, that as with other aspects of their perspective, Gottfredson and Hirschi are wise theoretical prognosticators. Nonetheless, the findings are not as tidy as they would predict because most studies report relationships that are not fully consistent with the parental management thesis. Some of this untidiness might be attributed to measurement error and the methodological idiosyncrasies of individual data sets. However, it also is likely that empirical reality is more complex than Gottfredson and Hirschi's parsimoniously stated general theory anticipates.

For example, Unnever et al. (2003) find that self-control is related to parental monitoring and consistency of punishment but that it is also associated with race, a measure of economic disadvantage, and attention-deficit/hyperactivity disorder (ADHD). They also report that parental monitoring has a direct inverse effect on delinquent involvement that is not mediated by self-control. Perrone et al. (2004) show that parental efficacy is related to self-control but that self-control only partly mediates the impact of parenting on delinquency and does not eliminate the criminogenic effects of deviant peers. Pratt et al. (2004) discover that the sources of self-control include not only parental management but also adverse neighborhood conditions. Blackwell and Piquero (2005) reveal that the effects of instrumental parental control are specified by gender and family power structure (e.g., "Among females in more patriarchal households, more parental controls were significantly associated with higher self-control, whereas among females in less patriarchal households, more parental controls were associated with lower self-control" [p. 7]). Hay (2001) presents support for the parental management thesis but then shows that a broader conception of parenting than that proposed by the general theory—"authoritative parenting"—explains more variation in levels of self-control than measures of monitoring and discipline. Hay and Forrest (2006) report that a composite scale of parental control and warmth is related to self-control. However, in contrast to Gottfredson and Hirschi's prediction, parental socialization continues to influence levels of self-control as youths move into adolescence; in fact, the association is stronger at age 15 than at age 13. As they conclude, "Parenting still matters for self-control beyond childhood" (Hay and Forrest, 2006, 757). Finally, in a study we will revisit, Wright and Beaver (2005) demonstrate that the effects of parenting on self-control are substantially reduced when the parents' potential genetic contribution to self-control is taken into account.

With regard to the parental mediation thesis, Hope et al. (2003) provide the most carefully designed study. Although previous research has reported that the effects of structural variables on delinquency are mediated by family process variables—including parenting—self-control has not been included in the causal chain (Sampson and Laub, 1993, 1994). Hope et al. (2003) are able to show, however, that "the structural family background variables exert their influence on self-control through the family process variables of attachment and supervision" (p. 307). This finding is consistent with the mediation thesis. Alternatively, Hope and her colleagues show that even with parental supervision in the model, gender, age, and parental education continue to exert significant influences on self-control among their sample of junior high and high school students. This result is inconsistent with the general theory.

Other empirical investigations do not conduct a systematic step-by-step analysis of background factors, parental management, and self-control. Still, these studies are relevant. The parental mediation thesis asserts that parenting mediates virtually all effects of family and background factors on self-control. Practically, this means that once parental management is entered into a multivariate analysis, the effects of other variables in the model should disappear. Again, this is because their effects should be either spurious or only indirect through the parenting variables. In the extant research, this does not occur; parenting affects self-control, but so do other individual, demographic, and social variables (Hay, 2001; Lynskey et al., 2000; Perrone et al., 2004; Pratt et al., 2004; Unnever et al., 2003; Wright and Beaver, 2005).

In short, the strength of the general theory—its boldness and fidelity to core principles—is its Achilles' heel. Reality is more complex than the general theory allows. Thus, although the theory offers keen insights into what affects parenting and why parenting matters, its us-versus-them approach results in a narrowness that leaves too much variation in the nature of parenting and in the nature of self-control unexplained. Its claims of generality are overstated, and its dismissal of alternative causal factors is indefensible.

Do Parental Management Practices Matter?

Beyond the criminological literature, there is another development that offers a challenge to Gottfredson and Hirschi's parenting perspective. Within psychology, scholars contend that the impact of parental management or socialization style on personality development in children is substantially overestimated (Harris, 1995, 1998; Rowe, 1994). This line of research has used samples of adoptees, twins, and siblings within the same home. In the field of developmental behavioral genetics, researchers have found that "about half of the variance in the measured psychological characteristics was due to heredity" (Harris, 1995, 458). But these studies reveal a "surprising conclusion": Little of the other half of the variance in personality "could be attributed to the home environments in which the participants of these studies were reared" (Harris, 1995, 458). This finding, of course, contradicts any perspective—including Gottfredson and Hirschi's general theory—that attributes to parental management the origins of a stable individual trait that has effects across situations and across the life course.

TABLE 5.2
Research on parental management and self-control

Study	Sample	Measure of parenting	Findings
Polakowski (1994)	411 London males, ages 8 to 9, followed until age 24 (Cambridge Study in Delinquent Development)	1. Supervision	1. Parental supervision related to self-control 2. Parental supervision mediated the effect of social services 3. Parental supervision mediated the effect of parental crime
Feldman and Weinberger (1994)	108 sixth-grade boys from San Francisco; 81 reinterviewed in tenth grade	1. Effective parenting (composed of measures of rejection, inconsistency versus child-centeredness, power-assertive/harsh discipline) 2. Effective mothering 3. Effective fathering	1. Effective parenting related to self-control in sixth grade 2. Effective mothering related to self-control in sixth grade 3. Effective fathering related to self-control in sixth grade
Gibbs, Giever, and Martin (1998)	289 college students	1. Overall parental management (including monitoring and discipline)	1. Parental management related to self-control
Cochran, Wood, Sellers, Wilkerson, and Chamlin (1998)	448 college students	1. Supervision	1. Parental supervision not related to self-control
Lynskey, Winfree, Esbensen, and Clason (2000)	5,935 eighth-grade students	1. Parental monitoring	1. Parental monitoring related to self-control for males and for females 2. Parental monitoring partially mediated the effect of intact families for males and for females
Hay (2001)	197 urban high school students, ages 14 to 18, from a southwestern state	1. Monitoring 2. Discipline 3. Combined monitoring and discipline scale 4. Authoritative parenting	1. Monitoring related to self-control 2. Combined monitoring and discipline scale related to self-control 3. Authoritative parenting related to self-control
Unnever, Cullen, and Platt (2003)	2,472 middle school students in a Virginia metropolitan area (grades 6, 7, and 8)	1. Consistency in parenting 2. Parental monitoring	1. Consistency in parenting related to self-control 2. Parental monitoring related to self-control

TABLE 5.2
(Continued)

Study	Sample	Measure of parenting	Findings
Hope, Grasmick, and Pointon (2003)	1,139 junior high and high school students in Fayetteville, Arkansas	1. Parental attachment 2. Supervision	1. Parental attachment related to self-control 2. Supervision related to self-control 3. Supervision partially mediated the effect of single-parent home
Perrone, Sullivan, Pratt, and Margaryan (2004)	13,536 adolescents in grades 7 to 12 in the United States (National Longitudinal Study of Adolescent Health)	1. Parental efficacy	1. Parental efficacy related to self-control
Pratt, Turner, and Piquero (2004)	463 youths, age 10, in the United States (National Longitudinal Survey of Youth)	1. Supervision 2. Monitoring/discipline	1. Supervision related to self-control at age 10 and at age 12 for both whites and nonwhites 2. Monitoring/discipline related to self-control at age 10 and at age 12 for both whites and nonwhites
Blackwell and Piquero (2005)	287 adults (Oklahoma City Survey)	1. Parental instrumental control	1. Parental instrumental control positively related to self-control for females in more patriarchal households 2. Parental instrumental control negatively related to self-control for females in less patriarchal households 3. Parental instrumental control positively related to self-control for males across household type
Wright and Beaver (2005)	310 twins in kindergarten, reinterviewed in first grade; and 1,000 (nontwin) kindergarten students, reinterviewed in first grade (Early Childhood Longitudinal Sample, Kindergarten Class of 1998–1999)	1. Parental involvement 2. Parental withdrawal 3. Parental affection 4. Physical punishment 5. Family rules	1. Parental withdrawal related to self-control in twin sample 2. Parental involvement, parental withdrawal, and parental affection related to self-control in nontwin sample
Hay and Forrest (2006)	3,793 youths, ages 7 to 15 (National Longitudinal Survey of Youth— Child and Young Adult Supplement)	1. Parental control 2. Parental warmth	1. Parental socialization related to self-control 2. Parenting/self-control association continued to exist in adolescence (found to be stronger at age 15 than at age 13)

With regard to self-control specifically, it seems virtually indisputable that a meaningful proportion of the variation in this propensity is biological. In developing the construct of self-control, Gottfredson and Hirschi failed to review the relevant developmental research and dismissed the importance of heredity. They argue, for example, that there is "strong evidence that the inheritance of criminality is minimal. . . . We conclude that the 'genetic effect' . . . is near zero" (1990, 60). Unfortunately, this assertion ignores the mounting neuropsychological evidence, including works that use brain imaging. This research shows that "executive control functions"—the ability to resist impulses, regulate emotions, focus on tasks, and delay gratification—are located in the frontal, orbital-frontal, and prefrontal cortex of the brain and thus have an identifiable physical or biological "home" (Aron et al., 2004; E. K. Miller and Cohen, 2001). Similarly, although the constructs of ADHD and self-control are not identical, they clearly overlap. ADHD produces impulsivity and a lack of restraint, and, like self-control, it predicts involvement in offending and a range of analogous behaviors across life (Barkley et al., 2002; Pratt et al., 2002; Unnever and Cornell, 2003; Unnever et al., 2003). It is instructive that the heritability estimates of ADHD average as high as 0.80 (Barkley, 1997); for parenting the influence on ADHD ranges from 0.00 to 0.06 (Neiderhiser et al., 1999).

This literature suggests that criminological research on parenting that does not control for potential genetic effects is likely to be misspecified, including the works surveyed in Table 5.2. A recent study by Wright and Beaver (2005) illuminates this problem specifically for self-control theory. In a traditional analysis of the data, Wright and Beaver first assessed the impact of five measures of parenting on a random sample of 1,000 children selected from the Early Childhood Longitudinal Sample, Kindergarten Class of 1998–1999 (ECLS-K). This research shows that, consistent with the general theory, three of the parenting measures were related to levels of self-control (parental withdrawal or emotional distance from their child; parental affection toward the child; and family rules about watching television, covering the amount, content, and time of day).

However, Wright and Beaver also analyzed the data for an ECLS-K subsample of 310 monozygotic and dizygotic twins (i.e., 155 twin pairs). Using hierarchical linear modeling to account for the clustering of observations—in this case, the nesting of twin dyads in the same household—they were able to eliminate any variance in low self-control resulting from genetic factors. In this analysis, only one parenting variable—parental withdrawal—had any significant effect on self-control; even here, the variable's effects were modest and could be detected in only some statistical models. Of course, further research, especially work designed specifically to measure Gottfredson and Hirschi's theory, is needed to confirm these results. Still, Wright and Beaver's research challenges the parental management thesis in suggesting that the major parental sources of self-control are likely genetic and thus cannot be traced to the style of child-rearing techniques used in a household.

CONCLUSION: THEORETICAL IMPLICATIONS

Gottfredson and Hirschi's general theory of crime is a formidable perspective. As a paradigm, it is internally consistent and arguably organizes much knowledge about crime, including not only family factors and crime but also the generality of deviance, versatility in offending, stability in wayward behavior, and the nature of crime and the nature of criminality. In science, when propositions are explicitly stated and then are supported, the whole theoretical paradigm gains credibility. Still, after nearly two decades in print, Gottfredson and Hirschi's paradigm may be close to exhausting its utility as a self-contained theory that explains almost everything. The general theory has explanatory power, but its ability to account for empirical reality is limited, not complete. With regard to parenting, we would suggest three areas for theoretical elaboration—two derived from our analysis in this essay and one implied by the recent work of Tittle et al. (2004).

1. *Parents have effects on offending not only through self-control but also through social learning.* Within the discipline, control and social learning—or cultural deviance—theories have a common heir in the Chicago school of criminology and, in particular, in the theorizing of Shaw and McKay (1929, 1972). As Kornhauser (1978) realized, Shaw and McKay offered a "mixed model" that viewed delinquency as the combined product of a breakdown in control and of the transmission and learning of criminal traditions. Hirschi's (1969) decision to divide this mixed model into competing theoretical camps—control versus cultural deviance—reified the two perspectives as incompatible opponents. Hirschi succeeded in placing the two theories at odds, largely by asserting that control theory assumed that humans had a universal motivation to seek gratification and thus would offend unless restraint was present. It is important to realize that Hirschi did not demonstrate empirically the existence of this underlying motivation or show that people's traits at birth—for example, temperament, impulsivity, or the ability to delay gratification—are universal in the sense of being equal across the population. In fact, there is evidence that they are not (Raine, 2002).

The point is that Hirschi's assumption of universal motivation has been a firm barrier to integrating control and social learning theories. This assumption that motivation is a given is a main reason that he (and Gottfredson) reject out of hand any need for positive learning for crime to occur. This view, however, no longer appears defensible. Gottfredson and Hirschi's parental management model is essentially a description of how parents use reinforcement to facilitate their children's *learning* self-control (Akers, 1998). It is also clear that children learn from their parents not only self-control but also prosocial and antisocial attitudes, among other things. Again, these attitudes or definitions have been shown in the research to be strong predictors of offending (Andrews and Bonta, 2006; Unnever et al., 2006).

This discussion suggests two points. First, it seems likely that the learning that occurs through parental management encompasses more than self-control. Second, Gottfredson and Hirschi's conception of parenting as having effects mainly through monitoring and discipline is overly narrow. Research should explore the effects of a broader view of parenting that involves, among other things, modeling, love, emotional and instrumental social support, informal social control, and the use of aggression (Cullen, 1994; Sampson and Laub, 1994; Unnever et al., 2004, 2006; Wright and Cullen, 2001).

2. *Parents are not the only source of self-control.* As we have seen, there is evidence consistent with the parental management thesis that monitoring and discipline are sources of self-control. However, the research also shows that self-control has more than one source, including a strong genetic component. The general theory will need to expand its borders to take into account this empirical reality.

3. *Parents may influence different dimensions of self-control differently.* Tittle et al. (2004) observe that "the conceptualization of self-control set forth by Gottfredson and Hirschi appears to be incomplete" (p. 168). They argue that self-control consists of two dimensions. First, there is the ability or *capacity* for self-control, "which is rooted in the personality, with few links to the contemporary social environment" (p. 165). Second, people can differ in their *desire* to restrain their behavior. Self-control desire, they contend, is "fundamentally sensitive to the external social context" (p. 165). Past research has tended to conceptualize and measure self-control as a capacity and thus has largely ignored individual differences in the desire to exercise self-restraint.

This innovative theoretical advance has implications for the parental management thesis. Research might now investigate how parenting is related to each dimension of self-control. For example, it is plausible that direct control (monitoring and discipline) is more related to developing the capacity for self-control, whereas the desire for self-control depends more on parents instilling prosocial values that motivate restraint. These possibilities are speculative, but they illustrate the kinds of inquiry that Tittle and his colleagues' work creates with regard to parental management.

Gottfredson and Hirschi's general theory is likely at a turning point in its career as a criminological paradigm. It will remain an important theory, summarized in textbooks and learned by the next generation of graduate students. The perspective's larger challenge, however, will be whether it will continue to generate fresh empirical research and theoretical developments. As the limits of the general theory are revealed—as occurs with all prominent theories—a rigid fidelity to the original statement of the general theory is likely to ensure its staleness if not decline. It might be too much to ask Gottfredson and Hirschi to consider the wisdom of theoretical integration. Even so, it appears that the time has come for the general theory to broaden its horizons so as to confront criminological realities that now rest beyond its boundaries.

II THEORIES OF CRIME

6 SELF-CONTROL AND SOCIAL LEARNING THEORY

Ronald L. Akers

In *A General Theory of Crime* (1990), Michael Gottfredson and Travis Hirschi argue that low self-control is the cause of criminality. They claim that their general theory explains all crime under all circumstances and at all times. The general theory of crime has been widely accepted by criminologists everywhere as a major explanation of criminal behavior, and research has provided considerable empirical support for it. I reviewed the book shortly after it was published (Akers, 1991) and referred to the "power, scope, and persuasiveness" of Gottfredson and Hirschi's argument; it represented, in my view, a "milestone in criminological theory" (p. 201).

My purpose here is not to analyze the strengths and weaknesses of the theory (for such an analysis see Akers, 1991; Akers and Sellers, 2004; and other chapters in this volume). Rather, I want to address the flaw in Gottfredson and Hirschi's (1990) argument that there is an incompatible and irreconcilable difference between "control" theory, which they portray as explaining *only* why people do not commit crime, and "positivist" theory, which they maintain explains *only* why people do commit crime. In Gottfredson and Hirschi's view control theory rests on the assumptions that motivation for crime is universal and invariant across individuals and that conformity can be expected only if this ever-present criminal motivation is self-controlled. Positivist theories on the other hand, they argue, are not capable of explaining crime because they ignore factors that constrain it and assume that deviance will not occur unless individuals are caused to deviate by forces and influences beyond their control. This is the same distinction that Hirschi (1969) made when he proposed his earlier social bonding version of control theory.

It is accurate to say that theories differ in the extent to which the explanatory scheme emphasizes risk or facilitative variables versus protective or restraining variables in crime and deviance. My disagreement is with the strong oppositional approach taken by Gottfredson and Hirschi; they go beyond a simple recognition of differences in theoretical emphasis and draw a qualitative and immutable distinction between control theory and positivist theory (a category into which they place virtually all other criminological theories except for rational choice and deterrence theories). I most especially object to the way that Gottfredson and Hirschi contrast their theory with social learning theory, which they portray as a prime example of a positivist theory and not at all compatible with control theory. This incompatibility was central to the 1990 presentation of self-control theory and continues to be asserted today. "Control theory is not compatible with 'social learning' or 'labelling theory,' and should not reap the benefits or bear the burdens of association with these illustrious perspectives" (Hirschi and Gottfredson, 2006, 116). They follow Hirschi (1969) and Kornhauser (1978) in depicting social learning theory as the prime example of "cultural deviance" theory. Cultural deviance theory is depicted as assuming that the only cause of crime is positive learning of and adherence to the values and norms of a deviant subculture or group that positively values deviant behavior and has a normative structure that contravenes the laws and norms of the larger society. Thus Gottfredson and Hirschi argue that social learning theory is incapable of explaining individual variation in criminal or conforming behavior. They believe that social learning theory assumes that socialization into group or subcultural norms is perfect and that no member of the group will violate those norms. As I have shown previously (Akers, 1996, 1998), this is a serious error. In fact, much to the contrary, social learning theory explains learning to engage in, as well as learning to refrain from, criminal behavior—learning to conform to and to violate norms, including norms of one's own groups. Indeed, the theory would propose that self-control is itself learned by processes stated in learning theory. Socialization takes place in such a way that it results in low self-control, which produces criminal behavior. Far from resting on diametrically opposed assumptions, both theories contain control and positivist dimensions. Social learning and self-control theories have differences, but the two theories overlap and have many similarities. Hirschi's (2004) recent modifications to the concept of self-control increase those similarities.

LOW SELF-CONTROL AS A GENERAL THEORY OF CRIME

Gottfredson and Hirschi's theory proposes that, given the opportunity, individuals with low self-control commit crimes of all kinds (and engage in certain acts, such as substance use, which they refer to as "analogous" to crime), whereas individuals with high self-control do not. Gottfredson and Hirschi propose a general theory that explains all individual differences in the propensity to commit crime at all times and places and under all circumstances. Individual differences in the tendency to commit criminal acts, they state, "*remain reasonably stable with change in the social location of individuals and change in their knowledge of the operation of sanction systems.* This is the problem of self-control, the differential tendency of people to avoid criminal acts whatever the circumstances in which they find themselves. Since this difference among people has attracted a wide variety of names, we begin by arguing the merits of the concept of self-control" (Gottfredson and Hirschi, 1990, 87; emphasis in original).

Individuals with low self-control have a preference for excitement and impulsive risk taking. They have low manual and academic skills, are self-centered, are indifferent to the suffering of others, possess minimal tolerance for frustration, and are short-term hedonists who focus on immediate gratification without regard to long-term consequences of their actions. Compared to them, people with high self-control will be "substantially less likely at all periods of life to engage in criminal acts" (Gottfredson and Hirschi, 1990, 89). Not only crime, defined by Gottfredson and Hirschi (1990) as "acts of force or fraud undertaken in pursuit of self-interest" (p. 15), but also all forms of "analogous behavior," such as smoking, drinking, drug use, illicit sex, and even accidents, are all and equally "manifestations of" low self-control. Therefore individuals with low self-control show great versatility in the types of crime and analogous behavior they undertake. Except for accidents, Gottfredson and Hirschi's list of analogous behavior is indistinguishable from the list of behaviors that sociologists have always included in the concept of deviant behavior (Goode, 2005). One's propensity for crime can be counteracted by circumstances and depends on opportunities to be activated; therefore low self-control does not require crime or analogous behavior.

Gottfredson and Hirschi endorse the view that the cause of low self-control is ineffective or incomplete childhood socialization, especially ineffective child rearing by parents. Parents who supervise their children closely and recognize and punish their deviant acts will socialize children into self-control. Children whose parents fail at this are unlikely to learn self-control. The explicit disapproval of parents is the most important negative sanction. Once self-control is formed in childhood, the theory proposes, across-individual differences in self-control remain stable throughout life. This would seem to rest on the assumption that an individual's self-control changes little over time, place, or circumstance or that, if such changes do occur, they have no effect on between-individual differences in self-control. Children who learn self-control tend not to become delinquent as teenagers or to engage in crime as adults. It is in the family during childhood where the most important socialization takes place. No such socialization occurs in peer groups, and as a point of particular contradiction to social learning theory, low self-control theory accords such groups no more than a trivial role in contributing to the commission of criminal and deviant acts.

Low self-control explains "all crime, at all times, and, for that matter many forms of behavior that are not sanctioned by the state" (Gottfredson and Hirschi, 1990, 117) including all forms of property and violent offenses, white-collar crime, and organized crime. Low self-control is "for all intents and purposes, *the* individual-level cause of crime" (Gottfredson and Hirschi, 1990, 232; emphasis in original).

SOCIAL LEARNING AS A GENERAL THEORY OF CRIME

Social learning theory is an integration of Sutherland's (1947) sociological theory of differential association with behavioral principles from psychology, as originally presented by Robert Burgess and Akers (1966) as "differential association-reinforcement" theory and as I have developed it since then. Social learning principles have been applied to criminal and delinquent behavior and to treatment and prevention by other social behaviorists in ways that are compatible with and differ only somewhat from social learning theory as I have proposed it. Although it refers to all aspects of the learning process, the theory relies mainly on four principal explanatory concepts: differential association, definitions, differential reinforcement, and imitation (Akers, 1998). The basic assumption in social learning theory is that the same learning process in a context of social structure, interaction, and situation produces both conforming and deviant behavior. The probability that individuals will engage in criminal and deviant behavior is increased and the probability of their conforming to the norm is decreased when they differentially associate with others who commit criminal behavior and espouse definitions favorable to it, are relatively more exposed in person or symbolically to salient criminal or deviant behavioral models, define criminal behavior as desirable or justified in a situation discriminative for the behavior, and have received in the past and anticipate in the current or future situations relatively greater reward than punishment for the behavior (see Akers, 1998, 50).

Differential association refers to the direct association and interaction with others in primary groups who engage in and/or support certain kinds of behavior as well as the indirect association and identification with secondary and more distant reference groups. Although differential peer association is emphasized both theoretically and in empirical tests, social learning theory is not simply a theory of peer group influence but includes the family and other intimate relationships as the most important primary groups. It also posits effects from neighbors, members of churches and other religious organizations, school teachers, the law and authority figures, and other individuals and groups in the community (as well as mass media and other more remote sources) that constitute real or "virtual" groups (Warr, 2002) with which one may be in differential association. *Definitions* refer to an individual's own general and specific, positive and neutralizing attitudes, values, orientations, rationalizations, definitions of the situation, and other evaluative and moral attitudes that orient the individual to the commission of an act as right or wrong, good or bad, appropriate or not appropriate, expected or not expected. *Differential reinforcement* refers to the balance of past, present, and anticipated future rewards and punishments that follow or are consequences of behavior. The most important of these are social, but the theory posits that at least some of the differential reinforcement may involve unconditioned or intrinsic "nonsocial" physiological or physical stimuli. The concept of social reinforcement (and punishment) goes beyond the direct reactions of others present while an act is committed to include the whole range of actual and anticipated, tangible and intangible rewards valued in society or subgroups. In self-reinforcement individuals exercise self-control, reinforcing or punishing their own behavior, in effect, taking the role of others, even when alone. *Imitation* refers to the engagement in behavior after the observation of similar behavior in others. The observation of salient models in primary groups and in the media affects both prosocial and deviant behavior, primarily in the initial acquisition and performance of novel behavior but also in the maintenance or cessation of behavioral patterns once established.

These social learning concepts define sets of variables that are all part of the same underlying process that is operative in each individual's learning history, in the immediate situation in which an opportunity for a crime occurs, and in the larger social structural context. This process is one in which the balance of learned definitions, imitation of criminal or deviant models, and the anticipated balance of reinforcement produces the initial delinquent or deviant act. The facilitative effects of these variables continue in the repetition of acts. After initiation the actual social and nonsocial reinforcers and punishers affect whether or not the acts will be repeated and at what frequency. Whether a deviant act will be committed in a situation that presents the opportunity (itself subject to definitions of the situation) depends on the learning history of the individual and the set of reinforcement contingencies in that situation. Past learning history produces habit and behavioral tendencies that lean in the direction of stability of behavior that is reinforced by similarities over time and place in social contexts, but to the extent that changes in the individual's social and personal situation result in changes in the learning variables, social learning theory expects changes in behavior. I have elaborated on the theory to produce a social structure and social learning (SSSL) model in which I hypothesize that social structural factors affect the social learning variables, which, in turn, have a direct impact on the individual's conduct. In this model social learning variables are proposed as the main ones in the social-psychological process mediating the effect of social structure on the individual's behavior that comprises rates of crime and deviance (Akers, 1998).

DIFFERENCES AND SIMILARITIES IN SELF-CONTROL AND SOCIAL LEARNING THEORY: CORRECTING MISCHARACTERIZATIONS

As I show in this overview, social learning is a general theory encompassing social, nonsocial, and cultural factors that explains the acquisition and maintenance of and change in criminal and deviant behavior. The theory embraces factors that operate both to motivate and to control or prevent criminal behavior and both to promote and to undermine conformity. The scope of its claims as a general theory of criminal and deviant behavior is as broad as if not broader than the scope of the claims for self-control theory. It is capable of accounting for the onset, continuation, and cessation, stability and change, and specialization and versatility in criminal and deviant behavior. Although it has positivistic elements in it, it should be clear from the foregoing that social learning theory does not fit the category of a positivist theory of crime as defined by Gottfredson and Hirschi. That is, it is not a theory solely of the positive causes of crime, addressing only "why they do it" and uninterested in or incapable of explaining "why they do not do it." Rather, social learning theory incorporates crime-facilitating as well as protective, preventive, or controlling factors. It rests on soft determinism and allows for human agency and choice. It does not "reject hedonic calculus in favor of the positivistic view that people are naturally social and must therefore be compelled to commit deviant or criminal acts by forces over which they have no control" (Gottfredson and Hirschi, 1990, 10–11).

Gottfredson and Hirschi (1990) seem to recognize in one place that learning theories "also assume that behavior is in large part shaped by contingencies of reinforcement, a view directly compatible with Bentham's classical theory of behavior" (p. 64), incorporate the hedonic calculus, and "assume that behavior is governed by its consequences" (p. 71). At the same time, they place social learning squarely in the sociological positivist category of theory, which in their schema is mutually exclusive with the control theory category into which they place self-control theory. Therefore, according to this categorization as a positivist theory, social learning theory cannot really recognize the effect of consequences on behavior. Rather, it conforms, as do *all* theories not categorized as control theories by Gottfredson and Hirschi, to "the positivist position on sanctions [that] is equally misinformed, assuming as it does that failure to document a strong effect of legal sanctions is evidence that sanctions in general do not operate to restrict criminal behavior.... [On the contrary] the evidence is fully consistent with the view that criminal, deviant, sinful, and reckless behavior flourish in the absence of negative consequences or in the absence of social control" (Gottfredson and Hirschi, 1990, 13–14).

Except for the recognition in one place (although contradicted in another) that social learning theory does truly invoke consequences of behavior in its explanation of crime, *nothing* in the description of a positivist theory by Gottfredson and Hirschi fits social learning theory (nor, I would argue, does it fully fit other theories that they place in the positivist category). Because the concept of differential reinforcement (balance of behavioral consequences) is central to social learning theory, it is clearly wrong to identify it as belonging to a category of theory in which sanctions in general are assumed to have no restrictive effect on criminal behavior. The notion that criminal, deviant, and reckless behavior will flourish in the absence of negative consequences is not foreign to social learning theory, although I would argue that a focus only on variations in negative consequences is incomplete because, unlike social learning theory, it says nothing about the impact of positive consequences. Social learning theory would not only propose the impact of negative sanctions but go beyond that to assert that such behaviors will flourish in the presence of positive rewards for them. To be more accurate, in social learning theory it is the *balance* of these positive and negative consequences (social, nonsocial, formal, informal, internal, external) over time, across circumstances, between and within individuals, that will determine the frequency, timing, pattern, stability, and versatility of a behavior and predict whether or not the behavior will flourish. The principle of differential reinforcement encapsulates variation in rewards and punishments for both motivation toward criminal (or noncriminal) behavior and control (social and self-) of criminal behavior. If Gottfredson and Hirschi define positivist theory in part by assuming that such a theory ignores negative consequences of behavior, it is beyond comprehension that social learning theory, which gives such a key role to the balance of rewards and punishment, could be characterized as a positivist theory.

Although self-control theory allows for no or only a limited role for variation in rewards or positive consequences to explain variation in criminal behavior, to the extent that self-control theory allows for behavioral impact of social sanctions, it is clearly in line with, not opposed to, social learning theory. Gottfredson and Hirschi say that control theory is grounded principally in classical theory with its interest solely in the nature of offenses and crime deterrence, whereas social learning theory is grounded in positivist theory, which they claim is focused solely on social or personal characteristics of offenders that cause the commission of crime. This characterization is wrong and does not negate theoretical overlap between control and social learning. I long ago connected the punishment function in classical and deterrence theories to social learning theory and included measures of both formal and informal deterrence in tests of social learning theory (Akers, 1977; Akers et al., 1979). I have shown that the notions of cost-benefits or rewards-punishment analysis in expanded versions of deterrence and rational choice theories are wholly compatible with and indeed are essentially partial statements of the differential reinforcement principle found in social learning theory (Akers, 1991). Moreover, social learning theory focuses on social context and cognitive-behavioral variables, not on individual personal characteristics (Akers, 1998).

The similarities and overlap of self-control theory with social learning theory and the fact that control theory recognizes positive behavioral consequences at least to some extent are seen in various statements such as "crime is caused or prevented by constellations of pleasurable and painful consequences" (Gottfredson and Hirschi, 1990, 5) and a "central element of self-control theory (and of all control theories) is the assumption that behavior is governed by its consequences" (Hirschi and Gottfredson, 2006, 115). These statements directly reiterate the principle of differential reinforcement in social learning theory. Indeed, far from being alien to social learning theory, they could have been lifted straight out of my earlier statements that "the principles of behavior theory of most interest to us are those which detail the way environmental consequences react on and affect behavior" (Akers, 1985, 43) and "whether deviant or conforming behavior [is committed and] persists depends on the past and present rewards and punishments and on the rewards and punishment attached to alternative behavior" (p. 57), and from similar statements of the theory made over the years (Akers, 1998). As noted, Gottfredson and Hirschi sometimes recognize this overlap but attempt to show how different self-control theory is by asserting (erroneously) that social learning theory makes only passing references to "negative reinforcement" and relies exclusively on learning through positive reward (Gottfredson and Hirschi, 1990, 71). Any reasonable reading of social learning theory would show that this characterization is wrong. Social learning theory explicitly includes positive reinforcement (strengthening of behavior through rewards) and negative reinforcement (strengthening of behavior through escape or avoidance of cost or punishment) as well as positive punishment (directly costly or painful consequences) and negative punishment (indirectly through removal of rewards) for both conforming and deviant behavior. Long before publication of *A General Theory*, I had explicitly proposed that deviant behavior can result from failures in learning conformity and from directly learning deviant behavior (Akers, 1973, 62; also see reiterations in Akers, 1977; 1985; and 1998, 59).

Proponents of self-control theory downplay (and often ignore) the effects of positive consequences on behavior, whereas social learning theory emphasizes the balance of positive and negative consequences. Therefore there are obvious differences in the centrality given to behavioral consequences in the two theories. Indeed, although behavioral consequences were given a central place in the original Burgess-Akers formulation and have maintained that place in social learning theory, the proposition that behavior is a function of its consequences was not explicitly endorsed by Hirschi until his later work on self-control theory with Gottfredson. The impact of sanctions was only implicit in Hirschi's (1969) original social bonding version of control theory. The only place where this social bonding version of control theory shows any recognition of behavioral consequences is found indirectly in the concept of commitment. The hypothesis in social bonding theory is that individuals who have a strong commitment to conformity refrain from deviance because that commitment represents a costly investment that would be lost by indulging in deviant acts. Soon after the theory first appeared, I pointed out that "little is said directly about sanctions" in social bonding theory, that the theory does not specifically utilize the knowledge that "social control is exerted through *sanctions*, both in direct external control and in training for self-control," and that it makes no reference to the "specific, deliberate efforts of the formal control system to deter deviance" (Akers, 1973, 28–29; emphasis in original). I saw compatibility and overlap between control and social learning theories. For instance, the social bonding concept of commitment and its effect on deviance assumes a process that is the same as the learning concept of negative reinforcement in which behavior results from avoiding aversive consequences. Another example is the concept of belief in social bonding theory overlapping with the social learning concept of definitions unfavorable to deviance. Nearly two decades before Gottfredson and Hirschi (1990) asserted the significance of consequences of behavior for self-control, I argued that control theory should be modified to incorporate formal and informal social sanctions and provide a place for sanctions and consequences in the formation of *self-control*. "Thus, the direct role of sanctions in the socialization process—the molding of the individual's commitment to conformity and *development of self-control*—could be made part of control theory. Also, control theory could include the type and effectiveness of informally applied sanctions by parents and peers as well as the formal application of sanctions by the legal and correctional system to control violations of norms. When this is done, *control theory becomes especially compatible with the social learning theory*" (Akers, 1973, 29; emphasis added).

The way that I first dealt (and still do deal) with the process of socialization and the concept of self-control and the way that Gottfredson and Hirschi later dealt with them are substantially similar. For instance, Gottfredson and Hirschi maintain that self-control is learned primarily through childhood socialization in the family. "Most people are sufficiently socialized by familial institutions to avoid involvement in criminal acts. Those not socialized sufficiently by the family may eventually learn self-control through the operation of other sanctioning systems" (Gottfredson and Hirschi, 1990, 105). Many years before publication of this statement, I maintained that "the direct role of sanctions in the socialization process—the molding of the individual's commitment to conformity and development of *self-control—could be made part of control theory*" (Akers, 1973, 29; emphasis added). "Over time, sanctioning behavior may lead to the development of *self-control*. . . . The individual learns from his parents, peers, and others what are considered the right and wrong things to say and do in a variety of contexts. . . . After the initial period of socialization most people conform by controlling their own behavior without further directly applied sanctions. Every social system relies to a considerable degree on socialization to develop self-control among the population" (Akers, 1973, 6; see also Akers, 1977, 8, 38; 1985, 6).

Not only is there no fundamental difference between these statements, but they say essentially the same thing about self-control and childhood socialization. Socialization and informal social control in the family have long been incorporated into the social learning process to produce conformity or deviance. The family is a key primary group with which one is differentially associated and in which learning takes place. The typical empirical measures of variables thought to be derived only from control theory, such as family parental control, discipline, and management (parental sanctions), are also transparently measures of social learning variables, such as differential social reinforcement, in which parents reward their children for conforming behavior and punish them for nonconforming or disobedient behavior. Given my long-standing theoretical recognition of behavioral consequences and the role of both positive and negative parental sanctions in the socialization (social learning) process to develop self-control and given self-control theory's later recognition of the same process, it is plain why I dispute Gottfredson and Hirschi's assertion that their theory is a purely nonpositivistic control theory that rests on a basic assumption about the importance of behavioral consequences, which places it in direct opposition to social learning theory.

Again, this is not to deny that there are differences between self-control theory and social learning theory. Both recognize that socialization can take place outside the family. However, self-control theory expects no important change in self-control, once formed in childhood, by any subsequent socialization. Social learning theory on the other hand allows for socialization and resocialization effects. If the social contexts and the learning variables remain relatively stable, then social learning theory expects relative stability in self-control and behavior, but if there are changes in the learning variables, then the theory expects some change in behavior and level of control. My SSSL model (Akers, 1998) specifically hypothesizes effects on the learning process from the social structure, a stance that is consistent with research findings on separate and independent effects of neighborhood context on self-control (Pratt et al., 2004). Another significant difference is the place given to peer influence in social learning theory versus the dismissal of peer influence in self-control theory. Gottfredson and Hirschi know that the research literature in criminology has over a great many years produced consistent findings of the strong relationship of one's own behavior to actual and perceived peers' behavior. They want to dismiss this relationship by stating that reports of peers' behavior is simply another measure of one's own deviance, but this assertion is not supported by research (Menard and Elliott, 1994). They repeat the commonsense adage, favored by Glueck and Glueck (1950), that birds of a feather flock together. This folk saying is cited in support of the proposition that peers' behavior has no effect on one's own delinquent or conforming behavior. The connection is merely the result of one's already established behavior prodding self-selection into deviant groups, not the result of any peer influence on learning of deviant behavior. I have usually responded with another aphorism, attributable to Benjamin Franklin, "If you lie down with dogs, you get up with fleas." "Social learning admits that birds of a feather do flock together, but it also admits that if the birds are humans, they also will influence one another's behavior, in both conforming and deviant directions" (Akers, 1991, 210). Thus social learning provides for both socialization and selection in delinquency, depending on what part of the process is being measured. Peers learn deviant (and conforming) patterns from one another, and similarities in behavior have an impact on selection of friends (which is itself affected by differential reinforcement, the rewards and costs attached to making and continuing those friendships), where there is a choice. But whatever one's pattern or level of prior deviance, it is escalated and increased after joining the group (or decreased if the associations in the group are primarily with conforming patterns).

Gottfredson and Hirschi believe social learning theory posits that only positive learning of deviance takes place in peer groups and that peer groups socialize the adolescent into a set of deviant values which require or compel the individual to commit deviance. As my outline of social learning theory shows, however, there is no such proposition in the theory. Social learning stresses differential association and differential reinforcement within and between conforming and deviant peers, family, and other groups. Learning of a set of specifically prodelinquent values to the exclusion of conforming values may occur, but it is not necessary for the peer group influence to affect behavior. This mischaracterization of the theory also ignores my statements that most of the peer influence is in a conforming direction and my references to the effect of deviant behavior on choice of friends and other feedback effects in social learning theory (Akers, 1985, 60, 116–117).

To Gottfredson and Hirschi (1990), both one's own deviance and the differential association with deviant peers are the result of low self-control; any relationship between one's own and peers' behavior is spurious. The only, or at least main, function of the peer associations is to "ease" or "facilitate acts that would be too difficult or dangerous to do alone" (p. 159). If it were not for this easing and facilitating function of the group, crime and deviance would be largely committed alone and without reference to friends. Thus self-control theory denies that deviance-relevant learning of any kind takes place in peer groups. Individuals do not learn or modify their attitudes or behavior in peer groups, and the effects of modeling or social reinforcement from peers are insignificant. Therefore peer associations do not affect the onset or the acceleration, or the continuation or cessation of crime and analogous behavior; nor do they have any effect to which theory needs to attend. According to self-control theory, "*taking up with delinquent peers is . . . without causal significance*" in the commission of delinquency or crime (Gottfredson and Hirschi, 1990, 258; emphasis added). The role accorded to peers in social learning theory and the insistence of Gottfredson and Hirschi that peers' behavior, attitudes, or reactions are inconsequential for one's own behavior constitute one of the major true differences between the theories. This difference is also one of the key points where the empirical evidence strongly favors social learning theory.

Although self-control and social learning theory have some clear differences, they also show many similarities and compatibilities. Contrary to Gottfredson and Hirschi's position, both self-control and social learning theory contain clearly positivistic and control elements. Both incorporate behavioral consequences in some fashion. Both postulate in-family socialization in the production of self-control. There are other commonalities. Given the differences between the two theories, one may properly object to efforts to integrate them or to claims that they offer exactly the same explanation of crime and deviance. However, given the clear similarities and overlap, it is not proper to place them in opposition as totally different kinds of theoretical explanations of crime.

BACK TO THE FUTURE: HIRSCHI'S SOCIAL BONDING MODIFICATIONS TO SELF-CONTROL THEORY

Hirschi (2004) has recently proposed a "slightly revised" version of self-control theory by offering a "new definition of self-control" (pp. 543, 545). If accepted as replacing the version put forth by Gottfredson and Hirschi (1990), the redefinition will have a major impact on the development of self-control theory in the future, an impact that is already being seen. This reconceptualization for the *future* goes *back* in time to the concept of social bonds in Hirschi's (1969) original social control theory in which deviance is said to be caused by weak or absent ties that bind the individual to society. To the control from social bonds Hirschi (2004) now adds the control that comes from the individual's consideration of the negative consequences of each act—a control that was not originally included in social bonding theory—and asserts that "social control and self-control are the same thing." Redefined, says Hirschi, "self-control becomes the *tendency to consider the full range of potential costs of a particular act*. This moves the focus from the *long-term* implications of the act to its *broader* and often contemporaneous implications" (Hirschi, 2004, 543; emphasis in original). Put another way, Hirschi adds, "Self-control is the set of inhibitions one carries with one wherever one happens to go. Their character may be initially described by going to the *elements of the bond identified by social control theory*: attachment, commitments, involvement, and beliefs" (pp. 543–544; emphasis added).

Whereas Hirschi (1969) subsumed self-control under the concept of attachment in social bonding theory, his 2004 statement equates all the elements of the social bond with, and perhaps subsumes them under, his newly defined concept of self-control. Unlike the earlier concept of social bonds that paid little attention to behavioral consequences, the bonds are now seen as describing the true meaning of self-control—the extent to which the individual does or does not take into account all the broader short-term and long-term implications of the act.

In short, the focus on impulsivity, short-term hedonism, and other "psychological" or "personality" elements of Gottfredson and Hirschi's (1990) concept of self-control is replaced by a focus on the full range of anticipated costs of behavior in Hirschi's (2004) new concept of self-control. It remains to be seen how far this new focus is taken by Hirschi himself or in collaboration with Gottfredson, but I believe that this recent reformulation of self-control theory, with Hirschi's accompanying discussion and presentation of empirical data, is highly significant and sets the stage for new contributions of control theory to the explanation of crime and deviance. In so doing, I believe Hirschi also addresses, at least in part, three of the main issues I have raised with regard to self-control theory in the past (Akers, 1991; Akers and Sellers, 2004). First, Hirschi offers a solution to the tautology issue in self-control theory. Second, he offers a response to the questions about the relationship between self-control theory, circa 1990, and social bonding theory, circa 1969. Third, and most relevant to my argument here, his reformulation enhances the already apparent similarities and compatibilities of self-control and social learning theory and opens the door for additional work on this issue.

Hirschi notes that his and Gottfredson's reaction to the question of tautology has had a "certain lawyerly quality about it," saying that "'yes' it is tautological, as it should be" and at the same time saying "'no,' it is not tautological." He believes that both answers are legitimate and that "the present effort should not be construed as an effort to deal with the tautology issue" (Hirschi, 2004, 550). But with apologies to Hirschi, I do construe his new effort as dealing with the tautology issue. I do not construe it as resolving the tautology problem for the 1990 version of self-control theory or the tautology created by the behavioral measures of self-control. Rather, Hirschi's redefinition of self-control solves the problems by changing the definition of self-control to refer specifically to the broader and contemporaneous negative consequences of deviant acts. The new concept of self-control is nontautological because (unlike the 1990 concept) it is not synonymous with criminal propensity or criminal behavior and because the new measures of it suggested by Hirschi (unlike the behavioral measures of self-control previously preferred by Gottfredson and him) are not indicators of the dependent variable converted to measures of the independent variable. Thus neither the new concept nor the new measures of self-control have any problem with tautology. Unfortunately, the measures Hirschi uses to offer an empirical test of the reformulated self-control theory do not directly measure the actual or perceived consequences of the acts as specified in the new definition. Rather, Hirschi (2004) constructs an indirect measure by using the same data he originally used to test social bonding theory (Hirschi, 1969) and newer data collected in 1997. In both cases he reassembles some items originally designed as measures of social bonds (mainly attachment) and renames them "self-control responses" and "measures of the social bond/self-control."

Although Hirschi maintains that he is simply moving closer to the true meaning of self-control, in so doing, he actually modifies both self-control and social bonding theory. In contrast to Gottfredson and Hirschi (1990), Hirschi's (2004) modified theory, by referring to attachment and other social bonds, goes a long way toward clarifying the link between the earlier social bonding theory and the later self-control theory. In addition, unlike the original social bonding theory, this merging of self-control and social bonding theory now explicitly includes differences in consequences of acts (albeit only or mainly negative consequences). I think the new concept is in line with my long-ago suggestion to modify social bonding theory by directly and self-consciously incorporating behavioral consequences into the theory (Akers 1973, 29) and moves control theory toward even greater compatibility with social learning theory.

Future research should build on Alex Piquero and Bouffard's (2007) research, which does not depend on recycling measures of social bonds but constructs new measures, namely, respondent's perceptions of the costs (salience and number) they might experience hypothetically if they were to engage in drunk driving and sexual coercion. Future research should also recognize that, although Hirschi's new definition refers only to "potential costs of a particular act," self-control as the tendency to consider "broader and often contemporaneous implications" of an act leaves the door open to incorporate both rewarding and costly outcomes. As I have argued, the already existing compatibility of control and learning theory is enhanced by explicit incorporation of behavioral consequences into control theory. If one sticks to Hirschi's concept of self-control that refers only to negative consequences, then this incorporation is only a partial iteration of differential reinforcement. If one adds consideration of both positive and negative consequences, then it comes closer to being identical to the broader concept of differential reinforcement. Either way it is difficult to deny the overlap and similarities of control and learning theories in this regard.

Yet, this is exactly what control theorists continue to do. In 2004 Hirschi stated that "our child-rearing model owes much to the work of Gerald Patterson" (Hirschi, 2004, 541). This reference to the work of Patterson and his associates on the effects of family relationships and parental disciplinary practices as a primary basis for control theory is also found in Gottfredson and Hirschi (1990) and elsewhere. This covers up the fact that Patterson is a prominent learning psychologist and the founder and long-time director of the Oregon *Social Learning* Center. The theoretical and empirical work of this center is and always has been self-consciously and unequivocally social learning (Patterson and Dishion, 1985; Patterson et al., 1992). To refer to the Center's research as an important basis for how control theory views child rearing, while at the same time claiming control theory has irreconcilable differences with social learning theory, as Gottfredson and Hirschi do, goes beyond inconsistency. It wrongly implies that, because the two theories are viewed as contradictory, the Oregon Social Learning Center's work supports control theory *rather than* social learning theory. To say, as I do, that the work of the Center is primarily supportive of social learning theory but also can be seen as consistent with control theory underscores again that the two theories share commonalities. If the future of self-control theory can be tied to going back in time to social bonding theory, as Hirschi does, then perhaps my argument from the past and the present of compatibility between control theory and social learning theory will be accepted and become the basis for future theoretical developments.

SUMMARY AND CONCLUSION

Control theory is rightly seen as one of the three (along with strain and social learning) perspectives at the core of criminological theorizing (Cullen et al., 2006). My attention here has not been on analyzing or evaluating the theory itself. Rather, I have argued against the position taken by Gottfredson and Hirschi in their defense of "control" theory and their rejection of "positivist" theories. They are most mistaken in their depiction of social learning theory. Social learning is not incompatible with or wholly in opposition to self-control theory. Indeed, I have presented the case here that, although the two theories have some clear differences in concepts and predictions, they show no fundamental difference in assumptions. Moreover, many similarities and overlaps between the two theories have been increased by recent modifications in self-control theory.

7 | SELF-CONTROL, ANOMIE,
AND SOCIAL INSTITUTIONS

Richard Rosenfeld and Steven F. Messner

On initial inspection Gottfredson and Hirschi's general theory of crime shares little in common with explanations derived from the anomie tradition in sociology. Gottfredson and Hirschi's theory is oriented to the individual or micro level of analysis, whereas anomie theory is indisputably a macrolevel perspective. Gottfredson and Hirschi's theory attributes the tendency to commit criminal behavior to low self-control, a personal attribute that is primarily a consequence of deficient parenting but is not otherwise subject to appreciable social influence. In contrast, anomie theory locates the sources of criminality in the structure and functioning of whole societies. Thus in a sense the two perspectives speak different languages. Nonetheless, the two theories overlap in two important respects. First, the concept of *control* is central in both theories, and second, the institution of the *family* plays a prominent role in each theory. Even so, the manner in which the two theories treat these issues differs fundamentally; those differences form the basis for our critical comparison.

CLASSICAL ANOMIE THEORY

Merton's (1938) classic formulation of anomie theory attributes crime to the gap or disjunction within the culture and between the culture and the social structure. (Our description of Merton's anomie theory and institutional-anomie theory draws from Messner and Rosenfeld [2007].) It subdivides culture into two parts: first, the society's central goal orientations, or ends, and, second, the institutionalized means for attaining them. In Merton's formulation the social structure differentially distributes access to the legitimate means for attaining highly valued, mainly economic goals. Crime tends to be high in societies with a strong cultural emphasis on attaining material success but a social and economic structure that grants only limited access to success goals.

A disjunction or gap within the culture results from a society's culture placing excessive cultural emphasis on success goals and correspondingly less emphasis on the legitimate means for achieving the goals. The greater the emphasis on goals relative to means, the stronger the pressure on individuals to deviate from established modes of behavior, including legal standards, in the pursuit of culturally defined success. A second disjunction or gap is between a society's culture, that is, its emphasis on success, and its social structure, that is, its unequal distribution of opportunities to achieve success goals. A social organization produces crime, according to Merton, in both these ways. Because of their privileged position in the social structure, by which Merton primarily means the class system, some individuals or groups have advantages over others in the pursuit of success. Yet all are striving for the same goals. People faced with this contradiction between cultural mandate and structural impediment are subject to pressures or "strain" to abandon legal but ineffective means of goal attainment in favor of illegal, effective ones. These pressures are particularly acute, Merton argues, for members of the lower class, who lack access to the legitimate means of attaining the goals shared by members of all classes.

Merton's article had little immediate impact on the fields of criminology and the sociology of deviance. Then, in the 1950s, following the publication of Albert Cohen's *Delinquent Boys* (1955), which made extensive use of it, anomie theory began to capture the imaginations of influential theorists and researchers. Scholars identified ambiguities in the original statement of the theory and proposed remedies. Prominent sociologists and criminologists integrated aspects of anomie theory with other criminological ideas to construct explanations of crime and deviance that were both more comprehensive and more precise than Merton's original formulation. Merton himself further advanced the anomie research program by responding to early criticisms and offering expanded and revised versions of the theory (Merton, 1964, 1968).

CRITICISMS OF ANOMIE THEORY

After flourishing in both the theoretical and research literature, interest in anomie theory dropped markedly in the 1970s and 1980s. Researchers were less likely to draw on the anomie tradition for theoretical guidance, and several highly respected scholars directed harsh criticisms at the perspective. In an influential monograph on juvenile delinquency published in 1978, Ruth Kornhauser dismissed the utility of "strain theory," the label given to anomie theory by many criminological theorists, on both theoretical and empirical grounds. She argued that the theory suffered from serious logical flaws and that its central empirical claims—for example, that the discrepancy between aspirations and achievements is a cause of delinquency—lacked support in the research literature. Kornhauser (1978, 180) concluded her review of the perspective with the blunt advice to colleagues to turn their attention elsewhere in efforts to explain crime and delinquency.

Gottfredson and Hirschi (1990) built their criticisms of anomic theory on Kornhauser's (1978) critique. Merton's suggestion that distinctive forms of deviance and crime result from differing adaptations to socially generated strains misconstrues the singular nature of crime and rests on logically dubious and empirically disconfirmed assumptions about the relationship between crime and social class. Sociologists persist in connecting crime to social class, they argue, out of a misguided advocacy of their "disciplinary interests" (Gottfredson and Hirschi, 1990, 79–80). The image of criminality in anomie theory, say Gottfredson and Hirschi, is plainly contrary to the facts. Criminals are not class warriors; they do not "strike out against their class enemies or people more fortunate than themselves; in fact, offenders tend to victimize people who share their unfortunate circumstances" (p. 152).

We believe that these criticisms rest on an incomplete reading and caricatured version of anomie theory. For example, although it is true that Merton concentrates on the criminal behavior of the lower classes, his basic argument can be extended to explain criminal behavior among those at the upper levels of the social hierarchy as well. Passas (1990) describes the strain toward anomie experienced by corporate executives, individuals who are under severe pressures to maximize profits under conditions of structural constraints. Such a situation, Passas suggests, is conducive to high levels of corporate deviance and white-collar crime. Passas thus explains how both upper- and lower-class crimes can be accounted for by reference to the same mechanisms that are described in the general anomie perspective. By contrast, the connection between corporate criminality and low self-control is far from obvious. How could people of such limited competence, people who lack the capacity to defer gratification and distinguish between short-term and long-term benefits (Gottfredson and Hirschi, 1990, 89), achieve the positions of influence and power necessary to commit corporate crimes?

In one sense we agree with Gottfredson and Hirschi and other critics that Merton and his early followers devote undue attention to the relationship between class and crime. For Merton the function of social structure is to distribute opportunities to achieve cultural goals. As Durkheim before him recognized, however, there is more to social structure than this. Social structure also functions to place limits on certain cultural imperatives so that they do not dominate and ultimately destroy others. This is the specific role of social institutions. Merton devotes little attention to institutions, beyond the system of social stratification, in his discussion of social structure and anomie.

The basic shortcoming of Merton's explanation of crime, and of the anomie tradition more generally, is the absence of a comprehensive account of institutional structure and functioning. Institutional-anomie theory begins to fill this gap in the anomie tradition.

INSTITUTIONAL-ANOMIE THEORY

We introduced the arguments of institutional-anomie theory in the early 1990s, when violent crime rates in the United States, already high by comparative standards, were rising (Messner and Rosenfeld, 1994). Institutional-anomie theory was intended to explain the sharply higher rates of serious crime observed in the United States compared to other developed societies. Following Merton, we argue that crime results from the intersection of particular cultural and structural features of society. Cultural values that define success or social standing largely in economic terms and that extol the virtues of economic success for all members of society are likely to be "anomic" to the extent that corresponding cultural emphasis is not placed on the normative status of the means for attaining success, and legitimate means are differentially distributed across the social structure.

To this point, institutional-anomie theory faithfully follows Merton's arguments. However, it extends those arguments by calling attention to features of the social structure beyond the stratification system that are conducive to high levels of serious crime. Crime results when the social controls and social supports of the major social institutions of a society (family, schools, political system, religion) are weak or when they operate in such a way as to directly promote crime. This is where the "institutional" component of the theory comes in. The theory's emphasis on the crime-facilitating properties of the full range of social institutions is a key element that distinguishes it from Merton's stratification-centered anomie theory—and, as we will see, from Gottfredson and Hirschi's general theory as well.

Culture and social structure intersect within the major social institutions of a society. The overriding function of all social institutions, regardless of their manifest content, is to orient the behavior of social actors to the society's dominant values, goals, beliefs, and norms. That is, all social institutions have both a socialization and a social control function. Institutions also provide members with many types of social support (Cullen and Wright, 1997). Socialization, social control, and social support are realized through the interrelated statuses and roles that constitute the structural component of social institutions.

Institutions do not and cannot exist in isolation from one another; they are strategically interdependent in the sense that the proper functioning of any one institution depends on inputs from all the others. However, institutions are rarely coequal in the claims they make on social actors and other institutional sectors and in the degree to which they embody a society's most cherished values and highly prized goals. Institutions typically stand in definite power relations to one another; that is, all societies can be characterized by a particular *institutional balance of power* (Messner and Rosenfeld, 2007; Rosenfeld and Messner, 2006). We argue that the free-market economy dominates the institutional structure of American society in the sense that noneconomic institutions and their respective functions are *devalued* compared with economic functions, are forced to *accommodate* economic perquisites and requirements, and are *penetrated* by the logic and language of the marketplace.

When the free-market economy dominates other institutions, they lose their capacity to exert social control and provide social support. Noneconomic institutions lose their fervor and force when their distinctive functions are devalued; they succumb to economic pressures and are subjected to the withering standards of market rationality. The family in particular has taken a beating in this regard. Its function as a unit of economic production was stripped away in the nineteenth century, and the homemaker role was attenuated in the twentieth century. But institutional control and support are not lessened simply because noneconomic institutions are weakened by the economy; the free-market economy also reduces control and support *directly*. By design, the free-market economy is much less constraining than other institutions. In the United States, where the principle of laissez-faire remains more persuasive than in other advanced industrial nations, economic controls, on business owners as well as on workers, are particularly permissive. "Ironically, then, Americans tend to be most strongly attached to the institution with the least restraining qualities" (Messner and Rosenfeld, 2001, 79).

Diminished social controls provide fertile soil for the cultivation of criminal propensities, for reasons well established in the long-standing "control" traditions in criminology (Hirschi, 1969; Kornhauser, 1978). Similarly, reduced social support stimulates criminal tendencies directly by weakening stakes in conformity and indirectly by decreasing the effectiveness of existing social controls (Cullen, 1994). Criminal propensity is also stimulated by a strong cultural emphasis on the goal of economic success and a weaker emphasis on the legitimacy of the means for attaining success (Merton, 1968). In short, anomic cultural tendencies are both realized and reinforced when the free-market economy dominates the institutional structure of a society. The result is a weakening of both external controls and internalized moral prohibitions against crime.

SELF-CONTROL AND ANOMIE: CULTURE MATTERS

Both Gottfredson and Hirschi's self-control theory and institutional-anomie theory recognize a need for restraint over individual desires and interests. Self-control theory focuses on the individual capacity to exercise restraint over personal interests and potential conflicts of interest among individuals. Institutional-anomie theory focuses on the strength of the normative order and difficulties in creating forms of social organization that enable actors to pursue their goals through normatively legitimized means. Further, given its sensitivity to cultural dynamics, institutional-anomie theory anticipates that the consequences of low self-control for crime may be conditioned by the larger societal context. For example, the extent to which the capacity to restrain aggression leads to crime will depend on the extent to which aggressive behavior runs counter to cultural values and norms as expressed in criminal law. Except insofar as opportunities for crime may be culturally determined, self-control theory rejects cultural explanations of any kind (Gottfredson and Hirschi, 1990, 169–179).

THE ORIGINS OF LOW SELF-CONTROL

Gottfredson and Hirschi derive their theory of self-control from an evaluation of the characteristics of crime. Crime, they say, is easy, requires little in the way of planning or skill, and promises short-run rewards for minimal effort. Everyone should be attracted to such acts, but only individuals with low self-control will succumb. Gottfredson and Hirschi's image of individuals with low self-control is not a pretty picture. Such individuals undervalue academic achievement, take impulsive risks, care little for others' suffering or opinions, and are prone to accidents, heavy drinking, smoking, and drug use. When opportunities are propitious, individuals with low self-control can be counted on to commit crimes. Regardless of opportunity, individuals with high self-control will refrain from criminal activity.

The sociological concept of anomie differs from low self-control in several important respects. Anomie is an attribute of social systems, whereas self-control is an individual trait. Anomie as most commonly used refers to the condition of normlessness or the weakening of moral norms. For Durkheim anomie tends to emerge in a context of conflicting values or rapid social change. Merton also uses the concept of anomie to refer to a weakened normative order and attributes its origins to the contradiction or disjuncture between universalistic cultural success goals and the normatively prescribed means to achieve them.

The conceptualization of anomie with reference to the weakening of the normative order, however, does not exhaust its meaning. As Orru (1987) has pointed out, anomie refers not just to the absence of cultural constraint but is "itself an 'ethic' that must be culturally motivated and socially sustained" (Messner and Rosenfeld, 2001, 7). The limitless pursuit of material and social success is part of the morality of modern capitalism. As Durkheim (1966 [1897]) put it, "It is everlastingly repeated that it is man's nature to be eternally dissatisfied, constantly to advance, without relief or rest, toward an indefinite goal. The longing for infinity is daily represented as a mark of moral distinction" (p. 257). Durkheim held that the unlimited appetites stimulated by modern capitalism would have to be restrained by new forms of institutional control to reduce their destructive consequences. This conception of culturally stimulated anomie subject to institutional controls is incorporated into institutional-anomie theory.

LOW SELF-CONTROL AND THE CONSUMER ROLE

We suggest that the principal structural locus of anomic cultural pressures in modern market societies is the *consumer role*. The Janus-faced nature of market society depicted in classical social thought—the capacity of markets to free people to pursue their own interests and to bind people in reciprocal exchanges (Hirschman, 1992)—is represented in the two major role complexes of the economy: consumption and work. These are the institutional mechanisms through which the economy exerts both its restraining and liberating power over the vast majority of the members of a market society and through which the dominant culture is brought into the flow of everyday social relations. Compared with those of legitimate employment, the expectations and obligations of the consumer role are highly permissive and provide considerable discretion with respect to how, when, where, and with whom the role is performed. Entry criteria are minimal, and opportunities for training and performance are plentiful. (The dress code generally amounts to little more than "shirts and shoes required.") The rewards of consumption are theoretically limitless. Moreover, whereas work necessarily draws individuals into the service of others, the self-oriented control over the conditions of material acquisition can free individuals from social obligation and restraint.

Consider Abelson's (1989) provocative account of the freedom entailed in consumption for middle-class women in the new department stores of the late nineteenth century and the implications of such freedom for crime. The appeal of the stores lay in the "freedom of the store environment [which] was not often duplicated in other areas of a woman's life" (p. 137). The connection between this freedom and the temptations of theft "was not lost on some shoplifters, who accused the stores of permitting too much freedom: they became 'over excited' and over stimulated in the large stores; they could not refrain from handling things, and no one bothered them. Everything led to temptation, shoppers complained, . . . and there was a 'deplorable liberty' to touch everything" (p. 139).

Now consider the situation of the Victorian department store ladies from the perspective of self-control theory. Self-control theory would predict that only ladies with low self-control would engage in shoplifting; no matter the degree of temptation or absence of external restraint, the ladies with high self-control would refrain from stealing. All the rest—the layout of the stores, permission to handle the goods, lack of surveillance—if addressed at all, would be consigned to opportunity factors interacting with self-control to produce crime. This interpretation, as far as it goes, is not necessarily incorrect, although self-control, as

Gottfredson and Hirschi define it, probably does not exhaust the individual-level factors associated with criminality. It would not be surprising if people with low self-control were more likely to shoplift or engage in other crimes than people with high self-control; nor would such a finding contradict arguments derived from institutional-anomie theory. Individuals with low self-control are likely to be more vulnerable than others to the anomic pressures inherent in the consumer role. The difference between the two perspectives lies in how each explains the social origins of low self-control.

Self-control theory assumes that the causes of low self-control are wholly negative. "No known social group," write Gottfredson and Hirschi (1990, 95), "actively or purposefully attempts to reduce the self-control of its members." We disagree. This is precisely what the so-called consumer culture seeks to do. From "Buy now, pay later" to "You are pre-approved," from the department store to the Internet, the relentless message of the market is to suspend self-control and gratify material desires. To be sure, not all dimensions or aspects of self-control are targeted to the same degree. Advertisers do not necessarily have an interest in making consumers indifferent to the suffering of others or in limiting their educational attainment, although some advertisers obviously make concerted efforts to encourage behaviors such as drinking and smoking, which Gottfredson and Hirschi attribute to ineffective socialization. And, again, some targets are likely to be more vulnerable than others. But the consumer culture does seek to overcome resistance to consumption, and it does so with positive appeals to life, liberty, and the pursuit of happiness through reduced self-control.

The argument that the causes of self-control are wholly negative appears to rest on the underlying premise that socialization is uniform across all domains. People are socialized to a greater or lesser extent and thus develop higher or lower self-control. Institutional-anomie theory is predicated on a multidimensional view of socialization that allows for the possibility that people may be well socialized in some respects but not in others. For example, although the shoplifter may have failed to develop proper respect for the culturally prescribed ways of obtaining merchandise—paying the clerk at the checkout counter—the act of shoplifting is itself testimony to effective socialization into the consumer role.

Gottfredson and Hirschi (1990) argue that no social group tries to lower self-control in its members because doing so would undermine "harmonious group relations and the ability to achieve collective ends" (p. 96). "These facts," they conclude, "explicitly deny that a tendency to crime is a product of socialization, culture, or positive learning of any sort" (p. 96). This explanation of low self-control overlooks the great historical drift of market societies away from the social discipline imposed by economic production toward the individual liberation permitted by consumption. Moreover, consumption incorporates a wide range of motivations and behaviors that are arguably as vital to the functioning of market societies as engagement in legitimate employment. No market economy could withstand for long a continuous drop in consumption.

Whether the anomic pressures of the consumer role raise levels of crime beyond what would be expected based on the existing distribution of low self-control (plus opportunity) ultimately is an empirical question. From the perspective of institutional-anomie theory the consumer role is less likely to generate anomie and accompanying criminal behaviors when it is embedded in relations of mutual obligation, dependence, and associated restraints. Shopping and purchasing gifts for family and friends are forms of what may be termed embedded consumption, which is unlikely to be criminogenic. As a ritual affirmation of social relationships, embedded consumption is more likely to reinforce social bonds and enhance concomitant social controls. Institutional-anomie theory also predicts that embedded consumption will vary with the prevailing institutional balance of power in society. Societies in which the free-market economy dominates the institutional structure should be subject to high levels of anomic consumption and attendant criminality, holding constant the personal traits of consumers.

THE ROLE OF THE FAMILY: THE CRUCIBLE OF SELF-CONTROL

Both self-control and institutional-anomie theory recognize that socialization plays a major role in the development of controls and the fostering of social order. Self-control theory directs attention almost exclusively to the family. Institutional-anomie theory also assigns an important role to the family but expands the institutional focus to encompass other social institutions on which the family depends for its effective functioning. In addition to its more restricted institutional focus, self-control theory depicts the causes of crime as characteristically negative; it is the absence of effective socialization that leads to crime. Further, institutional-anomie theory holds that both positive and negative socialization can take place in institutional contexts beyond the family.

Gottfredson and Hirschi maintain that low self-control is primarily the product of poor parenting. The principal parental deficit that produces low self-control in children is the inconsistent punishment of misbehavior, which in turn may result from low attachment to the child, inadequate monitoring and supervision of children's behavior, or lack of recognition of misbehavior. Adults who possess low-self control themselves make especially ineffective parents, which largely accounts for the intergenerational transmission of criminality (Gottfredson and Hirschi, 1990, 97–102). None of this is necessarily at odds with institutional-anomie theory, which also gives primacy to the family as a unit of socialization and control. However, institutional-anomie theory goes beyond self-control theory by pointing to particular cultural and social conditions that impede family functioning and emphasizing that crime-relevant socialization also occurs outside the family.

We have suggested that market forces may act as a positive stimulant to anomie and criminal behavior. The process begins early in life in the context of the family. Consider the modern American child. Nearly all American children occasionally participate in what Nightingale (1993) calls an intense "commodity worship" that can result in conflict with parents and the erosion of parental control. In some families these market-driven enticements and pressures are more intense and prolonged than in others. In the poor inner-city Philadelphia neighborhood that Nightingale (1993) studied, consumption pressures were unrelenting and sometimes destroyed the relationship between parents and children. Poor black American families, of course, are beset by hardships and pressures of many kinds, chief among them the destabilizing effects of chronic unemployment, low income, and racial exclusion (W. J. Wilson, 1987 1996). But the consumer culture aggravates those structural burdens with its promise of instant gratification and status elevation through participation in the abundance of American life beyond the ghetto. The poor parent may not stand a chance against such powerful cultural forces.

Nightingale (1993) proposes that competitive consumption is particularly intense, fraught with emotional content, and fateful among poor children because possessing and displaying fashionable commodities (clothing, jewelry, electronic devices, hairstyles, bicycles, and automobiles) constitute a form of "compensatory status." Achievement in the world of consumption compensates for children's feelings of failure and a sometimes profound disappointment in their parents. Conflicts erupt with parents who are perceived as ineffectual and weak, to which parents may respond with harsh and violent discipline, further alienating their children. The consumer culture thus acts on children directly, stimulating commodity worship, desire for instant gratification, and consumption-based status competition, and it weakens parent-child attachments, which further erodes parental controls over children. It would not be surprising if children had difficulty developing self-control under such circumstances. But it would be astonishing if the destabilizing effects of market forces were confined to the poor family.

MARKET EFFECTS AND EDUCATIONAL IDEALS

As noted, all social institutions depend for their effective functioning on the inputs from other institutions. The schools rely on well-functioning families to provide educable human capital in the form of students who are eager and willing to learn or at least who do not actively resist school officials and disrupt the learning of others. Employers rely on the schools to provide punctual, attentive, and literate workers. The polity relies on families and schools to produce citizens who will turn out to vote in sufficient numbers to maintain the legitimacy of existing political arrangements. Families rely on the economy for material resources, on the polity for a "social income" when adequate employment is unavailable, and on community institutions for charity when all else fails. Institutional dysfunctions in one area inevitably lead in domino fashion to weakened controls and supports in others. If market forces undermine the control and support functions of a particular institution, then the logic of institutional interdependence dictates that the consequences are ramified through the others. Thus anomic consumption pressures and the utilitarian logic of the marketplace are pervasive throughout the institutional order.

A commonsense view of the origins of crime and other social problems attributes great causal significance to the supposed breakdown of the family. To be sure, the size, structure, and functions of the family have been whittled down considerably over the past two centuries in Western societies. The material production functions of the family have been almost completely absorbed by a structurally differentiated economy, and other institutions have assumed some of the socialization and support functions that were once the exclusive prerogative of the family. The state seeks to maintain minimum health and welfare standards for children and disabled adults and provides retired workers with "social security." The functions of the school have been expanded well beyond the transmission of "academic" knowledge and skills to include training in basic "life skills," such as driving and developing healthy sexual relations. At the same time, however, the polity and the schools also must contend with the effects of market forces that erode their own capacity to carry out their traditional functions, much less assume new ones thrown off by the family. Consider the condition of the contemporary American school.

As with the family, education is a premarket institution both historically and in the role transitions characteristic of the modern life course. The school prepares students for the assumption of adult occupational roles and is the primary formal mechanism for status attainment in the modern world. In democratic societies the school also socializes the young for enlightened citizenship. Ideally, formal education is meant to socialize the young to cooperate with others in the pursuit of collective purposes, to exercise critical judgment, to respect wisdom, to appreciate beauty, and to value truth. The implicit but distinctively important message of education is that judgment, wisdom, beauty, and truth are values in and of themselves and not merely the means to achieve some other end. These values constitute inviolable institutional boundaries against encroachments from other realms. "No matter how much people are willing to pay," the philosopher Mark Sagoff has written, "three will never be the square root of six" (quoted in Kuttner, 1996, 49).

We have of course presented an ideal-typical view of educational values, as often as not honored in the breach or as embattled protest ideals rather than standards for daily living. Nonetheless, judgment, wisdom, beauty, and truth are what education, as opposed to mere training, stands for as an institution. They are the source of education's institutional sovereignty and legitimacy. To the degree that they are degraded, made to seem untenable and irrelevant, regarded as "revealed preferences" subject to negotiation, or treated merely as the means to realize other values, the intrinsic functions of education will suffer and the school's normative control over students will weaken. The resulting detachment from education was exquisitely expressed by a student who described her understanding of the intrinsic value of education this way: "School's important but so's money. Homework doesn't pay. Teachers say education is your payment, and that just makes me want to puke" (quoted in Messner and Rosenfeld, 2001, 70). This student had just increased her schedule at her two after-school jobs to thirty hours a week, which complicates the argument that her alienation from school was just a matter of low self-control.

Gottfredson and Hirschi (1990, 159–163) contend that sociologists have placed too much emphasis on the schools as a cause of crime and delinquency. Labeling and strain theories that blame ability grouping and other stratification devices for students' poor academic performance and weakened bonds to the school, they argue, essentially get the story backward. Students who show up to school with low self-control care little for what goes on in the classroom and cause trouble. If anything, the schools are made weak by having to contend with the products of poor parenting.

There is little question that education would improve if families provided the schools with more cooperative and compliant students. But that is not the whole story. In response to recalcitrant students and their own failures at normative control, American schools have strengthened the remaining forms of control available to them. They have increased both coercive and remunerative sanctions. Metal detectors, armed guards, and so-called zero tolerance policies are generally lamented as unfortunate but necessary to maintain order and discipline. However, offering students incentives to learn is applauded in some quarters as a positive development. An elementary school in Birmingham, Michigan, pays third-graders for doing homework and class work "with a bonus thrown in for good quality." The teacher explains the rationale for the program: "When I come to work, I get paid for it. We've really just likened it to the real world" (Walsh-Czarnecki, 2004). Paying students to learn may induce some of them to be attentive and work harder, but it is also likely to reinforce students' perception of learning itself as somehow "unreal," their tendency to work to rule, and the cynical and calculative orientation to education evidenced by the student quoted earlier. Because education is increasingly subject to market-based reforms—from monetary incentives to learn, to commercial television broadcasts now beamed to thousands of middle and high schools (http://channelonenetwork.com/about_us.html), to voucher plans that promise to make parents "active consumers in the educational marketplace" and drive out underperforming schools (http://www.schoolchoices.org/roo/vouchers.htm)—its distinctive institutional ideals and practices erode, and it becomes yet another training ground for the consumer role.

EMPIRICAL TESTS OF INSTITUTIONAL-ANOMIE THEORY

Institutional-anomie theory has not been subjected to extensive empirical investigation, but a growing number of studies lend support to some of its key arguments (see Messner and Rosenfeld, 2006; Pratt and Cullen, 2005). Self-control theory has received consistent support in the research literature in the form of significant associations between crime and various measures of self-control (Pratt and Cullen, 2000). However, the fact that other individual-level variables also predict crime when self-control variables are held constant raises questions about the empirical status of self-control theory, which holds that self-control is virtually the sole cause of criminal propensities. Research findings that show multiple causes of criminal propensities, therefore, technically disconfirm self-control theory. The evaluation criteria for institutional-anomie theory, by contrast, are not so onerous. The theory would be disconfirmed by evidence showing that rates of serious crime are unrelated or run counter to the theoretically expected configuration of cultural and institutional patterns. But institutional-anomie theory would not be disconfirmed if other characteristics of societies, groups, or individuals, including self-control, were also shown to predict serious crime. Self-control theory imposes much stronger assumptions on the data than does institutional-anomie theory, as would be expected from a perspective that explains "all crime, at all times, and, for that matter, many forms of behavior that are not sanctioned by the state" (Gottfredson and Hirschi, 1990, 117).

We noted earlier that institutional-anomie theory and self-control theory are directed toward different levels of explanation and thus speak different languages. Nevertheless we can envision a productive research agenda involving core insights from the two perspectives. Specifically, a multilevel research design would permit the assessment of the potential interconnections among institutional structures, individual self-control, and levels of offending. In such a research design the investigator would estimate multilevel models with data gathered on individuals and on nations or other macrosocial units in which the individuals are situated. Indicators of self-control and perhaps also child-rearing practices would be developed at the individual level. Indicators of culture and institutions would be formulated at the macro- or aggregate level in accordance with the specifications of institutional-anomie theory. Depending on whether the outcome of interest is criminal events or propensities, opportunity variables also could be specified at the aggregate level.

Self-control theory predicts that, with the exception of opportunity measures, any effects of the macrolevel indicators on levels of crime will disappear once the individual-level factor of low self-control is controlled. In technical terms the macrolevel correlation is a purely compositional effect. Aggregates have high levels of crime because they have relatively large numbers of people with low-self control. Such a finding would enhance the credibility of self-control theory as an individual-level explanation of crime. At the same time, if institutional structures foster low self-control in ways that are consistent with the logic of institutional-anomie theory, these findings would suggest that self-control theory can be enriched by an explicit and systematic consideration of the institutional context within which self-control is cultivated.

Another possibility is that the multilevel modeling might reveal that the macrosocial variables continue to have significant effects on the levels of crime with indicators of self-control controlled. This finding would imply that low-self control does not offer a complete explanation of offending and that insights from other individual-level theories are needed to develop a comprehensive explanation of variation in levels of crime. An additional intriguing possibility is that the strength of any self-control effects might vary according to institutional and cultural conditions.

The research agenda that we are proposing is not intended as a critical test for choosing between institutional-anomie theory and self-control theory. Indeed, framing the question in terms of whether self-control or institutional arrangements explain crime seems unproductive to us. A more fruitful approach is to ask how features of the institutional environment act in concert with individual propensities to account for the systematic patterning of crime across time and space. We invite Gottfredson and Hirschi and other self-control researchers to join us in conducting such an inquiry.

8 | ON THE COMPATIBILITY OF SOCIAL DISORGANIZATION AND SELF-CONTROL

Ross L. Matsueda

Ostensibly, social disorganization and self-control theories are compatible perspectives, merely operating at different levels of explanation—disorganization at the group or neighborhood level and self-control at the individual level. This apparent fact is reinforced by the compatibility of social disorganization and control theorists, who tend to affiliate, cite each other's work, and speak highly of each other. In this chapter I argue that the compatibility between theories of disorganization and self-control is more apparent than real. When classical theories of social disorganization are viewed in their totality and in historical context, they violate the crucial assumption of control theories—that the motivation to deviate is constant across individuals—which, according to Hirschi (1969) and Kornhauser (1978), separates control perspectives from all other sociological theories of crime. Indeed, early social disorganization theorists conducted qualitative studies, using naturalistic inquiry, direct observation, life history narratives, and ethnographies, to identify the roots of motivation for behavior, including criminal behavior. Those motivations were found to be rooted in concepts, such as the four wishes, moral codes of gangs, and cultural transmission, that violate the assumption of control theories. If, however, disorganization theories are shorn of their motivational component and the qualitative studies from which they derive—a strategy pursued by Kornhauser—the remaining concept of disorganization is more easily integrated with self-control theory.

In this chapter I describe self-control theory, quickly summarize the history of social disorganization theory, and then briefly evaluate Kornhauser's attempt to extract what she terms a "pure control" model from social disorganization theory. I then show that Kornhauser's pure control version of disorganization can be viewed as a macrolevel counterpart to self-control theory but that social disorganization theories, when taken in totality, are incompatible with self-control theory. Finally I evaluate some relevant bodies of research and speculate on ways of explaining the research findings.

FROM SOCIAL CONTROL TO SELF-CONTROL

In a career spanning more than thirty-five years, Travis Hirschi has been the leading proponent of control theories, although his theory changed in important ways when he teamed up with Michael R. Gottfredson.

Hirschi's Social Control Theory

In 1969 Hirschi published *Causes of Delinquency*, a remarkable monograph that developed a social control theory of crime at a time when the broader perspectives underlying the theory—social disorganization theory and Freudian theory—had fallen out of favor in sociology. The book not only developed social control theory, a theory that would dominate criminology for at least a decade, but also operationalized the theory and tested it empirically using original survey data and statistical methods of the period. *Causes* was a landmark study and helped to spawn a minor revolution in the study of crime, as criminologists increasingly collected survey data, used statistical methods of analysis, and subjected traditional theories of crime—including most notably, social control theory—to empirical tests.

The hallmark of control theories, as articulated by Hirschi (1969), is the assumption that the motivation for crime is constant across individuals and therefore not a cause of crime. This assumption, which derives from the assumption of value consensus—"a single moral order"—separates control theories from all others. The assumption has a number of controversial implications or corollaries: Crime is not learned but is natural; criminal peers are not a cause of crime; subcultural theories, which specify subcultural motives for crime, are empirically bankrupt; criminologists need not study the cause of crime but rather the cause of conformity; and theories that posit special or unusual motivations for crime are suspect. Hirschi (1969) was agnostic about the precise justification of natural motivation; it could just as easily have been due to Hobbes's animal impulses, the Freudian id, Briar and Piliavin's (1965) situationally induced motives, or Matza's (1964) "drift" followed by "will" and "desperation." The important point is that crime, and its motivation, is taken for granted; what is problematic—to be explained—is conformity. For Hirschi (1969) conformity is explained by strong bonds to conventional society, and these bonds consist of four additive variables: attachment to parents, commitment to conventional lines of action, involvement in conventional activities, and belief in the moral order. Delinquency results when a person's bond is broken or weakened. Hirschi (1969) found empirical support for his theory (his measures of attachment, commitment, and belief had strong effects on self-reported delinquency), although one finding contradicted the theory (delinquent peers exerted the strongest effect on delinquency, even controlling for social bonds) and supported subcultural, learning, and differential association theories. *Causes* became a classic in criminology.

Twenty years after the publication of *Causes*, Hirschi teamed up with Gottfredson to specify a new version of control theory. They maintained allegiance to the control perspective, as articulated in *A General Theory of Crime*. Again, the motivation for crime was assumed constant across individuals, but now a different mechanism justified the assumption. Gottfredson and Hirschi argued that the most efficient way of satisfying needs is through deviant or illegal behavior; therefore, if left to our own devices, we would all opt for such means. Merton (1957) argued an almost identical point earlier: Often, the most effective means to attain an individual goal entails the use of force or fraud, and hence institutional norms function to curtail such acts to ensure an orderly society. Moreover, the pleasures associated with crime, Gottfredson and Hirschi maintain, are obvious to all and require no special learning.

Self-Control Theory

Gottfredson and Hirschi (1990) begin with three empirical assertions: (1) The age-crime curve is invariant across all social groups, societies, and historical periods and therefore is beyond explanation by social theories; (2) criminals do not specialize in offenses but are versatile in their offending (and also engage in similar acts that are legal, such as having accidents, smoking, drinking, having premarital and extramarital sex, and gambling); and (3) crime is remarkably stable throughout the life course. They assert that most criminological theories imply that the age effect can be explained socially, that criminals tend to specialize, and that crime is unstable over time. Thus a new theory is needed to account for these facts.

Gottfredson and Hirschi (1990) define crime as acts of force or fraud committed for self-interested gain. They then examine the distribution of the dependent variable, street crimes (and embezzlement), and argue that for each offense we can focus on the statistical modal category and safely ignore the variation around the mode. Finding a common thread in the modal burglary, robbery, larceny, homicide, motor vehicle theft, rape, and drug and alcohol consumption, they go on to infer a link with criminality. Criminal acts provide easy gratification, are exciting and risky, provide meager long-term benefits, require little skill or planning, and involve pain or discomfort for the victim. Therefore criminals tend to be impulsive and unable to delay gratification; they seek excitement and risk, tend to have unstable jobs, friendships, and marriages, have little academic or manual skill, and are indifferent to the suffering of others.

From the versatility of offending Gottfredson and Hirschi conclude that the common characteristics of criminal acts reflect a latent trait that they term low self-control. From the stability in offending over time they conclude that low self-control is a trait that remains stable throughout the life course. From the age distribution of crime they conclude that low self-control increases the probability of crime but does not require it and that age and other factors also affect the likelihood of crime. Those other factors fall under the rubric of criminal events. If criminality is the stable trait underlying a variety of offenses over time, then criminal events (crime) refer to the elements of the immediate situation of offending that affects the likelihood of crime. This includes the objective opportunity for crime—including the presence of suitable targets and the absence of capable guardians (to use the terms of routine activities theory)—the physical ability to commit the crime, including age, and the immediate costs and benefits associated with the crime.

But where does self-control come from? Gottfredson and Hirschi (1990) are explicit about this: Self-control develops early in life (before the age of culpability) through socialization by parents. Parents who consistently identify undesirable behavior in their children and sanction that behavior informally—by frowning, shaming, disapproving—will inculcate high self-control in their children. Parents who fail to monitor their children or who fail to identify and sanction undesirable behavior will raise children with low self-control. By adolescence the trait of self-control has been set; it becomes a stable trait that will last a lifetime. Individuals low on self-control will always have low self-control and will always be at risk of crime and of other crimelike behaviors, such as smoking, drinking, gambling, lying, and engaging in premarital and extramarital sex. At this point nothing can alter the trait of low self-control; it is set in stone. People cannot change. It follows that conventional institutions—such as religion, education, and the labor market—are unable to alter low self-control and therefore will have no affect on a person's criminality beyond childhood.

Here Gottfredson and Hirschi (1990) make another strong assertion: Life course transitions, including education, entrance into a delinquent gang, marriage, divorce, and work, all have no causal effect on crime. Any correlation with crime is spurious because of selectivity. Delinquent peers and gangs are correlated with crime because individuals with low self-control commit crimes and select into delinquent peer groups; good marriages are negatively correlated with crime because individuals with high self-control refrain from crime and select into good marriages; good jobs are inversely correlated with crime because individuals with high self-control refrain from crime and select into good jobs.

But how do the two concepts, self-control and criminal events, produce crime? Gottfredson and Hirschi (1990) appear to discuss these effects as additive, with the relative magnitude of the components varying with the type of crime. Crimes that are more eventlike—that is, have more complex opportunity structures, such as burglary and robbery—will have a stronger component for criminal events, whereas crimes for which opportunity is ubiquitous, such as petty theft, will be dominated by low self-control. For this reason Gottfredson and Hirschi recommend using minor delinquent acts as a measure of self-control. But in their analysis of the structure of specific crimes, in which they reveal the relationship between self-control and criminal opportunities, they appear to suggest a complex set of relationships, including an interaction effect. Individuals low on self-control will be particularly vulnerable to crime when opportunities are plentiful and less so when opportunities are few. In contrast, individuals high on self-control will resist temptation even in the face of plentiful opportunities. Moreover, logically, self-control should be causally related to criminal events: Individuals low on self-control may self-select into criminal opportunities (e.g., staging areas for gang fights) or be selected by other individuals, groups, or institutions (e.g., schools segregating students with low self-control into a single classroom).

Finally, social structure or organization affects crime in two ways. First, it indirectly affects low self-control by affecting parents' ability to identify and discourage undesirable behaviors. For example, in close-knit neighborhoods with high social capital, parents assist other parents in supervising children. Such effects can transmit low self-control across generations, because impoverished neighborhoods impede parents' child-rearing practices, creating children with low self-control, whose reduced life chances impede their ability to raise their own children. Second, social structure directly affects criminal events by providing incentives and structuring criminal opportunities through its effects on routine activities of victims and offenders. This provides an avenue that links self-control theory to theories of social disorganization.

THE ROOTS OF SOCIAL DISORGANIZATION THEORY

It is instructive to review the history of the concept of social disorganization before assessing its compatibility with the general theory. I provide a brief synopsis here; for a more detailed presentation see Matsueda (2007). The concept of social disorganization can be traced to W. I. Thomas and Znaniecki (1958 [1927]), who define it as "a decrease of the influence of existing social rules of behavior upon the individual members of the group" and note that it refers "primarily to institutions and only secondarily to men" (p. 1128). Social disorganization is only loosely connected to "individual disorganization, which consists in a decrease of the individual's ability to organize his whole life for the efficient, progressive, and continuous realization of his fundamental interests" (p. 1128).

Social organization, then, consists of norms that govern the behavior of members of the group, and it is undermined by the introduction of new attitudes that give rise to new behaviors that are neither socially recognized nor socially sanctioned. If left unchecked, those behaviors, and the attitudes underlying them, produce social disorganization. But disorganization is not inevitable; social reorganization can create "new rules of personal conduct and new institutions" that correspond more closely to the new attitudes (W. I. Thomas and Znaniecki (1958 [1927], 1128). The new rules increase cohesion, cooperation, and organization. Thus societies are in constant flux, always undergoing some degree of disorganization, reconstruction, and organization.

But Thomas and Znaniecki were not merely attempting to explain macrolevel social change; they were also seeking a theory of motivation, social control, and the interplay between the individual and society. They posited the four wishes, which Thomas (1923, p. 4) later refined: the desire for new experience, security, response, and recognition. The problem of social control, for Thomas, is precisely how social institutions regulate the different means of fulfilling wishes. This is done through the definition of the situation: deliberating and examining a situation as calling for certain kinds of behavior. What is important is not the objective situation but rather the perceived definition of the situation: "If men define situations as real they are real in their consequences" (W. I. Thomas and Thomas, 1928). For Thomas (1923), "gradually a whole life-policy and the personality of the individual himself follow from a series of such definitions" (p. 42).

The organized society regulates conflict and competition by definitions of situations, which define a moral code—a "set of rules or behavior norms"—and compete with individual definitions of situations (Thomas, 1923, 43). Culture conflict is involved here: "One set of opinions would be rigoristic and hold that conformity with the existing code is advisable under all circumstances; another pragmatic, holding that the code may sometimes be violated" (p. 79). Thomas and Znaniecki used personal documents—life histories, diaries, and letters—to document the ways in which Polish peasants, underaged prostitutes, and wayward girls fulfilled their wishes using definitions of situations that sometimes conflicted with conventional definitions.

Park and Burgess showed how social disorganization was distributed spatially within urban areas. Park (1926) drew concepts of competition, dominance, invasion, segregation, and succession from plant biology to explain growth of cities. Influenced by Darwin's concept of the "struggle for survival," Park argued that competition among groups was the motor that led to segregation of areas into natural areas, which resulted from market forces rather than from conscious planning. At times, disequilibrium occurred, such as when groups invaded neighborhoods, inducing competition and possibly resulting in succession or accommodation.

Within this framework Ernest W. Burgess (1925b) developed his theory of residential patterns, in which the city was divided into a series of concentric zones. The inner zone, the central business district, has the highest land use values and is surrounded by the zone in transition, or "interstitial area," in which residential neighborhoods are under invasion from business and manufacturing. Encircling the interstitial area are three increasingly affluent residential zones. For Burgess urban growth occurs when industry invades contiguous residential areas, which become deteriorated and dilapidated. Rents and housing prices drop as stockyards, railroads, and factories are built. Those residents with sufficient resources flee the area, moving to the working man's zone, which in turn may result in more affluent working men migrating out to residential areas, and so on, creating a ripple effect until equilibrium returns. The ripple effect of geographic mobility creates a gradient in which socioeconomic status increases with increasing distance from the center of the city.

The zone in transition provides a residential neighborhood for newly arriving impoverished immigrant groups and a mechanism by which older immigrant groups are able to increase their affluence and move to better neighborhoods. The resulting population turnover, however, undermines incentives for residents to develop local community ties, commitments, and a sense of community. Consequently, "cultural controls over conduct disintegrate; impulses and wishes take random and wild expression"; and the "result is immorality and delinquency; in short, personal and social disorganization" (E. W. Burgess, 1925a, 150). This model set the stage for studies using natural histories and personal documents to examine how residents accommodated to their spatial situations.

Thrasher's (1927) landmark study of 1,313 gangs in Chicago was framed by Park and Burgess's human ecology approach. Using direct observation, interviews, and personal documents, Thrasher (1927) argued that gangs are rooted in the failure of local institutions to direct boys. Most gangs begin as spontaneous playgroups and develop an organization through conflict with the wider society, eliciting a group consciousness, leadership, rules, and an awareness of group history. The gang is an "interstitial group, a manifestation of the period of readjustment between childhood and maturity" (p. 492). Because of endemic conflict and competition, gangs tend to be unstable, adopting different forms ranging from diffuse, solidified, conventionalized, criminal, and secret society.

Thrasher uses Thomas's concept of "the wish for new experience" to show how society's inability to channel the energy of adolescent boys in socially desirable ways results in the boys being attracted to the gang, which provides a forum for spontaneous expression of natural impulses. He uses Thomas's concept of "the definition of the situation" to analyze social patterns, leadership, and control in the gang. Such patterns derive from the disorganized neighborhood, resulting in isolation from conventional cultural patterns and development of patterns within the gang's own social world. More established gangs, often with older members, constitute a key part of the "moral region" and often get younger boys involved in stealing, robbing, and other delinquent acts. This is the "education of the street," which forms "tastes and habits, ambitions and ideals" as well as a "universe of discourse," consisting of a gang language or argot, symbols, and signs (Thrasher, 1927, 265–267). This learning entails not only learning skills for crime (e.g., buying guns, picking pockets, or fencing stolen goods), which can be as elaborate as "the gang is capable of deliberation, planning, and cooperation in a highly complex undertaking" (p. 284), but also definitions of situations calling for crime: "The gang boy sees lawlessness everywhere and in the absence of effective definitions to the contrary accepts it without criticism" (Thrasher, 1927, 260).

Thrasher gives a nuanced analysis of social control in the gang, which begins with the unity of the gang developed from consensus over "habits, sentiments, and attitudes," an "*esprit de corps*," and solidifies through conflict with external groups. Group control is further achieved through use of a code of conduct for gang members, which if violated, is met with severe sanction. A rudimentary organization emerges around a natural leader, an "inner circle" of intimates surrounding the leader, and fringe groups of hangers-on. Moreover, demoralization develops through a "series of stages," beginning with "playing hookey"—which can lead to a few days in a juvenile detention home and which gives "great prestige with other boys"—followed by entrance in a gang, minor delinquent acts, occasional crime, and, "if nothing intervenes," development into "a seasoned gangster or professional criminal" (Thrasher, 1927, 369). Thrasher (1927, 381, 393) concludes that gangs are an important causal factor in crime and can lead to participation in organized crime, which he describes as having a hierarchical organization.

At about this time Shaw and McKay began their studies of delinquency, mapping official juvenile court rates by neighborhood and also collecting voluminous case studies, life histories, and personal documents. In *Delinquency Areas* Shaw et al. (1929) begin by outlining a "cultural approach to the study of delinquency," drawing on Chicago school concepts, describing Burgess's concentric zones, and mapping rates of delinquency and crime over time. They conclude that rates of truancy, delinquency, recidivism, and adult crime covary spatially, tend to be highest in the center of the city, and vary inversely with distance from the center. Their "tentative interpretation" was that city growth—whereby business and industry invade residential communities—leads to disorganization, which is intensified by the influx of immigrant groups, whose "old cultural and social controls break down." As a result, "delinquent and criminal patterns arise and are transmitted socially just as any other cultural and social pattern is transmitted" and in time "may become dominant" (Shaw et al., 1929, 205–206).

In a later report Shaw and McKay (1931) examine demographic characteristics of neighborhoods, analyze case studies, personal documents, and life histories, and extend their quantitative analyses to other cities. They begin with an extensive case study to illustrate culture conflict, in which a boy's behavior is "in conformity with the socially approved standards of the play group and neighborhood" but is a "violation of the family tradition and expectations," and therefore it is through "conflict of values, attitudes, and interests that the boy's temper tantrums, stubbornness, and open defiance of authority occurred" (Shaw and

McKay, 1931, 19–20). They then present in great detail their statistical analyses, finding that delinquency rates are highest in the zone in transition, which is characterized by "physical deterioration, decreasing population, high rates of dependency, high percentages of foreign and negro population in the total population, and high rates of adult crime" (p. 386). They also find that, despite the complete turnover of the racial and nationality composition of the area, the delinquency rate remained high. Moreover, as older immigrant families moved to the periphery, the delinquency rates of their children decreased. Shaw and McKay (1931) conclude that high delinquency areas are associated with city growth, in which industry invades residential areas, causing out-migration of less impoverished groups, drops in housing values and rent of vacated dwellings, and in-migration of impoverished immigrant groups. The result is that the community "fails as an agency of social control" (p. 387).

Shaw and McKay also studied the group nature of delinquency, finding high rates of copresence of older offenders with younger delinquents in areas of high delinquency (a correlation of 0.90). Moreover, they conducted a remarkable analysis of interlocking playgroups and delinquent gangs using official records. From these analyses Shaw and McKay (1931) conclude that "the groups serve as an agency for the transmission of the traditions of delinquency in high rate areas of the city" (p. 390).

To identify the mechanisms by which delinquency rates remain stable in inner-city neighborhoods despite turnover of their ethnic composition, Shaw and McKay (1931) analyze life histories and personal documents, presenting representative cases for illustration (p. 116). They identify two mechanisms: social disorganization, in which "the dissolution of the neighborhood organization is accompanied by a breakdown of the restraints and safeguards which normally surround the child" (p. 117), and cultural transmission, in which "various forms of lawlessness have become more or less traditional aspects of the social life and are handed down year after year through the medium of social contacts" (p. 126). Here they show that "crime among the older offenders is often highly organized" and that "these older offenders, who are well known and have prestige in the neighborhood, tend to set the standards and patterns of behavior for the younger boys, who idolize and simulate them" (p. 127). Delinquent behavior "in many instances" is "encouraged by parents" and siblings, so that in some cases "criminal patterns of behavior are transmitted through personal contacts within the family group" (pp. 127–135).

Finally, Shaw and McKay (1931) examine the process of "acquiring the delinquent code," noting that the standards of the group "may represent a complete reversal of the standards and norms of conventional society," so that conduct that would bring "dishonor in a conventional group, serve to enhance and elevate the personal prestige and status of a member of the delinquent group" (pp. 240–241). Echoing Thrasher, they argue that the delinquent group, "like all social groups," controls the behavior of its members with a code of conduct, eliciting punishment for violators and rewards for conformists. The function of the code is documented repeatedly in their case histories.

Drawing on Thomas's four wishes, Shaw and McKay (1931) show how the delinquent group, like other groups, satisfies universal desires of recognition, esteem of fellows, excitement and thrills, companionship, and security. The difference is in the "cultural traditions and social values" (p. 250). The delinquent group provides stimulation and thrills in illicit activities, security and protection from the police, and feelings of pride and superiority. Shaw and McKay (1931) conclude carefully that, although their data cannot "determine the extent to which membership in delinquent gangs produces delinquency," membership is probably "a contributing factor" to delinquency, given that often "the delinquent group marks the beginning of his career in delinquency and that his initial delinquencies are often identical with the traditions and practices of his group" (p. 256). Their cautious conclusion reflects a concern with selectivity into the gang. Although Shaw and McKay find little evidence that broken homes affect delinquency, their life histories suggest that "emotional tensions and conflicts within the family may be significant for delinquent behavior," especially "personality problems and offenses against the home" (p. 343).

In their final volume Shaw and McKay (1942) provide a more nuanced explication of social disorganization and cultural transmission. They use the term "differential social organization" to underscore how delinquency rates are the result of broader economic and demographic forces that undermine conventional local institutions of control, which allows divergent values (often from immigrants) a foothold, which in turn spawns a tradition of organized delinquency transmitted through interlocking peer groups on the street (as well as within families). Here, the crucial institution of the family is weakened by competition from peer groups, which undermines parental influence; new problems, such as delays in entering the labor force or more leisure time; and a family member or friend earning money illegally, which neutralizes the family's opposition to crime. Because of the divergent values present in the neighborhood, resulting in part from immigration and geographic mobility, the community is unable to identify problems of common interest, reach a consensus on how to address the problem, and carry out a collective solution. The result is differential social organization, in which the dominant system of values is conventional but in which a "powerful competing system of delinquency values exists" in some communities (Shaw and McKay, 1942, 317). In this context a delinquent tradition—consisting of "conduct, speech, gesture, and attitudes"— arises and is passed on through "intimate association with predatory gangs or other forms of delinquent and criminal organization" (p. 316). With respect to group delinquency, the delinquent is not disorganized but rather, "within the limits of his social world and in terms of its norms and expectations, he may be a highly organized and well-adjusted person" (p. 316).

A PURE CONTROL VERSION OF SOCIAL DISORGANIZATION

Social disorganization theory fell out of favor in the 1950s and 1960s, in part because it became associated with theories of social pathology, which were criticized for blaming the victim, and in part because the findings and concepts were subsumed under theories of differential association and differential opportunity. The theory, however, made a comeback in part because of the publication of Ruth Kornhauser's (1978) *Social Sources of Delinquency*, a brilliant essay in which she analyzes the assumptions of criminological theories, creates a typology within which to categorize the theories, and concludes that a "pure" control theory is logically and empirically superior to the others. Elsewhere, I have critiqued Kornhauser's (1978) interpretation of social disorganization theories (Matsueda, 2007); here, I briefly summarize those arguments.

To understand Kornhauser's treatment of social disorganization theories, we need to understand her typology of theories. For present purposes the relevant contrast is between what she terms "cultural deviance" theories and "pure control" theories. Earlier, I argued that her portrait of cultural deviance theories, of which Sutherland's (1947) differential association is the "pure" form, is a "caricature" of differential association theory (see Matsueda, 1988; see also Akers, 1996). Such theories, Kornhauser maintains, assume that human beings are entirely plastic, having no human nature, and that crime is entirely relative. They assume no consensus in society and therefore portray society as a set of warring subcultures; therefore, she argues, laws cannot reflect consensus but must reflect the subcultural values of the powerful. Furthermore, cultural deviance theories assume that socialization to subcultures is always perfect (not variable), that all subcultures (and conventional culture) are equally strong, and therefore that crime is solely the result of differences in the *content*, not *strength*, of competing subcultural norms. Because behaviors are always perfect expressions of subcultural values, there can be no deviant *behavior*, only deviant *cultures*. Hence the term *cultural deviance theory* (Matsueda, 1988, 290–291). Finally, because *subcultural* differentiation perfectly mirrors *structural* differentiation and because behavior is a perfect reflection of subcultural values, Kornhauser concludes that subculture is indistinguishable from social structure, which is a structure of values that perfectly mirror behavior. Because structure and culture do not vary, they are constants—present everywhere and therefore nowhere—and consequently are incapable of explaining behavior.

Kornhauser (1978) has created a caricature of theories of differential association and cultural transmission. In fact, processes of cultural transmission and differential association allow for variation in the strength of competing norms, acknowledge that conventional culture is generally stronger than any given subculture, and distinguish social structure from culture (see Matsueda, 1988, 2007). Indeed, the concept of differential social organization suggests that delinquency rates are high in areas where youth are relatively isolated from the controls of conventional institutions, which, in the context of conflicting values (also generated by weak conventional institutions), may lead to a tradition of delinquency (including availability of delinquent techniques, attitudes, and values). Thus delinquency is the result of the strength of contacts with the two kinds of values or behavior patterns (e.g., Shaw and McKay, 1942, 317–318).

Kornhauser (1978) rejects her straw man theory of cultural deviance and embraces a version of social disorganization as an alternative, in part because of the empirical and theoretical work of Hirschi (1969) in *Causes* (Hirschi, 1996). But the preeminent disorganization theorists of delinquency, Shaw and McKay as well as Thrasher, had emphasized the role of gang codes, delinquent attitudes, and cultural transmission, which Kornhauser categorizes under the rejected cultural deviance theory. To reconcile this contradiction, she extracts what she terms "a pure control theory" from the work of Thrasher and Shaw and McKay, which she argues is superior to cultural deviance theory. With respect to Thrasher, she emphasizes the role of community disorganization and conflict with the community in explaining the origin and persistence of the gang but discounts the role of gang moral codes in motivating delinquency. Rather than a casual mechanism, the gang provides group processes that reinforce what has already been caused by weak controls.

With respect to Shaw and McKay, Kornhauser identifies the macroprocesses of urban growth that give rise to social disorganization in inner cities, which in turn lead to loss of social control over youth. Such loss of control, she maintains, leads directly to delinquency, according to her pure control model. She rejects the role of cultural transmission, interlocking peer groups, and the learning of delinquent techniques and attitudes, because for her they fall under the rubric of cultural deviance theory. She concludes that the slum contains not only disorganized structure but disorganized culture as well (which is too weak to account for delinquency), and therefore we can dispense with the contradictory process of cultural transmission. Youth with weak controls "become delinquent *with or without* the influence of delinquent companions," but delinquent groups "explain additional variance in delinquency because of collective behavior processes and primary group processes that reinforce preexisting tendencies" (Kornhauser, 1978, 69).

Kornhauser's interpretation and transformation of Shaw and McKay's theory suffers from use of her cultural deviance type to characterize the process of cultural transmission. A delinquent tradition may exist on the street, but it need not be an autonomous subculture perfectly socializing its members in delinquent gangs organized solely for the purpose of crime. Rather than being autonomous subcultures, delinquent traditions are often interwoven in the very strands of conventional culture, for example, as situational exceptions to norms (Matsueda, 2007). To reject the role of criminal values, prestige hierarchies, and group control, Kornhauser must reject the voluminous qualitative data of Thrasher and Shaw and McKay that document these processes. Kornhauser (1978) concludes that "their own case-history data, and other data, do not provide convincing evidence of the existence of delinquent values" (p. 70). But rather than providing her own case history data to demonstrate that delinquent values are irrelevant, Kornhauser merely reinterprets the evidence they present. Kornhauser's arguments are strongest when they *explain* delinquency using Shaw and McKay's explanatory concepts and weakest when they try to *explain away* their theoretical mechanisms (cultural transmission) and the empirical findings on which they are based.

Thus a more convincing assessment of Shaw and McKay would not suggest that they misinterpreted their data or failed to realize that they combined incompatible models of delinquency. Rather, it would instead embrace their empirical research and theoretical interpretations by assessing cultural deviance theory as a caricature of cultural transmission, differential social organization, and differential association.

Kornhauser's (1978) interpretation of social disorganization theory has had an enduring effect on the subsequent treatment of the theory, perhaps reinvigorating research on the "pure control theory" aspects of the theory. An influential paper by Sampson and Groves (1989), which cited Kornhauser's (1978) writings on disorganization and cultural deviance, found empirical support for the causal structure of demographic characteristics of high-delinquency areas and the intervening mechanisms of loss of control and formation of spontaneous peer groups. Before that, Bursik and Webb (1982) and Heitgerd and Bursik (1987) had tied disorganization to the systemic approach to urban ecology and, using previously unanalyzed data from Shaw and McKay, had found support for the general theoretical approach, with some extensions.

The most ambitious and important advance on social disorganization theory is Sampson and colleagues' specification of "collective efficacy" as a mechanism of social disorganization. Collective efficacy is a neighborhood-level concept defined as "willingness of local residents to intervene for the common good," which is largely dependent on "conditions of mutual trust and solidarity among neighbors" (Sampson et al., 1997, 919). It is a collective counterpart to self-efficacy, and like self-efficacy is "relative to specific tasks such as maintaining public order" (Sampson, 2004, 108). Moreover, Sampson et al. (1999) link collective efficacy to the concept of social capital, arguing that intergenerational closure (ties between the parents of different children in the neighborhood) and reciprocated exchange (exchange of advice, favors, goods among neighbors) provides the "resource potential of personal and organizational networks" for children, which is realized in collective efficacy. They further link collective efficacy and social capital to the spatial structure of neighborhoods. Here they find that that high collective efficacy in one neighborhood can spill over and provide advantages in social control of a contiguous neighborhood (particularly for predominantly white neighborhoods). Conversely, low collective efficacy can disadvantage contiguous neighborhoods (particularly for predominantly black neighborhoods). In general, Sampson et al. (1999) find support for their theory, which integrates social disorganization and social capital: Neighborhood ties are associated with greater collective efficacy, which in turn is associated with lower rates of violence.

PURE CONTROL VERSION OF SOCIAL DISORGANIZATION AS A MACROLEVEL COUNTERPART TO LOW SELF-CONTROL

Having discussed the early classical work on social disorganization theory, we are in position to discuss its compatibility with Gottfredson and Hirschi's (1990) self-control theory. I first discuss the compatibility of self-control theory with Kornhauser's pure control version of social disorganization theory and then discuss the compatibility with the original formulation of the social disorganization perspective.

If we assume, as does Kornhauser, that crime is not learned or transmitted across individuals, that the motivation for crime is constant across individuals, that values or definitions of situations conducive to crime are impotent or nonexistent, and that peer networks affect crime only by increasing criminal opportunities, then the macrolevel concept of social disorganization can be shown to be compatible with the microlevel mechanisms of self-control theory. Indeed, Gottfredson and Hirschi (1990, 82) speak approvingly of this version of social disorganization.

But even if we grant consistency in assumptions, it remains to be seen whether the causal mechanisms presented in the two perspectives are compatible. The key is the link between the family and delinquency and the link between family and community. After noting that the family is the most important factor in developing attitudes and personality, Shaw and McKay (1931) state eloquently the important role of the family in delinquency:

> During the more plastic and impressionable years of his life, the child's vital contacts with other persons are largely limited to the members of his own family group. This group situation, with its different personalities and with its complex attitudes, relationships, and

social values, is not a matter of the child's own choosing; it is part of the order of things into which he is born and to which he must make some kind of adjustment. It exists prior to him, has certain expectations with reference to him, and seeks to regulate and control his activities according to its preexisting standards, values, and ideals. The family as an institution serves both as an agency for the transmission of cultural heritages and for the development of the attitudes and personality of the child. (p. 261)

Shaw and McKay (1931, 292–343) present two case studies showing that tension and conflict in the home are related to delinquency, conclusions consistent with Gottfredson and Hirschi. In an interview with a delinquent's father, they find that the father was isolated in childhood, never learned to participate in social groups, and was self-centered, critical of others, resistant to advice, and argumentative. From a second case study they conclude that "there is little question but that their failure to develop a stable life organization was due in part to the constant discord between the parents and the absence of consistent parental discipline and control" (p. 342). Such family processes have been supported by subsequent empirical evidence (Loeber and Stouthamer-Loeber, 1986).

Recall that for Gottfredson and Hirschi (1990), the source of high self-control—the stable individual trait that restrains individuals from crime throughout the life course—is early child socialization, in which they suggest that the "minimum conditions" are the following: "In order to teach the child self-control, someone must (1) monitor the child's behavior; (2) recognize deviant behavior when it occurs; and (3) punish such behavior" (p. 97). Caring parents who invest in their child in this way produce a child capable of delaying gratification, being sensitive to the interests of others, and being willing to accept restraints on behavior (p. 97). Unlike Shaw and McKay, Gottfredson and Hirschi (1990) rule out the possibility that parents can transmit delinquency to their children because "parents do not prefer their children to be unsocialized in the terms described" (p. 98). Punishment, they argue, "usually entails nothing more than explicit disapproval of unwanted behavior," and "rewarding good behavior cannot compensate for failure to correct deviant behavior" (p. 100).

Given that this form of informal sanctioning by parents is the key cause of all crimes, it is disappointing that Gottfredson and Hirschi do not provide us with more details about how this process works, except to say that punishment can be too lenient or too harsh. But parenting entails more than merely identifying and disapproving of unwanted behavior in a rigid or mechanistic way. In a complex society moral reasoning often requires making nuanced and difficult moral judgments. For example, Baumrind (1991) has developed a typology of more complex parenting styles, including the following: (1) Authoritative parenting is characterized by warmth, use of rules and inductive reasoning, consistency of words and actions, and use of nonphysical punishment; (2) authoritarian parenting is characterized by coldness, rigid adherence to rules, use of physical punishment, and power differentials; (3) permissive parenting lacks consistency, entails a lack of monitoring and permissiveness, and approximates a peer relationship rather than an authority relationship. The permissive parenting style can be decomposed into indulgent versus neglectful parenting (Maccoby and Martin, 1983). Baumrind suggests that authoritative child rearing leads to well-adjusted children, a prediction supported by research. For example, Lamborn et al. (1991) found that children with authoritative parents were better adjusted and had fewer behavior problems than other children; children with indulgent parents had high self-confidence but had substance and behavioral problems in school; and children with authoritarian parents were obedient but had low self-confidence. Thus a more nuanced theory of child rearing may help refine the mechanism by which children adjust to life exigencies.

But how are families linked to communities, and more generally, how is low self-control linked to the dynamics of urban growth and social disorganization, which leaves a spatial gradient of delinquency rates centered in the zone in transition? Given that delinquency rates are highest in the inner city and, according to Gottfredson and Hirschi, that delinquency is highly correlated with low self-control, it follows that the inner city must have high rates of individuals with low self-control. How did this happen? I can think of two overlapping mechanisms, one entailing social causation and the other, social selection.

First the causal mechanism. High rates of in-migration of immigrants and disadvantaged families coupled with out-migration of families with resources to move to more desirable neighborhoods leave the inner city with high rates of poverty, deterioration, residential instability, and ultimately social disorganization. With weak and unlinked institutions, residents are unable to achieve consensus, solve common local problems, and achieve shared values—in short, positive organization, or collective efficacy, is missing in the neighborhood. Property values remain low, the base for property taxes remains low, and poverty remains high. Low family income impedes families' ability to rear their children. To make ends meet, parents likely work longer hours, late shifts, and two jobs. Difficult work schedules, frequent layoffs, and the complications of being unable to pay bills on time induce stress and tension in the family. Such processes undermine child rearing, the formation of warm attachments to children, the ability to monitor the child's undesirable behavior, and the capacity to sanction that behavior using authoritative, rather than authoritarian, styles of parenting.

Such handicaps may be further compounded by the context of disorganized neighborhoods. High rates of transience, immigration, and ethnic heterogeneity undermine formation of social relationships and hence community social capital. For James S. Coleman (1990) lack of closure in social relationships can directly undermine social capital and thus the monitoring and socialization of children. For example, in organized, well-functioning neighborhoods the parents of children who form friendships form their own social ties; therefore, when a child misbehaves, not only the child's parents but also the parents of the child's friends have the capacity to identify the unwanted behavior. This process gives rise to a multiplier effect for monitoring in the neighborhood. This is a neighborhood with high collective efficacy. Sampson et al. (1999) find intergenerational closure (structural ties between parents and children) and child-centered social control strongly interrelated. They also find each to be undercut by high rates of neighborhood residential instability, concentrated immigration, and concentrated disadvantage—the structural processes associated with social disorganization. Thus, social disorganization, which is a product of neighborhood structure, produces high crime rates, and the mechanism is low collective efficacy. As Shaw and McKay emphasized, in examining family functioning and child rearing, it is important to examine how families are embedded in communities.

The second mechanism by which spatial location in disorganized neighborhoods is associated with high rates of low self-control is one of selection. This is partly a process of self-selection but mainly a process of selection by other groups, organizations, and institutions (Gottfredson and Hirschi, 1990, 159–168). As Gottfredson and Hirschi argue, individuals low on self-control suffer from impulsivity, indifference to the suffering of others, inability to delay gratification, attraction to risk, and lack of manual and academic skills, and consequently they will have difficulty sitting still in school, doing their homework, and learning the material. Their lack of human capital will hamper their labor market chances, as will their inability to meet deadlines, show up for work on time, and get along with co-workers. If they do get a job, they will have difficulty keeping it. Their negative traits will also interfere with personal friendships and handicap them in the marriage market. They are less likely to attract a quality spouse and are more likely to have marriages that are rife with conflict and end in divorce. Caspi et al. (1987) provide evidence of such selection: Early child temper tantrums can lead to later problems in life, including downward occupational mobility, erratic work lives, and divorce. They posit two distinct selection mechanisms. First is cumulative continuity, whereby the maladaptive behavior selects for negative environments (dropping out of school, getting fired from a job, divorce) that perpetuate the behavior. Second is interactional continuity, in which negative reciprocal interactions with others (acting out in class, fighting with classmates, arguing with a spouse) sustain the maladaptive behavior.

Such selectivity leaves the person with low self-control relatively isolated and without resources, which leads to secondary selection effects. Lacking resources, they are ill-equipped to compete in the housing market and are relegated to precisely those low-rent, high-crime, disorganized neighborhoods studied by Shaw and McKay. Given their own lack of self-control and their lack of resources, they will have difficulty inculcating self-control in their children. Surrounded by other families who are, on average, low on self-control, they cannot benefit from community social capital. But even if they were surrounded by capable parents, their own deficits in social skills and ability to develop trust would make it difficult. The result is children low on self-control and high on crime, which creates at the aggregate level high rates of delinquency in inner-city neighborhoods across generations. Conversely, parents high on self-control will enjoy good jobs and marriages, have resources to afford to live in affluent neighborhoods with high average self-control, create flexible work schedules (or have a spouse stay at home), and benefit from community social capital—all of which allows them to use authoritative parenting and build high self-control in their children.

But can this explain Shaw and McKay's findings about race, nativity, and immigration? Recall that they found, first, that rates of delinquency in interstitial areas remained high despite a complete turnover of ethnic and immigrant groups and, second, that the delinquency rates of children of immigrant groups declined as they moved up the socioeconomic ladder and out to the city's periphery. It is possible that selection plays a role here: Many immigrants may be motivated to leave their country of origin because they have not found success in adjusting to their homelands. Thus, on average, newly arriving populations, such as Irish, Scandinavian, Italian, and Jewish immigrants, may have lower self-control than their homeland contemporaries and possibly slightly lower self-control than their American-born counterparts. But it seems unlikely that such selection effects could explain much of the elevated delinquency rates of their children. Instead, causal processes may be involved. Thomas and Znaniecki (1927) identified problems of adjustment for new immigrant groups, including language barriers, unfamiliar events, habits and attitudes no longer being appropriate, group support no longer present, and children being exposed to a variety of perspectives and values, all of which may hamper attempts at rearing children (see also Shaw and McKay, 1931, 99–106). Such processes will persist across generations, as new immigrants or impoverished groups continue to settle in the inner city. But what about the finding that rates of immigrant groups decline as they move to the periphery? Here, Shaw and McKay invoked the process of cultural transmission: Immigrant groups moving to the periphery have fewer problems of delinquency because a tradition of delinquent values and attitudes is absent. Such processes, of course, are inadmissible for control theories. Nevertheless, we can draw on the concepts of social organization, social capital, and collective efficacy to explain this finding. Immigrant families who move to the periphery still suffer from higher rates of parents with low self-control but benefit somewhat from the collective efficacy of their new community, which consists of a critical mass of parents with high self-control. Their children will benefit, have a greater chance of learning control, and have a higher probability of an upward life trajectory, including earning a high income and residing in a low-crime neighborhood.

Finally, net of the effects of individual self-control on individual delinquency and of the effects of aggregate self-control (aggregated to the neighborhood level) on delinquency rates, community social disorganization will exert a contextual effect on delinquency. The mechanism is one of opportunity and rational choice. Recall that Gottfredson and Hirschi (1990) draw on lifestyle, opportunity, and routine activities theories to specify criminal opportunities as a necessary but insufficient condition for crime. A person low on self-control and thus free from conventional constraints will deviate, given the opportunity, if short-term benefits outweigh the short-term costs of crime (costs with a long time horizon are discounted). Consequently, the presence of suitable targets and the absence of capable guardians will play an important role in crime. Moreover, because individuals low on self-control are incapable of planning or delaying gratification, their crimes tend to be situationally induced spur-of-the-moment acts committed during their routine activities. Therefore their criminal opportunities will lie primarily near their own places of residence (Gottfredson and Hirschi, 1990, 13). Criminal opportunities will be greater in socially disorganized inner-city neighborhoods. Again, social capital and collective efficacy will be lower in disorganized areas marked by high rates of mobility, renters, poverty, and ethnic and immigrant groups. Neighbors are unlikely to know one another, have a sense of community pride, and monitor the streets—and if they do see problems, they are unlikely to intervene. Distrustful of conventional institutions, which are unresponsive to their individual needs, they are less likely to call the police in the event of a crime. Although the poverty of the neighborhood means that average targets are not very attractive, the relative absence of external controls (capable guardians) makes crime relatively attractive to local youth. The result, then, is a contextual effect of social disorganization on crime rates.

ORIGINAL VERSION OF SOCIAL DISORGANIZATION
AS A MACROLEVEL COUNTERPART TO LOW SELF-CONTROL

Peers, Gangs, and Subcultures

If we consider social disorganization theory in its totality and the way that it was developed by Thomas and Znaniecki and applied to delinquency by Thrasher and Shaw and McKay, then social disorganization theory is inconsistent with the major tenets of self-control theory. The concepts of gang codes, delinquent values and attitudes, and cultural transmission of delinquent traditions from youth group to youth group violate the assumptions of control theories, as defined by Hirschi (1969) and Gottfredson and Hirschi (1990). Let me briefly review some research that examines these questions. On the role of delinquent peers in delinquency, Gottfredson and Hirschi (1990) argue that the correlation between peers and delinquency could be spurious because of selection or reverse causality (i.e., delinquency causes delinquent peers) or measurement artifacts (i.e., the reports of delinquency of one's peers reflects one's own delinquency). Matsueda and Anderson (1998) examined this assumption using longitudinal data and found strong selection effects and correlated measurement errors in reports of delinquency and delinquency of one's peers, but they still found a significant effect of delinquent peers on future delinquency controlling for prior delinquency (which captures self-control). Using a stronger research design, in which delinquent peer groups were identified using network data and self-reports from the peers, Haynie (2001) found that, net of attachment to schools and parents, delinquent peers significantly affect delinquency, and this effect is larger for cohesive peer networks (see also Kreager, 2004).

With respect to the effects of gangs, research based on both quantitative and qualitative designs shows complicated results. Statistical analyses of longitudinal self-reported survey data suggest that stable gang members have higher rates of delinquency than non–gang members, particularly while they are in the gang (Thornberry et al., 1993, 2003; Esbensen and Huizinga, 1993). Moreover, the individual characteristics of gang members do not fully explain their crimes, implying that gang processes may be important. Although Yablonsky's (1962) classic study of gangs suggests that gang members are impulsive, unable to distinguish right from wrong, aggressive, and lacking in empathy, other studies suggest that street gang members are "socially disabled" but not pathological (Short and Strodtbeck, 1965). Klein (1995) argues that pathological types would be selected out of the gang if they showed unreliability, conflict with other members, or actions bringing attention of police.

Although some research, such as Yablonsky (1962), finds gangs to be relatively disorganized near-groups, others find some semblance of organization depending on the type of gang, with drug gangs more organized than violent gangs. Perhaps the strongest case for gang organization is found in Venkatesh's (1997) analyses of gangs associated with housing projects in Chicago. Venkatesh uses Taylor's concept of corporatization of gangs—the shift to entrepreneurial activities usually involving drug sales—to analyze the embeddedness of gangs in the local community. The gang's success in drug sales provided it with resources with which to become a part of the community, including funneling some money to tenant leaders and resident organizations and offering services in kind, such as security escorts and recreational programming. Venkatesh (1997) traces the dynamics of corporatism and infiltration into the politics of the housing project by presenting precipitating events, coalition formations, and interactions between residents, leadership, and gang members. Furthermore, Levitt and Venkatesh (2000) provide a fascinating economic analysis of a drug-selling gang, using the gang's financial books. They characterize the gang's organization in terms of a hierarchical structure resembling Cressey's (1969) analysis of the Mafia; they describe the gang structure as "a franchised company," whereas Cressey used the term "loosely organized federation." At the top of the gang are 100 gang leaders, each of whom has three officers, an enforcer, a treasurer, and a runner. At the bottom are foot soldiers, ages 16–22, and at the periphery are the "rank and file," who pay to consume drugs, for protection, and for status. Levitt and Venkatesh (2000, 781) describe how the organization functions to reduce risk, note that gang wars are costly, and explain how—in the context of norms such as "if a gang member is assaulted or shot, the gang must retaliate"—gang leaders try to avoid escalation into a gang war.

In general, research does not find that gangs are part of an autonomous subculture containing a value system completely at odds with conventional culture. Nevertheless, studies do find, over and over again, that gang members are preoccupied with status, honor, and respect, which they define in ways they can attain. For example, Short and Strodtbeck (1965) find that gangs value being cool and having high status, which can lead to "satisficing" decisions to engage in violence when status is threatened (see also Klein, 1995). Horowitz (1983) examines culture and identity in a Latino neighborhood and posits two cultural codes that structure an inner-city neighborhood. The instrumental code of the American Dream, organized around economic success, is espoused by community members but conflicts with the realities of poor experiences in lower-class schools and in available jobs, which each fail to link residents to the broader culture. The code of honor among men, organized around respect, manhood, and deference, is espoused by young men on the streets. Violations of the code of honor can lead to violence, particularly among Latino men. Street identities of young men are shaped by their responses to insult, negotiations of threats to manhood, and ability to maintain honor. For Horowitz (1983) Latino youth must balance the instrumental code of the American Dream (which requires being "decent" from the standpoint of the larger community) against the honor code of the streets (which entails gaining status in ways that are often violent and illegal).

Notions of honor and respect are key to crime and violence on the streets of inner-city neighborhoods. Anderson (1999) identifies a "code of the street" operating on the streets of Philadelphia, which he argues is rooted in the local circumstances of ghetto poverty as described by W. J. Wilson's (1987) underclass thesis. Cut off from gaining success in mainstream institutions, alienated African American youth come to distrust the legal system for resolving their disputes and turn to violence and an emphasis on "manhood" to resolve disputes and gain status. Status is derived from developing a reputation as a "badass" or "man," which is based on showing toughness, nerve, and physical prowess, and by adhering to the code of the street: never backing down from a fight, always coming to the defense of one's crew, and exacting revenge or "payback" when one or one's loved one is disrespected. Indeed, street youth manipulate the status system by "campaigning for respect" to increase their "juice" or status, that is, by challenging, assaulting, or disrespecting others by stealing their material possessions or girlfriends. Katz (1988, p. 81) argues that "badasses" demonstrate a "superiority of their being" by dominating and forcing their will on others and by showing that they "mean it." Anderson (1999) finds that even youth from "decent" as opposed to "street" families must learn the code of the street to protect themselves from episodes in which they must fight or suffer loss of status on the street. Recent survey research finds that there is support for the existence of the code of the street in inner-city neighborhoods and that it is related to structural disadvantage and violent crime (Matsueda et al., 2006).

Immediate Pleasures of Crime

We can take another angle on the assumption that all individuals have the same motivation to deviate by examining the assumption that the "momentary benefits" provided by crime are "obvious," and therefore crime does not require specialized learning for motivation or execution (Hirschi and Gottfredson, 1994a, 9). It follows that because the pleasures from crime are "immediate consequences," they will "tend to be more pleasurable than those whose consequences are delayed" (Gottfredson and Hirschi, 1990, 12). But there is evidence that such benefits from crime are not obvious but require specialized learning, even tutelage, which results in motivation to deviate. We can illustrate this point with marijuana smoking, which to outsiders may appear to have obvious physiological benefits that require no learning. In his classic participant observation study on becoming a marijuana user, Becker (1963) shows that learning is indeed relevant.

Becker (1963) found that novice smokers must learn how to smoke marijuana, including how to inhale and hold the smoke in the lungs, how to recognize the effects of being high, and how to define the effects as pleasurable. In this way an inherently ambiguous physiological experience—dizziness, nausea, euphoria, or comicality—is transformed and redefined into a social object defined as being high and, more important, as being pleasurable. Such definitions are built up in interaction in groups, as other experienced members help demonstrate how to smoke properly, how to recognize the feeling of being high (including having the munchies), and how to interpret the high feeling as pleasurable and even euphoric. Thus "marihuana acquires meaning for the user as an object which can be used for pleasure," and with repeated experiences of this sort "there grows a stable set of categories for experiencing the drug's effects" (Becker, 1963, 56). In this way "deviant motives actually develop in the course of experience with the deviant activity" (p. 42).

Moreover, because marijuana is illegal, whether the beginner progresses to an occasional user and then to a regular user depends on how he or she adapts to social control attempts to limit supply of the drug, detect drug users, and define the behavior as immoral. Through interaction regular users develop contacts with drug dealers, learn verbalizations that neutralize definitions of the behavior as immoral, and deal with the possibility of being caught by segregating acquaintances into users versus nonusers, withdrawing into groups who condone marijuana, or concluding that detection would not be so bad. Through these processes regular users adopt a stable self-concept as a marijuana smoker. Becker's interpretations have been widely accepted, and his theoretical framework is consistent with the perspective of W. I. Thomas, and in particular, his concept of the definition of the situation. Here, if the novice user defines the situation of smoking marijuana as aversive rather than pleasurable, in the absence of group sentiment to the contrary, he or she will not become a smoker.

A Sociological Theory of Psychopathy

Finally, we might consider another interpretation of low self-control. In identifying the manifestations of low self-control, Gottfredson and Hirschi (1990, 93) cite a long passage from Harrison Gough (1948), who uses terms such as "impulsive," "inability to form attachments," "poor planning," "lack of anxiety and distress in maladjustment," "blame other for failures," "emotional poverty," and "unwilling to take responsibility." Gough was describing psychopathy, about which he was trying to develop a sociological, as opposed to psychiatric, explanation. Given the affinity between this concept and low self-control, it might be useful to compare the two. One of the leading experts on psychopathy is Robert Hare, who has conducted extensive research on psychopaths and who has developed an instrument for measuring psychopathy. Hare (1993) argues that symptoms of psychopathy appear in childhood, including chronic lying, cruelty to animals, aggression, and indifference to the pain of others. At the same time psychopaths often evidence intelligence, cunning, and ability to manipulate. Psychopathy is highly correlated with crime, especially violence, and has a prevalence rate of about 1 percent. Sibling correlations are low, suggesting that parenting and family background are not strong causes (Hare, 1993). Some evidence points to biological factors, because electroencephalograms of psychopaths differ from those of nonpsychopaths. If this research is correct, it suggests that a good deal of crime is committed by psychopaths (Hare estimates that nearly half of imprisoned violent offenders can be classified as psychopathic), but the majority of crimes are committed by nonpsychopaths. Could it be that a good deal of the typical crimes described by Gottfredson and Hirschi (1990), which correspond to characteristics of psychopathy, are crimes committed by psychopaths? And perhaps the nonmodal crimes are committed by nonpsychopaths through other social mechanisms?

The title of Gough's (1948) article is "A Sociological Theory of Psychopathy." His theory is quite provocative. He begins with Mead's (1934) theory of the self, noting that through taking the role of others, one is able to take the self as an object and see oneself as an object from the standpoint of others—which gives rise to a "me," a self-conception. In time the self-conception involves the "generalized other," which includes "abstract rules and standards" that appear in games and organizations. The self involves a dynamic between the "I" and the "me," which occurs through role taking, and entails self-criticism by the "me." Gough (1948) hypothesizes that "the psychopathic personality is pathologically deficient in role-playing abilities," which means "the capacity to look upon one's self as an object (Mead) or identify with another's point of view" (p. 363). He further states:

> The psychopath is unable to foresee the consequences of his own acts, especially their social implications, because he does not know how to judge his own behavior from another's standpoint. When confronted with disapproval, the psychopath often expresses surprise and resentment. He cannot understand the reasons for the observer's objection or disapprobation. The psychopath cannot grant the justice of punishment or deprivation, because this

involves an evaluation of his behavior from the standpoint of the "generalized other," or society. (Gough, 1948, 364)

Gough suggests using therapy to improve role-taking skills; however, more recent research suggests that psychopathy is rooted in neurological deficits, and such therapies are unsuccessful (Hare, 1993).

There is some evidence that the key feature of psychopathy is not inability to engage in role taking but the inability to inhibit impulses. For Mead (1934) role taking and cognition—the dialectical inner conversation of gestures between the "I" and the "me"—occur when habitual behavior no longer suffices because an impulse has been blocked, causing the situation to become problematic. It is here, with the inhibition of an impulse, that a self arises and cognitive processes are used to solve the problem. Specifically, one takes the role of others, considers a solution from their standpoint ("me"), and then reacts to that possible solution with the "I," which if inhibited, calls out another "me," and so on, until a solution is found that works. It follows that if a person is unable to inhibit an impulse and delay response, the person will be unable to engage in cognition. A series of intriguing experimental studies by Joseph Newman and his colleagues provides some support for this conception.

Newman et al. (1987) conducted an experiment to examine the effects of response inhibition in psychopaths. They hypothesized that psychopaths are unable to inhibit punished responses because of response perseveration, which could be neurologically rooted in septohippocampal functioning. The research design consisted of a card-playing video game in which subjects were allowed to play for money. They were given 100 cards, which they could play one at a time, and after each play they were given a chance to quit. The probability of losing was increased by increments of 0.10 for every ten cards. Therefore the rational response would be to quit sooner rather than later. Newman et al. (1987) took a sample of thirty-six psychopaths, assessed using the Hare psychopathy checklist, and a sample of thirty-six control subjects from a minimum security prison in Wisconsin and randomly assigned them to three conditions. One experimental condition provided a running visual feedback on wins and losses, which could help subjects realize that their losses were increasing. A second experimental condition forced the subjects to pause 5 seconds before deciding whether to continue playing. The control group received neither of these treatments. Newman's group found that, as expected, psychopaths played more cards and lost significantly more money than nonpsychopaths. Cumulative feedback by itself had no effect on this difference. However, when cumulative feedback was paired with a 5-second pause, the psychopaths performed nearly as well as the nonpsychopaths. In other words, psychopaths are unable to inhibit impulses and engage in cognition; but if forced to delay a decision, they are capable of engaging in cognitive processes (role taking) like nonpsychopaths and make more rational decisions.

This conceptualization of psychopathy is consistent with the finding that siblings show low correlations in psychopathy and the conclusion that parents are not entirely to blame for their children's life trajectories (Hare, 1993). Instead, neuropsychological deficits or other determinants of a colicky child may be in part responsible for the child's unresponsiveness to disapproval by parents. This underscores that parenting is a social interaction in which the child is an important player (Bell and Harper, 1977). Or, as Scarr and McCartney (1983) argue with respect to genetic effects, genes affect outcomes in part by selecting their environments—as when a colicky child selects for parent behavior.

Psychopathy, or something similar to it (such as inability to inhibit responses), may help account for the high incidence of delinquency in disorganized inner-city neighborhoods. Faris and Dunham (1939) found high rates of a variety of mental disorders in disorganized neighborhoods and suggested a selection mechanism, in which the mentally ill "tend to fail in their economic activities and as a consequence drift into slum areas" (Faris, 1955, 337). Moreover, if correct, this sociological interpretation of psychopathy would help explain the characteristics of typical street crimes using the same framework—the Chicago school of Mead, Dewey, Thomas, Thrasher, and Shaw and McKay—that gave rise to theories of social disorganization and cultural transmission. Furthermore, psychopathy and other mental disorders, such as attention-deficit/hyperactivity disorder, probably account for a small percentage of criminals but perhaps a substantial number of crimes. Moreover, as Hare implies, they are probably more likely to be arrested and incarcerated for their crimes and thus are more visible. A key question is whether psychopathy is a discrete trait or whether it is a description of the tail of a continuous distribution.

An important puzzle, thus far unaddressed, is, What happens when such individuals are mixed in with the rest of the population? The result is likely to depend on context. For example, during adolescence, when youths are caught between the constraints of childhood and the impending transition to adulthood, popularity and peer status are often given to youths of the "fast crowd" who defy authority, take risks, and act like reckless adults—precisely the behaviors characteristic of those with attention-deficit disorder, psychopathy, and perhaps low self-control. In this context peer dynamics may exert pressure to affiliate, emulate, and acquire the culture of the fast crowd through cultural transmission. Conceivably what Gottfredson and Hirschi (1990) are observing when they characterize the modal or typical crime is in part the activity of the 2 or 3 percent of the population afflicted with psychopathy and other mental disorders, plus their emulators, whose delinquency is acquired through group processes and cultural transmission.

DISCUSSION

Perhaps a judicious evaluation of Gottfredson and Hirschi's (1990) theory of self-control would state that it has effectively challenged the criminological community, contains important insights, arguments, and findings but also makes strong assumptions that are questionable in light of research results, and derives equally strong implications that are questionable given faulty assumptions. The assumptions are that there is constant motivation to deviate, that self-control is a stable trait and explains crime, and that the age-crime curve is invariant. Implications include that life course events have no effect, delinquent peer effects are an artifact, crime is never learned, and crime is not organized. These faulty assumptions notwithstanding, self-control theory is picking up an important empirical regularity. A number of research studies find some support for the basic hypothesis of low self-control affecting crime. Pratt and Cullen (2000) conducted a meta-analysis on studies of the theory and concluded that "regardless of measurement differences, low self-control is an important predictor of crime" (p. 931). But they also noted that the effect is weaker in longitudinal designs and that, moreover, attitudes favorable to crime and delinquent peers also have strong effects, even net of self-control measures. Consequently, Pratt and Cullen (2000) conclude that "it is unlikely that Gottfredson and Hirschi's perspective can claim the exalted status of the general theory of crime" (p. 953).

This then shifts the puzzle to the following question: How can low self-control, delinquent peers, and attitudes favorable to delinquency all have strong effects on crime? Of course, one can always quibble about measures, arguing that measures of low self-control are surrogates for the dependent variable, crime itself, which leads to circularity and tautology (see Akers, 1991). But a more challenging and stimulating question takes the research results at face value and tries to explain them. Here are three points that may help form the basis of such an explanation.

First, a substantial number of street crimes share the characteristics that Gottfredson and Hirschi (1990) describe. Some, but not all, of these crimes may be committed by individuals suffering from psychopathy, attention-deficit disorder, low self-control, and other disorders. This does not mean that they are born with the idea of crime but rather that their crimes are mainly a result of their inability to inhibit impulses, engage in cognitive imaginative rehearsals before acting, and thereby control their actions. Whether this personality is due to neuropsychological deficits, brain functioning, or parenting is a research question for clinical psychology. But this would explain none of the nonmodal crimes and only a fraction of the modal crimes described by Gottfredson and Hirschi (1990). Why do so many street crimes not committed by psychopaths share these characteristics?

This leads to the second point, which is an institutional explanation for modal characteristics of crime. According to Gottfredson and Hirschi, such crimes entail few skills—manual, social, or academic—little delayed gratification, little planning, little respect for others, and little geographic distance from place of residence because of the institutional configuration of conventional society. Most industrial societies have erected elaborate social institutions—schools and the labor market—that handsomely reward those who have skills and other attributes (such as planning, delaying gratification, manipulating abstract concepts, and empathizing with others) of individuals with high self-control. Those who lack these skills and attributes will be selected out of school achievement, college, and good jobs. Part of their predicament can be explained by the lack of mobility that characterizes most capitalist economies. Their parents may suffer similar characteristics, which has left them in the secondary sector labor market and in inner-city neighborhoods, resulting in the child starting out disadvantaged. Unlike their skilled counterparts, they start out at greater risk of a negative future trajectory.

When a segment of the population shares attributes that are not rewarded by conventional institutions—and worse yet, share visible attributes such as racial minority, disadvantaged family, and immigrant status that are not legitimately associated with lack of opportunity—they will be at risk of crime. As Shaw and McKay show, because of residential patterns resulting from urban growth, they are likely to come into contact with each other on the street and learn more refined ways of committing crimes and getting away with it.

Shaw and McKay also show that the backdrop of adult organized crime in the community provides illicit opportunities for such individuals. Thus prohibition led to incentives for local gangs to coalesce over bootlegging and then, with legalization of alcohol, to diversify into other realms, such as loan sharking, gambling, and drugs. Levitt and Venkatesh (2000) show that some gangs are able to corporatize when presented with strong incentives. The gang leaders earn a handsome income, higher than they could earn in legitimate jobs. Here, then, illegal enterprises are able to compete with legitimate firms and attract some skilled individuals who can plan and delay gratification into illegal rackets. Moreover, as revenues come in, they are able to expand their organization into a hierarchical structure, with an authority structure and internal controls, which increases the safety of their illegal actions. Such structures include positions for nonskilled impulsive street hoodlums, such as rank and filers and some foot soldiers. But to move up in the ranks, one must be capable of controlling indiscriminant impulses to violence and yet be willing to resort to violence when the organizational occasion calls for it (Levitt and Venkatesh, 2000).

Such illegal enterprises, however, have a definite ceiling over which the organization cannot expand. When such enterprises develop elaborate structures to reduce risk and increase profits, including infiltrating the political and legal systems through donations, bribery, and kickbacks, their activities become increasingly visible, subject to negative publicity and media coverage. Citizens become enraged and political leaders see a campaign issue that always sells. As a consequence, the political system responds with a vengeance (Sutherland and Cressey, 1978). Thus, when organized crime became lucrative and threatening, RICO laws were passed; these laws undermined the individual rights of the accused but resulted in dismantling much of the syndicate's monopolization. The events of September 11 mobilized a nation against terrorism, again undermining the rights of the accused with domestic wiretapping, secret prisons, and denial of due process. The reason that contemporary terrorism is so frightening to the average citizen is not because there are a number of impulsive individuals carrying out unplanned acts of suicide bombing. Rather, it is because, I suspect, that Al Qaeda has shown extensive networks, organized cells, command of technology available to them, and extremely persuasive rhetorical devices—based on practical appeals to religious ideology and anti-Americanism—which may be succeeding in recruiting not just extremist fanatics but a broader cross-section of the Muslim world.

The key point here is that institutional processes that reward high self-control also ensure that illegal enterprises remain embryonic and at a severe competitive disadvantage. The result is a pool of potential criminals dominated by characteristics of low self-control. Furthermore, the crimes of the rank-and-file and isolated unskilled criminals will be visible and likely to be apprehended. In contrast, crimes that reflect organized enterprises will be difficult to detect, and the leaders, who depart from the description of modal crimes, will be difficult to find.

Third, a substantial proportion of crimes probably depart from characteristics of the typical crime. These crimes are committed by individuals with moderate to high self-control. It is a heterogeneous mix of offenses. It includes the crimes of leaders of criminal enterprises, crimes committed by confidence artists, and crimes committed by white-collar workers (Cressey's embezzlers) and politicians, such as presidential cabinet members seeking a political edge or presidents having histories of drinking and driving and criminal fraternity pranks. Such crimes involve cultural transmission and vocabularies of motive that justify the behavior.

To conclude, Travis Hirschi and Michael Gottfredson are truly luminaries of the discipline of criminology. Hirschi's *Causes of Delinquency* was brilliant in constructing an innovative theory of crime—at a time when notions of control had gone out of style—and in bringing empirical data to bear on competing hypotheses derived from the theory. It also served as the exemplar for criminological research, inspiring other criminologists to follow suit, collecting data, finding ways of testing theories of crime, and specifying theories in falsifiable form. His *Measuring Delinquency*, with Hindelang and Weis (Hindelang et al., 1981), was a landmark study that justified the use of self-reports to a skeptical research community and thereby stimulated a massive body of important self-reported empirical research. Gottfredson's work on victimization surveys and development of an opportunity theory of crime was equally seminal (Hindelang et al., 1978), as was his elegant empirical test of Black's behavior of law (Gottfredson and Hindelang, 1979). Most scholars would rank *A General Theory of Crime* with the rest of this work, as it is beautifully written and brilliantly argued. Although these brilliant arguments are capable of convincing us that up is down or that "black is white," they have also "forced the authors into intellectual contortions" (Tittle 1991, 1610). Such brilliance, however, would be unnecessary if Hirschi and Gottfredson would free themselves from the restraints of control theory and concede important roles for longitudinal data, delinquent peers, criminal organization, life course events, and the learning of crime. In this way their individual-level theory would be fully compatible with the rich research tradition of social disorganization theory.

NOTE

This paper was written while I was on sabbatical from the University of Washington and an Honorary Fellow in the Sociology Department at the University of Wisconsin, Madison, in 2005–2006. The research on which this paper is based was supported by grants from the National Institute on Drug Abuse (R01DA18148) and the National Science Foundation (SES-0004323). All points of view in the paper are mine and do not reflect the positions of the funding agencies. I thank Avery (Pete) Guest and Erich Goode for comments on an earlier draft.

9 | A FEMINIST CONSIDERATION OF GENDER AND CRIME

LeeAnn Iovanni and Susan L. Miller

Consider the following cases of women's criminal activity from a study based on interviews with incarcerated women: "Tanya's boyfriend started wanting to rob banks. She didn't want to, and he beat her up—said she was going to do it or he'd kill her. He had a drug habit now. So they ended up robbing banks, and that led up to Tanya serving time. . . . Laura started getting in trouble a lot after her mother's boyfriend had touched her. She began throwing stuff at cars, starting fires, tearing stuff up, and raising hell. Now that she thinks back on it, she thinks she was trying to make someone ask what was wrong" (DeHart, 2004, 19, 27). And consider this incident during Beth's sixteen-year violent marriage:

> Sam came in from work about midnight and started all over again. I asked him why he was doing this when he knew how tired and run down I was. He said, "because I caught you at your lowest point; I can beat, defeat you now." The hair pulling hurt me terribly because I had kept my hair long for him all the years of our marriage. . . . That night, when I thought he was finished, I went into the bathroom and started cutting my hair. . . . [He] saw what I was doing, grabbed me by the hair, and dragged me into the kitchen. He threw me on my back on the floor, straddled and pinned me, and continued to punch and slap me. (Sipe and Hall, 1996, 62)

What do these situations mean for self-control theory? Based on insights from feminist and gender-focused literature, in this essay we critically explore the general theory's essential neglect of gender. Here, we comment on empirical research as it relates to self-control and gender and examine self-control as an explanation of crime committed by women as well as crime committed by men, particularly those crimes that victimize women. We also examine the implications of Gottfredson and Hirschi's emphasis on parental supervision as the key element in crime prevention. We conclude that feminist perspectives call into question the utility of self-control theory for understanding the relationship between gender and crime.

Criminologists who examine gender traditionally have concerned themselves with two issues: the gender gap in crime (males commit more crime overall than do females) and generalizability (the ability of a theory to explain crime equally well for males and females).

The general theory of crime easily deals with generalizability as it "is meant to explain all crime, at all times" (Gottfredson and Hirschi, 1990, 117) and then gives a perfunctory nod to the gender gap, one that downplays the role of opportunity. Gottfredson and Hirschi (1990) neatly dispense with the issue, noting that "male-female differences in the use of force or fraud emerge early in life, well before differences in opportunity are possible, and persist into adulthood, where differences in supervision by the agents of social control are minimal" (p. 148). Moreover, the fact "that gender differences for all types of crime are established early in life and that they persist throughout life . . . implies a substantial self-control difference between the sexes" (p. 147). Their theory implies that girls develop greater self-control because parents, more attuned to the consequences of deviance for females on their life chances, are more likely to make daughters the targets of their supervision and thus more likely to recognize and correct antisocial behavior. When females do commit crime, presumably it has the same source, low self-control, an apparently gender-neutral explanation. But "what does it mean to develop a gender-neutral theory of crime . . . when neither the social order nor the structure of crime is gender-neutral?" (Daly and Chesney-Lind, 1988, 516).

Champions of simplicity and parsimony, Gottfredson and Hirschi are well known for their critique of theoretical efforts that embrace "the complexity of human behavior" (Hirschi and Gottfredson, 2004, 66). But a fuller understanding of crime and delinquency, as with any other social phenomenon, must take into account the fact that the social world is organized by gender as well as by race, ethnicity, and class and reflects differences in power, resources, and opportunities. Gottfredson and Hirschi similarly theorize racial and ethnic differences in crime as most likely the result of differences in self-control. They recommend that "research on racial differences in crime should focus on differential child-rearing practices and abandon the fruitless effort to ascribe such differences to culture or strain" (Gottfredson and Hirschi, 1990, 153). In their view we have little need to consider social location, economic marginalization, or power relations in a theory of crime.

Regarding gender, Gottfredson and Hirschi (1990) conclude that "it is beyond the scope of this work and beyond the reach of any empirical set of data to attempt to identify all of the elements responsible for gender differences in crime" (p. 149). In contrast, we argue that gender in the general theory of crime is rendered virtually invisible. The general theory raises important questions, such as what circumstances put individuals in crime situations in the first place or, once in these situations, what factors constrain their choices or influence their decisions? Gendered power relations and their intersection with race, ethnicity, and class play a role in shaping the patterns of men's and women's criminal behavior. In our view it is the job of criminological theory to take these factors into account.

MAINSTREAM ISSUES AND METHODOLOGICAL CONCERNS

The Gender Gap and Generalizability

Theory is informed by empirical research, and the choice of method can influence what kinds of questions we ask and what kinds of concepts we develop. The original statement of self-control theory was bolstered primarily with reference to quantitative data, much of which was based on male samples, and with reference to theoretical statements originally developed to explain male behavior. Subsequent tests of the theory have also been quantitative, a common practice in criminology for hypothesis testing and theory building. Tests of self-control theory with respect to gender concern themselves with the theory's ability to account for the gender gap in crime and the theory's generalizability for males and females. Other work examines how well researchers have interpreted and defined the theoretical concept of self-control, particularly in terms of survey items. Although some theoretical insights result, a mainstream approach to research questions and methods does little to expand Gottfredson and Hirschi's ideas about self-control and gender.

We can spell out the logic of research examining the gender gap as follows: If the effect of gender on offending behavior becomes smaller in magnitude or statistically insignificant when researchers introduce self-control into the model and shows a significant effect on offending, this is evidence that we can explain the gender gap in crime in part by gender differences in self-control. Some studies also take the opportunity to offend into account and opportunity is allowed to interact with low self-control. Indeed, some research supports the ability of self-control to account for the gender gap (Burton et al., 1998; LaGrange and Silverman, 1999; Tittle et al., 2003a). Offending behavior in females is also partly attributed to lower opportunity (Burton et al., 1998; LaGrange and Silverman, 1999). The tests are generally consistent with the notion that gender differences in crime are due to gender differences in self-control and, to some degree, opportunity. The results, however, are not entirely straightforward, and the gender effect can vary according to the way self-control is measured (behavioral vs. attitudinal measures; Tittle et al., 2003a); by offense type (general delinquency, property, violent or drug offenses; LaGrange and Silverman, 1999); or by interaction effects (e.g., the interaction of self-control and social control; Nakhaie et al., 2000).

With respect to generalizability, if the magnitude or statistical significance of self-control is similar in gender subgroups, then this is evidence that self-control can explain criminal behavior equally well for males and females. Inconsistent findings across gender subgroups, however, have led some researchers to question the generality of the theory. LaGrange and Silverman (1999) analyzed separate elements of self-control (preference for risk seeking, impulsivity, temper, present-oriented, and carelessness) where risk seeking and impulsivity were among the strongest predictors overall, but the results were not entirely similar across gender and offense types. These researchers uncovered enough differences across gender subgroups to suggest that "there may be different patterns of causality leading to male and female offending" (LaGrange and Silverman, 1999, 63). Burton et al. (1998) also found differences across gender subgroups in a study that compared the effect of self-control with variables from rival criminological theories (strain, social bonds, and differential association). Self-control was the only variable significantly related to criminal involvement for males, but for females measures of differential association and the interaction of low self-control and opportunity were significantly related to crime. Burton's group speculated that women are placed under greater constraints and that having criminal friends may provide access to illegitimate opportunities. Finally, in a roadside traffic study Keane et al. (1993) reported that the same risk taking variables (such as not wearing a seat belt) were related to drinking and driving (observed blood alcohol content) for both males and females, results interpreted as support for the generalizability of self-control theory for gender.

Construct Validity

As predicted by the theory, the tests mentioned earlier also generally show that males score lower on measures of self-control. However, fundamental questions have been raised about construct validity—how well a theoretical concept is translated into operational definitions and survey items—and gender. Researchers have defined the components of self-control as impulsivity, simple tasks, risk seeking, physical activity, self-centeredness, and temper (Grasmick et al., 1993). Longshore et al. (1996) statistically analyzed different combinations of measures of self-control across gender. Not only did risk seeking in combination with either impulsivity/self-centeredness or temper emerge as the most important predictor of crime, but measures of self-control were also less statistically acceptable (thus less theoretically tenable) for women. Among the items performing less well for women: looking out for self first; almost always doing something physical rather than mental; feeling better when on the move rather than sitting and thinking; and losing one's temper easily. The researchers noted that "it will be difficult to make much headway in understanding the relevance of self-control for gender differences in crime until there are satisfactory measures of self-control among women" (Longshore et al., 1996, 223). We note that self-control as a general construct may be so at odds with female life experience that it may not even vary enough among girls or women for it to be a useful predictor of female involvement in crime. Indeed, a concept may be "inscribed so deeply by masculinist experiences" that even attempts to modify it could "prove too restrictive, or at least misleading" (Daly and Chesney-Lind, 1988, 519).

Risk Preference and Risk Perception

Given the primacy of the risk-seeking component, low self-control may simply be a less precise conceptualization of risk seeking (Longshore et al., 1996, 222–223) and in terms of gender and delinquency researchers have raised questions about what the broader concept adds to our understanding in the face of power-control theory (LaGrange and Silverman, 1999, 63; Nakhaie et al., 2000, 51). Power-control theory essentially links structural gender inequality in the labor market, power differences between parents, differential familial control of sons and daughters, and thus differences in risk preference and perception to account for the gender gap in common delinquency (Hagan et al., 1987). In this view the general theory's notion of self-control, an individual trait devoid of social context and perhaps preference for risk seeking in disguise, does not advance even the state of mainstream criminological theory as it relates to gender.

In addition, the related notion of risk perception has implications for *perceived opportunity*—the extent to which individuals *subjectively* see a situation lending itself to action. Although Gottfredson and Hirschi downplay the role of opportunity, their theory appears to embrace an objective notion of opportunity. However, in a potential elaboration of the theory, if individuals with low self-control are more likely to *interpret* situations as ripe for crime (i.e., a low risk of getting caught), females, theorized to have higher self-control, would be less likely to perceive opportunities for crime because they perceive a greater risk of apprehension. Again, explanations for women's higher risk perceptions have been suggested: Women find criminal punishment more threatening to the female role and overestimate risks; women have less need to downplay risks than do men attempting to live up to masculine roles by lawbreaking; women have been subject to more supervision and feel more visible and accountable to others; women are more likely to view crime as immoral; women have led more sheltered lives and have less information about criminal activity or less confidence in their information (Richards and Tittle, 1981); or women perceive greater risks of informal sanction, such as losing the respect of people whose opinion is valued (Finley and Grasmick, 1985). These hypotheses question the utility of self-control in understanding gender differences in perceived opportunity.

It is important to point out that a mainstream approach that simply includes gender as a control variable or analyzes gender subgroups in statistical analyses hampers our ability to theorize gendered power relations or the *meaning* of gender for criminal behavior. Quantitative studies, although useful, are limited in the information they provide. They are driven by conceptualizations that lend themselves easily to survey questions and thus can obstruct our view of a problem. With the advantage of typically larger samples, they can tell us about general patterns and trends but can mask important distinctions within and across diverse groups. Although feminist criminologists use different types of methods, they have been drawn to qualitative research, such as in-depth interviews or observational techniques, to a greater degree than have mainstream criminologists. These methods allow participants to articulate their experiences more clearly in their own terms, potentially providing more accurate and valid information, and allow researchers to capture experiences as participants live them. Qualitative findings can supplement those from quantitative data or allow for alternative interpretations and new conceptualizations.

One approach to this type of research is known as standpoint theory (D. E. Smith 1990). Standpoint theorists argue that women and men perceive the world in different ways and that knowledge depends on social location and life experience. Women and members of ethnic and racial minorities (i.e., anyone not in the hegemonic majority position) have a unique standpoint as outsiders in an unequal, patriarchal society; the standpoint approach privileges "outsider" voices. The general theory of crime is uninformed by insights from research conducted with qualitative methods and the voices of the less powerful, especially those of women.

Clear conclusions about the ability of self-control theory to account for the relationship between gender and crime are not forthcoming from the available research. The evidence suggests that self-control may not be the general explanation it claims to be, that its current measurement may not fully reflect female experience, and that self-control may simply be a restatement of existing theoretical ideas. Moreover, the theory's limited focus does not take into account the structural forces that produce differences in the internalization of self-control through socialization processes (Nakhaie et al., 2000, 52). Even if self-control is applicable for both males and females in some general sense, we question whether and to what extent it is applicable in the same way or to the same degree. The theory does not address how gender relations operate to structure self-control or opportunity, and the empirical tests do not build on the theory. The theory also cannot address what the sources of gender differences might be beyond low self-control and opportunity (LaGrange and Silverman, 1999, 62). Essentially ignoring gender, the theory actually tells us little about the nature of gender differences in crime rates, differences in the kinds of criminal situations that women and men become involved in, or the different social processes that lead to crime.

FEMINIST PERSPECTIVES AND GENDER SCHOLARSHIP

The general theory's agnosticism and dismissal of the role of gender is a serious flaw. In our view the theory falls short of an adequate explanation of participation by women in some kinds of crimes as well as some criminal activity by men, particularly when considering crimes of violence committed against women. This omission of women and gender is not entirely uncommon. Historically, most theoretical developments in criminology have taken place with boys or men in mind or have used male-only samples. Generalizations were routinely made about women's criminal activity by simply extending knowledge about men with no empirical verification. However, more sophisticated feminist work on women and crime has emerged and has revealed differences in the nature of female crime compared to that of males. The feminist perspective calls our attention to gender and power in the explanation of criminal behavior. Women who commit violent acts such as assault or homicide have often been victims of violence themselves. Women who commit welfare, check, or credit card fraud and minor acts of theft are often doing so to support children and dependents. Thus the victimization of women and their economic marginality are explored as the contextual conditions of female offending. The feminist perspective has also been instrumental in including the viewpoint of victims in the conceptualization of crime. Interviews with battered women have shown that researchers need to be more sensitive to the motivations and consequences of intimate partner violence and not simply count its frequency. Improved surveys on rape have revealed that the stranger in the bushes is not the most likely scenario. In sum, feminist theory would conclude that the general theory ignores the life experience of half the population, some of whom commit crimes or are a primary target of men's violent crimes, challenging Gottfredson and Hirschi's claim to explain "all crime."

Masculinity

Perhaps Gottfredson and Hirschi have posited a theory that is more useful to understanding male crime. However, feminist-inspired efforts foreground *gender*. Messerschmidt (1993) brings together existing theoretical concepts to view masculinity as a key element in understanding crime. His structured action theory draws on the notions of social structures as patterned forms of interaction that constrain and enable behavior; gender as situated, social, and interactional accomplishment; and "hegemonic masculinity" as a culturally idealized construction of masculinity that men must constantly demonstrate or accomplish. Hegemonic masculinity involves "work in the paid-labor market, the subordination of women, heterosexism, and . . . driven, uncontrollable sexuality," as well as "practices toward authority, control, competitive individualism, independence, aggressiveness, and capacity for violence" (Messerschmidt, 1993, 82).

In this view crime is a "resource" for boys and men to situationally accomplish masculinity. Robbery, for example, is a rational practice not only for getting money but also for "provid[ing] an ideal opportunity to construct an 'essential' toughness and 'maleness' . . . a certain type of masculinity—hardman" (Messerschmidt, 1993, 107). Some men will resort to crime if conventional avenues for accomplishing masculinity are unavailable. Structural location based on race and class plays a part in the extent to which masculinity is challenged and in the salience of particular criminal behaviors used to accomplish the goal. In a different vein, by examining the gender gap through in-depth interviews with high-risk youth, Bottcher (2001, 925) frames gender as "social practices"—what males and females actually do based on the rules and resources available to them—and views delinquency as interpersonal youthful activity in the context of social life where male dominance is all pervasive. Bottcher offers that gender is not simply enacted through crime; rather, crime *becomes* a resource for accomplishing masculinity through the social practices of gender (Bottcher, 2001, 925). Risk taking was especially prominent for males; structural opportunity factors (theoretically downplayed by Gottfredson and Hirschi), such as males' greater access to privacy and nighttime, were also important, as were males' sex-segregated peer groups that encouraged crime. But Bottcher's analysis of social practices questions the view of risk taking as an individual trait produced by socialization. Messerschmidt's and Bottcher's works suggest that crime is *meaningful* behavior and not simply the result of a lack of restraint implied by low self-control.

Crime Committed by Women

Feminist and gender-focused research on the nature and context of girls' and women's lawbreaking emphasizes the impact of gendered power relations on behavior. An important theme in recent research, both quantitative and qualitative, is the connection between childhood victimization and offending. Widom and colleagues followed two cohorts of courtprocessed children, comparing victims of abuse with nonvictims (English et al., 2001). They found that although the experience of childhood abuse (physical or sexual) or neglect made an arrest for a violent crime (juvenile or adult) more likely for both males and females, the impact was much greater for females. Females experiencing childhood trauma were 7.5 times more likely than female nonvictims to have a violent arrest, compared to 2.5 times for males. In another cohort study abused or neglected females were more likely than female nonvictims to have a juvenile or adult arrest for violence; males with childhood trauma were not *more likely* to be arrested compared to male nonvictims, but they were more likely to have a larger *number* of arrests (Widom and Maxfield, 2001). The effect of childhood trauma on offending appears to work differently for males and females, amplifying male criminality, which may start for other reasons, but serving to push girls into crime.

Running away from an unsafe home often propels girls into delinquent offenses, such as petty theft, substance abuse, and prostitution, as a means of survival on the street, paving the way for adult criminality. Indeed, research finds that girls are much more likely to be the victims of child sexual abuse than are boys and that this abuse is more likely to be committed by a family member, often a stepfather (Chesney-Lind and Pasko, 2004, 23–28). Girls are generally more vulnerable to family-related abuse by men who hold patriarchal attitudes, and girls are more governed by rules requiring them to stay at home where their abusers have access to them. Widom and colleagues have also found that females who were abused (physically or sexually) or neglected were three times more likely to have engaged in prostitution than were females without this background and that the relationships of child-hood sexual abuse and neglect to prostitution were significant only for females (Widom and Kuhns, 1996). They noted that these results "reinforce the importance of viewing prostitu-tion in a victimization context" (Widom and Kuhns, 1996, 1161).

Prostitution is overlooked in Gottfredson and Hirschi's framework. We must assume either that women involved in prostitution lack self-control or that self-control theory is not meant to explain involvement in prostitution, a prominent aspect of female criminal activity. If self-control does apply to women's involvement in prostitution, a line of logic would be that prostitution provides "easy or simple" gratification of desires and is "exciting, thrilling or risky." We find it difficult to conceive of prostitution in these terms. Prostitu-tion routinely exposes women to violence and coercion and often entails the risk of being beaten, raped, or exposed to AIDS and other sexually transmitted diseases because clients are often resistant to using condoms (Pyett and Warr, 1999). Women in prostitution in the desperate environment of inner-city crack cultures often face the possibility of having to perform degrading sexual acts (Erickson et al., 2000). Women's involvement in prostitution, substance abuse, and violence are also often linked. The general theory explains drug use as providing "immediate, easy, and short-term pleasure" (Gottfredson and Hirschi, 1990, 41); assault provides "relief from momentary irritation" (p. 90). But these activities occur within complex situational and structural factors where it is difficult to see the place of low self-control.

The socioeconomic and cultural aspects of women's street crime have been elucidated with ethnographic fieldwork by Maher and colleagues in urban, minority, underclass areas in Brooklyn, New York. The widespread use of crack cocaine has increased the number of women engaged in street-level sex work—the only source of income in the gender-stratified informal economy, where high-level drug distribution is the domain of men—and has caused both a shift in the type of sex acts and a price deflation for sexual services. Increas-ingly economically marginalized and at risk for violent victimization, these women often resort to "viccing" (robbing) their clients. Albeit an instrumental robbery, its complex mo-tivations are "intimately linked with women's collective sense of the devaluation of their bodies and their work. Viccing can be viewed as a way of contesting this devaluation and simultaneously as a means of adaptation to the changed conditions of street-level sex work" (Maher and Curtis, 1992, 246). Moreover, these women rarely initiated violence and were more often responding to actual or anticipated harms perpetrated against them by male attackers. Thus women's crime and violence are situational acts of resistance contextual-ized "within the terms of the sometimes conflicting and often complementary structures of patriarchy, racism and capitalism" (Maher and Curtis, 1992, 251).

Although drug use may provide some "immediate gratification," research indicates that women's drug use is often intertwined with trauma and with relational concerns. For in-stance, women are often introduced to drugs by their male partners (Amaro and Hardy-Fanta, 1995), whereas male initiation occurs in context of male friends. Interviews with women drug users in Miami showed that women are more likely to drink or use illegal drugs as a form of self-medication to cope with histories of physical and sexual abuse; men on the other hand are more likely to use drugs for thrills, excitement, or pleasure or because of peer pressure (Inciardi et al., 1993, 25). Moreover, although prostitution can provide a means of supporting a drug habit, drug use can also provide a way of coping with the traumatic experience of prostitution (Sanchez, 2001).

Ethnographic research by Laidler and others (see Chesney-Lind and Pasko, 2004) on Asian American women drug users in Hawaii describes an intricate path to illegal drug use. These women generally came from economically marginalized families where parental alcohol and drug use, family violence, and girls' physical and sexual abuse were not uncommon. Peers and extended family members often introduced these women to alcohol, tobacco, and marijuana in their early teen years. Later, they also provided the source for cocaine and methamphetamine, the latter being useful for appetite control or used with a partner for sexual enhancement. Depression and paranoia from prolonged drug use often led to strained family relations and isolation, which in turn increased drug use as a coping strategy.

The connections between victimization and offending are especially evident in female gang participation. Although male gang involvement provides an avenue for masculinity confirmation, research on female gangs consistently reveals that gangs often serve as a refuge from sexual victimization in the home, and one study found that female gang members were more likely than male gang members to come from homes with drug users and individuals arrested for crimes (Moore and Hagedorn, 2001). Gang membership is also influenced by racial, ethnic, and class position. According to the U.S. Department of Justice, women of color are disproportionately involved in gangs, with most gangs either African American or Latina (Moore and Hagedorn, 2001). This composition reflects the economic pressures on women to rely on their own resources to support themselves and their children, given high male unemployment and the male incarceration rate along with the elimination of AFDC and other welfare reforms. Moreover, female gang members attach a great deal of importance to a reputation as a good mother and are most likely to fight to defend challenges to their honor around maternal roles than for reasons having to do with gang issues (Campbell, 1984).

Jody Miller's (2001) qualitative study shows how young women knowingly exchange powerlessness and random violence in the home for the predictable violence on the street. Miller contends that "gang violence is governed by rules and expectations. As such it does not involve the same kind of vulnerability that being on the streets without a gang might entail. . . . Moreover, in principle, it provides a contrast to many young women's previous experiences of victimization in their home . . . where many found themselves vulnerable and unable to control the actions of the adults who victimized them" (J. Miller, 2001, 158). Miller also found that young women were reluctant to engage in violence unless deliberately challenged by a rival gang. Even the "initiation" violence associated with entrance into a gang was purposeful, where girls actively consider the costs and benefits of being "sexed in" versus "beaten in." Other male and female members saw young women as weak, promiscuous, and deserving of abuse if they made the decision to be sexed in. The use of physical violence is often an alternative to sexual victimization, and decisions to be beaten into the gang translated into greater respect for a woman's fighting ability. Thus females' gang membership and related behaviors exemplify resiliency in the face of adversity and entail careful consideration of the long-term benefits of gang protection and the trade-offs to surviving on one's own.

The importance of a gender analysis is underscored with regard to women's use of violence in intimate relationships. In stark contrast to men's violence to control, intimidate, subordinate, or punish their (typically) female partner, women who use violence against their male partners rarely instill fear or achieve control over them. In a three-year study exploring women arrested for domestic violence, Susan Miller (2005) found that only 5 percent of her sample of arrested women were violent without provocation. The remaining 95 percent used violence when it seemed that nothing else would work with their abusers, when trying escape a violent incident or attempting to leave to avoid one, or in response to a threat to them or their children. Thus women use violence in ways that rarely resemble men's controlling violence in intimate relationships, neither of which is adequately accounted for by low self-control.

Neighborhoods and poverty can also affect women's affinity to violence. Poor women living in urban areas, who are also disproportionately women of color, are more likely to live in dangerous areas where gangs are active, where gun and knife violence is not uncommon, and where the risk of violence outside the home is great (Hooper, 1996). In the home fighting back is an available and desirable alternative to feeling powerless and trapped in an abusive relationship, especially when calling the police means an encounter with a system that is perceived as racist and that is also likely to blame these women for the violence. Recent research also suggests that there may be racial or cultural differences in how women respond to violent partners. For instance, African American women may more often use violence against their intimate male partners in response to experiencing severe physical and sexual aggression and psychological abuse (C. M. West and Rose, 2000). In a study comparing white and black women, black women were more likely to fight back when physically assaulted (Moss et al., 1997). This tendency of black women to fight back may be attributed to a "long history of physical abuse and oppression, both within their homes and in the larger society, [such that] they had to be prepared to defend themselves" (C. M. West and Rose, 2000, 488).

The experience of physical violence and sexual victimization in intimate relationships can combine with the impact of racism. Richie's (1996) life history interviews with incarcerated women show that they were often forced to engage in crimes such as petty theft, fraud, drug dealing, or prostitution by their batterer or saw these crimes as an avenue for their own economic survival. Some were forced by their batterer to take drugs and did so as a means of creating intimacy. Some used violence against their batterer in retaliation or self-defense. African American women living in poor communities can be especially trapped in relationships with abusive men, despite coming from loving families with hopes for their futures. Women's situational violence and offending in these contexts seem a far cry from the result of low self-control because their options are structurally conditioned by the oppressions of gender, race, and class.

Crime Committed by Men Against Women: Battering and Rape

The general theory of crime masks the way gender and power operate within personal relationships and social institutions, raising serious questions for its ability to account for crimes of interpersonal violence committed by men against women. Significant features of battering and rape are also at odds with the notion of low self-control, particularly as it manifests as impulsivity and risk taking.

With respect to battering, we distinguish between a one-time hit and an ongoing pattern of domination and control over an intimate partner that includes not only physical assault but also real and perceived threats, intimidation, and emotional and psychological violence. The Gottfredson and Hirschi framework does not directly address this particular behavior, but it effectively serves to trivialize intimate partner violence by men by explaining that "the major benefit of many crimes is not pleasure but relief from momentary irritation" (Gottfredson and Hirschi, 1990, 90) and by positing that "crimes of personal violence, such as . . . assault . . . are by their nature incapable of providing more than short-term gratification for the offender" (p. 20). Although masculinity notions would question self-control as an adequate explanation of even typical male-on-male violence scenarios (the barroom brawl or street fight), we note that male battering of female partners has little in common with these one-time events. Battering is deliberate behavior with intended effects and serves as a long-term mechanism of male control, ensuring proper domestic behavior of female partners. Research reveals that the battering cycle becomes increasingly more violent, frequent, and injurious, resulting in long-term benefits of absolute power, authority, and control exercised by the offender over the victim or household (Walker, 1979). Although the one-time use of partner violence might be indicative of expressive "out-of-control" behavior that *could be* interpreted as consistent with self-control theory, the intimate partner violence that is gendered, patterned, frequent, and instrumental seems to be instead "in-control" behavior (Sellers, 1999) that has little to do with low self-control or impulsiveness.

The treatment of rape also suffers in the general theory. First, according to Gottfredson and Hirschi (1990, 89), rape meets the criteria for a crime of low self-control: "Criminal acts provide *easy or simple* gratification of desires . . . [such as] sex without courtship." In our view this is a mischaracterization; it effectively reduces rape to a purely sexual act rather than a violent sexual offense and obscures the force inherent in power relations where traditional notions of violence may not apply. The reality of rape can be an ultimate submission out of fear, terror, or the inability to demonstrate nonconsent (because of drugs, alcohol, or mental or physical disability), but rape occurs in the absence of *consent*, not in the absence of dating.

Second, empirical research challenges Gottfredson and Hirschi's claims that non-stranger rape is statistically uncommon or that most nonstranger rapes involve parties who know each other only slightly. For instance, Koss et al. (1987) asked 6,100 students on 32 college campuses whether they had experienced or committed unwanted sexual intercourse or other sexual victimization (anal or oral intercourse or penetration by objects) in situations of physical force or the plying of alcohol or drugs. The study found that 15 percent of the women had been raped and that 12 percent had experienced an attempted rape since age 14; it was estimated that this could be as high as one in four women. Importantly, the study also found that 84 percent of the women knew their attacker and that in 57 percent of these cases the attacker was a date. More recently, Fisher et al. (2000) surveyed a national random sample of 4,446 college women with detailed questions about their sexual victimization experiences; they found that nearly 5 percent of college women are victimized in any given year on college campuses. In actual cases of completed and attempted rapes committed by single offenders, approximately 90 percent of the offenders were known to be a classmate, friend, ex-boyfriend, or acquaintance. In addition, gang acquaintance rapes on college campuses are not uncommon. The Koss data revealed that 16 percent of the male students who committed rape and 10 percent of those who attempted rape participated in incidents involving more than one attacker (Warshaw, 1988, 101).

Research also finds evidence of planning that raises questions about impulsivity. In an early study based on police records, Amir (1971) found that 71 percent of rapes in police records were planned, although rapists searched for the most convenient victims. Scully's (1990) in-depth interviews with incarcerated rapists revealed that for stranger rapes by a single offender, the majority of the rapists indicated that it was their original intent to rape versus to rob or burglarize. Although the choice of an actual victim could be based on "randomness and convenience" (Scully, 1990, 175), the rape itself had been planned for hours or sometimes days. In the case of rapes that occurred in conjunction with a robbery or burglary, "the decision to rape was made after a sense of control over the situation was established" (Scully, 1990, 174). In the somewhat more spontaneous acquaintance rapes, offenders likely had been previously rejected by the victim, and a third of these cases involved instrumental use of violence to create fear and gain compliance (Scully, 1990, 179). Moreover, acquaintance rapes that occur in dating situations (less likely to be represented in an incarcerated sample) are often characterized by a degree of manipulation and coercion (Sanday, 1996), suggesting that rapists are not merely more "vulnerable to the temptations of the moment" (Gottfredson and Hirschi, 1990, 87).

Finally, battering and rape occur within a risk scenario that differs from other types of offenses. Gottfredson and Hirschi (1990, 168) agree with the deterrence notion that informal sources of social control (conventional peers, school, job, marriage, and family) are more effective than formal criminal justice processing at restraining individuals from crime and deviance—but only insofar as individuals are "within their sphere of influence." In their framework people with low self-control avoid attachment to or involvement in all social institutions, precluding an informal deterrent effect. However, informal costs may not play a role for reasons other than a lack of attachment to these sources. In the case of battering some degree of societal ambivalence remains—lingering attitudes of provocation or deservedness on the part of the woman, feelings that this is a private matter, or difficulty in believing victims. Thus conventional others in the batterer's sphere may not directly condemn the behavior, rendering informal costs low or nonexistent. In the case of rape informal attachments may even encourage the behavior, such as the cultural support for sexual conquest in college fraternities (Sanday, 2007).

Both batterers and rapists also generally face lower risks of detection, formal apprehension, prosecution, and punishment in the criminal justice system. These crimes typically occur in private without witnesses. Victims of both battering and rape are often reluctant to report their attackers for reasons such as embarrassment, stigma, and self-blame, as well as understanding that the criminal justice system is either unlikely to take them seriously or reluctant to vigorously pursue their case. Battering victims, particularly those with children, may be economically dependent on their partners. In addition, because women are on average not as strong as men and because many women are socialized not to fight back, perpetrators of these crimes are at little risk of injury vis-à-vis male-on-male crimes of violence. Rape and battering carry low risk and high reward.

The general theory's conceptualization of rape as an act of low self-control and its similar implication for battering ignores the highly rational nature of these crimes and effectively absolves men of responsibility. Devoid of social context, the theory is incapable of recognizing these acts of violence as embedded in the gendered power relations that operate at all levels of a patriarchal society. These acts reflect a gender and offense specificity inherently at odds with the general theory of crime.

SOCIALIZATION AND SELF-CONTROL

Gottfredson and Hirschi attribute criminal propensity to the failure to establish self-control during a child's first six to eight years, emphasizing the salience of parenting in crime causation. For these theorists "the major 'cause' of low self-control thus appears to be ineffective childrearing" (Gottfredson and Hirschi, 1990, 97). However, feminist scholars have challenged Gottfredson and Hirschi's representation of family labor and parenting and their implicit critique of mothers in child rearing (S. L. Miller and Burack, 1993).

First, although Gottfredson and Hirschi acknowledge that effective child rearing can be accomplished in settings other than "traditional" families, they generally portray the family as a dual-headed heterosexual one where parenting does not vary by gender. Moreover, although they do note that single-parent families are usually headed by females, they view mothers and fathers as interchangeable, noting "we could substitute 'mother' or 'father' for 'parents' without any obvious loss in child rearing ability. Husbands and wives tend to be sufficiently alike on such things as values, attitudes, and skills" (Gottfredson and Hirschi, 1990, 103). However, these theorists fail to appreciate the patterned inequities of family and social life, namely, regardless of whether a household is single-headed or dual-headed, women are the primary child care providers. Despite the increased involvement of fathers in child rearing in recent years (Kurz, 1997; Siranni and Negrey, 2000), men tend not to rear children because "men don't want the job" (Polatnik, 1983) and continue to see this as "women's work" (Arrighi and Maume, 2000). Some research shows that following the birth of a child, men tend to "help out" rather than share child-raising responsibilities (Belsky and Kelly, 1994; Walzer, 1996). Recent changes in men's employment, such as number of hours employed, job flexibility, and job stability, have no effect on their involvement in child care and housework (Gerstel and Gallagher, 2001). Findings from the National Survey of Families and Households revealed that single, divorced women receive even less help from fathers: Roughly 30 percent of divorced fathers did not see their children in the previous year, 60 percent saw their children several times or less during the year, and only 25 percent saw their children weekly (Seltzer, 1991).

Second, economic disparities between women and men continue to be the norm and shape parenting. Women in the labor market continue to be remunerated less well than men. Income figures for 2005 show that women working full-time and year round earned a median income of $31,858 compared to $41,386 for men (DeNavas-Walt et al., 2006). These economic realities are compounded for women of color, who face the additional burdens of institutional racism and workplace discrimination that translate into lower salaries and fewer job prospects compared to white women. In addition, women remain ghettoized in clerical, sales, and service occupations that are lower in status and lower in pay than men's occupations. Such inequities reinforce the economically feasible practice of women in dual-headed households participating less in the paid-labor market and assuming the brunt of child-rearing responsibilities at home. Women's primary caregiving role and resulting economic dependence reinforce women's structurally weaker social, legal, and political position vis-à-vis males, both in their positions as "heads of households" and in general (Hartsock, 1985). Moreover, one-third of all households headed by women with children live below the poverty line. Race and gender interact where, among female-headed households, 19 percent of white families, 35 percent of black families, 37 percent of Hispanic families, and 15 percent of Asian American families live in poverty (Proctor and Dalaker, 2002). These statistics speak to the "feminization of poverty" (Pearce, 1993), which compounds the problems faced by women in their maternal and child-rearing roles.

The picture presented here undermines the Gottfredson and Hirschi assumption of gender neutrality in child rearing and speaks to the social and economic forces that shape family dynamics and challenge mothers. Implicit in the story of law-abiding behavior presented by the general theory is a construction of the "good" mother. However, this ideal mother, financially supported by a husband, working at home, socializing children to hegemonic values, is a race- and class- as well as gender-based standard. The general theory abstracts the family and parenting from social context and essentially takes a mother-blaming stance in its explanation of the development of adequate self-control.

CONCLUDING REMARKS

Gottfredson and Hirschi's parsimonious theory has not brought us closer to understanding the gender-crime nexus. When gender relations and differences in power, resources, and opportunities are considered, it becomes clear that the relationship between gender and crime is more complex than the one portrayed by the general theory. Qualitative studies on gangs, drugs, battering, and rape that have explicitly incorporated gender and race provide us with evidence of criminals who act with more self-control than the theory would suggest. Crime and delinquency ultimately reflect gendered power differences. Girls are at higher risk of sexual victimization in the home than are boys, where the only means by which they can exercise power is to run away. All too often the result is crime as street survival in the form of prostitution, drugs, or gang membership for support. Women strike back violently in self-defense or retaliation against their abusive male partners; women often engage in economic and drug-related crime in the context of abusive relationships, and these crimes as well as other violence can occur within the context of gang membership. Men engage in both sexual victimization and physical abuse of women, some of whom they know or are in relationships with, as an affirmation of male power and a means of intimidation and control. When crime is viewed in these terms, it is difficult to see the contribution of self-control. The general theory lacks a complete consideration of gender and its relationship to crime and its implications for parenting, and any policy implications derived from it will, in our estimation, remain misguided.

III | TYPES OF CRIME

10 | LOW SELF-CONTROL AND HIGH ORGANIZATIONAL CONTROL: THE PARADOXES OF WHITE-COLLAR CRIME

David O. Friedrichs and Martin D. Schwartz

In *A General Theory of Crime*, Gottfredson and Hirschi (1990) claim to have identified a valid scientific solution to explaining crime. They argue that all forms of crime can be explained principally as a function of low self-control: When an opportunity arises, individuals with low self-control will engage in crime. We argue that low self-control is a simplistic, one-dimensional explanation for what is ultimately a complex phenomenon. In particular, a sophisticated understanding of white-collar crime does not lend itself to such a simplistic, one-dimensional explanation. It requires a complex, multidimensional explanation.

DEFINITIONS AND TYPOLOGIES OF WHITE-COLLAR CRIME

Criminologists agree that white-collar crime occurs in a legitimate occupational context, is motivated by the objective of economic gain or occupational success, is not characterized by direct, intentional violence, is committed by offenders who do not have a criminal self-image, and tends to activate milder criminal justice responses than is true of conventional crime (Friedrichs, 2007, 4–5). However, criminologists continue to debate a number of definitional issues, including the following: whether white-collar crime should refer only to violations of criminal law or to violations addressed by civil and administrative law as well; whether it should refer to acts committed by higher-status individuals and institutions or to acts committed in the context of any legitimate occupation; whether it should refer only to acts involving financial and economic activities or to acts involving physical as well as financial harm; and whether it should refer only to the acts of individuals or to acts committed collectively, that is, by organizations as well.

The definitional problem goes to the core of Gottfredson and Hirschi's problems with theories of white-collar crime. Gottfredson and Hirschi claim that such theories cannot account for ordinary crime. Sutherland's (1949) theory of differential association was put forth as a *general* theory of crime, and hence some observers reason that, if an explanation is not general, it is not valid. Sutherland's basic proposition was that both ordinary criminal behavior and white-collar crime are learned behaviors: If one associates with gang members, one will acquire their values and behavioral patterns, and if one associates with corporate executives, one will acquire their values and behavioral patterns. Sutherland's theory was inspired by his concern that the focus of the criminological theories of his time on social pathology and poverty as causes of crime made it impossible to explain the crimes of the middle classes and the wealthy. Rather than trying to understand crime by looking at people who are different, Sutherland was focusing attention on processes whereby anyone could conceivably be drawn into some form of criminal activity.

Gottfredson and Hirschi (1990) argue that their self-control theory is superior to Sutherland's theory of differential association because "it begins with an image of crime that is consistent with good research" (p. 199). Gottfredson and Hirschi endorse the approach to white-collar crime taken by Wheeler et al. (1988), who selected eight federal statutory offenses as representative of white-collar crime and then compared convicted white-collar and conventional offenders; Wheeler's group found that most are "banal, mundane" activities of the kind that are most likely to be committed by individuals with low self-control, as Gottfredson and Hirschi suggest.

The problem is that not all criminologists agree with this approach to defining and measuring white-collar crime. Crime and criminal behavior can be defined in other more complex, far richer ways, for instance, as manifestations of harmful conduct (Henry and Lanier, 2001). Contrary to Wheeler and his colleagues, such critics argue, white-collar crime is not best conceived of as offenses that federal prosecutors have found easiest to pursue. By some measures the most harmful and consequential activities of corporations, businesses, and professionals have been the least likely to be clearly defined as crime by the law and, when so defined, have proved to be the most difficult to investigate and prosecute.

Even if one resolves the question of how best to define crime, another issue arises. Historically, much less attention has been devoted to explaining criminalization—that is, why certain forms of harmfulness but not others are formally designated crimes—than to explaining criminality, or the causes of criminal behavior. Gottfredson and Hirschi (1990) adopt a definition of crime as "force and fraud in pursuit of self-interest" (p. 15) but use specifically legalistic definitions of crime when they cite data in support of their theory. Many criminologists believe that the distribution of power explains why certain violators of laws are formally identified as criminals and processed by the criminal justice system while others are not. Explaining criminalization is especially important in relation to white-collar crime because white-collar harms have been less vulnerable to being classified as crimes in the first place, and harmful (and illegal) activities carried out in a white-collar context are less vulnerable to detection and adjudication than is typically true of street crime activities. In short, Gottfredson and Hirschi's first and most fundamental problem is conceptual: Their definition of white-collar crime is flawed because it is skewed.

ARE CRIMINALS DIFFERENT FROM THE REST OF US?

Gottfredson and Hirschi's general theory argues that criminals are fundamentally different from the rest of us. The difference, they say, can be traced back to poor parenting and the consequent development of low self-control. To our knowledge this claim is not supported by the evidence on white-collar crime. Indeed, we are unaware of any study documenting that white-collar offenders are products of poor parenting or afflicted with low self-control. One major study of a cohort of convicted white-collar offenders concluded that these offenders were not very different from nonoffenders (Weisburd and Waring, 2001). Rather, their lawbreaking was principally a function of situations and circumstances. Although Weisburd and Waring adopted the operational definition of white-collar crime favored by Gottfredson and Hirschi, this finding contradicts the claims of their general theory.

Furthermore, adopting Gottfredson and Hirschi's view pushes us to focus on some forms of crime over others and to exclude vast territories of criminal activities that somehow do not correspond to their theory. Essentially by definition, low self-control theory would have us think of crime mainly in terms of impulsive, instrumental, simplistic actions (such as smash and grab thefts and assaults) while largely discouraging our interest in other forms of crime. This fits in with the historical tradition that criminologists, the general public, and governmental policymakers have focused on street crime while white-collar crimes have received far less attention. Gottfredson and Hirschi (1990) contend that their general theory applies to the understanding of white-collar crime and of conventional crime. However, it is our claim in this chapter that this contention is fundamentally flawed and does not help us to develop a sophisticated understanding of contemporary white-collar crime.

There is a superficially plausible logic to Gottfredson and Hirschi's claim that low self-control plays a critical role in relation to certain forms of conventional lawbreaking, mainly the FBI's index crimes. Certainly a tendency toward impulsivity and the inability to defer gratification correlate with run-of-the-mill violations of the law. But individuals with low self-control violate laws only selectively, episodically, at certain times, and in certain situations. And surely different crimes can vary greatly in terms of the amount of planning and skill involved, with a wide range of variables coming into play. Furthermore, low self-control manifests itself in many contexts apart from conventional lawbreaking. Let's look at self-control as it relates to the corporate context.

LOW SELF-CONTROL OR ADHERENCE TO CORPORATE NORMS?

Gottfredson and Hirschi (1990, 181) concede that the concept of white-collar crime has made it clear that criminal behavior is not necessarily tied to poverty or social pathology. Indeed, white-collar crime demonstrates that, although the privileged have been less vulnerable to legal prosecution, they do engage in criminal behavior. Gottfredson and Hirschi suggest that this does not really take us very far, and it feeds into the unfortunate tendency to classify crimes in accordance with the characteristics of their perpetrators. But is this tendency really unfortunate, or does it lead us to a more sophisticated understanding of criminal behavior? For Gottfredson and Hirschi white-collar crimes are principally committed by individuals with commonplace occupations. And Gottfredson and Hirschi do not pay any attention to the activities of high-level corporate executives who act on behalf of corporations. But if their theory truly is general in scope, it should account for the actions of such executives as well as more conventional offenders. It is difficult to imagine that the criminal motivations and crime patterns of inner-city teenage males are not fundamentally different from the criminal motivations and crime patterns of upper-class middle-aged corporate executives. It may be true that both upper-level corporate offenders and conventional offenders could be breaking the law for economic gain, but for the most part this attempt to find common elements serves mainly to distort our understanding of the broad, complex phenomenon we know as crime. High-level white-collar offenders typically define themselves as law-abiding respectable members of society; they engage in selective forms of lawbreaking, generally make risk-benefit calculations regarding the forms of violations of the law they engage in, and rely heavily on rationalizations of such violations to maintain a respectable self-image.

The wave of high-level white-collar crime revealed early in the twenty-first century in the United States is explained better by "the structural features of the investment-banking industry that created powerful incentives for misbehavior" (Stelzer, 2004, 25) than by the low self-control of criminal actors. More specifically, three major changes in the financial markets that took place between 1985 and 2000 promoted such crime: the increasing complexity and lack of visibility of financial instruments, the increasing gap between the control and ownership of companies, and the overall deregulation of markets (Partnoy, 2003, 3). Gottfredson and Hirschi's explanation is essentially irrelevant to such crimes; it neglects the type of social control that operates to encourage such acts and is incapable of understanding a different form of social control that fails to operate here.

From a broad perspective social control refers to deliberate efforts by individuals, such as state officials and corporate executives, who have the power to control the behavior of their subordinates. In this sense white-collar crime is a product of social control, as seen from two distinctly divergent dimensions: first, highly successful organizational control, that is, the exercise of the power of executives in corporations to control the behavior of subordinates so that they can achieve corporate goals while skirting or violating the law; and second, the failure of social, professional, and legal institutions to prevent or deter corporations and individuals from engaging in socially harmful conduct. These dimensions of social control are distinctly different from Gottfredson and Hirschi's microlevel concept of self-control, and they are generated by distinctly different causes and have distinctly different consequences.

Thus, ironically, white-collar crime may reflect the high level of control over individual human conduct that organizations achieve. Such crimes often result from conformity to— not a violation of—organizational norms. So when Gottfredson and Hirschi (1990) claim that, to the extent that white-collar crimes occur at all, they are best understood as a function of individuals with low self-control, the critical observer can counter: On the contrary, much of the most significant and consequential white-collar crime occurs because lower-level corporate employees are conforming to the expectations and priorities established by their corporate superiors, who control their behavior to a high degree. High organizational control refers to this key aspect of how such white-collar crime differs from much conventional crime. It is the exceptional corporate or organizational employee rather than the typical one who displays an unwillingness to participate in unethical or illegal conduct when pressured by higher management to do so. Only a small number become whistle-blowers and with good reason: Those who do blow the whistle are typically punished for their Good Samaritan behavior. In contrast to Gottfredson and Hirschi's approach, the notion of low self-control is problematic here, because the degree of control by others rather than impulsivity or a focus on immediate benefits seems to be the key factor in compliance or noncompliance with organizational efforts to control the behavior of employees.

OPPORTUNITY AND WHITE-COLLAR CRIME

Gottfredson and Hirschi (1990) argue against what they characterize as an "occupation theory" of white-collar crime, that "a finding that the employed are more likely to steal because of their employment no more justifies a unique theory of theft (white-collar crime) than a finding that the unemployed are more likely to steal justifies a theory focusing exclusively on the lower class (deprivation or strain theory)" (p. 186). But this proposition wholly misrepresents the thrust of white-collar crime theory. It does not claim that white-collar offenders are more likely to steal because of their employment. Rather, it suggests that white-collar employment provides opportunities to engage in certain forms of crime, from embezzlement to corporate price-fixing.

Any credible theory of white-collar crime recognizes that many (or most) of those in a position to commit white-collar offenses do not engage in it, just as any credible theory of conventional crime must recognize that many (or most) of those in circumstances conducive to conventional lawbreaking (e.g., poor inner-city residents) do not engage in such lawbreaking. When Gottfredson and Hirschi (1990, 187) suggest that white-collar crime can be explained only by turning to individualistic levels of explanation—to account for why some of those in white-collar occupations commit offenses and some of their peers do not—they do not effectively attend to the notion of organizational crime, or white-collar crimes carried out on behalf of organizations such as corporations. They disregard the fact that a complex of external and internal factors—on many different levels and interacting in different ways—may account for why white-collar crime occurs in some circumstances but not in others, why some individuals (and organizations) engage in white-collar offenses and others do not.

A number of case studies (e.g., Faulkner et al., 2003) have revealed the external and internal pressures on some corporations and how the pressure on individuals is socially structured. Criminal conspiracies in certain industries may well be "sustained by authoritative decisions, inter-organizational leadership, and adroit management of intra-firm staff in other kinds of hierarchical, authority-based settings engaged in crime" (Faulkner et al., 2003, 548). This type of approach to explaining a significant form of corporate crime is persuasive and sophisticated.

CAN CORPORATIONS COMMIT CRIMES?

Can corporations, or organizations, commit crimes? Although the white-collar crime literature has debated this question, Gottfredson and Hirschi (1990, 187–188) are generally dismissive of the issue. They claim that students of white-collar crime have not really focused on corporations as criminal actors, treating the corporation only as the setting within which some white-collar crime occurs. But since the 1970s and especially since Gottfredson and Hirschi's book was published (1990), a number of significant studies have specifically focused on corporations as offenders and have made comparisons between corporations where high and low rates of offending appear to occur (Jenkins and Braithwaite, 1993; Shover and Bryant, 1993; Simpson and Piquero, 2002). In a literal sense, of course, a corporation (a chartered entity) cannot "do" anything; on some level humans must implement corporate policy and actions. But it does not follow that a corporation is no more than a setting for some forms of white-collar crime. When crimes that simply cannot be carried out by an individual or even by groups of individuals are committed through the corporation and require the resources of the corporation, then it is meaningful to claim that corporate—not simply individual—crime has occurred.

Admittedly, it is not always easy to discriminate between illegal actions carried out on behalf of the corporation and those carried out in the interest of key corporate executives. However, over time a corporate culture develops, including value systems and incentives, and this tends to play a key role in promoting corporate crime. It is a long-established tenet of sociology that groups (or societies) are more than simply the sum of the individuals who constitute them, and so it is with corporations. Thus many illegal, unethical, or harmful corporate actions, such as evasion of pollution regulations, toleration of dangerous working conditions, and marketing of unsafe products, are most accurately characterized as corporate crimes carried out in the interest of maximizing corporate profit or minimizing corporate loss. And such crime is simply not helpfully explained or understood in terms of putative low self-control as an attribute of corporate executives.

WHITE-COLLAR CRIME AND CONVENTIONAL CRIME

Gottfredson and Hirschi (1990) ask, "What is the theoretical value in distinguishing a pharmacist's theft of drugs from a carpenter's theft of lumber?" (p. 189). If either the pharmacist or the carpenter is stealing drugs or lumber from their place of employment, these actions could be classified as occupational crime; if one or the other is stealing drugs or lumber independently of their place of employment, in both cases conventional forms of crime are involved. Assuming that Gottfredson and Hirschi are really asking, What is the theoretical value of distinguishing occupational theft from conventional theft, one can answer: Occupations structure special opportunities for theft quite different from conventional opportunities for theft; theft within an occupational setting is likely to occur on a significantly larger scale and with more diffuse harmful consequences than is true of conventional forms of theft; and occupational theft involves a different form of violating a trust than is true for conventional forms of theft. If one accepts the axiom that a crime is a function of both motivation and opportunity, it makes sense that theories applicable to situations involving some types of opportunities are less applicable to situations involving other types of opportunities. A valid theory of occupational theft must take account of a workplace (or professional) culture that may promote theft on some level. Gottfredson and Hirschi ask, "What is the theoretical value in distinguishing a doctor's Medicaid fraud from a patient's Medicaid fraud?" Again, the scale of opportunity, the consequences of the fraud, and the nature of trust violation differ in these two cases and accordingly call for a different dynamic.

Near the outset of their chapter on white-collar crime, Gottfredson and Hirschi (1990) make the following remarkable claim: "Our general theory of crime accounts for the frequency and distribution of white-collar crime in the same way as it accounts for the frequency and distribution of all forms of crime, including rape, vandalism, and simple assault" (p. 181). Rape is typically characterized as a crime of domination, humiliation, and degradation, although many include motivations fueled by appalling attitudes toward women and inhibitions unleashed by alcohol. It is profoundly difficult to see meaningful connections between such crime and the actions of corporate executives signing off on practices that will enhance profit or cut losses by evading environmental laws. Such crimes are different in many respects. Vandalism is intentionally destructive, often irrational, and unrelated to material gain; white-collar crime may have destructive consequences but is oriented toward material gain (or minimizing loss) and is rational and carefully planned, and destructive consequences are avoided if they do not compromise these material objectives. Aggravated assaults tend to be personal, expressive, and impulsive; white-collar crime is almost uniformly impersonal, instrumental, and calculated.

HOW RARE IS WHITE-COLLAR CRIME?

Because the attributes necessary to succeed in white-collar occupations are inconsistent with the characteristics associated with criminality, Gottfredson and Hirschi (1990, 191) predict a relatively low rate of offending among white-collar workers. If conventional crime, such as burglary and robbery, is disproportionately concentrated among inner-city residents, it obviously does not follow that most such residents engage in these activities. But is the proportion of white-collar workers who engage in some form of white-collar crime really lower than the proportion of inner-city residents who engage in some form of conventional crime? Criminologists and sociologists from Sutherland on have argued differently. Merton (1968, 198–199) reasoned that white-collar criminality was the norm among legitimate businesspeople, not the exception. More recently, Callahan (2004) has claimed that cheating is epidemic in America—among students, doctors, lawyers, taxpayers, auto mechanics, job applicants, stock analysts, file sharers, and corporate executives, probably as a result of high payoffs and weak punishments.

Gottfredson and Hirschi complain that white-collar crime researchers make inappropriate comparisons (e.g., comparing organizational rates of lawbreaking with individual blue-collar offender rates). But because a high proportion of white-collar crime is undetected and unreported, fully valid comparisons of white-collar offenders and nonoffenders (on both the individual and the organizational level) may simply not be obtainable. Gottfredson and Hirschi (1990, 191) acknowledge the problem of unavailable data but do not adequately explore the implications of this fact. White-collar crime, by definition, occurs "in the suite," not "on the street," by people who are generally more sophisticated than typical conventional offenders.

What evidence is there, then, for the claim that white-collar crime is common? Admittedly, the methodological challenges of establishing rates of offending for white-collar workers in general and corporate executives specifically are formidable and perhaps ultimately insurmountable. Nevertheless, there is much reason to believe that such rates are roughly equivalent to those for inner-city residents in relation to the commission of conventional crimes. First, one can consider the prevalence of offending among corporate executives. Surveys of corporate involvement in a broad range of illegal and harmful conduct, from Sutherland's (1949) pioneering study on, have provided much evidence of the pervasiveness of such conduct (Clinard and Yeager, 1980; Friedrichs, 2007; Rosoff et al., 2006).

In the 1980s a wave of savings and loan frauds occurred, as did high-level insider trading cases, that were clearly not isolated instances of serious lawbreaking (e.g., Calavita et al., 1997). Following the exposure of massive financial misrepresentations and fraudulent activities at Enron Corporation in 2001, parallel activities were exposed in numerous other corporations, including WorldCom, Global Crossing, Rite Aid, Adelphia, Xerox, and Health-South (Friedrichs, 2007; Rosoff et al., 2006). The fraudulent activity involved many, if not all, of the top executives in these corporations and many other managerial employees as well. Studies of middle managers have produced much evidence that unethical or illegal practices have been far from uncommon on this level (e.g., Clinard, 1983; Jackall, 1988; Reed and Yeager, 1996). At Enron many energy traders engaged in massive manipulations of California's energy markets in 2000 and 2002 in ways that cost the state billions of dollars. Furthermore, it came out that corporate board members, auditors, stock analysts, investment bankers, corporate lawyers, and various other parties were involved to varying degrees in the fraudulent activities or the illegal concealment of these activities. For every participant in these fraudulent activities who were successfully identified, how many more have gone undetected?

At the same time various investigators have exposed fraudulent activities in other financial sectors, such as the vast mutual funds industry (Labaton, 2003). In the United States $7 trillion is invested annually by close to 100 million investors, generating $70 billion in fees. In the 1990s investors lost two-thirds of their high-tech investments while the mutual funds earned $50 billion in fees, with significant evidence of misrepresentations to investors and insider manipulations to benefit the mutual funds and their managers. During the same period of time a pattern of deep-rooted and long-running fraud was uncovered within the foreign currency exchange industry (Fuerbringer and Rashbaum, 2003). In 2005 New York State's attorney general characterized the level of fraud in the insurance industry as "vast," with systematic market manipulation and other forms of fraud (Treaster, 2005). The Martha Stewart insider trading case of this period was simply the highest profile of a number of insider trading cases (Hays and Eaton, 2004; Labaton and Leonhardt, 2002). Indeed, whenever regulators and journalists scrutinize any segment of high-finance industry, broad patterns of illegal and unethical conduct are found. White-collar crime on this level seems to be anything but rare.

Extensive fraud has also been documented within a wide range of retail and service-related businesses. Participant observer reports involving a large number of retail businesses in New York City, over a period of years, found that deceptive practices were the norm, observed in more than 70 percent of the businesses included in the sample (Blumberg, 1989). A famous early study found that more than 60 percent of auto mechanics engaged in some level of fraud with regard to repairs, and we have other studies supporting this kind of finding (Friedrichs, 2007, 91–92). Furthermore, significant levels of fraudulent conduct of some sort can be found in virtually all occupational settings.

Rather than predicting that corporate executives and those working in a wide range of financial industries, retail and service-related businesses, and professions have a low rate of offending relative to some other segments of society, we should concede, first, that white-collar offending in some form appears to be widespread and in some contexts the norm; second, that the vast majority of white-collar offenders are never formally identified (or prosecuted); and third, that we simply do not have the data—and are unlikely to have it soon, if ever—that could reliably affirm that offending is lower in the white-collar crime strata of society than in other strata or segments of society, including unemployed inner-city residents.

EMPLOYEE THEFT

Studies of employee crime likewise indicate that employee theft is common and for retail businesses accounts for more of the shrinkage than is caused by shoplifters and other non-employees (Friedrichs, 2007, 105). Although Gottfredson and Hirschi (1990, 191) cite a Clark and Hollinger (1983) study that 90 percent of retail employees reported never having stolen store merchandise of any value, Clark and Hollinger (1983) themselves reported that property theft is fairly common in the workforce with a "conservative estimate" that "about 35 percent of the surveyed employees reported theft involvement in the half-dozen or so items included in the theft index" (p. 12). Some estimates suggest that workplace theft costs retailers in the United States up to 25 percent of sales and that up to $400 billion a year is lost in the United States to workplace theft (Payne and Gainey, 2004, 63). A vast amount of fraud exists in the workers' compensation system, which is funded by employer premiums; cheating is involved in an estimated 20 percent or more of the claims (Kerr, 1991).

Gottfredson and Hirschi (1990, 197) claim that Cressey's (1953) celebrated study of embezzlers proved incorrect Sutherland's assertion that white-collar crime was a natural extension of ordinary business values, because Cressey's "embezzlers reported that they had not learned embezzlement from a 'business culture' but that, in fact, their criminal behavior resulted from efforts to cover problems created by their own prior misbehavior." Their analysis here is off the mark. White-collar crime researchers do not claim that corporations deliberately encourage employees to steal from the business, except perhaps for some employers who allow some employee theft to compensate for low wages and poor working conditions (Ditton, 1977). Employee theft involves activity thoroughly at odds with the values promoted within the business (and corporate) world.

But Sutherland's (1949) *White-Collar Crime* was not at all focused on this form of white-collar crime. Rather, Sutherland focused on violations of criminal, civil, and regulatory law undertaken *on behalf of* corporations, by corporate executives and employees, in the interest of maximizing profit and minimizing loss. And *that* form of white-collar crime—in the larger scheme of things a much more consequential form of white-collar crime than embezzlement—is indeed quite consistent with long-standing "business values" that throughout the history of modern industrial corporations have privileged profit making over all other considerations, including scrupulous compliance with laws, regulations, and ethical principles (Bakan, 2004).

Accordingly, when Gottfredson and Hirschi (1990, 198) assert the "rarity" of white-collar crime on the logical argument that a high level of such crime would be devastating over time to the pursuit of profit, that white-collar offenders receive little support for their criminal activity from the organization and their fellow workers, and that "the victim of white-collar crime is typically the organization itself," they conflate forms of occupational crime that victimize businesses with the far more significant forms of corporate crime that victimize workers, consumers, competitors, creditors, shareholders (in some cases), and citizens. Much corporate crime activity is consistent with enhancing profit, not diminishing it, and, we have reason to believe that that activity succeeds in achieving this objective much more often than not.

As Sutherland demonstrated long ago and as many more recent studies have demonstrated as well, even when corporations are caught violating laws or regulations, and penalized, they invariably continue such practices; this finding strongly suggests that the profit enhancement involved outweighs even the costs of being caught and fined, in some cases in the tens or hundreds of millions of dollars (Friedrichs, 2007). Contrary to Gottfredson and Hirschi's assertions, the corporate culture—be it of the Ford Motor Company or Enron or any number of other corporations—plays a central role in promoting much of the most consequential forms of white-collar crime.

Gottfredson and Hirschi (1990) ask, "If the white-collar work force is actually socialized to the virtues of embezzlement, bid-rigging, and fraud, what accounts for the extraordinarily high level of law-abiding conduct among white-collar workers?" (p. 198). First, most white-collar workers spend most of their time engaged in law-abiding conduct, but of course it is surely also true that most inner-city residents spend most of their time engaged in law-abiding conduct. Second, the claim of much of the white-collar crime literature is not that white-collar workers are socialized within the corporate environment to commit specific crimes but rather that they are socialized to focus on maximizing profit and minimizing loss at the expense of legality, which pressures them to commit crimes.

Accordingly, when these objectives can be accomplished by legal means, as is often the case, this is all to the good. Indeed, virtually any legitimate business recognizes a potential downside to lawbreaking activity, including possible criminal indictments, fines, prison time, collateral civil lawsuits, and bad publicity. And virtually by definition, a legitimate business does not encourage or promote lawbreaking for its own sake, because if it does, it really takes on the form of an organized crime enterprise and is no longer a legitimate business. It is also true that across many industries a broad sense of contempt or resentment exists with regard to regulatory law in particular, and evasion or outright violation of such law may indeed be encouraged. Finally, we simply have no reliable way of fully measuring the pervasiveness of lawbreaking behavior among white-collar workers, although we have various indicators—as suggested throughout this chapter—that it is hardly insignificant.

AGE, RACE, INTELLIGENCE, AND WHITE-COLLAR CRIME

On the basis of data from the yearly Uniform Crime Reports issued by the FBI, Gottfredson and Hirschi (1990) report that for fraud and embezzlement, "arrest rates for these white-collar crimes peak in the late teens and early twenties, and they decline sharply with increasing age. . . . By about age 41, the rate of fraud has declined to half its peak value" (p. 192). Their point is that patterns of lawbreaking for white-collar offenses parallel patterns for other types of crimes. They find such parallels for males and females and for whites and blacks. But Gottfredson and Hirschi's conclusions about demographic parallels between conventional and white-collar offenders are possible only by neglecting the crimes of those at the higher end of the white-collar crime pyramid. What the statistics they cite tell us has less to do with rates of offending than with how federal authorities choose to define and classify crimes and how certain segments of the population are far more vulnerable to arrest than others. Many of those arrested for fraud or embezzlement are engaged in low-level crimes, such as welfare fraud or check cashing fraud at the grocery store, which are hardly white-collar crimes. The vast majority of white-collar crimes committed by corporate executives and professionals never result in arrests that would be included in the Uniform Crime Reports, and we have many indications that the most serious white-collar crimes are disproportionately committed by white older males.

Gottfredson and Hirschi (1990, 194–195) also claim to find support for their age hypothesis in studies of tax evasion, suggesting that young people are more likely to underreport income than older people. This appears to be a remarkably naïve interpretation of actual patterns of tax evasion. There are substantial reasons to believe that the most consequential tax law evaders are dramatically different in demographics from conventional crime offenders. Although Gottfredson and Hirschi claim to be interested in rates of offending, not consequences, we dispute the conclusion that there is any clear evidence of a lower rate of offending for wealthy offenders. Wealthy individuals (who are typically older) have evaded billions of dollars in taxes by a wide range of maneuvers and strategies, including the use of blatantly illegal offshore accounts and tax shelters (D. C. Johnston, 2003, 262–273). Meanwhile, the IRS has audited the working poor at a rate many times higher than it has audited well-off and wealthy people (D. C. Johnston, 2003, 128–144). Much evidence suggests that this has allowed tax cheating among the wealthy to remain epidemic.

Regarding intelligence, Gottfredson and Hirschi (1990) assert that "it is obvious that intelligence is positively related to white-collar success, and it should therefore be positively related to white-collar crime. In all cases where data are available, however, those data suggest that the reverse of these assumptions is more near correct" (p. 196). Because Gottfredson and Hirschi do not give their data source for this assertion, it is hard to assess its validity. Still, even if it were true, one could make the argument that less intelligent white-collar criminals are the ones being caught and that more intelligent ones are evading detection.

Finally, on inherent ethics Gottfredson and Hirschi (1990) regard the attributes necessary for conventional success and for engagement in criminal behavior as essentially incompatible, and accordingly "selection processes inherent in the high end of the occupational structure tend to recruit people with relatively low propensity to crime" (p. 191). This proposition strongly suggests that the higher up people are in the occupational structure, the less likely they will be to engage in crime; a higher proportion of lower level employees will commit illegal, unethical, or harmful acts than higher level managers. The epidemic of wrongdoing at the highest levels of numerous corporations, as exposed by the corporate scandals of the recent era, and the pervasive wrongdoing at the highest levels of many financial and professional occupations strongly suggest that this proposition is simply wrong. The data that we have come from "the very slim fraction of people who are caught" (Dubner and Levitt, 2004, 64). In an attempt to test the validity of this assertion, Spahr and Alison (2004) used data sets collected in connection with the savings and loan frauds of the 1980s. Gottfredson and Hirschi's theory would predict that a higher percentage of cases would involve employees rather than directors, but in fact the data revealed the opposite. One can argue that such data inform us more about prosecutorial priorities in pursuing major cases of fraud than about criminality or lawbreaking itself.

LEVELS OF EXPLANATION

It is tempting to believe that crime can be explained simply by focusing on individual attributes, such as low self-control. But for white-collar crimes and especially those carried out within an organizational context, much accumulated evidence supports the claim that a sophisticated understanding of such crime requires attention to different levels of explanation. Vaughan (1999) in particular has argued for the need for attention to microlevel, mesolevel, and macrolevel factors. Microlevel factors focus on individuals, mesolevel factors focus on situations and organizations, and macrolevel factors focus on the structural or societal context. How would a multilevel approach apply to understanding the Enron case, one of the high-profile white-collar crime cases of the early twenty-first century?

When Enron filed for bankruptcy in December 2001, it was described as the seventh largest American corporation in terms of earnings (Oppel and Sorkin, 2001). With $60 billion in reported assets, it was also described as the largest corporate bankruptcy filing in American history up to that time (the subsequent bankruptcy of WorldCom was even larger). The collapse of Enron was attributed, at least in part, to its taking on massive debt and to issuing highly misleading reports about its profits and overall finances (Sloan, 2001). Much of the debt had been shifted into secret partnerships, which had the effect of grossly distorting the relationship between Enron's assets and profits and its losses and debts. The collapse of Enron led to devastating losses to Enron employees and pension plan participants, to investors, and to many other constituencies affiliated in some way with Enron. It also contributed to a significant loss of confidence in the securities markets. Enron's auditing firm, Arthur Andersen, was found guilty on obstruction of justice charges related to its complicity in the Enron case, and many high-level Enron executives were indicted for various criminal offenses. Massive civil lawsuits were also filed against many different parties involved in the matter in some way, including investment banking houses.

To attempt to explain the complex series of actions that constituted the Enron case by reference to low self-control would appear to be extraordinarily simplistic and wrongheaded. Assuming that we could make valid empirical studies of high-level corporate executives who do and do not engage in corporate fraud, we would hypothesize no significant differences in parental practices and patterns of self-control. Of course, *individualistic* factors may well play some role, because at least some decision makers may be amoral risk takers or greedy, egocentric, or sociopathic individuals with delusions of grandeur. Far from being "impulsive" individuals with low self-control, their success in completing demanding postgraduate programs and rising rapidly in a fiercely competitive corporate environment suggests significant attributes of high self-control and discipline. Their involvement in blatantly unethical and in at least some cases clearly illegal schemes would appear to be more associated with arrogance, hubris, and an assumption of invulnerability to criminal investigation and prosecution.

On a *dramaturgic* level Enron exemplified the projection of an image of ultrarespectability through, for example, chairman Ken Lay's top-level political contacts, conspicuous local philanthropy, and the naming of Houston's stadium as Enron Field. This image may have reinforced the sense within the company that its business practices were legitimate and immune from serious external oversight.

On an *organizational* level an environment of intense competitiveness, intimidation toward compliance with the organizational agenda established by the company leadership, and the promotion of a strong ethos of corporate pride, loyalty, and superiority was also significant. Executive retention plans, pay incentive structures, rejection of old economy models, and the use of complex financial instruments such as derivatives contributed to an environment that fostered the relentless pursuit of higher returns, however fabricated, over integrity and other considerations.

Finally, on a *structural* level Enron was a product of a capitalist political economy promoting free-market competition, the pursuit of profit, and the expansion of markets, or growth. In the most recent era an enormous emphasis on stock price maximization has emerged. Deregulatory legislation promoted by politicians who in many cases were receiving large political campaign funding donations from corporate interests contributed to a sense of immunity by corporate executives and auditors for financial manipulations they might undertake.

The crimes of Enron, then, are best understood as a product of a complex interaction of various different factors, operating on quite different levels. It is far from clear that we have any methodology available to us that could establish definitively exactly how these different factors interact. Many parallel factors are surely involved in other corporate crime cases, but of course it does not follow that all large-scale corporations involve such criminal activity. It is suggested here that the factors identified, on different levels, can interact with each other in a virtually infinite number of ways. The specific configurations that will give rise to corporate crime within a specific corporation are complex, not simple. We have no reason to believe that low self-control, as conventionally defined, plays any significant role in such white-collar crime.

CRIMES OF THE STATE AND CRIMES OF CORRUPT DICTATORS

Gottfredson and Hirschi (1990) argue that theirs is a general theory that can explain *all* crimes. But their definition of crime does not encompass crimes of the state—or planned crimes against the state. Hence they cannot explain what are usually the worst forms of crime: the purposeful acts of evil and corrupt dictators that result in physical harm to human beings, abuses of civil liberties, and economic loss (Friedrichs, 1998; Green and Ward, 2004). It should be noted that Gottfredson and Hirschi's neglect of such crime is shared by the field of criminology as a whole; nonetheless, we take serious exception to such neglect. In all likelihood, such crimes are common, no less frequently enacted as other forms of crime. Crimes of the state are the public sector equivalent of corporate crimes, and crimes of corrupt political officeholders are the public sector equivalent of occupational crime.

By some estimates more than 350 million people worldwide died in the twentieth century because of deliberate actions of the state (Heidenreich, 2001). A large proportion of these deaths were caused by genocides, massacres, and mass executions (Markusen, 1992). Hitler and Stalin represent just two of the most notorious megacriminals of the twentieth century, each complicit in tens of millions of deaths. Even with the fall in 2003 of Saddam Hussein of Iraq—a contemporary dictator with much blood on his hands—many countries of the world continue to be ruled by dictators complicit in massive violations of human rights, typically against their own people, including acts of violence and torture, wanton neglect leading to starvation, and a wide range of abuse or exploitative practices. These dictators include Kim Jong Il of North Korea, Than Shwe of Myanmar, Hu Jintao of China, Robert Mugabe of Zimbabwe, and Crown Prince Abdullah of Saudi Arabia. To explain their evil careers and activities in terms of poor parenting practices and consequent low self-control seems wrongheaded. Even if they were afflicted by low self-control, their large-scale crimes can be understood only within particular sociohistorical contexts and organizational structures.

State leaders have been complicit in not only large-scale crimes of violence but also theft on a monumental scale. In addition to his many other crimes, Saddam Hussein skimmed billions from aid programs (Sachs, 2004). Many other state leaders of recent decades have embezzled massive fortunes from their countries. A partial list, compiled in 2004 by the Agence France-Press, includes Suharto of Indonesia (1967–1998, $15–$35 billion), Ferdinand Marcos of the Philippines (1972–1986, $5–$10 billion), Mobutu Sese Seko of Zaire (1965–1997, $5 billion), and Sani Achaba of Nigeria (1993–1998, $2.5 billion). Again, low self-control theory does not help us explain how criminality on such a scale takes place. More important, both Gottfredson and Hirschi's general theory of crime specifically and criminological theory in general pull our attention away from such crimes.

CONCLUSION

Rather than accepting Gottfredson and Hirschi's argument that we can explain criminality by means of a single factor, we should recognize that accounting for crime entails a multitude of factors, that we are highly unlikely to realize a comprehensive explanation of crime, and that the complex of factors explaining different forms of white-collar crime is not the same complex of factors that can be invoked to explain the different forms of conventional crime. In our view Gottfredson and Hirschi's low self-control theory fosters an erroneous explanation and understanding of crime and contributes to the adoption of white-collar crime policy that is highly unlikely to be effective. It is more honest—and accurate—for criminologists to concede that explanations of white-collar crime must be complex and inevitably must be incomplete.

NOTE

A version of this chapter was presented at the American Society of Criminology meeting in Nashville, Tennessee, in November 2004. We benefited from discussions with Michael Benson, Thomas Bernard, Harry Dammer, Richard Hollinger, and David Weisburd. Jennifer Gibbs provided helpful research assistance in connection with this chapter. We are especially indebted to Erich Goode for numerous constructive suggestions, many of which we adopted. Needless to say, we alone take responsibility for the arguments put forth here. Work on this chapter was partially supported by a University of Scranton Faculty Research Grant.

11 | VIOLENT CRIME

Richard B. Felson and D. Wayne Osgood

From Gottfredson and Hirschi's perspective we have no business writing a special chapter on violence in a volume on self-control and crime. Why write about violence when violent offenders commit a variety of crimes—they rarely specialize? Gottfredson and Hirschi would not object to a chapter on situational factors and violence because the situational factors leading to violent crime are different from those leading to other crime. However, this book focuses on individual differences—why one person commits crime and another does not. And from Gottfredson and Hirschi's perspective only one individual difference factor matters: low self-control, or the offender's inability to regulate his or her behavior. Therefore we are writing about the wrong dependent variable.

Identifying the proper dependent variable is an important problem in criminology, and Gottfredson and Hirschi deserve credit for addressing the issue. The choice of dependent variable affects what theories we use to explain the phenomenon. For example, researchers who focus on domestic violence develop specialized theories to explain it. However, if these offenders also tend to commit other crimes, a more general approach is required (Moffitt et al., 2000). Similarly, if violent offenders also commit other offenses, then a more general approach is required. For example, the versatility of offenders calls into question socialization theories that focus on the modeling of violent parents or violent heroes and villains on television.

Violent crime is both violence and crime. Hence the question arises, is our dependent variable violence or crime? Moreover, examining the pattern of offending is important in determining what type of theory is most useful. If an offender engages in violence but not other deviant behavior, then a theory of aggression is necessary to understand the behavior. If an offender engages in criminal behavior in general, then we need a theory of crime or deviance. The good news is that, because different theories imply different effects, such an analysis provides a way of testing those theoretical explanations. This method of theory testing has been called discriminant prediction (R. B. Felson, 2002). It is the method Gottfredson and Hirschi use when they argue that self-control can account for versatility.

Gottfredson and Hirschi (1990) sometimes use self-control to refer to a loose amalgam that seems to include all individual difference factors that might be associated with crime. In this chapter we ignore all those other individual differences that they sometimes lump together. We think it is a mistake to use self-control to include such a broad range of traits. Instead, we address the portion of Gottfredson and Hirschi's work that is most directly a theory of self-control.

We begin this essay by describing evidence indicating that self-control has a causal effect on violent behavior. We then discuss the idea that low self-control is ubiquitous among offenders and suggest that it has some unlikely implications. We suggest that attitudes toward risk provide an additional explanation of why many offenders are versatile. We also argue that Gottfredson and Hirschi exaggerate the offender's level of versatility. Most offenders commit only minor offenses; they avoid serious offenses, many of which involve violence. We suggest that this strong pattern is likely to be due to attitudes toward differences in risk, not differences in self-control. We then discuss how violent crime is different from nonviolent crime. We argue that some attitudes and personality factors should be more strongly associated with crimes that involve committing intentional harm than with other crimes, and therefore some specialization can be expected. Finally, we discuss evidence showing that attitudes matter. Our general conclusion is that self-control is only one of a number of individual difference factors implicated in violent and nonviolent crime.

THE CAUSAL EFFECT OF SELF-CONTROL

Numerous studies show that self-control is correlated with criminal behavior (Pratt and Cullen, 2000). The measurement of self-control is problematic, however, and causal inference is difficult with correlational data. Criminologists are generally unaware of a body of experimental research in social psychology that uses mirrors to assess effects of self-control on behavior. When people stand in front of a mirror, they are better behaved. The focus of their attention is inward, and their behavior is more likely to conform to their values or standards (Wicklund, 1975). In other words, they are more likely to use self-control. Experimental research has shown that the presence of a mirror inhibits male participants from delivering shocks to women, a behavior that is likely to violate their values (Scheier et al., 1974; Carver, 1974). On the other hand, the presence of a mirror leads participants to deliver more intense shocks when the target is a man and the delivery of shock is legitimated by the experimenter. These results suggest that self-control may either inhibit or facilitate violence depending on the individual's attitudes toward the use of violence in a particular context.

The effect of self-control on the relationship between internal standards and violence has also been demonstrated in experiments carried out by Froming et al. (1982). In the first experiment only college students who opposed the use of physical punishments as a means of gaining compliance from others were selected. A second criterion for selection was that these students believed that most other people were favorable to the use of physical punishments. In a teacher-learner situation the presence of a mirror inhibited the use of shocks, but the presence of an evaluative audience facilitated aggression. In the second experiment the criteria for selection of subjects were reversed. Only students who were favorable to the use of physical punishments but believed most others were unfavorable were selected. The results were exactly the opposite of those found in the first experiment. When a mirror was present, participants gave more shocks than control subjects, whereas the presence of an evaluative audience decreased shock delivery. Again, the results showed that the effect of self-control depends on individual attitudes and that individuals vary in whether they view violence as an appropriate response in a particular circumstance. Attitudes determined the direction of self-control's impact on behavior.

This experimental literature suggests that self-control is not simply an individual difference variable but a process that varies across situations and is relevant to everyone. In that sense Gottfredson and Hirschi have made a rather narrow use of the concept, and there is a need for criminological work on situational factors that promote or diminish people's immediate capacity for self-control. For example, research shows that individuals use less self-control when they are tired (Baumeister et al., 1994); it is a capacity that can be used up. Also, individuals have lower self-control when they are highly aroused, as they are when they are under threat in a violent situation.

THE IMPULSIVE OFFENDER

These experiments suggest that attitudes matter. In contrast, Gottfredson and Hirschi suggest that the attitudes of criminals are no different from the attitudes of the rest of us. The criminals' problem is a faulty time perspective. Because they are immersed in the immediate situation, because they live in the here and now, they think about immediate benefits and forget about future costs. Because crime and other risky behaviors typically have immediate benefits and long-term costs, offenders are more likely to engage in risky behaviors than those of us who have a broader temporal perspective. In other words, although everyone's rationality is bounded, offenders' rationality is much more so. Like the family dog, typical offenders think only of the stimuli they face and the immediate payoff. Dogs and criminals live in the present and therefore have difficulty resisting temptation and waiting.

From Gottfredson and Hirschi's perspective, if everyone counted to ten before behaving, crime would be rare and criminologists would go out of business. Fortunately for us, some people are too impulsive to count to ten. They are careless decision makers who do not think about future costs or moral implications in the criminogenic situation. As a result, they do things they do not really want to do, that are contrary to their values or beliefs. They are similar to those of us who have bad habits, only more extreme. Many of us would like to stop overeating, smoking, gambling, drinking, or buying things we do not need, and we often fail at self-control (see Baumeister et al., 1994). Many of us have problems with self-regulation, but we can at least take pride in the fact that we have more self-control than the common criminal, or the family dog, for that matter.

Gottfredson and Hirschi (1990) state that offenders seek "relief from momentary irritation" (p. 90). Their scheme implies that offenders are more likely than nonoffenders to immediately attack when insulted but that they are no more likely to come after the adversary or seek vengeance the next day. A drive-by insult of an offender should not be particularly dangerous. Because offenders do not plan for the future, they would not carry weapons in anticipation of an altercation or opportunity.

Gottfredson and Hirschi's emphasis on self-control also has some surprising implications for the way offenders should feel after they have committed a crime. Freud said that the most righteous feel the most guilt, but Gottfredson and Hirschi imply otherwise. Because offenders have similar values and standards as the rest of us, they should have just as much remorse afterward as we would. They know they have done wrong, and presumably they sincerely regret what they did on impulse; it was out of character. After they commit an assault, they should be more likely to excuse their behavior than the rest of us, to say "I lost my temper." They should be no more likely to justify it, however. You won't hear them say, "The son of a bitch deserved it." Moreover, after a history of violating their own standards, the poor souls should develop low self-esteem.[1] On the other hand, perhaps they are better able than the rest of us to explain away their bad behavior.

This description of the offender as having similar standards as the rest of us, as just as forgiving, as unarmed, as lacking in nefarious plans, or as remorseful and self-critical, does not ring true. We find it difficult to believe that offenders are the same as us, differing only in that they are more impulsive. In our view Gottfredson and Hirschi's argument that self-control is the only significant factor separating the offender from the nonoffender is extreme. Of course, low self-control is *a* causal factor in crime. Psychologists have been talking about self-control all along, and there has been a recent resurgence in interest in what is called self-regulation in psychology (Baumeister et al., 1994). However, it is doubtful that it is the *only* individual difference factor involved in crime.

Gottfredson and Hirschi led the reaction against sociological determinism in criminology. They (along with some developmentalists) seem to have rediscovered for criminologists, blinded by their sociological big brother, that not all individuals are alike. They helped bring the individual difference side of psychology back into criminology, countering the sociological bias in the field. A personality trait could help explain why two social behaviors are related. For example, low self-control could produce a spurious relationship between academic performance and crime. Gottfredson and Hirschi countered an "oversocialized concept of man" as well as an "overspecialized concept of crime" (Wrong, 1961).

The concept of self-control helps us to understand the offender's decision-making process and bounded rationality. Many acts of violence involve careless decisions and an offender's failure to consider consequences. The concept of self-control also helps us to understand why many offenders do such stupid things and how someone can commit an offense even when it violates their own moral standards. Finally, it can explain the versatility of offenders. However, we argue that other processes are involved as well.

THE VERSATILE OFFENDER

Gottfredson and Hirschi have been influential partly because they are so damn smart and partly because they could explain versatility in offending. Most criminals engage in many impulsive behaviors, criminal and noncriminal; they do not typically specialize in any particular type of offense. For Gottfredson and Hirschi the common element is low self-control.

There is considerable evidence that individuals who commit violent crime tend to also commit nonviolent crime and other deviant acts. Studies of arrest histories based on both official records and self-reports show a low level of specialization in violent crime. For example, Blumstein and Cohen (1979) examined the arrest histories of individuals who had been arrested for aggravated assault. They found that the probability of arrest in a given year was 0.19 for aggravated assault, 0.14 for robbery, 0.11 for theft, 0.10 for drugs, and 0.08 for burglary. These results show that the probability that violent offenders will be arrested for additional violent crimes (assault and robbery) is only slightly higher than the probability that they will be arrested for nonviolent crimes. Knowing the type of crime that violent offenders have committed is not very helpful in predicting the type of crime they will commit next (Kempf, 1987; Lattimore et al., 1994; Paternoster et al., 1998).

In another study, D. J. West and Farrington (1977) found that 80 percent of adults convicted of violence also had convictions for crimes involving dishonesty. Violent acts were related to noncriminal forms of "deviant" behavior, such as sexual promiscuity, smoking, heavy drinking, and gambling. Noticeably absent from the list is overeating. For some reason offenders use self-control at the dinner table, and there are relatively few endomorphs in prison. It raises the issue of to what extent self-control is a personality trait and to what it extent it is situationally variable.

Studies investigating associations among crimes or deviant acts also indicate that individual differences in criminal violence reflect a general tendency toward crime (Donovan and Jessor, 1985; Osgood et al., 1988). Yet these same studies also make clear that Gottfredson and Hirschi exaggerate the amount of versatility in crime and deviance. For instance, Osgood et al. (1988) found that roughly half of the stable and reliable variance in a variety of deviant behaviors was general or shared variance. More recently, Deane et al. (2005) found much stronger evidence for offense specialization than versatility among adolescents. Using marginal logit models, they showed that violent offenders are much more likely to engage in additional violent offenses and that nonviolent offenders are much more likely to engage in additional nonviolent offenses. Furthermore, Osgood and Schreck (2007) have demonstrated that proper statistical modeling reveals sizable individual differences in the tendency toward violence versus property offending that are stable and predictable, even when holding overall offense propensity constant. Overall, these studies indicate that there is enough versatility to suggest that a general theory such as Gottfredson and Hirschi's is needed. They also show, however, that there is a clear need for explanations that address specificity.

ANOTHER EXPLANATION OF VERSATILITY

Versatility is not necessarily due to low self-control or impulsiveness. Risk preferences could also lead people to engage in a variety of risky activities. Two interrelated attitudes toward risk could be involved: (1) thrill or sensation seeking (a preference for risk) and (2) fearlessness (versus an aversion to risk).[2] Thrill seekers find risky activities more rewarding or enjoyable (Katz, 1988). A preference for risk is a motivating factor, not a disinhibition. Thrill seekers are not necessarily impulsive—that is, they do not necessarily have low self-control. They can make plans to go bungee jumping or commit robbery.[3] Their behavior is unrelated to their ability to consider costs when contemplating the crime. Second, individuals who are fearless, who experience less anxiety over negative consequences, are more likely to engage in risky activity. Either they are optimists—they attach a low estimate to the probability of incurring costs—or they perceive the costs as less negative than nonoffenders do. Fearless individuals are not necessarily impulsive. They may actually have more self-control when they are in a risky situation. They may be cool, calm, and collected and less likely to panic than those who are risk averse. On the other hand, those people who lose control of bodily functions when faced with danger are not good candidates for a life of crime. They may be particularly likely to avoid violent crime because the counterattack of an adversary and the risk of bodily harm are much greater. The nonviolent offender mainly has to fear the police.

Risk preference and risk aversion affect different aspects of the decision-making process than self-control. From the perspective of bounded rationality, individuals will commit crime if they perceive that the rewards are greater than the costs, based on the information they consider. From Gottfredson and Hirschi's perspective the impulsive decision maker does not consider the costs because they occur in the future, whereas the rewards of crime are immediate. People with low self-control attach the same weights and probabilities to rewards and costs but are careless in their thinking. It is also possible, however, that some offenders *do* consider all the information but attach different values to the rewards and costs of crime than nonoffenders do. Thrill seekers find crime and other risky activities more rewarding. Fearless individuals find the costs less aversive because they tend to be less anxious about anticipated costs. For example, the prostitute may enjoy the thrill of her lifestyle and be willing to accept the costs—the danger and stigma—but she is not necessarily impulsive. Women sometimes have sex on impulse, but the career choice to join the oldest profession seems a more considered decision.

Research suggests that attitudes toward risk reflect, at least in part, biological differences (see Raine et al., 1997). People who engage in crime tend to be physiologically underaroused, as indicated by lower resting heart rate levels.[4] Raine et al. (1997) argued that either thrill seeking or fearlessness (or both) may explain the link between criminal behavior and arousal levels. First, it may be that individuals seek out exciting activities to compensate for their physiological underarousal and bring some physiological balance to their system. Second, individuals with low resting heart rates may experience less fear and anxiety. As a result, they may be more likely to engage in risky behaviors.[5]

Attitudes toward risk do not necessarily lead to versatile offending. Resting heart rates have also been shown to be lower for violent offenders than for nonviolent offenders (e.g., Farrington, 1987). This suggests that thrill seeking is a more important motive for violence than for other criminal behavior—violence is more exciting. It may also be that fear is more likely to inhibit violent crime than nonviolent crime because of the danger resulting from the confrontation with the victim.

Although Gottfredson and Hirschi's emphasis on self-control enables them to explain the versatility pattern, it makes it difficult for them to explain crimes in which there is some premeditation. Many crimes, including violent crimes, involve some planning (see Birkbeck and LaFree, 1993). An overemphasis on self-control also leads to a misrepresentation of the crime of assault. Offenders may have a history of conflict with an adversary, and they may bide their time, delaying their vengeful attack until an opportunity presents itself. Adding attitudes toward risk to the equation makes it easier to explain crimes that are premeditated, crimes committed over a period of time, and crimes committed by organized groups. In addition, it helps to explain why many youth age out of crime: The young are more likely to value risk and feel invulnerable. It is difficult to explain age patterns in offending by positing differences in self-control.

THE LIMITED OFFENDER

Serious crime, which includes many acts of violence, is *much* less frequent than minor crime. This may be the most prominent pattern of criminal behavior. The versatility evidence suggests that serious offenders usually commit minor crime. However, most offenders who commit minor crimes do not commit serious crime. Even they have their limits. For example, although most violent offenders also use drugs and commit theft, the reverse is not necessarily true. If most crime is petty, then most criminals are not so versatile in this sense; they limit themselves to minor crime. They have a buffet-style approach to crime, but they do not put everything on their plate.

So why don't most criminals commit serious offenses? Can Gottfredson and Hirschi account for the low rates of serious crime among most offenders? What is the difference between serious offenders and minor offenders? To explain this prominent pattern, Gottfredson and Hirschi would have to argue that serious offenders have lower self-control than offenders who commit more minor crime. Most offenders have enough self-control to stop themselves from killing but not stealing. They have moderate levels of self-control. Only those with extremely low self-control are unable to stop themselves from doing the most serious crimes.[6]

Gottfredson and Hirschi cite evidence that most offenders engage in a variety of risky behaviors. However, the reverse is not true: Most smokers, alcoholics, gamblers, and accident-prone people do not engage in crime. Why not? Gottfredson and Hirschi would have to argue that these people have moderate levels of self-control, enough self-control to avoid crime but not enough to avoid bad habits. Their approach implies a self-control continuum with Guttman scaling. At the low end are the hardened criminals, who commit both serious and minor crime, who do so with high frequency, and who have bad habits as well. At the next level are the petty criminals with moderate levels of self-control who also have bad habits. Third are those people who have bad habits but do not commit crime. Finally, those people with the highest self-control have only good habits and certainly do no crime. They do only what they want to do, what they know is good for them. They are the self-control elite whom many of us envy and resent.

Attitudinal differences provide an alternative and straightforward explanation of petty crime specialization. Many offenders are inhibited from committing serious or violent crime because of their moral values. They'll assault people, but they won't kill them. They'll shoplift, but they won't engage in robbery or even steal from individuals. They'll use drugs, but they won't get involved in trafficking. Attitudinal differences can also explain why most people with bad habits do not become offenders. Gluttons may lack will power, but they still have moral character.

How does one determine to what extent these patterns are due to individual variation in attitudes or self-control? One method is to examine the relationship between the frequency and seriousness of a person's offense record. Gottfredson and Hirschi's approach implies that these variables should have a strong relationship because of the impact of low self-control. They would also predict a strong relationship between frequency and the proportion of the offender's offenses that are serious. Examining this relationship might be more interesting because it would exclude the artifactual relationship between frequency and seriousness: People who commit frequent crime are more likely, by chance, to have committed some serious ones.

Frequency is related to seriousness (Capaldi and Patterson, 1996; A. Piquero, 2000; Farrington, 1991), but there are many exceptions to the rule. Imagine a 2 × 2 table involving frequency and seriousness as dichotomous categorical variables. There are many frequent offenders who do not commit serious forms of violence and presumably a fair number of serious offenders who are infrequent offenders. Individual differences in self-control cannot explain the behavior of frequent minor offenders and serious but infrequent offenders. We would argue that it is necessary to examine the attitudes of these offenders to understand their behavior. A frequent offender who would not kill or rape has different attitudes than a frequent offender who does commit these crimes. An infrequent offender who kills has different attitudes than one who won't kill. Note that attitudes toward risk can explain the frequent petty offender. Perhaps these offenders tolerate moderate levels of risk.

VIOLENCE VERSUS CRIME

Following Gottfredson and Hirschi's lead, we think it is important to pay close attention to the nature of the dependent variable. In particular, it is important to consider the nature of violent crime and how it is different from other crime or risky behavior. Is there any reason to expect it might have different causes? Addressing this issue requires a consideration of the nature of aggression.

Violence and criminal behavior are overlapping domains. Some violence is criminal, some is not, and some crimes involve violence and some do not. Because both are risky behaviors, they are likely to have some common causes. Individual differences in self-control and attitudes toward risk should be related to all types of risky behavior. However, they are also different phenomena and therefore should have different causes as well.

Violence is physical aggression—that is, a type of aggression involving the use or threat of physical force. Aggression involves behavior in which individuals intentionally harm another person. They deliberately impose some outcome on the victim that they know the victim would rather avoid. Criminal behavior, on the other hand, is deviant behavior—that is, the violation of rules that have been codified in law. Although criminal behavior typically involves behaviors that lawmakers judge harmful, many crimes do not involve aggression, that is, intentional harm-doing. Crimes in which no harm is intended include victimless crimes and accidents resulting from the offender's negligence. For example, drunken drivers, illegal drug users, and prostitutes do not intend harm. Harming others is not on the minds of these offenders and is irrelevant to their motivation.

For crimes involving aggression, on the other hand, harm is intended. Some of these acts of aggression are dispute-related and some are predatory, depending on the offender's attitude toward harming the victim. In dispute-related aggression harm is the proximate goal, desired because it achieves some distal goal (e.g., face-saving, justice, deterrence). These offenders have grievances with their victims, they are angry, and they want to see their victims suffer. Most homicides and assaults stem from disputes, but so do some robberies, rapes, thefts, and frauds (Black, 1983). Insults and other verbal attacks also stem from disputes, although they are not usually considered violations of law.

For predatory offenders harm is incidental and not their goal. They deliberately harm victims but do not have a particular desire to do so. Rather, they have some other goal in mind, and they are willing to harm the victim in order to achieve it.[7] For example, robbery and rape typically involve predatory violence. Most robbers and rapists are indifferent to the victim's suffering. They use violence to force the victim to comply because compliance will allow them to get something else they want (e.g., money or sex). Most predatory offenders use nonviolent methods (e.g., theft or fraud).[8] Harm is incidental to most thieves; they desire the stolen object but could not care less whether the victim's insurance can replace it.[9] Note, however, that nonviolent offenders may not believe that their behavior has harmed anyone when it has (Sykes and Matza, 1957). For example, shoplifters may not think they have harmed anyone, whereas they might if the victim was an individual. It is important to take into account the offender's subjective viewpoint in considering whether their behavior involves aggression.

It is likely that the tendency to deliberately harm others has some distinctive causes. Any characteristic that increases a person's desire or indifference to harming others is likely to lead to crimes involving deliberate harm but not necessarily to victimless crimes or crimes of negligence. For example, people who are empathic—who "feel the pain" of others—are less likely to engage in violence (e.g., Mehrabian, 1997). Some are more punitive when they think they have been mistreated (Markowitz and Felson, 1998). Some are more selfish than others. One should expect a negative correlation between aggression and altruism, at least altruistic behavior with no external reward. Some have hostility biases and easily interpret the behavior of others as aggressive and respond accordingly (Dodge and Somberg, 1987). On the other hand, people who are empathic and tolerant may take drugs and drink and drive, but they will not intentionally harm others. They may shoplift, thinking there is no victim, but they will not steal from individuals. They will be limited offenders.

Attitudes and personality factors may also have different effects on predatory and dispute-related violence. The desire for thrills should provide more of an incentive for predatory violence than dispute-related violence. Predatory offenders may enjoy a certain degree of physical danger or the risk of getting caught by the police. Self-control may play a greater role in dispute-related violence—these are the crimes of passion where adversaries lose their temper, typically during a verbal dispute.

Note that the study of individual differences is complicated by the fact that variables that cause one individual to be violent may cause potential adversaries to show deference. Others may be careful in how they treat an individual with a temper or a reputation for violence. The implied threat is often sufficient and no overt act is observable or reported. As a result, the relationship between attitudes and violence is likely to be weaker than the relationship between attitudes and other types of crime.

One suspects that the propensity to engage in selfish behavior approximates a normal distribution. Some people are extremely selfish, some are saintly, but most are a mix, so their actions will vary depending on the situation. Gottfredson and Hirschi imply that low self-control distinguishes the bottom end of the moral distribution, but what about the other end of the distribution? Do these individuals have the highest level of self-control, or are their attitudes different? How are the most righteous, law-abiding, and altruistic people different from the average person? It seems more likely that their attitudes are different in that they have extremely high levels of self-control. If attitudinal differences matter at the high end of the distribution, they should matter at the low end.

Finally, violence is not necessarily deviant behavior. In dispute-related violence offenders often feel self-righteous and view their behavior as an act of justice (see Black, 1983). The victim has wronged them and deserves punishment. To fail to punish the misdeeds of others would be morally wrong. Although pacifists view violence as a clear moral evil, for most people moral values regarding the use of violence are ambivalent and context dependent. They describe harm doing as just punishment when they approve of it and as aggression or violence when they do not (Tedeschi and Felson, 1994). Recall that looking in the mirror can lead to more or less violence depending on the participant's attitude.

CAUSES OF VIOLENT AND NONVIOLENT CRIME

To some extent violent crime and nonviolent crime have similar causes. For example, testosterone (Booth and Osgood, 1993) and pubertal development (Felson and Haynie, 2002) are associated with a variety of crimes, not just violence. To understand these effects, we need to know why testosterone and puberty lead males to break rules, not only intentionally harm others. Similarly, evidence suggests that the modeling of parental violence by children cannot explain the intergenerational transmission of violence. Children who are physically abused by their parents are just as likely to engage in nonviolent offending as violent offending when they become adults (e.g., Widom, 1989). Modeling also cannot explain why physical abuse has no greater effect than parental neglect on the likelihood that the child will become a violent adult. These studies suggest that any type of parental mistreatment results in a greater likelihood of a broad range of misbehavior by offspring. If a variable is correlated with crime in general, not just violent crime, then a theory of crime, not violence, is needed to explain the relationship (see also Capaldi and Patterson, 1996; A. Piquero, 2000; Farrington, 1991).

On the other hand, some research shows that violent crime and nonviolent crime have different causes. Some demographic factors are associated with violent crime but not other crime. For example, Zimring and Hawkins (1997) find that rates of homicide but not theft are higher in the United States than in most other developed nations. We have a violence problem, not a crime problem. Demographic factors also have different effects on violent and nonviolent offending. Evidence from the National Longitudinal Study of Adolescent Health suggests that black adolescents have higher rates of violence, particularly armed violence, when controlling for other demographic factors, but that they do not have higher rates of property or drug crime (R. B. Felson et al., 2001). Effects of socioeconomic status are also observed for violent crime but not for nonviolent crime. Gender effects are observed for both violent and nonviolent crime, but they are much stronger for violent crime (see also A. Piquero, 2000). Finally, the age of the adolescent is negatively related to violence but is positively related to drug use and most property crime.

THE HYPOCRISY HYPOTHESIS

From Gottfredson and Hirschi's perspective offenders are not deviant in their attitudes; they are just hypocrites. When asked, they express proper values, but they are too impulsive to act in terms of those values. Because of their impulsivity, their words do not match their deeds. We all have the same thoughts and impulses, but only some of us act on them. Actually, the social psychology literature on the relationship between attitudes and behavior shows that offenders are not alone in the tendency to do one thing and say another (e.g., Liska, 1975).

As evidence for attitude consensus Gottfredson and Hirschi point to the fact that most offenders agree that crime is wrong. However, it may be that offenders are just providing lip service or managing impressions for the squares who question them. In addition, attitudes vary in strength and salience, and offenders may not hold these attitudes as strongly as the rest of us. Although everyone may agree that in most circumstances killing and stealing are wrong, some may hold these attitudes more strongly than others. Finally, people are ambivalent about the use of violence. For example, they believe in both retributive justice and turning the other cheek. As indicated earlier, attitudes toward the legitimacy of violence depend on context. Whether a violent act is viewed as legitimate or not is likely to depend on the nature of the adversary and the provocation. Individuals are likely to vary in their attitudes regarding violence. Good measurement, which takes context into account, should reveal these differences.

Evidence clearly shows that attitudes are related to self-reported violence and that there are attitudinal differences between offenders and nonoffenders. For example, Markowitz and Felson (1998) found that ex-offenders are more likely than the general population to emphasize the importance of showing courage in a fight and getting retribution when someone wrongs you. Ex-offenders are also more disputatious, according to evidence based on their responses to hypothetical scenarios. Luckenbill and Doyle (1989) describe disputatious individuals as more likely to assign blame when someone else produces a negative outcome for them, to express their grievance to the blameworthy party, to demand reparation, and to use physical violence if their demand for remedial action is not satisfied.

One might question whether attitudes have a causal effect on behavior. Evidence for causality comes from a longitudinal study of high school students (Liska et al., 1984). Feelings of resentment and attitudes toward revenge produced changes in violent behavior over time. Moreover, the effects of attitudes on behavior were stronger when the attitudes were strongly held.

There is also evidence that attitudes mediate at least some of the relationship between social demographic factors and violence. Markowitz and Felson (1998) found that respondents with lower socioeconomic status were more likely to engage in violence to a large extent because they were more punitive and placed greater emphasis on showing courage in conflicts. These attitudes mediated all the status differences in disputatiousness and much of the status differences in frequency of violence. They also found that men were more punitive than women and that younger adults were more punitive than older adults. Attitudes toward retribution mediated some of the age and gender differences in disputatiousness and violence. Thus the evidence suggests that one of the reasons young males commit more violence than older people and females is that they tend to be more punitive.

Attitudes related to machismo have been shown to help explain gender differences in violence. Richard B. Felson and Liska (1984) asked junior high school children to rate themselves on adjective pairs, such as sensitive-unfeeling, cowardly-brave, and rough-smooth, and to indicate which children in the class fought the most. The analyses indicated that the strong gender difference in frequency of fighting was greatly reduced when self-ratings were controlled.

Sexual attitudes have been shown to be related to rape. Kanin (1985) found that young men with high sexual aspirations were more likely to engage in sexual coercion. These men masturbate frequently and spend a lot of time searching for sexual partners. The study suggests that at least some sexual coercion is sexually motivated and that individual variation in sexual interests affects the likelihood of offending.

CONCLUSION

Careless or impulsive thinking is a factor that leads people to engage in crime and other risky behavior. In front of a mirror they behave more consistently with their attitudes. However, attitudes also have an impact. Some people either enjoy risky activities or at least are not as anxious about negative consequences. Risk preference and risk aversion as well as self-control help explain the versatility of offenders and the tendency of offenders to engage in legal but irresponsible behavior. The level of versatility, however, is exaggerated. Violent offenses involve intentional harm doing, and some offenders are inhibited about committing crimes that hurt others. In addition, some attitudes are likely to affect violence but not victimless crimes or crimes of negligence. Those who are more punitive and concerned with showing toughness are more likely to use violence, whereas empathy and moral attitudes act as inhibitors. Self-control may play a greater role in dispute-related violence, but thrill seeking may play a greater role in predatory violence.

In addition, petty offenders usually avoid more serious offenses, including crimes of violence. Although there may be few specialists in violence, there are many limited offenders who avoid serious forms of violence. We argue that risk aversion is a better explanation of limited offending than self-control. However, we believe that attitudinal differences better explain why most offenders have restricted repertoires.

Gottfredson and Hirschi took an extreme position that opened them up to criticism. But they were countering an extreme position: the sociological construction that there are no meaningful individual differences between offenders and nonoffenders. They altered the course of criminology in a more realistic direction, and we hope that the present chapter contributes to further advances in the movement they initiated.

NOTES

1. On the other hand, perhaps they are better able than the rest of us to rationalize bad behavior. However, an examination of neutralization techniques goes beyond the theory of self-control.

2. It is not clear whether risk preference and risk aversion are opposite ends of the same continuum or whether they vary independently. Those who are fearless do not necessarily have a preference for risk.

3. Note that Gottfredson and Hirschi sometimes imply a broad definition of self-control that includes thrill seeking.

4. Low arousal has long been viewed as a component of psychopathy.

5. Research also suggests that self-control has a strong biological component. Recent experiments based on MRI data suggest that short-term and long-term thinking engage different parts of the brain (McClure et al., 2004). When people choose a delayed over an immediate reward, the calculating part of the brain (the cortex) is more active. When they choose a short-term benefit, the part of the brain associated with emotion (in the limbic region) is more active.

6. Rowe et al. (1990) provide a conceptual and statistical framework for showing how an underlying propensity such as self-control would translate into the frequency of committing offenses of varying seriousness.

7. Behavior has multiple consequences; some of these consequences are goals while others are incidental outcomes. In addition, a consequence that is incidental to the offender may be quite costly for the victim. The victim's experience of harm should be the focus in treating the victim, but it is irrelevant to an understanding of the offender's behavior.

8. Behaviors involving deception or stealth are not generally treated as examples of aggression, although they involve intentional harm doing.

9. Note that those scholars who take a frustration-aggression approach treat offenses in which harm is deliberate but incidental to the offender as instrumental aggression.

12 PROPERTY CRIMES

Marc L. Swatt and Robert F. Meier

The theory of self-control has generated substantial interest and application in criminology. Our purpose in this chapter is to examine the theory's ability to account for property crimes. We use data largely from the Uniform Crime Reports on reported property crime and the National Crime Victimization Survey on reported victimizations involving property crime, although other data are brought to bear as well. We have been necessarily selective in the property crimes we discuss here, but we believe strongly that the crimes discussed are, in many respects, representative of property crimes as a whole. There are notable exceptions to this claim, and we will point them out in our discussion.

In this chapter we stress the implications of patterns of property offending for Gottfredson and Hirschi's self-control theory. In so doing, we wish to be sensitive to several points of low self-control theory. First, the theory of low self-control is a general theory of crime, as the title to Gottfredson and Hirschi's 1990 book states. This means that it should serve to explain all criminality. However, Gottfredson and Hirschi demur on this point and indicate that there are some offenses that are beyond the scope of the theory. The reason for this is that Gottfredson and Hirschi do not use a legal definition of crime as the meaning of their dependent variable. Rather, they indicate that the theory is an effort to explain "acts of force or fraud undertaken in pursuit of self-interest" (Gottfredson and Hirschi, 1990, 15). Some of these violate the criminal law, some do not. Although virtually all property crimes fit Gottfredson and Hirschi 's definition, some do not.

Second, Gottfredson and Hirschi conceive self-control, as Goode also notes in Chapter 1, in dichotomous rather than interval terms. One either has self-control or not. This constriction of the notion of self-control raises serious issues about the ability of self-control to explain or predict changes in crime rates, whether property or otherwise. Simply put, can a constant (or something close to a constant) explain a variable?

Low self-control theory is an unusual theory in a number of respects, not the least of which is the dependent variable it attempts to explain. Most theories are concerned with the antecedents (causes) of criminal behavior, but Gottfredson and Hirschi largely ignore these and instead concentrate on the crime itself. Crime, they say, is caused by criminality, the propensity to commit crimes and other acts that ignore long-term negative consequences. But to consider criminality as a tendency or propensity harkens back to something akin to instinct theory.

In this chapter we examine property crimes and their trends. Our objective is to see to what extent the distribution and trends in property crimes are best explained by the theory of low self-control.

PROPERTY CRIMES IN THE UNITED STATES

Property crime is the most common kind of crime everywhere. Property crime usually involves some kind of theft (e.g., burglary), but it can also involve some kind of property loss, such as that involved with vandalism. Some property crimes are defined by the object that is stolen (e.g., auto theft), whereas others are defined by the nature of how the property is lost (e.g., arson). Given the variety of different property offenses, we have limited our discussion to a relatively small number of offenses.

Most criminologists use either the Uniform Crime Reports (UCR) or the National Crime Victimization Survey (NCVS) to answer questions about nationwide crime frequency. Here we review both of these sources. We also examine these sources with respect to information at one point in time and with respect to possible changes over time.

In the following section we examine two major sources of information about the extent and the distribution of crime in the United States, the UCR and the NCVS. The UCR have supplied crime information since their inception in 1930. Begun with the realization that information about crime in one community would be of interest in another, the UCR provide information about property crimes reported to the police. The data for the UCR are collected by individual police departments and are submitted to the Federal Bureau of Investigation (FBI) and consist of crimes reported and individuals arrested by each participating police agency. The FBI uses this information to create estimates for the extent and distribution of crime, although it really measures only reported crime.

The NCVS, on the other hand, is collected by the U.S. Census Bureau and consists of a victimization survey that is given to the members of households selected for inclusion. Surveys of crime victims began in 1967 with the first national victimization survey commissioned by President Johnson's Commission on Law Enforcement and the Administration of Justice. That survey, conducted by the National Opinion Research Center at the University of Chicago, demonstrated the utility of large-scale national surveys to measure crime. The first survey questioned 10,000 individuals and found that the extent of unreported crime was much higher than suggested by the UCR. The Bureau of Justice Statistics uses the responses to these surveys to create estimates of the extent of crime victimization in the United States. It is important to remember that because the estimates of the UCR and the NCVS are derived from different methodologies, the results do not always agree because each provides different information regarding the distribution of crime. Examining both measures simultaneously, however, allows researchers to have increased confidence in the results when they do agree. A detailed discussion regarding the methodologies, advantages, and limitations of these measures can be found in Mosher et al. (2002).

For the purposes of this discussion the property crimes under consideration are three of the index crimes of the UCR, specifically, larceny-theft, motor vehicle theft, and burglary. These crimes include many of the types of incidents that are commonly considered property crime. Robbery was not included because it contains an element of personal contact and is rightly included with violent crime. Arson was excluded because the UCR only started to include arson as a type 1 crime in 1979 and because the NCVS does not collect information on arson. Finally, Gottfredson and Hirschi (1990) specifically mention burglary and motor vehicle theft when discussing the nature of the typical crime. If Gottfredson and Hirschi (1990) are correct, their theory should be able to explain the patterns that are seen in the distribution and trends of these crimes.

DISTRIBUTION OF CRIME

According to the FBI, larceny-theft is "the unlawful taking, carrying, leading, or riding away of property from the possession or constructive possession of another" (Federal Bureau of Investigation, 2003, 497). Of the three crimes under consideration, larceny-theft is the most common: 66.7 percent of all property crime reported to the police in 2005 (Bureau of Justice Statistics, 2007). This is not surprising because many disparate types of theft incidents are included in this category, including shoplifting, purse snatching, pickpocketing, theft from buildings, bicycle theft, theft from coin-operated machines, theft from a motor vehicle, and theft of motor vehicle accessories. Of the different types of theft that have been categorized separately, theft from a motor vehicle is the most common (25.8 percent of all reported larceny-theft), followed by shoplifting (13.9 percent of all reported larceny-theft).[1] Although larceny-theft covers such a broad number of categories of theft, these crimes resulted in the smallest loss per incident, averaging $691 in 2005 (Bureau of Justice Statistics, 2007).

Although criminologists are interested in statistics that detail the nature and extent of larceny-theft, what is much more interesting are the differences in the rates that segments of the population either commit larceny-theft or are victimized by it. When examining the relative rates of offending, criminologists look at the demographic characteristics of the individuals arrested for each offense. It is important to emphasize that arrest statistics necessarily contain hidden biases because the police apprehend only a fraction of the offenders when crimes are reported. Specifically, the percentage of property crime cleared by arrest was only 16.3 percent in 2005 (Bureau of Justice Statistics, 2007). Although a substantial proportion of offenses went uncleared, the arrest statistics, if used with caution, can provide us with tentative conclusions regarding the differences in arrest rates by different demographic groups.

One consistent finding in criminology is that younger individuals are arrested at higher rates than older individuals. In fact, Gottfredson and Hirschi (1990) specifically discuss the age-crime curve when describing their theory. These age-rate differences are clearly visible when examining the crime of larceny-theft. In 2005 juveniles younger than age 18 accounted for approximately 25.8 percent of arrests for larceny-theft (Bureau of Justice Statistics, 2007). Juveniles are slightly overrepresented in the arrest statistics, considering that individuals younger than age 18 constituted only 24.8 percent of the U.S. population in 2005 (U.S. Census Bureau, 2007).

Another consistent finding in criminology is that minorities are overrepresented in arrest statistics. In 2005 blacks constituted 28.0 percent of the individuals arrested for the crime of larceny-theft (Bureau of Justice Statistics, 2007), but they made up only 13.4 percent of the U.S. population in 2005 (U.S. Census Bureau, 2007). This discrepancy is also seen when examining arrests by race and age. Blacks younger than age 18 accounted for 7.3 percent of arrests for larceny-theft (Bureau of Justice Statistics, 2007), yet they constitute only 4.2 percent of the population (U.S. Census Bureau, 2007).

Crime is mainly a male-perpetrated activity. This finding is reflected in the differences in the percentages of males and females arrested for larceny-theft. Specifically, in 2005 males were arrested in 61.4 percent of the cleared cases of larceny-theft, whereas females were arrested in only 38.6 percent of the cases (Bureau of Justice Statistics, 2007). Again, given that males constituted only 49.3 percent of the U.S. population in 2005, they are clearly overrepresented in the arrest statistics (U.S. Census Bureau, 2007). This overrepresentation also is seen when examining sex and age. In 2005 males younger than age 18 accounted for 13.5 percent of arrests for larceny-theft (Bureau of Justice Statistics, 2007), yet they constituted only 12.7 percent of the U.S. population (U.S. Census Bureau, 2007).

In addition to examining the relative distribution of offenders, it is possible to use the data from the NCVS to examine the relative risk of victimization of property crimes. It is important to note that, although both the UCR and the NCVS provide measures of crime, their respective numeric rates are not directly comparable (see Mosher et al., 2002). Although methodological differences prevent direct numeric comparisons, similarities between the patterns of relative victimization risk and the patterns of relative arrest risk can be detected.

Given that the NCVS rates for property crimes are calculated by households rather than by individuals, it is not possible to compare victimization by age. By definition, juveniles cannot be considered the head of a household. Further, data for household victimization by the sex of the head of household is generally not tabulated.[2] It is possible, however, to compute the relative risk of victimization by the race of the head of the household. According to the 2004 NCVS data, blacks had a slightly higher risk of victimization (130.6 per 1,000 households) than did whites (121.6 per 1,000 households) (Bureau of Justice Statistics, 2007).

Examining household risk for victimization also provides some other interesting differences. First, rented households had a lower risk for victimization for larceny-theft (110.8 per 1,000 households) than did owned households (148.9 per 1,000 households). Not surprisingly, urban households had a much higher rate of victimization (159.4 per 1,000 households) than did suburban (111.2 per 1,000 households) or rural households (103.2 per 1,000 households). Finally, there are some notable differences in the rates of larceny-theft at different household income levels. Households with incomes between $15,000 and $24,000 were victimized the least (119.0 per 1,000 households), and households with incomes over $75,000 were victimized the most (145.1 per 1,000 households) (Bureau of Justice Statistics, 2007).

Now let's look at burglary. The FBI defines burglary as "the unlawful entry of a structure to commit a felony or theft" (Federal Bureau of Investigation, 2003, 497). Burglary is the second most common property crime reported to the police. In 2005 burglaries made up 21.2 percent of all property crimes reported to the police (Bureau of Justice Statistics, 2007). Interestingly, most burglaries of residences occurred during the daytime (47.2 percent of all residence burglaries), and the majority of nonresidence burglaries occurred at night (41.4 percent of all nonresidence burglaries) when people are least likely to be there, suggesting that many burglaries involve some planning.[3] The average property loss in 2005 from burglaries was $1,725, more than twice as much as the average for larceny-theft (Bureau of Justice Statistics, 2007).

When examining the patterns in UCR arrest statistics for burglary, many of the same patterns emerge as were seen for larceny-theft. In general, the levels of overrepresentation were higher for burglary than they were for larceny-theft. In 2005 juveniles were overrepresented in the arrest statistics; 26.2 percent of all arrests for burglary involved juveniles (Bureau of Justice Statistics, 2007). Likewise, males were overrepresented; they constituted 85.5 percent of all burglary arrestees (Bureau of Justice Statistics, 2007). Males younger than the age of 18 were also overrepresented; 20.4 percent of arrests involved male juveniles (Bureau of Justice Statistics, 2007). Blacks were also overrepresented in these arrest data, accounting for 28.5 of all arrests for burglary. Finally, black juveniles were overrepresented, accounting for 8.1 percent of all burglary arrests (Bureau of Justice Statistics, 2007).

When examining the NCVS victimization statistics, a different pattern emerges regarding the relative risk of victimization by the race of the head of household. In 2005 black households were victimized at a much higher rate (44.3 per 1,000 households) than were white households (27.6 per 1,000 households) (Bureau of Justice Statistics, 2007). Rented households had a much higher risk of victimization (39.9 per 1,000 households) than owned households (24.9 per 1,000 households). Similarly, urban households had a higher rate of victimization (49.1 per 1,000 households) than did suburban (23.2 per 1,000 households) or rural households (27.8 per 1,000 households). A striking pattern emerges concerning the rate of victimization and household income. Households with lower incomes have a much higher rate of victimization than households with higher incomes. This is most pronounced for the extreme categories. Households earning less than $7,500 were victimized at a rate of 59.3 per 1,000 households, compared to households earning more than $75,000, which were victimized at a rate of 23.9 per 1,000 households (Bureau of Justice Statistics, 2007).

The final crime that we examine in detail is motor vehicle theft. The FBI defines motor vehicle theft as "the theft or attempted theft of a motor vehicle" (Federal Bureau of Investigation, 2003, 497). Of the three crimes discussed in this section motor vehicle theft is the least common. In 2005, 12.2 percent of the property crimes known to the police were motor vehicle thefts (Bureau of Justice Statistics, 2007). Not surprisingly, the average value of property loss with this crime is substantially higher than either larceny-theft or burglary, with an average of $6,173 lost per incident in 2005 (Bureau of Justice Statistics, 2007). Looking at population rates for motor vehicle theft can be misleading, because many individuals own either no cars or more than one car. It is possible to adjust for this by using a denominator based on the number of vehicles in the United States. In 2005 one motor vehicle theft was reported for every 200 registrations. This ratio has been generally increasing since 1991, indicating that the relative risk for motor vehicle theft has been decreasing (Bureau of Justice Statistics, 2007).

Many of the differences in arrest rates previously discussed are also present regarding motor vehicle theft. Again, in 2005 juveniles were overrepresented in arrest statistics and accounted for 25.6 percent of all arrests for motor vehicle theft (Bureau of Justice Statistics, 2007). Males were also overrepresented and constituted 82.4 percent of all arrestees for motor vehicle theft. Juvenile males were overrepresented and accounted for 15.0 percent of arrests for motor vehicle theft (Bureau of Justice Statistics, 2007). What is striking is the level of overrepresentation regarding race compared to the other crimes examined. Blacks were arrested in 34.8 percent of cases involving motor vehicle theft. Even more pronounced is the overrepresentation of juvenile blacks, accounting for 11.1 percent of all motor vehicle theft arrests (Bureau of Justice Statistics, 2007). This is approximately three times the rate that would be expected based solely on the size of the population.

When examining the 2004 NCVS victimization statistics for motor vehicle theft, we see similar patterns emerge as those for burglary. Black households have a higher rate of victimization (15.6 per 1,000) than white households (7.6 per 1,000) (Bureau of Justice Statistics, 2007). Similarly, renters had a higher rate of victimization (12.5 per 1,000 households) than homeowners (7.1 per 1,000 households). Likewise, urban households were victimized at higher rates (13.4 per 1,000 households) than were suburban (8.8 per 1,000 households) or rural (3.4 per 1,000 households) households (Bureau of Justice Statistics, 2007). Surprisingly, the relationship between household income and motor vehicle theft appears different from the relationships observed for larceny-theft and burglary. The middle-income category, households earning between $25,000 and $34,000, had the highest rate of victimization (11.1 per 1,000 households), and households with annual incomes less than $7,500 had the lowest rate of victimization (4.9 per 1,000 households) (Bureau of Justice Statistics, 2007).

In general, it would appear that the distributions of these three crimes closely mirror many of the important findings from criminology. Furthermore, in many cases the more severe the crime, the more pronounced the differences. For all these crimes juveniles and males, especially male juveniles, are consistently overrepresented in the arrest statistics. Blacks, and especially black juveniles, were overrepresented in all the arrest statistics. In addition, in terms of victimization, blacks had inflated levels of victimization for the crimes of burglary and motor vehicle theft. Rented households had the highest rates of victimization for burglary and motor vehicle theft. Households in urban areas had the highest levels of victimization for all crimes. Finally, concerning the relationship between household income and crime, no consistent patterns emerge across these crimes.

CRIME TRENDS

In addition to investigating the differences in the distribution of crime across demographic categories, criminologists are often interested in the trends in the rates of crime over time. Often, criminological theories are invoked to explain shifts in the frequency of crimes. For the purposes of this section we examine the trends in larceny-theft, burglary, motor vehicle theft, and total property crime over the period 1973–2005. The data used come from the NCVS victimization rates and the UCR reported crime rates. Although the trends in these two measures cannot be directly compared numerically, similarities in the trends between these two data sources can be explored. It is expected that the general theory of crime (Gottfredson and Hirschi, 1990) can be used to explain any patterns detected in these trends over time.

Figure 12.1 presents the trends in the victimization rate for property crime from 1973 to 2005. When examining these trends, we see some clear patterns emerge. First, property crime victimization in general has been decreasing since 1973. Although this trend is most pronounced for the victimization rate for total property crime, the victimization rates for all the component crimes have been decreasing as well. Decreases in larceny-theft contribute a large amount to the trend in overall property crime. This is evident as the trend for larceny-theft largely mirrors that of the trend in total property victimization. Although it is much more difficult to observe because of the scale used in Figure 12.1, the rate of burglary victimization over this time period has substantially decreased as well. Again, although it is difficult to tell because of the low baseline rates, motor vehicle theft victimization has exhibited a slightly different trend over time. After a period of slow decline, the rate of motor vehicle theft victimization began to rise rapidly in 1987, reaching a peak in 1991. After this peak the trends in motor vehicle theft experienced a large decline, mirroring the rest of the property crime trend for the remainder of the time period.

The trends for UCR reported crime from 1973 to 2005 are presented in Figure 12.2. One thing is strikingly clear: The trends observed for the UCR data are substantially different from the trends seen in the NCVS data. Instead of a general downward trend for total

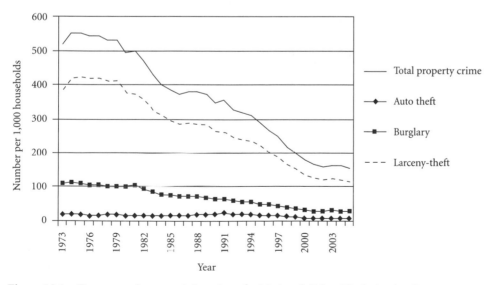

Figure 12.1 Property crime trends based on the National Crime Victimization Survey, conducted by the U.S. Census Bureau. Data for the figure were adapted from Bureau of Justice Statistics (2005b, 2007).

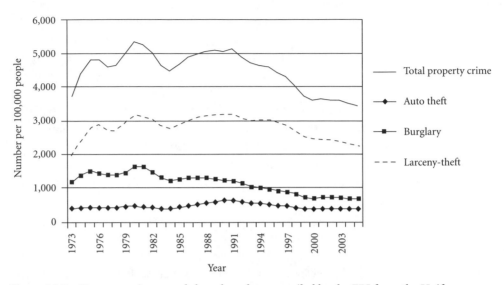

Figure 12.2 Property crime trends based on data compiled by the FBI from the Uniform Crime Reporting Project. Data for the figure were adapted from Bureau of Justice Statistics (2005b, 2007).

property crime, the levels of property crime reports fluctuate throughout the time period, reaching peaks in 1975, 1980, and 1991. After 1991 the trends follow a general downward trend for the rest of the time period, so the UCR and the NCVS agree on the general trend in property crime since 1991. The trends for both larceny-theft and burglary largely mirror what is seen for total property crime, although their curves appear muted as a result of the difference in scale. Finally, although it is difficult to detect at this scale, the trends for motor vehicle theft reports are nearly identical with the trends in motor vehicle victimization. This is not surprising because auto theft is one of the best reported crimes (because of insurance requirements) and therefore the amount of auto theft that is undetected by the police is minimized. Earlier studies of crime trends have found similar results for auto theft (O'Brien, 1985).

DISCUSSION

Property crimes represent a diverse collection of crimes, although most of them share the common characteristic of being committed by force or fraud in the context of self-interest. This is good news for Gottfredson and Hirschi, but this observation did not require data on property crimes; it required only a decent nominal definition. So, although much in property crimes is consistent with the theory of self-control, we explored patterns of property crimes to see whether Gottfredson and Hirschi's theory was consistent with those patterns.

As with violent crime, there is a clear pattern in property crimes: Juveniles, blacks, and males have elevated rates of offending. This observation is consistent with a large volume of previous criminological research establishing that individuals with these demographics are overrepresented in arrest statistics. Given that results such as these are ubiquitous throughout criminology, even when examining different types of crime, it is curious that in its current formulation Gottfredson and Hirschi's (1990) theory is not capable of providing any substantive explanation for the inflated arrest rates of juveniles, males, and minorities. Instead, as Goode pointed out in Chapter 1, Gottfredson and Hirschi balk at offering any explanation in terms of low self-control but rather state that given the universality of these findings, an explanation is unnecessary. This approach seems to dance around the issue instead of addressing it directly and therefore limits the applicability of the theory to explaining the differences in crime rates.

Although Gottfredson and Hirschi (1990) do not provide an explanation for the differences among demographic groups in offending, this does not mean that the theory per se is not capable of addressing these questions. The concept of opportunity is relatively undeveloped in self-control theory and could potentially offer a much more satisfying explanation of the differences in crime rates by demographic groups. Concerning the age-crime relationship, it is possible that dramatic changes in autonomy from parents and other authority figures during the early and late teenage years contribute to a rise in property crime violation for this group. A similar change in the frequency and quality of recreation time in adult years could lead to a decrease in property crime among this demographic group. Differences in the opportunity to offend between young males and females may be related to differences in supervision early in life (males tend to experience less direct parental control). Finally, the differences between racial demographic groups could possibly be explained by the differences in criminal opportunity (decreased guardianship) between individuals living in urban versus suburban areas. These explanations are by no means exhaustive, but they serve to illustrate that the opportunity aspect of self-control theory can be elaborated to construct explanations for the differences in offending and victimization seen in official statistics.

A lack of criminal specialization is often associated with low self-control theory. The evidence to support the notion that property offenders specialize is not strong. Even a cursory examination of police rap sheets discloses that an individual who commits one property crime is likely to have committed other, relatively dissimilar property crimes. Such crimes are dictated more by convenience and opportunity than by more distant causes. This is consistent with low self-control theory, although it is consistent with other theoretical perspectives as well.

Gottfredson and Hirschi view crime by definition as impulsive, spur-of-the-moment behavior. It is guided by short-term intentions and the need for immediate gratification. Although much property crime can be so characterized, there are some offenses and offenders for whom this depiction is simply incorrect. Some crimes involve prolonged planning and the postponement of potentially quick and easy payoffs.

There are some property crimes for which specialization is not only desirable but necessary. Confidence swindles and professional pickpockets all tend to specialize only in that form of property crime. Professional criminals have better role-playing and verbal skills than nonprofessionals who may commit the same kind of crime. Safe cracking is a highly technical offense that is committed only by professionals who have been specially trained in this offense. Most people, no matter how highly motivated to commit this crime, simply cannot do so physically. Some other property offenders, such as the one Gibbons (1965, 102–104) called the "professional 'heavy' criminal," seem to specialize in armed burglary (and robbery).

In our discussion of burglary we noted that many burglaries took place when there was a greater chance that the building or structure was unoccupied. How can this be interpreted? Gottfredson and Hirschi (1990, 25–27) imply that this is an opportunity condition. Burglaries are more likely when no guardians are present. One could also interpret this finding, as we suggested earlier, as meaning that most burglaries are planned to increase the offender's opportunity to commit the burglary. Of course, planning need not represent a lengthy process. A quick check to see whether a door is unlocked might be a relatively spontaneous event. But surely that does not cover all burglaries. Gottfredson and Hirschi (1990, 26) note that less than one-third of burglaries involve forcible entry, suggesting that most burglars were simply taking advantage of the situation, a plausible interpretation.

We have seen that the rates of most, but not all, property crimes declined during the past decade. This is true of burglary, larceny-theft, and auto theft as measured by the UCR and by the NCVS. The declines appear to have been experienced in all parts of the United States, although the rate of decline has differed for each crime and from region to region. It is also worth mentioning that, although beyond the scope of this paper, in the United States the decline in property crime is similar to that in violent crime.

Different theories handle changes in crime rates in different ways. Social learning theory, for example, would examine both the content of what is learned and the method by which it is learned. If the rate of crime is declining, then patterns of learning have changed or the content of what is learned has changed. Social disorganization theory might explain crime rate changes by exploring changes in the extent to which communities (particularly high crime rate communities) have changed and become better organized.

How does low self-control theory handle changes in crime rates? A decline in crime should indicate a decline in low self-control. In other words, it should indicate an increase in high self-control. What might bring this about? Well, better parenting, we presume, would result in fewer individuals with low self-control and a subsequent lowering of the property crime rate. The problem is documenting that parents have become more effective in raising their children.

What can be documented is that parenting is easier when there are two people doing it. In 2002, 10 percent of the population of the United States was divorced, up from 8 percent in 1990 and 6 percent in 1980 (*Divorce Magazine*, 2005). There are also differences in the divorce rate by state and region, with Massachusetts having the lowest divorce rate and Texas and Nevada having the highest (D'Antonio, 2004). In fact, the highest divorce rates are found in the Bible Belt South and among born-again Christians. There are a number of reasons for this. More couples in the South enter first marriages at a younger age, and average household incomes are lower in the South. Also, there is a lower percentage of Roman Catholics in the South, among whom divorce rates are lower, and a high percentage of Southern Baptists, among whom divorce rates are higher.

The divorce rate in the United States today is more than twice what it was in 1960. In 1960 the rate was 9.2 divorces per 1,000 married women ages 15 and older (National Marriage Project, 2001). The divorce rate peaked in 1980 at 22.6 and has generally declined since then. But the declines have been so modest that they would appear not to explain the declines in property crime.

Or does the general decline in property crimes result from a decline in opportunities to commit these crimes, leaving the relative amount of low self-control the same? It is difficult for us to conceive of the kind of wholesale changes in criminal opportunities that would be required to explain the reductions in crime that we have seen, but it is not impossible. Although Gottfredson and Hirschi (1990, 270) do not believe that changes in police tactics or procedures affect crime rates, changes in the way communities are policed that are consistent with the objectives of problem-oriented policing may have been a factor in reducing criminal opportunities, although this is difficult to measure. Zhao and Thurman (2003), in an evaluation of the Community Oriented Policing Services (COPS), report that COPS grants were associated with reduced crime, both violent and property, in communities with populations larger than 10,000 but not in small communities.

Are there any large-scale social trends that could account for the decline in property crimes? One possibility that might explain the trends seen in property crime is the trends in female participation in the workplace. According to Lawrence E. Cohen and Felson (1979) female labor force participation can lead to an increase in crime because fewer guardians are available to monitor the activities of motivated offenders. In the terms of Gottfredson and Hirschi's (1990) theory, this translates to an increase in the opportunity for crime for individuals with low self-control. The NCVS victimization data show a clear decrease in the amount of property crime victimization since 1973. If female labor force participation affected crime trends through opportunity, we would expect a corresponding decrease in female labor force participation over time. Data from the U.S. Bureau of Labor Statistics indicate that female labor force participation has dramatically and consistently increased since before 1970 and has continued to increase into the twenty-first century (Bureau of Labor Statistics, 2003). Clearly, this social trend cannot account for any changes in opportunity that may be occurring with property crime, but other social changes may warrant future investigation.

Another possible explanation for the reduction in crime is that the "distribution" of low self-control is concentrated in certain individuals who were incarcerated beginning in the 1980s. Some attribute the decline in crime rates to the high rate of incarceration starting about this time (Conklin, 2002).

The NCVS informs us that crime rates began to decline in the 1970s (Rand et al., 1997). Total property crime reached a peak in 1973, with a rate well over 500 thefts per 1,000 households. By 1995 total property crime was less than 300 thefts per 1,000 households. By 2003, it was 163 thefts per 1,000 households (Catalano, 2004).

The Bureau of Justice Statistics (2007) informs us that, although prison populations increased in the 1970s, it was not until the 1980s that incarceration rates began to increase significantly, even from year to year. It also appears that the percentage of inmates who had been convicted of a property crime decreased in the 1990s (Bureau of Justice Statistics,

2005a). As a result, we conclude that the downward trend in crime preceded and was not the result of an increasing prison population.

There is another consideration. Donohue and Levitt (2001) argue that the crime decline was caused by the legalization of abortion in the 1970s. Assuming that legalized abortion reduces the number of unwanted babies and assuming that unwanted babies are more likely to be abused and neglected, Donohue and Levitt claim that as much as 50 percent of the crime decline is a result of legalized abortion (see also Levitt and Dubner, 2005, ch. 4). Now, if true, and assuming that unwanted babies are more likely to have low self-control because of inadequate parenting, it could be argued that Gottfredson and Hirschi's theory can account for at least some of the crime decline. That's a lot of assumptions, of course, and this would not explain the property crime decline that began in about 1973.

SUMMARY AND CONCLUSION

Many property crimes are precisely the kind of crime that the theory of low self-control is designed to explain: unsophisticated, spur-of-the-moment acts guided by the desire for immediate gratification. But not all property crimes are of this kind; some demand long-term skill and the ability to defer gratification. Yet, to the extent that offenders take advantage of immediate opportunities to steal or vandalize property, the theory of low self-control provides a satisfying explanation. This is not to say, however, that other theories do not provide the same level of explanatory power.

Our biggest objection to the theory of low self-control is that it does not appear to account for trends in property crimes or the distribution of property offenders by major demographic groups. The inability of the theory to explain crime occurrences over time and differences in offending by age, gender, and race may be a result of the theory not devoting sufficient attention to criminal opportunities, their distribution, and availability over time.

NOTES

1. In 2005, 32 percent of all larceny-thefts were categorized as "all other."

2. There is tabulated data for personal property victimization (namely, purse snatching and pickpocketing) by age and sex; however, this is not consistent with the definitions applied earlier. Further, this information is unavailable for burglary and motor vehicle theft. For the purposes of consistency these statistics will not be examined.

3. These numbers are smaller than 50 percent because there were a number of incidents for which the time of day was unknown.

13 | DRUG USE AND CRIMINAL BEHAVIOR

Erich Goode

Gottfredson and Hirschi's general theory of crime is predicated on the assumption that drug use and crime are but different manifestations of one and the same behavior; both are an expression of impulsiveness, low self-control, and the predisposition to engage in hedonistic, short-run pleasures without regard to their long-run consequences. There is no need, Gottfredson and Hirschi reason, to account for why they are related; their relationship is explained by the intrinsic qualities they share. The predilection to use drugs is simultaneously a predilection to engage in criminal behavior, and vice versa. Gottfredson and Hirschi hold that the drugs-crime link is not forged by structural or cultural factors—that is, it is not *contingent* on the configuration of a particular society's legal or normative structure; for instance, whether or not heroin possession and sale are crimes, marijuana is encouraged in certain social circles, or violence is a fixture of certain drug-selling contexts. Gottfredson and Hirschi believe, therefore, that traditional sociological explanations of the drugs-crime nexus are futile and in error (1990, 40–42, 93, 233–234).

In this chapter I address the issues of whether and to what extent self-control theory adequately accounts for the connection between drug use and crime, whether Gottfredson and Hirschi's critique of the explanations provided by other perspectives is balanced and valid, and whether the contention that the theories accounting for this connection are as mutually exclusive as is argued in *A General Theory of Crime*.

THE EMPIRICAL RELATIONSHIP BETWEEN DRUG USE AND CRIME

The statistical relationship between the consumption of psychoactive drugs and criminal behavior is one of the most robust and firmly established in the criminological literature. It is in fact completely unproblematic; hardly any criminologists or sociologists of deviance or drug use question that drugs and crime are *empirically* related. In nearly every systematic study ever conducted, individuals who engage in criminal or delinquent behavior, especially frequently, are statistically more likely to use illicit drugs, drink alcohol, and smoke cigarettes than individuals who do not engage in criminal or delinquent behavior—and vice versa. And the more frequently individuals use drugs for recreational purposes, the greater the likelihood that they engage in criminal behavior, the greater the likelihood that they will do so frequently, and the more serious the criminal behavior they engage in. In this chapter I do not address the relationship between drug use and drug-related crime—that is, the possession and sale of controlled substances or drug involvement as crime—because they are so definitionally intertwined as to render their causal links intuitively obvious. Of course, drug selling does influence *nondrug* crimes, such as violence; in contrast, that relationship *is* worth exploring.

Empirically, the drugs-crime relationship is so strong, consistent, and statistically significant that documentation seems almost superfluous. Nonetheless, the Youth Behavior Risk Surveillance study, a nationally representative survey of 15,000 teenagers in grades 9 through 12, provides ample evidence that the two behaviors are intimately related.

To choose a few relationships almost at random, consider the following facts:

Females who smoked more than twenty cigarettes a day in the month before the survey were 125 times more likely to say they drank while driving six or more times during the previous month (50 percent) than was true of those who did not smoke at all (0.4 percent); males who smoked twenty or more cigarettes were 45 times more likely to have done so (17.9 percent vs. 0.4 percent).

Females who drank five or more drinks on twenty or more days during the prior thirty days were 26 times more likely to carry a weapon to school on six or more days (44 percent) than those who never drank five or more drinks during that same period (1.7 percent); males who drank five or more drinks were just shy of 10 times more likely to have done so (75 percent vs. 7.6 percent).

Females who used cocaine more than ten times during their lives were 51 times more likely to have gotten into twelve or more fights during the previous year (36 percent) than was true of those who did not use cocaine at all (0.7 percent); males who used cocaine ten or more times were 16 times more likely to have done so (36 percent vs. 2.3 percent).

These relationships are consistent and remarkably robust. It hardly matters which indicator of drug use, legal or illegal (the purchase of alcohol is illegal to individuals under 21, and the purchase of cigarettes is illegal to everyone under the age of 18), or which indicator of crime and delinquency we choose, the two dimensions are so intimately related that they almost seem to be measures of the same phenomenon. Precisely the same relationship holds between drug use and risky sexual behavior (such as having sex at an early age, having sex without the use of a condom, drinking alcohol before having sex, getting pregnant or causing a pregnancy, having sex with multiple partners) and between delinquency and risky sexual behavior. In addition, the correlation between the use of alcohol and tobacco, which are inexpensive, and delinquent behavior, is extremely strong, on a par with that between illicit drugs and delinquency. These findings are entirely consistent with Gottfredson and Hirschi's contentions about the drugs-crime nexus.

These data are illustrative but not definitive. But the sheer weight of the available evidence, from multitudinous sources, including survey data (whether based on randomized samples or not), arrest data, overdose data, and data drawn from drug tests, confirms precisely the same generalization: People who use psychoactive drugs, both legal and illicit, for recreational purposes are substantially and significantly more likely to commit criminal offenses, and vice versa. "Many data sources," say policy analysts MacCoun, Kilmer, and Reuter, "establish a raw correlation between drug use and other criminal offenses" (MacCoun et al., 2003, 65). At this point, further documentation seems redundant.

EXPLANATIONS OF THE DRUGS-CRIME LINK

The empirical relationship between drug use and criminal and/or delinquent behavior is not at issue; it is as consistently documented as any we might find in any literature in the social sciences. But as every student of an introductory social science course quickly learns, correlation does not demonstrate causality. What is problematic is what *causes* this strong and consistent relationship between drug use and criminal behavior, and this issue is extremely contentious. How do we explain or account for the relationship?

Inciardi (2002) refers to the drugs-crime nexus as "the riddle of the sphinx" (p. 182)—an intellectual puzzle that seems fiendishly difficult, that demands an answer upon pain of death, yet whose answer may be simpler than we realize. Logically, the relationship between these two variables could be one of the following: Drug use causes crime; crime causes drug use; both are the effects of a common cause. But in real-world terms, what exactly do these mechanistic causal sequences *mean*? There is a spectrum of possibilities.

As all researchers know, convincingly establishing a precise cause-and-effect relationship between two or more variables is tricky and troublesome. With respect to the relationship between drug use and crime, this problem may be even more problematic than usual because of not only the complexity of the variables but also the quality of the research. Drugs and crime research, says Tonry (1990) in a widely cited passage, "is a minor scholarly activity and is poorly funded. The literature is scant, much of it is fugitive, the research community is fragmented, and too much of the research is poor in quality and weak in design" (p. 2). But after writing this passage, Tonry went on to co-edit a volume attempting to accomplish the very thing he had stated was next to impossible (Tonry and Wilson, 1990). In this chapter I do the same: Gather and assess the available evidence and attempt to reach a reasonable conclusion. These efforts will be in the service of weighing their relevance to Gottfredson and Hirschi's general theory of crime.

Among many vexing issues we might consider is the following: The relationship between drug use and criminal behavior is "probabilistic, not deterministic. Most drug users are not otherwise criminally active, and the vast majority of drug-using incidents neither cause nor accompany other forms of criminality" (MacCoun et al., 2003, 65). Moreover, the drugs-crime link "varies across individuals, over time . . . , across situations," and, possibly, "over time periods" (p. 66) and from one neighborhood or community and demographic group to another.

In addition, drugs are differentially linked to crime on a drug-by-drug basis. With respect to sheer volume, alcohol is implicated in more criminal behavior than any other psychoactive drug, but it is consumed on a monthly or more basis by more than half the American population, and the overwhelming majority of drinking episodes result in no criminal behavior whatsoever. On an episode-by-episode basis cocaine and heroin, compared with other illicit drugs, are extremely intimately linked with criminal offending; in contrast, the use of Ecstasy hardly ever appears in police records as implicated in criminal events. And last, the role of drug use in *being* criminally victimized further complicates the drugs-crime picture. Individuals who are under the influence of alcohol and illicit drugs stand a significantly greater chance of becoming victims of a predatory crime than individuals who are not under the influence. This issue is especially important for women (MacCoun et al., 2003, 71; Hindmarch and Brinkmann, 1999). The drugs-crime link is as complex as any in the social science literature.

The field of criminology offers several models or theories to explain the drugs-crime connection. In fact, the field offers several *sets* of explanation for different *aspects* of the link—one for the drugs-crime link in general and a separate one for the drugs–violent crime link. This is, of course, an elaboration that Gottfredson and Hirschi would most emphatically reject, because they view drug use and crime as a seamless garment and typologizing as a meaningless exercise. Still, these are the models that the field of criminology has produced, and as a consequence, these are the waters in which Gottfredson and Hirschi swim and against which the validity of the general theory of crime must be measured.

First, I address the four major models of the drugs-crime link in general. In the next section I address the three models of the drugs–violent crime nexus. The four models for the drugs-crime link are the enslavement model; the cultural deviance, subcultural, learning, socialization, or peer interaction (or "peer values") model; the predisposition model; and the intensification model.

The Enslavement Model

Gottfredson and Hirschi (1990) refer to the enslavement model as the "economic or cash nexus" model (p. 41). It applies most specifically to narcotic addiction but, in principle, could apply to any expensive, dependency-producing substance. The enslavement explanation of the drugs-crime link dominated sociological thinking at least as far back as the 1930s, when Alfred Lindesmith conducted his research on opiate addiction (1938, 1947). Among researchers seeking a drastic reform of the punitive drug laws, this model remains influential. The enslavement model has two varieties. The first can be referred to as the "out of character" model (Bean, 2002, 9). It argues that through a variety of paths more or less ordinary people become trapped into the use of and eventually addiction to opiates. The less radical psychiatric model argues that individuals suffering from certain mental disorders find refuge in addicting drugs and, like the ordinary person, come to be ensnared by the hook of addiction. In both varieties crime follows addiction almost inexorably: Because narcotic drugs are illegal, they are expensive, and as a result, addicts must resort to a life of crime to support a habit. In other words, because they are "enslaved" to narcotics, addicts are willy-nilly forced to engage in money-making crimes—thus the drugs-crime nexus. If opiate addiction were treated as a medical problem, not a criminal one, addicts could receive doses of narcotics in a clinic and not have to resort to criminal behavior to support their habit; as a result, the drugs-crime link would be severed (Schur, 1962; Lindesmith, 1965). Under legalization, this theory's advocates claim, "the black market would disappear, the prices of heroin and cocaine would decline significantly, and users would no longer have to engage in street crime to support their desired levels of drug intake" (Inciardi, 2002, 288).

Empirically, the enslavement theory is wrong because it is based on two egregiously fallacious assumptions. The first of these fallacies is that through a variety of fortuitous circumstances ordinary people (i.e., noncriminals) become ensnared in drug abuse and eventually addiction. The fact is, ordinary people do *not* become fortuitously ensnared in drug abuse or addiction. Instead, people who eventually use have *sought out* drugs because the use of psychoactive substances provides an easy, hedonistic, self-interested means of attaining short-term gratification and thus is immensely appealing to individuals lacking in self-control. Even if this "out of character" assumption is discarded, the assumption that enslavement to narcotic or other illicit drugs causes crime is equally fallacious.

Drug abusers and addicts are not criminal *only* because they need money to support their drug habit. If illicit drugs were inexpensive, this line of reasoning continues, drug abusers and addicts would not engage in criminal behavior any more than is true of the population at large, an obviously and almost self-evidently false assertion. This is because most people who come to abuse drugs committed delinquent acts *before* they took illicit, controlled substances, and they commit crime even when they are *not* using drugs. In other words, drug use "does not initiate criminal careers." For most heavy users of street drugs "their criminal [or delinquent] careers were well established prior to the onset of [taking] either narcotics, cocaine, or crack use" (Inciardi, 2002, 288). In addition, most drug experts have abandoned the idea that addicting drugs are used because of the terror of withdrawal. Positive reinforcement or pleasure seeking, they believe, is the factor that generates drug dependency, not physical addiction (Ksir et al., 2006, 34–39). Moreover, during periods of abstention long-term drug abusers still commit criminal acts vastly in excess of the population at large. Indeed, the criminal behavior of drug abusers and addicts is extremely wide-ranging, taking in not merely money-making crimes such as theft and drug dealing but also violence. The enslavement theory is invalid, fallacious, and in all likelihood politically motivated, underpinning, as it does, the argument to legalize the currently illegal psychoactive drugs. (Evidence for these assertions can be found in Inciardi [2002] and McBride and Swartz [1990]. Gottfredson and Hirschi do not make all these arguments, but they would endorse most of them.) Moreover, as Gottfredson and Hirschi (1990) say, criminals are more likely to use cheap, legal, and readily available drugs, such as alcohol and tobacco, than is true of the man and woman on the street (p. 41), an inconvenient fact for the enslavement theory.

The Cultural Deviance/Learning Model

The cultural deviance, subcultural, learning, or socialization theories, into which category Gottfredson and Hirschi group Sutherland's differential association theory (1939), labeling theory (Becker, 1963), conflict theory (Turk, 1969), the subcultural approach of Albert Cohen (1955), and the social learning theory of Ronald Akers (1973) and others (Elliott et al., 1985), see deviance as the outcome of a kind of tug-of-war between two sets of socializing groups or collectivities—conventional versus deviant—in which the deviant group emerges triumphant. Deviant values are instilled in individuals who interact the earliest, the most frequently, and the most intimately within and among social circles in which deviant values are promulgated. As a consequence, the close relationship between drug use and crime is caused by the fact that the positive value of both is promulgated in the same, deviant, social circles and the negative value of both is promulgated in the same, conventional, social circles. Individuals who use drugs and commit delinquent and criminal acts are those who have learned the positive value of such behavior in the social circles in which they have interacted most.

Drug use and criminal or delinquent behavior are connected, many sociologists say, because the social circles whose members engage in them heavily overlap. It is the factor of "peer pressure and adolescent values" that forges the link between them. The same friendship networks that endorse the one also support the other (Johnson, 1972). This perspective argues that "there is no *inherent* connection between drug use and crime" (Gottfredson and Hirschi, 1990, 41). The relationship between the two could be positive or negative, depending on the circumstances and the social circle in question. In other words, engaging in both or either—or neither—is entirely a function of the norms of the intimate groups or social circles in which people interact.

For instance, in certain circles of drug users (e.g., Indian holy men, or *sadhus*, who use marijuana to achieve an ecstatic state), criminal behavior is discouraged; likewise, among certain social circles of criminals (e.g., terrorists or revolutionaries) drug use tends to be discouraged. In these cases subcultural norms generate a *negative* relationship between drug use and crime. Hence the connection between drug use and criminal behavior may be positive or negative, depending entirely on the norms of the subculture of drug users or of criminals. It happens that in the United States at the present time, the norm among drug users tends to support violations of the law; likewise, among individuals who engage in delinquent and criminal behavior, norms favor the use of psychoactive drugs.

Of course, Gottfredson and Hirschi strongly *reject* the cultural deviance formulation of the drugs-crime link. They deny the validity of the very foundation of all learning theories of deviance. Gottfredson and Hirschi assert that getting high is so intrinsically and viscerally appealing to individuals with low self-control that what needs to be learned is the value of *not* getting high. Like the person who eschews criminal behavior, the drug abstainer has to learn that it is good *not* to take drugs. Taking drugs—and committing crime—is what "comes naturally" and does not have to be learned. It is not necessary for peers to teach anyone their positive value. Drug use and crime are, to use the words of behaviorist psychologists, "natural reinforcers": Their value does not have to be learned. That anyone would have to *learn* the value of deviance, crime and drug use included, runs counter to the data of one's senses, Gottfredson and Hirschi argue.

According to Gottfredson and Hirschi (1990), the cultural deviance/learning theory is also wrong because it fails to recognize "similarity across criminal acts" (p. 41) as well as the similarity between criminal acts and drug use. In other words, cultural traditions wrongly assume that the behaviors endorsed by the norms that prevail in offending groups and categories are to some degree arbitrary and need not have an inherent appeal to certain social circles in the population. In contrast, say Gottfredson and Hirschi, there is an inherent—not an arbitrary—link between the predispositions of actors and the behaviors they enact. The behaviors enacted by drug users and by criminals are linked because something about them is appealing to individuals lacking in self-control: "Drug use and delinquency are both manifestations of an underlying tendency to pursue short-term, immediate pleasure" (Gottfredson and Hirschi, 1990, 93). This underlying tendency, they say, "has many manifestations," of which two are crime and/or delinquency and drug use (p. 93).

Moreover, Gottfredson and Hirschi argue, deviants do not choose crime because they learn to do so from the criminal teachings of their intimates. The reality is precisely the other way around: They engage in deviant behavior because of an *absence* of friends, because they are *asocial* rather than social, because they act on their own individual predilections. In addition, Gottfredson and Hirschi state, in no human grouping are the acts we refer to as deviant—delinquent behavior, illicit drug use, crime—positively valued.

Of course, we do know that many acts included in Gottfredson and Hirschi's compass of deviant behavior are positively valued in many social circles in this and other societies: speeding, drag racing, adolescent drinking, marijuana use (even taking harder drugs), the consumption of pornography, shoplifting, vandalism, fighting, assault, and the sexual abuse and even the rape of females. In practically no social collectivity are the most horrific extremes of deviance and crime valued or encouraged, it is true, but as the example of rape demonstrates, in some collectivities many *very* serious and, for their victims, harmful crimes are positively valued and encouraged.

Gottfredson and Hirschi dismiss the enormous research literature supporting the view that a great deal of deviant, delinquent, and criminal behavior is caused by peer influence (Akers, 1985, 1998). They argue that the findings of such research are based on a "methodological artifact." Asking respondents in surveys about the deviant behavior of their peers, Gottfredson and Hirschi contend, is simply a stand-in measure for the respondent's *own* deviant behavior. Moreover, they say, the fact that one's peers are similar with respect to deviance versus conformity is little more than an empirical verification of the age-old adage "Birds of a feather flock together." It does not, they argue, demonstrate that peers *influence* one another to engage in illicit behavior (Armstrong, 2003, 47–49). Miscreants would engage in the same behavior, separately or in concert.

It is not clear what manner of evidence would falsify Gottfredson and Hirschi's contention that social learning/cultural deviance theory is invalid. It seems that they have formulated the truth or falsity of self-control versus learning theory in axiomatic terms, insisting that if control factors operate, then learning factors cannot possibly take place. They insist that learning theory argues that intergroup variation in the crime rate (i.e., males vs. females, blacks vs. whites, young vs. old) indicates that each category holds a separate and distinct set of norms with respect to engaging in criminal behavior, that the norms in the higher-crime rate category *demand* that its occupants engage in illegal behavior, and that no other causes of the higher crime rates account for this behavior (Gottfredson and Hirschi, 1990, 76, 151; Hirschi, 1969, 197; Kornhauser, 1978, 195–196; Akers, 1996). Not one of these contentions is true, say learning theory advocates. Indeed, in their critique of learning theory, Gottfredson and Hirschi do not quote any of the relevant texts from the theories they attack—although they do quote Kornhauser's characterization of cultural deviance theory. And as Akers points out (1996, 234), Kornhauser's use of a Sutherland quote is disingenuous, because it omits the necessary qualifications that would make that position far more moderate and reasonable.

In addition, Gottfredson and Hirschi (1990) characterize cultural deviance theories as being defined by "the transmission of [deviant] values from one generation to the next" (pp. 81–82). But this is false for *most* of the perspectives they characterize as deviance theories. It certainly does not hold for Becker's subcultural approach to the socialization of novices into drug use (1953; 1963, 41–58); here, the socialization processes take place as a result of a discontinuity from one generation to the next. And it does not hold as well for Sutherland's differential association theory (1939, 1947), which argues that positive normative definitions of criminal behavior can occur at any time in the actor's life (although earlier socialization processes tend to be more influential than later ones), need not entail generational continuity, may occur in any context or social assemblage (e.g., on the job, in a friendship network, in a gang, in school), and may bypass the usual generationally associated collectivities, such as family, ethnic group, or neighborhood. As Akers says (1996), not all the theories that Gottfredson and Hirschi characterize as cultural deviance theories fit their typification.

The Predisposition Model

Gottfredson and Hirschi endorse the predisposition model. The predisposition to commit crime and use drugs, say Gottfredson and Hirschi, is what fuses these two behaviors in the same individuals. In short, "the relation between drug use and delinquency [and crime] is not a causal question" (Gottfredson and Hirschi, 1990, 93). The two are correlated because they are in fact one and the same behavior—at least, manifestations of one and the same underlying tendency—not two separate and independent dimensions. Drug use and crime "are the same thing—that is, manifestations of low self-control. If we are correct, longitudinal research designed to determine the causal relationship between crime and drug use is a waste of time and money" (pp. 233–234).[1]

What generates this underlying predisposition, this impulse to engage in these two interlocked behaviors, is, as we have seen, low self-control—the tendency to seek short-term, easy, simple, immediate gratification of desires; as Gottfredson and Hirschi say, "Money without work, sex without courtship, revenge without court delays," acts that are "*exciting, risky, or thrilling*," that provide "*few or meager long-term benefits*," that require "*little skill or planning*," and often result in "*pain or discomfort for the victim*" (Gottfredson and Hirschi, 1990, 89). In other words, low impulse control is the mechanism, vehicle, or *means* by which the tendency to engage in criminal behavior and drug use is expressed. And what breeds low self-control is, as we have seen, poor, inadequate parenting—that is, the inability or unwillingness of parents to monitor or sanction the untoward behavior of their children. Low self-control is a lifelong characteristic of the individual, modified but not substantially altered by the aging process, which obtains for males and females separately and independently.

In sum, the link between drug use and criminal behavior is forged by their common, inherent appeal, by the fact that they both satisfy the same impulse, the thirst for immediate gratification, which is appealing for individuals lacking self-control. Both behaviors are risky, often entailing harm both to the actor and to victims, but both behaviors get the actor what is desired in the short run. Gottfredson and Hirschi's answer to the "why" question—Why is the link between drug use and criminal behavior so empirically robust?—is that there is a *predisposition* to engage in both behaviors. They are manifestations of the same underlying tendency; no other explanation explains as many aspects of this empirical link as does self-control theory. Accordingly, the other models that explain their correlation, say Gottfredson and Hirschi (1990, 41), are wrong.

The Intensification Model

As an explanation of the *origin* of the drugs-crime link, the classic Lindesmith-Schur enslavement model is clearly erroneous. Whether and to what extent it was valid in Chicago in the 1930s (when Lindesmith conducted his research) in the United Kingdom (where Schur conducted his research in the late 1950s) or whether it was valid as an explanation for why contemporary drug abusers and addicts began committing crime, the theory is invalid, as nearly all criminologists would agree. The illegality of narcotics is not what got eventual addicts *started* on criminal behavior. But is the enslavement model *completely* invalid? Does it explain *no* features of the drugs-crime nexus? Does the predisposition model account for *all* the major features of why drug abusers and addicts commit so much crime?

Researchers studying the careers of drug users have found strikingly higher rates of criminal behavior during periods of use, abuse, and addiction than during periods of abstention. Same individuals, same predispositions, very different rates of crime. The number of days when Baltimore addicts committed crime was substantially higher during periods when they were not taking methadone than during periods when they were (Ball et al., 1981, 1983; Nurco et al., 1985). Johnson et al. (1985) examined the drug use and criminal behavior of a sample of Harlem street heroin abusers and concluded that "crime increases with drug involvement" (p. 6). After conducting a study of Miami street cocaine abusers, Inciardi (1992) concluded that, "although the use of heroin and other drugs did not necessarily initiate criminal careers, it tended to intensify and perpetuate them. In that sense, it might be said that drug use freezes its devotees into patterns of criminality that are more acute, dynamic, unremitting, and enduring than those of other offenders" (p. 158).

The intensification model combines the enslavement and the predisposition models. Each perspective addresses a somewhat different aspect of the drugs-crime nexus. Clearly enslavement to addicting drugs cannot explain why the individuals who eventually become addicted engage in acts of delinquency and crime long before their addiction takes hold. In all likelihood, not one of the high school students in the Youth Behavior Risk Surveillance survey was addicted, yet the respondents who used drugs were immensely more likely to engage in delinquent behavior than those who did not. But origin of the drugs-crime link is not the only issue in which researchers are interested. Predisposition theory cannot explain the sharp decline in the crime rate during periods of abstention among drug addicts or during periods when addicts use methadone (Hubbard et al., 1989, 99–106). In short, Gottfredson and Hirschi adopt a too-narrow test of the best explanation for the connection between drug use and criminal behavior. They assume that if the predisposition model explains the *origin* of the drugs-crime link, the enslavement model must be wrong about the connection between drug use and criminal behavior *over time*. The predisposition model cannot explain why variations in drug use account for variations in criminal behavior; for that reason Gottfredson and Hirschi's declaration that the enslavement model is wrong in all its particulars must be regarded as premature.

One way of dismissing the relevance of these data on lower crime rates with lower levels of drug use for the *same* users is to argue that addicts who are motivated to seek treatment, or to cut back on use, are different from those who do not. They are more likely to desist from crime during treatment or abstention than those who refuse to enter a treatment program, drop out of one, or do not cut back on use and remain on the street, using drugs at the same, customarily high levels. As a consequence, treatment data do not adequately test the validity of the thesis that what causes the drugs-crime link is low self-control. At this point the interested researcher is forced to raise the question of falsifiability: What data could possibly falsify the proposition that low self-control is the only explanation linking drug use and criminal behavior? What would a true test of this hypothesis consist of? Most drug researchers find these treatment data sufficiently persuasive and argue that drug treatment programs take a swath of drug abusers and addicts—all characterized by low self-control, nearly all of whom engage in a wide range of crimes—and drastically lower their rate of using drugs and committing predatory crime. If that does not seriously qualify the predisposition model, they would ask, what would?

THE DRUGS-VIOLENCE NEXUS

As with crime in general, we are led to ask what causes or makes for the relationship between drugs and violence, or violent crime. As I said earlier, Gottfredson and Hirschi would reject the very premise of this question, because they regard crime and violence as inseparable, two heavily overlapping manifestations of precisely the same phenomenon. But the fact is, if the two have significantly different causal links with drug use, this might challenge Gottfredson and Hirschi's assumption of their seamless conjunction. Moreover, this characterization of the drugs-violence nexus is firmly entrenched in both the drug use and the criminology literature and therefore cannot be ignored. Goldstein (1985) proposed three possible models to explain the drugs-violence connection, or nexus: the psychopharmacological, the economic-compulsive, and the systemic models. The reader should be warned, however, that Goldstein's delineation of these models fudges a bit on conceptualizing the drugs dimension. By that I mean that two of the models refer specifically to drug *use*, whereas the third shifts conceptual ground and addresses the connection between drug *selling* and violence.

The question of which of these three models best explains the strong relationship between drug use and violence was tackled by a team of researchers who examined the dynamics of criminal homicide in New York City during the height of the crack crisis (Goldstein et al., 1989). A homicide was classified as drug related if it was decided by both the researchers and the police that drugs contributed to the killing "in an important and causal manner" (p. 662). Roughly one-fourth of all criminal homicides that took place in 1988 were selected for the study sample. The sample was made up of 414 "homicide events," because some of these events involved more than one perpetrator and more than one victim. Just over half (53 percent) of these events were classified as primarily drug related; just under half (47 percent) were deemed not to be drug related. Studying each event case by case, the researchers and the police determined that 60 percent of the drug-related homicides involved crack cocaine; an additional 22 percent involved powder cocaine.

The question that dominated the focus of this research team was, Which of the three models best explains the intimate connection they observed between drugs and criminal homicide?

The Psychopharmacological Model

The most commonsensical and traditional model or explanation of why drugs and violence are connected is that it is the psychological and physical effects of psychoactive substances that cause users to become violent toward others. As a result of ingesting one or more substances, users "may become excitable, irrational, and may exhibit violent behavior" (Goldstein, 1985, 494). The psychopharmacological model, which during the crack epidemic in the late 1980s attracted so much media attention and is so intuitively appealing to much of the public, did not offer an adequate guide to reality. In fact, of the 118 crack-related homicides, only 3 (3 percent) were deemed to have been caused by the psychoactive effects of the drug. This particular study did not examine the role of alcohol in inducing violence.

However, when the Goldstein team examined the drugs-violence link in the *precrack* era (1984), looked at homicide data throughout New York state, and included alcohol in the equation, it became clear that the psychopharmacological model accounted for the majority of the homicides that took place (59 percent) and that alcohol was the primary drug responsible (79 percent), verifying the proposition that the causal relationship between drug use and violence may differ from one era to another (Goldstein et al., 1992). Drug researchers insist, however, that with respect to violence, the psychopharmacological effects of alcohol are moderated by a variety of factors, including the predisposition of the person under the influence (Parker, 1995).

The Economic-Compulsive Model

Another explanation or model for drug use often leading to violence is that, because addicts need to raise large sums of money quickly, they engage in high-risk crimes, including theft, robbery, and burglary, that often escalate into acts of physical harm against the victim. For instance, in a robbery both the perpetrator and the victim may be nervous; the victim may resist, struggle, and attempt to retaliate against the offender and may be accidentally stabbed or shot. In a burglary the offender may be confronted by the resident and may attempt to flee, resulting in a struggle; suddenly, a crime of stealth becomes assault or even murder. Economic crimes to support a drug habit do not always remain simple property crimes; inadvertently, a certain proportion turn into crimes of violence. This model is obviously an elaboration of the enslavement model, with the admission that, currently, opiate addicts are more likely to be violent than was true in the past (McBride and Swartz, 1990). In any case,

Goldstein and his team (1989) judged only eight (7 percent) of the homicides to have been economic-compulsive in origin. Whether and to what extent the economic incentive of heavy drug use is instrumental in escalating property crime, it does not seem to be a major factor in violent crime. Few homicides are committed "by drug users in the context of committing property crimes to get money to buy drugs" (Goldstein et al., 1992, 473).

The Systemic Model

The world of drug dealing is thoroughly saturated with violence. Not having the protection of the law, dealers often resort to taking the law into their own hands. Drug sellers carry or stash drugs—a commodity much more valuable than gold—and handle large sums of cash. The temptation is for all manner of street people to rob dealers of both the cash and the drugs. Drug sellers are vulnerable to arrest, and informers often turn them in to avoid long prison sentences; violent retaliation is a common response to such betrayal. Drug sales may result in disputes over the quality and quantity of the goods sold. One gang may decide to muscle into the turf or territory of an already established gang, resulting in a shooting war. Buyers may receive a shipment of drugs, use most of it themselves, and be unable to pay for what they consumed.

Systemic violence, then, refers to "the traditionally aggressive patterns of interaction within the system of drug distribution and use" (Goldstein, 1985, 497). In fact, systemic violence is "normatively embedded in the social and economic networks of drug users and sellers. Drug use, the drug business, and the violence connected to both of these phenomena, are all part of the same general lifestyle. Individuals caught in this lifestyle value the experience of substance use, recognize the risks involved, and struggle for survival on a daily basis. Clearly, that struggle is a major contributor to the total volume of crime and violence in American society" (p. 503).

Except for a few "multidimensionally" caused homicides, all of the remainder of the New York homicides examined (100 out of 118, or 85 percent) could be explained by the systemic model (Goldstein et al., 1989). The circumstances of systemic homicides included territorial disputes, the robbery of a drug dealer, efforts to collect a drug debt, a dispute over a drug theft, and reactions to a dealer selling poor, weak drugs. In other words, typically, killings connected to crack (and powder cocaine as well) were caused not by the effects of the drug but by the violent and conflictual nature of the crack *business.*

What makes the crack business an especially disputational enterprise? Why was the crack trade in comparison with, for example, the heroin business, an arena in which murder took place with special frequency? Goldstein's team trace the volatile nature of the crack trade to its unstable, unorganized distribution system. Because cocaine hydrochloride can be extremely easily converted into crack, there need not be a hierarchy or organizational structure to hold dealing networks together. In fact, the marketplace is made up of "many small-scale entrepreneurs," independents who are able to start up a business for themselves and compete in the same territory for a clientele. For that reason boundary disputes are plentiful, and there are no higher-ups—indeed, no organization at all—capable of controlling violence when it does erupt. Moreover, in addition to the simplicity of the cocaine-to-crack conversion process, because crack is so inexpensive per dose, anyone with a small cash investment can set up a business. As a result, extremely young dealers entered the crack trade, many of whom were fearless, reckless, and lacking in judgment.

How does the Goldstein tripartite drugs-violence nexus shed light on the general theory of crime? The systemic model is entirely consistent with self-control as *a* key explanatory factor in the drugs–violence crime connection. It is entirely possible that a cause for the predisposition to sell drugs and resort to violence under a wide range of circumstances can be located to low self-control. (On the other hand, Goldstein's data do not automatically rule out the relevance of anomie, social disorganization, social control, learning, or conflict theory.) But whether and to what extent drug sellers resorted to violence is as structural as it is predispositional. The configuration of the drug market is such that violence is demanded of the dealer. If he is unable or unwilling to meet threats with violence, his options are limited: Quit the business or be killed. No one acquainted with the crack trade in the late 1980s questions the fact that selling *demanded* a specific predilection for violence. But predisposition does not *explain* the high levels of violence among crack dealers during that era. Indeed, the fact that crack-related rates of violence have plummeted since 1990 indicates that predisposition alone cannot account for the systemic drugs-violence nexus we observed in the 1985–1989 era. As we saw with accounting for the drugs-crime link in general, with the drugs-violence nexus we see Gottfredson and Hirschi's tendency to adopt an either-or position; they assume that if the predisposition to low self-control can explain a major feature of this nexus, any competing explanation must by definition be wrong. Most researchers see this assumption as incorrect and accommodate a more elaborate explanatory model for the many facets of the multiform terrain of drug use and criminal behavior.

There is relatively little discussion of opportunity in *A General Theory of Crime*; perhaps Gottfredson and Hirschi are satisfied that predisposition creates opportunity. They seem to assume, in any case, that criminal opportunities—and by implication, opportunities to use illicit (and for minors, legal) drugs—are so abundant that one need only reach up on the tree of temptation and pick the apple. But this is an empirical assumption that seems unwarranted. In any case, if one is weaving a systematic argument of the causation of deviant behavior, the ubiquity of illicit opportunity has to be established. Such lopsided attention to predisposition over opportunity is far from unique to the work of Gottfredson and Hirschi; it also tends to prevail in both the drug use and the crime literature, which hugely emphasizes predisposition and practically ignores opportunity. How does considering the role of opportunity modify the way we think about the drugs-crime connection?

Illicit drug use is a consensual act, that is, in the usual case no force or coercion is involved. In contrast, by definition, predatory crime, such as rape and robbery, is nonconsensual; it is coercive by its very nature. Thus the opportunity to engage in these types of acts is likely to have markedly different dynamics. The opportunity to use or purchase illegal drugs presents itself in the form of a motivated offender encountering someone with an illicit substance being willing to share or sell it. Opportunities to engage in predatory crimes present themselves in the form of a motivated offender being presented with a suitable target that lacks a capable guardian. With collaborative predatory crimes—whose import Gottfredson and Hirschi underplay—opportunity comes in the form of interacting with one or more other motivated offenders (A. K. Cohen, 1955, 1965).

Unfortunately, accounting for the role of opportunity to use illicit drugs runs into the same methodological problem we encountered when assessing Gottfredson and Hirschi's criticisms of the subcultural deviance theories: How do we separate the influence of predisposition from that of one's companions?

Wagner and Anthony (2002; Martin, 2003) conducted a secondary analysis of the data collected by a national survey, the National Comorbidity Study, to illuminate the role of opportunity in the "escalation" from legal to illegal drugs and from marijuana to cocaine. Among respondents ages 12 to 25, alcohol and tobacco users were more likely than nondrinkers and nonsmokers to have been presented with the opportunity to try marijuana by the age of 18, and, among those who were presented with the opportunity, more likely to have accepted. Roughly three-fourths of respondents who had used alcohol and tobacco said that by their eighteenth birthday, they were offered the opportunity to use marijuana, and more than 85 percent accepted. But this was true of only one-fourth of nonsmokers and nondrinkers; and of those who were offered the opportunity, only a quarter accepted. The same pattern prevailed for the transition from marijuana to cocaine. Of those young people who had never used alcohol, tobacco, or marijuana, only 13 percent had an "exposure opportunity" by age 25. The corresponding figure for those who had used alcohol and tobacco but not marijuana was 26 percent; it was 51 percent for those who had used marijuana but not alcohol or tobacco; and it was 75 percent for the ones who had used marijuana and alcohol or tobacco. The researchers attempted to eliminate respondents who sought out the opportunity to use cocaine by eliminating those who transitioned from marijuana to cocaine in the same year ("rapid transition" youths), and argued that, independent of background and motivation, opportunity *by itself* prompts higher levels of drug escalation (Wagner and Anthony, 2002).

Is opportunity a function of low self-control; that is, do individuals characterized by low self-control find opportunities where they can? Or is opportunity a function of being implicated in a network of like-minded and like-acting peers? Are we seeing predisposition or peer pressure and social influence at work here? Cultural deviance, social interactionists, and learning theorists are likely to interpret these gateway-drug data as supporting their position; Gottfredson and Hirschi are likely to disagree. Either way, although Gottfredson and Hirschi have not fully elucidated the role of opportunity in crime—or drug use—in *A General Theory of Crime*, they do stress its importance. Perhaps future researchers will follow up on their lead and more fully and systematically tease out the influence of opportunity on deviant actions and the degree to which opportunity is intertwined with predispositional and motivational factors. To paraphrase Albert K. Cohen (1965): "Given opportunity, what does a person do about it?" (p. 7).

NOTES

I would like to thank Jo Anne Grunbaum from the Centers for Disease Control and Prevention for assisting me in obtaining the raw data for this study. See Grunbaum et al. (2004).

1. Gottfredson and Hirschi's view on this matter is not shared by criminologists or drug use specialists. In a mail-in survey I conducted of the members of the Drinking and Drugs division of the Society for the Study of Social Problems, three-fourths of the respondents said that the study

of drug use and crime is the most widely investigated topic among sociologists who study drug use—more than was true for any other topic I asked about. The literature on the subject is immense. See, for example, the collection of position papers and their references in *Toward a Drugs and Crime Research Agenda for the 21st Century* (U.S. Department of Justice, September 2003). An online bibliography of nearly 900 "drugs and crime" references, all published before 2000, can be found at http://www.jhu.edu/~anthony/eldic/techrep.0801. See also Anthony and Forman (2003).

IV CONCLUDING THOUGHTS

14 | SELF-CONTROL:
A HYPERCRITICAL ASSESSMENT

Gilbert Geis

It seems essential to me that I begin with a mea culpa, an admission that I am aware of and uncomfortable with the fact that my criticisms of self-control theory and the tone of the present chapter may strike some readers as unacceptably harsh and ill-tempered. I have sought with some diligence through various drafts of this chapter to de-escalate my rhetoric, to eliminate the sarcasm, and to locate elements in the monograph on self-control theory about which I can say kind things. I fear that readers may conclude that flaws in my personality, professional jealousy, or perhaps an attempt to show off have driven me to attack a landmark contribution to the study of crime. Any or all of those explanations may contain some truth, but I would like to believe, such considerations aside, that what I say is accurate or, at least, challenging and that those put off by any infelicity of the style will indulgently shrug that off and concentrate on the substance of the critique.

I have read Gottfredson and Hirschi's *A General Theory of Crime* (1990) cover to cover at least half a dozen times and must say that I often was bothered by the manner in which the book sets forth its thesis, which, I hasten to add, bears not at all on the integrity of the theory itself. I found *A General Theory of Crime* often dogmatic and categorically dismissive of matters that deserved much more nuanced treatment. Take the core concept of self-control. Surely, the idea of a population indoctrinated by child rearers with great chunks of self-control—even presuming such an achievement is possible and could significantly reduce crime—would also have other consequences that deserve serious consideration before a public policy based on such a formula is advanced.

Truth be told, as an old-fashioned out-of-style liberal I also found irritating Gottfredson and Hirschi's dismissal of social injustice as a concomitant of crime, which, again, does not mean that they are not correct. And I began and ended the present analysis of *A General Theory of Crime* with the conviction, shared by numerous scholars who are wiser than I am, that the search for a single cause of all crime is a feckless enterprise.

I should also add that for a long time I was immersed in research about witchcraft in seventeenth-century England (Geis and Bunn, 1997). In those days tough invective was a common ingredient of debate. Thus a commentator on a work by the then renowned dissenting minister, Richard Baxter, noted crudely that Baxter had the ability to "distinguish himself into a fart" (Browne, 1681, 16), and the prebendary of Exeter thought that one of Baxter's treatises was marked by "putrid, pestilent stinks and corruptions and so unlike the breathing of a mortified Christian, that the like never proceeded from any dying man, except such a one as hath been dying twenty years altogether" (Long, 1697, 132). Perhaps some of that style has become too ingrained in my psyche. If so, I offer a sincere apology for not having exercised sufficient self-control to keep it under wraps, despite efforts to do so. This, after all, is not seventeenth-century England.

Theorists, like theologians and parents, notoriously develop a vested interest in their doctrine and offspring. The dogmas and the kin come to be viewed as surrogates; critiques are seen as personal attacks. Such a protective stance has been characteristic of debates between Gottfredson and Hirschi and those who take exception to elements of self-control theory. The roots of this condition can best be understood by juxtaposing the positions taken by Nobel Prize–winning physicist Richard Feynman and by Charles Darwin to the position enunciated by Hirschi. Feynman insists that full disclosure is a prerequisite for the responsible promotion of a theory: "Details that could throw doubt upon your interpretation must be given, if you know them," he writes. "You must do the best you can—if you know anything at all wrong, or possibly wrong" to explain it. "If you make a theory . . . then you must put down all the facts that disagree with it" (Feynman, 1985, 341).

Charles Darwin said that he discovered that he quickly forgot any fact that appeared to contradict his theories. He therefore made it a rule to write down such information so that he would not later overlook it (Darwin (1958 [1869], 123). Of Robert Dicke, an esteemed physicist, it was said: "That's why he was such a hero. When the data said the theory was wrong, then for him his theory was wrong. It was as simple as that" (Bartusiak, 2000, 66).

Compare these positions with what Hirschi declared in regard to his social control theory:

> A major mistake in my original oppositional comparison of social control and social learning theory was to grant a gap in control theory that might possibly be filled by social learning theory. Almost immediately, hordes of interactionist and social learning theorists began to pour through the holes I had pointed out to them, and control theory was to that extent subsequently ignored. It was here that I learned the lesson. . . . The first purpose of oppositional theory construction is to make the world safe for a theory contrary to currently accepted views. Unless this task is accomplished, there will be little hope for the survival of the theory and less hope for its development. Therefore, oppositional theories should not make life easy for those interested in preserving the status quo. *They should at all times remain blind to the weaknesses of their own position and stubborn in its defense.* (Hirschi, 1989, 45; emphasis added)

Hirschi's strategy detours attempts at an honest give-and-take discussion. One can expect Gottfredson and Hirschi to start with a conclusion "that what they have said is the gospel truth" and then to seek whatever evidence they can marshal to shore up that position. This tactic may make for energetic forensic duels, but it would be more helpful to acknowledge gaps and imperfections in one's formulation and, if possible, try to shore them up.

Old-timers in criminology probably recall that this same defensive tactic was used with considerable but not enduring success by Donald Cressey when he inherited stewardship of the differential association theory promulgated by his mentor, Edwin H. Sutherland. Sutherland was famously aware of the deficiencies of his theory and enunciated them in an unpublished paper satirically subtitled "The Swan Song of Differential Association" (Sutherland, 1956). Nonetheless, it was at the risk of a scolding letter from Cressey, who had an especially keen mind to go with a sharp tongue, that one dared to suggest that differential association was a feeble excuse for a theory seeking to explain all criminal behavior.

It is doubtful that the hordes that Hirschi envisioned assaulting his unprotected theoretical flank were quite as numerous as he indicates. Nor for that matter did the social control theory flounder: It may well enjoy more unqualified acceptance today than self-control theory, which, oddly, never attempts to reconcile or integrate the postulates of this earlier effort to interpret criminal behavior. Hirschi (1969) ends his lesson for promulgators of new (i.e., "oppositional") theories with the observation that those who seek to establish such viewpoints "should never smile" (p. 45). Perhaps he was aware of André Maurois's observation: "Dumas was a charming fellow," it was the general view, "but he is not serious minded." Maurois adds: "In France, if a man does not carry his head like the Blessed Sacrament, he may be regarded as an amusing character, but he is not respected. Bores enjoy priority" (Maurois, 1957, 160). For Feynman an injunction against a theorist smiling would have seemed ludicrous. Among other things he often repaired to a topless bar in Pasadena, declaring it to possess an ambience that best allowed him to think creatively (Feynman, 1985; Gleick, 1993).

The strikingly different positions of Darwin and the two physicists and the position of Hirschi represent two different kinds of strategies with regard to the promulgation and promotion of theories. But perhaps there is something in Hirschi's unwillingness to admit gaps in his theory's reach that is understandable and forgivable. Are theories in the hard sciences, such as physics, ultimately dependent on their empirical strength, whereas those in the human sciences, such as criminology, will go unattended unless launched and protected by a camouflage of invulnerability? Would this situation, if accurate, be traceable to the fact that criminology and its disciplinary cousins will never truly be able to construct an exception-proof formula so long as human beings act, or appear to act, with free will? Natural scientists, dealing with inanimate objects, confront no such obstacle, and therefore their theories can battle for suzerainty in an open marketplace. Put another way, it may be true that the survival and health of social science theories, at least to a point, must rely on legerdemain and lobbying. David Riesman (1957), who held degrees in law and sociology, once remarked that law professors teach law, whereas eminent social scientists train disciples who they hope will foster their mentors' own slant on subject matter and theory. The vulnerability of social science theories may have been captured by Ortega y Gasset when he observed that "to create a concept is to invite reality to leave the room" (Epstein, 1997, C14).

ON SELF-CONTROL THEORY

Gottfredson and Hirschi (1990) observe that they "intend our theory to explain all crime, at all times, and, for that matter, many forms of behavior that are not sanctioned by the state" (p. 117). This is the most vulnerable statement in *A General Theory of Crime*. Only a few pages later we are informed that there are crimes that are "rare" and "complex" and "diffi-cult" and that such crimes offer "an inadequate basis for theory and policy" (p. 119). Nor is it accurate that only rare and complex and difficult crimes fail to come within the embrace of self-control theory. Numerous proscribed acts are not complex or rare or difficult, and yet they have little or no relationship with either the presence or the absence of self-control, such as the failure to realize that passengers in the backseat of your car have not fastened their seat belts. Other such glaring exceptions will be noted as this chapter proceeds.

Although they almost totally rely on Anglo-American sources, Gottfredson and Hirschi claim that what they advance is accurate for all places at all times. A pair of scholars focus-ing on crime in Nigeria have challenged this position, noting that self-control theory does not travel well because it contains "unacknowledged value assumptions" that "undermine its claim to universality" (Marenin and Reisig, 1995, 501).

On the domestic scene Gottfredson and Hirschi see cigarette smoking as a consequence of a lack of self-control, not a decision to do what you please so long as you do not in-fringe on others' rights to the same prerogative. Unmarried sex signifies a similar character deficiency.

Gottfredson and Hirschi (1990) also observe that "if a society defines an act as criminal, our definition should be able to comprehend the basis for that society's definition" (p. 175). Surely, the ebb and flow of denominated outlawed behavior would challenge such an idea. How, for example, does self-control theory advance our understanding of legislative en-actments that penalize some drug usages and ignore others? Does the answer lie in the Gottfredson-Hirschi formulation, or would it be better understood by a focus on power relationships?

Gottfredson and Hirschi (1990) maintain that criminal behaviors provide "immediate, easy, and certain short-term pleasure" (p. 41). "We are careful," they note, "to avoid an image of crime as a long-term, difficult, or drawn-out endeavor" (p. 115). There is a dif-ference between being careful and being accurate. There obviously are numerous criminal activities, such as antitrust conspiracies, that are long term and quite complex. Enron's lawbreaking was not an impulsive, spur-of-the moment enterprise (Fox, 2003; Schwartz and Watkins, 2003). The "certain" label that is attached to the portrait of this short-term lawbreaking also is puzzling. Few of us know with assurance the outcomes of our endeav-ors, short or long term. Is an act to be excluded from the theory's ken if the pleasure it promises is not certain? We are additionally told that "*in all cases* the behavior [crime and cognate acts] *tends* to entail long-term costs" (Gottfredson and Hirschi, 1990, 8; emphasis added). It is difficult, as least for me, to understand how the categoric "in all cases" can be joined with the imprecise "tends." And how does one determine such a tendency absent its appearance?

Criminal acts are said to "often" produce "pain or discomfort for the victim" and that such consequences are of indifference to those with low self-control because they "tend" to be self-centered and insensitive to the needs of others (Gottfredson and Hirschi, 1990, 89). But there are legions of noncriminal acts, beyond those inventoried by Gottfredson and Hirschi, in which harm-inflicting indifference prevails. In their overview of the pan-orama of criminological theory, Vold et al. (1998) take exception to what Gottfredson and

Hirschi have decided are the core characteristics of all crimes and analogous behavior. Vold and colleagues point out that at least some crimes are "complex and involve delayed gratification of desires and few short-term benefits, are dull and safe while requiring considerable skill and planning, and generally produce large benefits for the offender while causing little pain and suffering for the victim." (p. 333). To cheat on an income tax return, a not uncommon practice, is unlikely to have long-run harmful consequences. Crimes of omission, such as not registering for selective service during the Vietnam War or failing to install safety equipment in a workplace as well as strict liability offenses also represent matters beyond the boundaries of Gottfredson and Hirschi's theoretical embrace. Other serious criminal acts unlikely to be tied tightly to self-control theory are terrorism, campaign finance finagling, and call-girl prostitution. Note, for instance, Hoffman's (1998) summary of the roots of terrorism with regard to self-control: "The wrath of the terrorists is rarely uncontrolled. Contrary to popular belief and media depiction, most terrorism is neither crazed nor capricious. Rather, terrorist attacks are generally both premeditated and carefully planned" (p. 157).

In a later contribution Gottfredson and Hirschi sought to deal with this problem by noting that terrorist acts were to be excluded from self-control theory because terrorists were operating not out of self-interest but to advance a political and organizational agenda. It could be argued, on the contrary, that it is their consuming self-interest in promoting that agenda that sends terrorists into action. Nor does the Gottfredson-Hirschi argument that terrorists are dedicated to long-term concerns provide persuasive grounds to have them excluded from self-control theory (Hirschi and Gottfredson, 2001, 94). What this argument conveys is that a crime that does not meet their definition of a crime is to be consigned to limbo. The theory thereby can be said to explain only what it can explain, not all that it claims to explain.

A recent episode connected with terrorism suggests the limits to the reach of self-control theory. Thirteen American CIA agents operating in Milan, Italy, seized an Arab religious leader who apparently had been engaged in terrorist activities. They sprayed something in his face, pushed him into a van, and in short order had him flown to Egypt, where he was tortured by the police to obtain information about his activities. The Americans were charged by an Italian judge with kidnapping (Grey and Van Natta, 2005; DiMento and Geis, 2006). Could what the CIA agents did in any way be tied to their level of self-control or, for that matter, opportunity, or were they merely hirelings who had been told to carry out a criminal act and did so?

Essentially, what Gottfredson and Hirschi enumerate as the elements of criminal activity as well as the elements of self-control often are the same thing. In this sense the theory may be regarded as tautological: The answer is the same as the question. Question: What causes acts that are marked by an absence of self-control? Answer: A lack of self-control. Gottfredson and Hirschi have sought to refute the allegation of tautological thinking: "In our view," they write, "the charge of tautology is in fact a compliment; an assertion that we followed the path of logic in producing an internally consistent result" (Hirschi and Gottfredson, 1993, 52, 54). The aim is not to produce an internally consistent result but a theoretical product that contains ingredients that mesh with external reality.

BASHING OTHER CRIMINOLOGICAL THEORIES

Much of Gottfredson and Hirschi's treatise effectively critiques other criminological theories. Doing so has become an indoor sport that was first brought to near perfection by Taylor et al. (1973). Since then, as each new theoretical entry is paraded, its designer traditionally highlights, besides its striking virtues, the obvious deficiencies of its rivals.

Charles Tittle's advocacy of what he labels control-balance theory offers a recent example. Tittle describes earlier theories, including that of Gottfredson and Hirschi, as "simple" (his is inordinately complex) when he seeks to push them into the wings and place his own ideas center stage. He tries to soften his stinging critiques with praise. Hirschi, for instance, is identified as a "genius" (Tittle, 1995, 55). Notwithstanding his genius, Hirschi's (and Gottfredson's) self-control theory is faulted because it is "too simplistic" and "too shallow" and lacks "precision" and "depth." If that is not enough, self-control theory, it is declared, "flies in the face of logic, evidence, and experience," is "unrealistic," and "incomplete and perhaps misleading" and has been put together "at the expense of credibility" (pp. 57–60). Tittle concludes that self-control theory is "inherently limited and incomplete, often rigid and stultified" (p. 71). This jousting among leading theorists can, as one prefers, be regarded as a sign of vigor and health in the field or as an indication of the considerable vulnerability of the current theories.

ACTS ANALOGOUS TO CRIMES

Gottfredson and Hirschi (1990) maintain that their theory can embrace matters such as "accidents, victimizations, truancies from home, school, and work, substance abuse, family problems, and disease" (p. ix) along with a tendency "to smoke, use drugs, have children out of wedlock, and engage in illicit sex" (p. 90). Disease? Tell that to cancer victims with no history of smoking or other apparent etiological precursors that reasonably could be tied to self-control. One study suggests that lack of self-control may be statistically related to gambling and drinking, but it failed to locate a difference in self-control between smokers and nonsmokers. The researchers suggest that "the theory may not be as general as [its] authors would like" (Arneklev et al., 1993, 241).

The absence of self-control is said to explain so wide a range of what its promulgators obviously regard as unwholesome actions that presumably all "decent" human behavior can be interpreted by the presence of self-control. Gottfredson and Hirschi imply as much. Crime, they say, is causally indistinguishable from all other behavior except that they do not carry the "notion of political sanctions; pleasures and pains manipulated by the state" (Gottfredson and Hirschi, 1990, 10). If infants and young children were only trained effectively into exercise of self-control, presumably we would discover the formula for satisfactory human existence.

The Gottfredson and Hirschi formulation ignores what for a large number of Americans represents the quintessential absence of self-control: overeating. It may be unfair to fault the theorists for failure to address gluttony: They cannot be expected to provide a roster of every imprudent act. But overeating is such a commonplace demonstration of low self-control that it would appear to merit consideration. But there could be difficulty in seeing food addicts as the same individuals who engage in burglary, reckless driving, and white-collar crime. Nor can overeaters handily be grouped with the unwed who do not have their sexual urges suitably tamed or those who show the absence of self-control by "quitting a job" (Gottfredson and Hirschi, 1990, 179).

Gottfredson and Hirschi's roster of noncriminal behaviors seems an odd lot that includes matters often having implications beyond the range of self-control theory. Take gambling, for instance. Clyde Brion Davis (1956) noted that gambling is an omnipresent condition of human existence. "You might say," Davis observed, "that life itself is a one-armed bandit slot machine, which in the end, takes all your nickels" (p. 12). Illustratively, he points out that insurance companies "bet you at what might be called pari-mutuel odds that your house will not burn down within the next three years." Perhaps this is off target. What Gottfredson and Hirschi primarily may be referring to is gambling for stakes, although it is not certain whether they would include stock market wagers in the category. For the lottery winner the denominated absence of self-control can turn into an enormous beneficence. And how can the theory incorporate the criminal abortions undergone by women before the procedure was legalized (Howell, 1969; Polgar and Fried, 1976)? Surely, it would be stretching matters to maintain that women who opted for illegal abortions did so because of an absence of self-control. Yet a theory that declares that it can explain all crime cannot ignore what likely amounted to about 1 million criminal acts each year in the United States.

It is possible that Hirschi was traduced with regard to his formulation of self-control theory by his earlier observations regarding the power of the idea of gravity to provide a sound scientific understanding of a great number of scattered facts. A quarter of a century earlier, Hirschi (1973, 165) had pointed out that the theory of gravity explains the movement of tides, the erect posture of trees, and the difficulty of writing on a ceiling with a ballpoint pen. A primitive person or a child might say that a stone dropped because it wanted to. A profound thinker in Aristotle's time probably would have said that the stone fell because it possessed the property of gravity. But after Newton we could declare that the stone dropped because it existed in a field of forces of which the most relevant were the mass of the stone, the earth's gravitational pull, and the relative insubstantiality of the intervening variable, in this case, air (Nisbett and Ross, 1980, 205). The theory of gravity allows understanding of the extraordinary demands on the erect human body for blood circulation and explains why some quadrupeds not adapted to the upright position may be killed by suspending them vertically (Engel, 1962, 28). But self-control and gravity are not equivalent things: One admits of no exceptions to the theory; the other can be said to involve an array of exceptions. Gravity does not change direction on a whim; people do.

ON EXCEPTIONS

Unlike Newton, Gottfredson and Hirschi tend to have a strong tendency to use the word *tend*. Thus among innumerable other examples: "Offenders . . . tend to be involved in accidents, illness, and death at higher rates than the general population; they tend to have difficulty persisting in a job regardless of the particular characteristics of the job" (Gottfredson and Hirschi, 1990, 94). One has to be reminded of Robert Merton's (1949) observation that "sociologists (including the writer) may discuss the logical criteria of sociological law without citing a single instance which fully satisfies these criteria" (p. 92).

The difficulty with such equivocations lies in assessing how much tolerance ought to be permitted a theory that proclaims that it is general, a term used (Gottfredson and Hirschi, 1990, 117) to indicate that there are no exceptions. How much variance from categoric pronouncements is to be permitted before the theory can be said to have been falsified? Certainly, if a theory is to be used to support public policy, it has to contain an acceptable level of accuracy before remedial measures are inaugurated.

The Gottfredson-Hirschi concern with seeking to explain all crime needs to be contrasted with the observation of the President's Commission on Law Enforcement and Administration of Justice (1967): "Each crime is a response to a specific situation by a party with an infinitely complicated psychological and emotional makeup who is subject to infinitely complicated external pressures" (p. 1). Such a pronouncement implies, misleadingly, that there is no possibility of generalizing about criminal behavior, at least about homogeneous categories of crime. In this regard note the observation of James Q. Wilson and Richard Herrnstein: The word *crime* can be applied to such varied behavior that it is not clear that it is a meaningful category of analysis. Stealing a comic book, cheating on a tax return, murdering a wife, punching a friend, robbing a bank, bribing a politician, hijacking an airplane: "These and countless other acts are all crimes. Crime is as broad a category as disease, and perhaps as useless" (J. Q. Wilson and Herrnstein, 1985, 21).

Unfazed by such warning signs, Gottfredson and Hirschi let us know that disease is not so difficult a condition to explain. It is the consequence of the lack of adequate of self-control. Elsewhere, James Q. Wilson (1997) observes: "People are complex, changeable creatures often better described by good poetry than good science" (p. 14). I would interpret this observation as a warning against hubris, not as a stricture against efforts at limited generalizations.

"In our view," Gottfredson and Hirschi (1990) observe, "lack of self-control does not require crime and can be counteracted by situational characteristics or other properties of the individual" (p. 89). This is saying, in essence, that absence of self-control causes all crimes except those that it does not cause. And the exceptions (what happened to that *all crime* phrase?) can be regarded as lying in an amorphous range of possibilities either within the social setting or within the person.

The same point is made in a different manner later in the monograph: "Specific crimes have causes distinct from properties of offenders; they require victims, opportunity, substances, and the like. These crime properties *may obviously* account for variation in specific offenses from time to time and place to place" (Gottfredson and Hirschi, 1990, 127; my emphasis). Ambiguity abounds here: If particular crimes have causes distinct from offenders' lack of self-control, may not these causes be manipulated to produce an alteration in the crime rate without attending to issues of self-control? Similarly, how can there be a general theory of crime that says that "self-control is only one element in the causal configuration of a criminal act, and criminal acts are, at best, imperfect measures of self-control" (p. 137)?

ARE CRIMINALS POLYMORPHOUS PERVERSE?

Gottfredson and Hirschi (1990) maintain that "specialization in particular criminal acts" is "contrary to fact" (pp. 77, 226). Criminals are said to perform any of a variety of lawbreaking behaviors. But this is far from absolutely true. Research clearly indicates that a great many criminal offenders are not polymorphous perverse and that the nature of their lawbreaking does not represent a response only to what is available when the self-control they failed to acquire before the age of 6 or 8 (p. 272) prompts them into an illegal action.

How much specialization is necessary to render self-control theory's position unacceptable? "Our portrait of the burglar applies equally well to the white-collar offender, the organized-crime offender, and the assaulter: they are, after all, the same people," Gottfredson and Hirschi (1990, 7) insist. "They seem to do just about everything they can do: they do not specialize" (p. 190). Ken Lay a murderer? Shoplifters exhibitionists? Richard Wright et al. (1995) found that burglars often specialize in that offense because they acquire a certain expertise. Interviews with forty-seven active residential burglars showed "strong evidence of technical and interpersonal skill and knowledge relevant to specific crime opportunities" (p. 40). Murder was not one of those preferred performances; neither was insider trading.

Gottfredson and Hirschi (1990) scoff at the idea that "maturational reform" lies at the heart of desistance from criminal activity, saying that it and other such concepts leave the data "an unexplained process" (p. 131). They maintain that writers confuse change in crime with change in the tendency to commit crime, which may not change at all (pp. 137, 144). This is the kind of errant reasoning that underlay Freud's idea of latent homosexuality and Marx's false consciousness. The tendency is invisible, lying dormant, but well known to the theorists by some sensory process that allows them to keep upright a theory that might otherwise tumble.

RESEARCH ON SELF-CONTROL THEORY

There has emerged, as this volume documents, a flourishing cottage industry of researchers who have seized on self-control theory as a topic. This deluge of published empirical material has been in part a consequence of an accurate reading of the requirements for academic advancement rather than a necessary appraisal of the integrity of the theory. One can define self-control, find this or that sample (generally juveniles or students), administer self-report queries about behavior, and then determine by the use of elegant statistical tests the relationship between self-control and criminal activity and/or some of the cognate behaviors specified in the theory. The results have never fully supported self-control theory. Harold Grasmick and his colleagues, to take but one example, found "inconsistencies" and noted that "the theory is in need of modification and expansion" (Grasmick et al., 1993, 22). The body of research on self-control theory engages in lusty debates regarding the adequacy of measures of self-control and almost inevitably includes strikingly similar disclaimers. The investigators apologize for the shortcomings of their measurement (e.g., my research "should in no way be regarded as a complete and definitive test" [Brownfield and Sorenson,

1993, 259]). They also emphasize that, just because they found the theory wanting, the reader should not conclude that it truly lacks scientific merit.

Gottfredson and Hirschi (1990) offer a hypothesis that might be tested: "Holding propensity constant," they write, "communities in which schools enforce attendance rules would be expected to have lower crime rates than communities in which such rules were ignored" (p. 252). This seems to conflict with a later observation by the theorists that "we do not recognize propensity to commit crimes" (Hirschi and Gottfredson, 1993, 53). Nor is it clear how one goes about "holding propensity constant." Many alternative hypotheses might explain why one school and not another enforces truancy regulations, but no one apparently has seized on this research suggestion. Indeed, if this volume nudges the progenitors of self-control to launch or supervise the kind of research they believe is core to their concept, it will have advanced matters considerably.

CHILD REARING AND SELF-CONTROL

For Gottfredson and Hirschi (1990) "the major cause of low self-control . . . appears to be ineffective child-rearing" (p. 97), although an escape hatch is appended thereafter: "Family child rearing practices are not the only causes of crimes" (p. 101). Whether these other causes represent only different ways in which a person is not satisfactorily indoctrinated into the realm of self-control or other etiological items is not clear.

The cure for crime involves training adults, but "not . . . in one or another of the various academic disciplines" (an odd pejorative). Adults "need only learn the requirements of early childhood socialization, namely to watch for and recognize signs of low self-control and to punish them" (Gottfredson and Hirschi, 1990, 269). If they fail to inculcate self-control, the "enduring consequences" must fall upon "parents and adults with responsibilities for child-rearing" (p. 269).

IDEOLOGICAL ISSUES

Some aspects of the Gottfredson-Hirschi theory seem to sacrifice firm logic at the altar of ideology. All theories, of course, carry with them implicit or explicit ideological offspring, but it is essential that the ideological and policy recommendations be tied in a reasonable fashion to the theory. So unanchored at times is the ideological element in the exposition of self-control theory that adherents to its full sweep might well be positioned in that cadre demarcated by Supreme Court justice Oliver Wendell Holmes: "Proper geese following their propaganda" (Howe, 1957, 25).

It is not poverty, not discrimination, not absence of equal opportunity to live a decent life, but poor parenting that must assume the blame for criminal behavior by different segments of the population. Efforts need to be made to suppress behaviors such as "whining, pushing, and shoving (as a child)" (Gottfredson and Hirschi, 1990, 71) in order to develop a self-controlled person. If this is not accomplished early enough, "there are about eight relevant years from birth," then the game is lost. Other explanatory paths are said to be fruitless.

Hirschi (1969) previewed parts of his ideological leanings in his social bonding theory when he indicated his belief that "positive feelings toward controlling institutions and persons in authority are the first line of social control" (p. 83). This may be true, but social control for what? If the authorities are not admirable, is there not something to be said for defiance? An element of judgment would seem necessary to be inserted into the formula. Self-control and attachment to authority during the Nazi regime is not the kind of behavior most of us would advocate being inculcated into infants and youths to keep them from smoking and having nonmarital sex. Simon Wiesenthal illustrates this theme in his portrait of Adolph Eichmann: "I had been wrong to look for a motive in his earlier life," Wiesenthal observes. "He was simply the perfect product of the system. . . . He would have done the same job if he had been ordered to kill all men whose name began with P or B, or who had red hair" (Askenasy, 1984, 287). These observations do not in any way undercut the possible accuracy of self-control theory or, for that matter, the ideological predilections of its formulators. What they do maintain is that it would be nice to have a fuller and more humane and philosophical exposition of the full implications of adopting the theory as a public policy.

Ideology rather than science intrudes into the self-control monograph's argument that, because inculcation of self-control is the path to reduction of crime, gun control policies are beside the point. It is maintained that guns inevitably will be available to those who want to use them for lawbreaking. Such guns, they say, typically are acquired by real or likely criminals from individuals who possess them legally. But if guns were not readily obtainable by those who legally have them, it would follow that criminals would have a more difficult time acquiring them. But what is most puzzling about this argument is why it is made. Gun control, at best, is peripheral to the core of the self-control thesis, and that thesis is hardly likely to contribute in any important way to the debate about weapons. It is difficult to avoid the conclusion that Gottfredson and Hirschi stray afield to try to score an ideological point.

Equally ideological is the following statement: "We see little hope for reduction in crime through modification of the criminal justice system. We see considerable hope in policies that would reduce the role of the state and return responsibility for crime control to ordinary citizens" (Gottfredson and Hirschi, 1990, xvi). Decreases in reported crime showing up in recent statistical reports, although they may not altogether represent the efforts of the criminal justice system, are even less likely to be the product of escalating self-control in American society. If anything, the reverse would appear to be true regarding the level of self-control manifest in the country today.

The "ordinary citizens" term is an ideological buzzword, and precisely how such citizens would exercise their control of crime would seem to call for at least some qualifications and restraints before our neighbors might undertake this task. Equally ideological is the insistence that "policies that seek to reduce crime by the satisfaction of theoretically derived wants (e.g., equality, adequate housing, good jobs, self-esteem) are likely to be unsuccessful" (Gottfredson and Hirschi, 1990, 256). Surely, even if it is as important as Gottfredson and Hirschi proclaim, the exercise of self-control would appear to bear some relationship to cultural conditions and cultural values. It likely is a great deal easier to be self-controlled if you have what you desire.

PUBLIC POLICY

Gottfredson and Hirschi (1990) devote twenty pages to "Implications for Public Policy" (pp. 255–274). All but a few of them are taken up with critiques of views other than their own, most notably selective incapacitation, the focus on career criminals, and rehabilitative emphases. They also argue that attention to policing will largely prove unproductive, because the presence of the police does not inhibit lawbreaking (although watching speeding cars slow down on freeways when a patrol car comes into sight might call that position into question).

According to Gottfredson and Hirschi (1990), the "motive to crime is inherent or limited to immediate gains provided by the act itself" and "there is no larger purpose behind rape, or robbery, or murder, or theft, or embezzlement, or insider trading" (p. 256). Policies that promote equality, adequate housing, good jobs, and self-esteem "are likely to be unsuccessful" in affecting crime rates. But people who have good jobs assuredly are less likely to break the law than those who are living hand to mouth. The risk of the loss of what a person has would seem to be a pivotal element in crime control.

The authors of *A General Theory of Crime* maintain that short periods of incarceration as well as employment "are incapable of producing any meaningful change in criminality. . . . Theories based on contrary assumptions are wrong" (Gottfredson and Hirschi, 1990, 232). The term *meaningful* offers problems: How meaningful does something have to be to prove meaningful? A sizable literature suggests that some crime offenders will desist from their lawbreaking after a short term of incarceration (Cullen and Gilbert, 1982), and the idea that legitimate employment in a decent job would inhibit crime to some degree (albeit perhaps not a meaningful degree) would seem to be beyond question. It is difficult to believe that the game is lost if adequate amounts of self-control are not instilled in human beings before they reach the age of 8.

The policy implications of self-control theory are rather easy to discern: They are preventive measures rather than treatment regimens, albeit they are unlikely to be implemented on any significant scale. For one thing in the United States there is a commendable reluctance to interfere in domestic family doings. The Gottfredson-Hirschi doctrine would advocate programs that instructed child rearers in methods to recognize signs of nascent low self-control and to reverse them. They summarize their proposed program in a short paragraph: "The intervention we have in mind . . . assume[s] that trouble is likely unless something is done to train the child to forego immediate benefits gratification in the interest of long-term benefits. . . . [Adults] need only learn the requirements of early childhood socialization, namely, to watch for and recognize early signs of low self-control and punish them. . . . Such intervention does not suffer from coming too soon or too late in relation to when crime is committed; it does not suffer from potential illegality; and few serious objections can be raised to it on justice grounds" (Gottfredson and Hirschi, 1990, 269).

The unidentified nature of the "few serious objections" is a bit unnerving. *Any* serious objection would, I presume, be a death blow. If such programs were launched, I would predict that the most common occurrence would be an increase in severe physical punishments by frustrated child rearers seeing innumerable accurate or misleading signs of potential low self-control in their charges. Nonetheless, it needs noting that Gottfredson and Hirschi are acutely sensitive to the ethical issues involved in involuntary interventions and the problem of the high level of false-positives that invariably characterize the operation of programs based on predictive premises.

All told, the prospect for self-control theory to enter and influence mainstream parental behavior does not look promising. But the impact that the theory has had on the minds of individuals dealing with crime and deviance suggests that it could be worthwhile, if human subjects committees could agree on details, to launch experiments to see what long-term consequences might result from indoctrination into practices to counteract early evidence of low self-control. Perhaps premarital instruction of random couples could offer a suitable study sample.

CONCLUSION

It was said by the eminent biologist Thomas Huxley that nothing is more tragic than the murder of a grand theory by a little fact. But Huxley hastened to add that nothing is more surprising than the way in which a theory will continue to survive long after its brains have been knocked out (H. S. Thomas, 1960). Part of the problem lies in the fact that the grander a theory of human behavior becomes, the less likely it is able to account for more than the obvious. I would endorse Jack Gibbs's observation regarding the cause of criminal acts that "each theory should be limited to one type of crime if only because it is unlikely that any etiological or reactive variable will prove relevant for all crime" (Gibbs, 1987, 830). Gibbons (1994) echoes Gibbs: "If we take seriously the claim that criminology deals with lawbreaking in all of its forms," Gibbons writes, "we may well discover that the more modest goal of developing a family of theories makes the greatest sense for the criminological enterprise" (pp. 196–197).

"The wish to establish a natural science of society, which would possess the same sort of logical structure as the science of nature probably remains, in the English-speaking world at least, the dominant standpoint today," Giddens (1976, 13) has written. "But those who are waiting for a [social science] Newton are not only waiting for a train that won't arrive; they're in the wrong station altogether." Giddens adds that the lay public frequently responds to social science claims with the remark that they tell us "nothing that we did not already know—or, at worse, dress up in technical language that which is perfectly familiar in everyday terminology." Giddens notes that there is a disinclination among social scientists to take this sort of protest seriously: For his part, he says, "I want to suggest that we have to take the objection very seriously" (Giddens, 1976, 14–15). Put another way, we can quote the response of a chair during a committee meeting: "That was a blinding glimpse of the obvious" (Kluger, 1996, 595).

A Nobel Prize–winning biochemist, Kary Mullis, had something to say about the matter of constructing theories that we should keep in mind when assaying self-control theory postulates: When you get the hang of it, science, like everything else people do for a living, is pretty straightforward. You are in the business of solving puzzles. The way to approach a puzzle is to think about it for a while, look at all the facts you can find out about it, and then take a guess. Propose a solution. The next step is to try your best to disprove your solution. Show that the pieces don't fit together in the way that you have proposed. If you can do that, then propose another solution. And then do the same thing. Realty is a tricky little puzzle. Sometimes a few pieces will fit together, but they really don't belong together. Some solutions will seem to be right for a time, but then they fail. The one that accounts for all the relevant facts and cannot be disproven, "all the pieces fit together without squeezing them too hard and new pieces fit together on top of them," is probably right. (Mullis, 1998, 50)

I can summarize what I believe is going on today with regard to self-control theory by repeating the title of an article bearing on a different subject: "Ours Is Not to Question Why, Ours Is to Quantify" (Heiman, 1997). And yet, I do not want to finish without recognizing the intellectual ferment, discussion, debate, and theoretical introspection and energy that has emerged from the work of Gottfredson and Hirschi. That is a quite dazzling achievement.

NOTE

This chapter has cut, added to, and considerably reworked material that appeared in my paper "On the Absence of Self-Control as a Basis for a General Theory of Crime" (*Theoretical Criminology* 4: 35–53 [2000]). Hirschi and Gottfredson respond in the same issue: "In Defense of Self-Control" (*Theoretical Criminology* 4: 55–69 [2000]).

15 CRITIQUING THE CRITICS: THE AUTHORS RESPOND

Travis Hirschi and Michael R. Gottfredson

> About thirty years ago there was much talk that geologists ought only to observe
> and not theorize; and I well remember some one saying that at this rate a man
> might as well go into a gravel-pit and count the pebbles and describe the colours.
> How odd it is that anyone should not see that all observation must be for or
> against some view if it is to be of any service.
> *Charles Darwin, 1861*

Theories should be judged by the adequacy of the answers they give to the questions they ask (Hirschi, 2006a). With this principle our theory does just fine (Marcus, 2003, 2004a, 2004b; Schulz, 2006). Without it there is no limit to the number of criticisms a theory may be asked to endure. Without it our theory is particularly vulnerable. It seeks to identify the common element in crimes and the nature of the general tendency to engage in them. Most criminologists ask very different questions and therefore conclude that our "answers" are unsatisfactory. As a result, the theory has sustained considerable attack, much of it found in the chapters in this book and some of it exceedingly harsh. Indeed, critics of the theory have been known to "take on a tone that is rarely heard in scientific discussions" (Marcus, 2004a, 649). As we will show, a substantial portion of these critiques address matters that our theory does not raise and that are, in fact, irrelevant to its scope or adequacy.

The theory deals with the connection between crime and criminality (self-control). The bulk of commentary here and elsewhere focuses on self-control and pays little attention to our concept of crime. As a result, self-control cannot retain its theoretical meaning. Concepts borrow meaning from one another. They are not "things" that exist independent of the context in which they are found. In our theory crime and low self-control are derived from one another. To this extent the relation between them is definitional or tautological. To the extent that crime and criminality are defined independently of one another, their relationship is in no sense tautological. Neither, then, is it theoretical. It is an empirical question whose answer acquires whatever meaning it may have from ad hoc speculation. In practice, the meaning imputed to observed associations between "variables" so defined may be predicted from the observer's favored perspective—and the benefits of more research are hard to see.

It follows that the practice of attaching concepts to theories on the grounds that they are important or of special interest to the critic makes no theoretical sense. This practice confuses the logic of multivariate analysis with the logic of theorizing. Theories simplify. They are weakened by concepts that add complexity without adding explanatory power. They are ruined by the imposition of concepts that embody incompatible or compromising assumptions. For example, our theory submerges motive and opportunity, concepts traditionally central to explanations or discussions of crime. Missing the point, many of the essays in this volume express concern for the whereabouts of such concepts. To the extent that they do so, it would seem incumbent on us to respond, but there is little reason a priori to believe that the theory will benefit from this exercise.

Standard empirical tests of theories multiply this problem. The logic of multivariate analysis requires that researchers throw into the pot as many variables as they can measure. Measures of a theory's concepts are thus typically joined by measures of concepts from competing theories, by sets of established control variables, by variables suggested or required by editors and referees, and, finally, by measures designed to represent the researcher's personal explanatory scheme—for an example in this volume, see Piquero's Chapter 2. As a result, much current theoretically oriented research is, in effect, antitheoretical, sacrificing parsimony, meaning, clarity, and the straightforward results of prior research on the altar of quantitative criminology.

Such demographic correlates of crime—for example, sex, age, race, and social class—raise a different set of issues. Theories are expected to explain these correlations and are faulted for failure to do so. If, the critics say, self-control is a general explanation of crime, then differences in levels of self-control should account for observed differences in rates of crime across categories of age, sex, race, and social class. We began our quest for a general theory of crime by arguing that no theory, including our own, could explain the robust effect of age on crime. We subsequently participated in an attempt to explain sex differences in crime that could *not* be accounted for by sex differences in levels of self-control. All of this led critics to conclude that established demographic effects require that we admit serious limitations of the theory or allow specifications and complications we had previously resisted. We now believe that the critics are wrong and that demographic factors, real and imagined, pose no threat to the theory.

A final source of persistent critical concern is the failure of the theory to recognize traditional categories of crime. Accordingly, this book has essays on white-collar crime, violent crime, property crime, and drug use. Any focus on a single type of crime will inevitably produce results apparently contrary to a theory that has no use for typologies, a theory based on the premise that all crimes tend to be engaged in by the same people and therefore have something in common. Goode (Chapter 13) finesses this problem by accepting an often striking connection between drug use and crime and assessing the theory's ability to account for it. The writers of the remaining crime-type chapters are stuck. They must attempt to demonstrate that their kettle of fish has neither kettle nor fish in common with other kettles of fish.

If acceptance of types of crime does not beg the question (and, in effect, automatically doom the theory), the fact remains that it fosters acceptance of subtypes, which leads to further distinctions, with no natural stopping point. In the end, the theory is too often asked to confront actual crimes with named perpetrators. If these are not enough, hypothetical, even fictional crimes and criminals are brought into play. In our view, it is unbelievable that serious scholars would introduce single or unique events as evidence against an abstract or general theory of crime. No one would use the behavior of a feather in a gust of wind in Nebraska against the theory of gravity. Or would they? Events equally are cited by Greenberg (Chapter 3), Iovanni and Miller (Chapter 9), Felson and Osgood (Chapter 11), and Swatt and Meier (Chapter 12). And Geis (Chapter 14) introduces air as an "intervening variable" in Newton's theory!

THE CRITICS CONCEPTS

Opportunity

Before *A General Theory of Crime* was published, Gottfredson presented an outline of the theory in a public debate. His famous adversary instantly reduced the theory to *motive* and *opportunity*, treated it as old hat, and argued accordingly. The first published test of the theory took the same tack, making opportunity and self-control equal or even competing explanations of crime (Grasmick et al., 1993). We objected (Hirschi and Gottfredson, 1993), but to no avail. A concept we all but ignored had risen to coequal status with a major concept of the theory.

We do not share our critics' enthusiasm for the concept of opportunity. And no wonder. In all cases their concept discredits the theory. In some cases (Simpson and Geis, Chapter 4), the goal is obvious: Opportunity is a transparent Trojan horse, a gift offered with ulterior motives and hopes of disastrous consequences. In other cases (Matsueda, Chapter 8; Friedrichs and Schwartz, Chapter 10; and Geis, Chapter 14), the goal appears worthy, but the effect on our theory is the same: Opportunity becomes a property of individuals, a perception that displaces self-control and overrides objective elements of the situation and the actual consequences of crime. For still others it is a perfectly above-board device for discrediting the theory—indeed, any theory that requires an assumption of individual differences. The last group, not represented in this volume, are champions of situational crime prevention, of rational choice and routine activities theories. They hold that "opportunity makes the thief" (M. Felson and Clarke, 1998). They are therefore not averse to the idea that the search for "criminal man" has failed (M. Felson, 2006, 21–22). They might not say that even to consider "criminality" as a tendency is to "harken back to something akin to instinct theory," but they explicitly disavow interest in the concept.

We have no essential quarrel with advocates of situational crime prevention or the theories that support it. But the ends they seek and the means they would use to attain them are not ours. We grant the value of crime-specific analysis for crime prevention. We specifically agree that potential offenders are often easily dissuaded and that displacement from one crime to another is more often the exception than the rule. But their heuristic assumption that we are all "middling in morality, self-control, in careful effort, [and] in pursuing advantage" (M. Felson and Clarke, 1998, 10) does not gainsay our grounded assumption that we are not. It is true, as they say, that research has failed to identify meaningful or useful categories of offenders, but this is not evidence against the view that some people are more likely than others to commit criminal acts.

For routine activity theorists opportunity is an objective property of the situation: a shrub hiding a window, an unlocked bicycle, a lone woman on an empty street. For our critics in this volume opportunity is said to be matter of perception. The basis of their conclusion is the famous dictum: "If men define situations as real, they are real in their consequences." Its not necessarily logical extension soon follows: "What is important is not the objective situation but rather the perceived definition of the situation" (Matsueda, Chapter 8; Schulz, 2006). Once again, "what is important" is decreed by a disciplinary perspective. And where does this conclusion lead? Tests of self-control theory now routinely include measures of opportunity. Respondents are asked about prior opportunities to commit a specific crime, where an opportunity is *defined* as a *situation* in which commission of the crime would be easy and safe (Grasmick et al., 1993; Longshore, 1998). Such measures leave us where we were. Is opportunity a definition or an objective situation? A second disciplinary decree is that "structure matters," and testers therefore teeter between the two interpretations. The data, it seems to us, favor perception. The correlations between opportunity measures are stronger than the correlations between measures of the crimes in question. More significant, opportunities to commit one type of crime are major predictors of actual commission of other types of crime. It would appear, then, that opportunity as measured resides not in the situation but in the eye of the beholder.

This puts the competition between opportunity and self-control in a new light. When, as is common, measures of opportunity outperform measures of self-control in predicting criminal behavior, this "finding" is said to "weaken considerably the appeal of [self-control] theory as presently formulated" (Grasmick et al., 1993, 24). Per contra, we would say, these findings show that the measure of opportunity is the better measure of self-control. If, within the limits set by objective conditions, there are stable differences between individuals in their tendency to perceive opportunities for crime, this fact would not modify our definition of self-control. It would remain the tendency to consider (see) the long-term consequences of one's acts. The higher the individual's level of self-control, the less likely he or she will see opportunities for crime (Schulz, 2006, 187). If such differences in perception are unstable or vary from one crime to another (as is assumed by the use of crime-specific measures), they would be irrelevant to the theory, which is, after all, an effort to identify the *common* element in criminal and delinquent acts.

Choice of a long-term costly act (a crime) presupposes the existence of means and conditions that allow it. Means and conditions known to affect the likelihood of crime include guns, gangs, cars, drugs, age, sex, strength, intelligence, agility, marriage, occupation, locks and bars, and governmental permission. These contingencies may facilitate crime, or they may make it more difficult or even impossible. They are the stuff of external reality. Individuals may choose to avoid or embrace some of them, but they cannot perceive them away. Our theory recognizes them for what they are: factors affecting choice (causes) that may mask or distort differences in levels of self-control. In this context the idea of opportunity is superfluous or worse.

By the same token our theory denies that crimes are matters of perception or social definition. According to the theory, the connections between such acts and future states of the actor are not governed by the definitions of the actor, by the criminal law, or by the (middle-class) morality of the observer. They are independently verifiable scientific facts. Murder has consequences. So do burglary and smoking. So do embezzlement and income tax evasion. In our theory the defining feature of crimes is their long-term costs, their negative consequences. A man found talking to another man's girlfriend is shot at point-blank range in full view of numerous witnesses. The act is made possible by a gun. Instantly, the shooter's days as a star athlete are over. And that is just the beginning of his troubles. Our theory sees in this event a quick and easy crime, the means necessary for its commission, low self-control, and disastrous consequences for the offender. It does not see or require opportunity in any meaningful sense of the term.

Motivation

"A factor . . . does not become a cause unless and until it becomes a motive" (Glueck and Glueck, 1962, 153). Such conflation of cause and motive is a common feature of what we have called substantive positivism. The positivists replaced choices with causes. Causes produce effects. A scientific explanation of behavior identifies its causes. Motives are causes. A scientific explanation of behavior therefore identifies its motives. Thus did science replace the choosing actor with a driven subject, a conforming individual, a disadvantaged person. Thus did science dictate the content of substantive theory, something it is not authorized to do (Gottfredson and Hirschi, 1990b, 64–84; Hirschi and Gottfredson, 1990; Gottfredson and Hirschi, 1993). Of course we accept the idea of causation. We have already listed a dozen or so established causes of crime (that is to say, factors that reliably affect choice). Our theory accepts commonsense or face-value motives for particular crimes—money, sex, revenge—but does not require them: "The motive to crime is inherent in or limited to immediate gains provided by the act itself" (1990, 256). It opposes explanations of crime built on deep, hidden, or theoretically derived motives. These explanations produce expectations contrary to fact. Offenders are versatile; they do not require crime; they are easily dissuaded from a given act; their choice of targets and victims does not square with their alleged motives; deep and strong motives laboriously constructed inexplicably go away; early lack of motivation for much of anything is a common characteristic.

More important, the theory opposes motive explanations because it cannot coexist with them. They are "the fundamental mistake of modern theory" (Gottfredson and Hirschi, 1990, 24). They beg the question. They assume the theory is false. The theory requires that crime be understood without reference to motives or benefits. This requirement is not understood by our critics or by those who would test the theory. Most of the essays in this volume fault us for failing adequately to deal with these concepts. As shown by Iovanni and Miller (Chapter 9) and Friedrichs and Schwartz (Chapter 10), the writers' level of interest in benefits and motives tends to coincide with their level of rejection of the theory. Researchers often remedy this supposed deficiency by ascribing unusual or strong motives to offenders and erroneously citing the theory as justification for doing so.

Recently, the worldwide criminological community was informed of the discovery in Great Britain that street robbery is not just about money.[1] Instead, we were told, the motives behind street robbery may be money for particular purposes, such as partying, buying and using drugs, or nonessential "status-enhancing" items. Indeed, they may have no connection to money. Robbers may rob for excitement, dominance, fun, fights, anger, and "informal" justice. The significance of these findings, we were further told, is that they challenge rational choice explanations that "focus . . . on the role of cost-reward calculations" and refocus attention on "characteristics of street culture."

Note that the general theory in question is vulnerable because, in the form imputed to it, it is insufficiently general. Desire for money does not subsume "just for kicks" or a desire to hurt someone. Bentham's solution, noted by us, was to raise the level of abstraction: "Crime, like non-crime, satisfies universal human desires" (Gottfredson and Hirschi, 1990, 10). Another solution is to identify a single motive or a universal goal and be done with the whole business. An example of a single motive is that given by Ludwig von Mises (1996, 13): "The incentive that impels a man to act is always some uneasiness." An example of a universal goal is that given by Thomas Jefferson, among others: happiness. None of these solutions may be disputed by alleging differences. Neither of these solutions may be disputed by alleging differences in motives among crimes or between criminal and noncriminal acts.

The theoretically relevant difference between crimes and noncrimes is not in the motives or goals of those committing them but in their consequences. The motives behind force and fraud do not differ from the motives behind persuasion and honesty. The relevant difference between the two classes of acts is that one of them is less likely and the other more likely to have long-term costs. And the same may be said of distinctions between drugs and food and between reckless and careful driving. Motives are irrelevant. Long-term outcome differences are not.

Those who wish to read the minds of offenders or to accept their accounts of their motives as sufficient explanation of their behavior will of course continue to do so. And it will continue to be true that such efforts say nothing about the validity of a general theory of crime.

Criminal Propensity

According to Ronald Akers, a "central proposition" of our general theory of crime is that "low self-control is the cause of criminal propensity." At the same time, he says, we "define low self-control and criminal propensity as essentially the same thing." So, in a nutshell, we argue that "low self-control causes low self-control." Thus the theory is both tautological and untestable (not to mention ludicrous). In the present volume Piquero (Chapter 2) in particular raises this red herring of an objection to the general theory. Akers's position is repeated and expanded in this volume by Piquero (Chapter 2).

As noted, the concepts matched with crime in interpretations of our theory vary from critic to critic and from one researcher to another. Our own second element evolved over time. We began with *criminality*. At one point we tried *propensity*—and still occasionally use it for ease of exposition (Gottfredson, 2006). At one point we dug up and quickly reburied *criminality*. We even briefly considered *conscience* before settling finally on *self-control*. As we came to use the term, self-control is the *choice* version of the *causal* concept of propensity (and/or criminality). It is our new and improved version of a discarded concept. The two may have occupied the same location in the theory at various times but never at the same time. If the theory uses one of them, it cannot use any of its variants. We could therefore never say or imply that self-control causes criminal propensity. Akers's first mentioned and most influential tautology is thus of his own making.

Akers tentatively resolves his tautology by suggesting separate measures of "the two concepts." Interestingly, the two concepts he proposes to measure are self-control and crime. The concept previously added to the theory, criminal propensity, disappears. So, the core concepts of the theory are not the same *and* can be measured separately. The theory would thus appear to be free of the tautology virus. Unfortunately, this is not the end of the matter. Thought requires concepts and definitions, and, sure enough, Akers and Piquero have detected additional tautologies in and around the theory. We will deal with them in our discussion of measurement issues later in this chapter.

DEMOGRAPHIC CORRELATES OF CRIME

Our theory is a choice theory. (We would no longer refer to it as a *rational* choice theory because we see no point in worrying about a perfectly extraneous issue.) Unlike traditional choice theories, it presupposes stable differences (whether innate or acquired) across individuals in their evaluations of the elements of situations in which crime is possible. Some are consistently more likely than others to choose crime (the quick and easy way). Current situational explanations of crime distinguish between "immediate situational variables" and "more remote variables such as family background and upbringing" (Clarke and Cornish, 2001, 33). The model to which we subscribe makes this distinction problematic. It assumes that long-established (i.e., "remote") variables may be in fact immediate situational variables and may be perceived as such by the actor. It thus allows us to understand why some background variables are *not* factors in crime and why others have effects *over and above* those explained by differences in levels of self-control. Put another way, choice theory, properly interpreted, supplements our theory and protects it from needless complication.

Friendly critics have convinced us that our discussion of such robust "correlates" of crime as age, sex, and race in *A General Theory* was too much influenced by our background in quantitative research and too little influenced by the presuppositions of our own theory. The substantive positivist in us tends to focus on statistical relations between variables, explaining the association between cause and effect by locating the intervening variables that account for it. The control theorist in us should have adhered to an image of actors making choices in situations where the factor in question (the presumed cause) plays a role in the decision-making process. The two explanations of the same empirical fact may have little in common.

The causal approach of necessity considers one background factor at a time. The choice approach could in principle examine the effects of the various "demographic categories" as a set: "The body of the actor forms, for him, just as much a part of the situation of action as does the 'external environment.'" Among the conditions to which his action is subject are those dealing with his own body, while among the more important of the means at his disposal are the 'powers' of his own body and, of course, his 'mind'" (Parsons, 1949, 47). Lacking the mental power to do otherwise, we too must consider the important factors one at a time.

Age

Schulz (2006) argues that our "age theory," criticized here by Greenberg (Chapter 3), is a "screen to shield self-control theory from the necessary consideration of the social environment beyond its significance during the ontogenesis of the actor" (pp. 121–122). He is probably correct. We were just smart enough to see that age (and, for that matter, sex and race) were quagmires we really did not wish to enter. We were trained to think in terms of variables and their interrelations. And we could see that age, sex, and race are composites of so many variables that parsimonious multivariate explanation of their effects on crime is a contradiction in terms. We could see, too, that advancing such an explanation was unlikely to advance understanding of the theory. Still, we tried to explain sex and race in these terms, with the expected results. We do not wish to go there again.

Schulz argues that it is unnecessary to do so, that selection principles implicit in the idea of self-control explain the age effect. In his example, put crudely, the situation of a youth at 13 is not the same as the situation of the same youth at 18. He or she may have acquired knowledge that affects the calculation of the costs and benefits of a particular crime and its alternatives. In other words, as people age, their definition of their situation changes. They acquire knowledge and a "moral conscience" and participate in the "social timetable of the life course (e.g., entry into marriage, retirement), which is defined by age criteria in norms and social roles" (Schulz, 2006, 137, quoting Elder, 1975, 165).

Schulz's solution marries our theory to the ever popular life course perspective. We have devoted some effort to resisting this match (Hirschi and Gottfredson, 1986, 1995; Gottfredson and Hirschi, 1990). We are tempted to accede and reap the benefits. But something is amiss. We *believe* that age affects crime and that attempts to assign its effects to its by-products or to some as yet unknown variable are a mistake.

We divided a very large sample ($N = 3,710$) of junior and senior high school students into two categories, those born before and those born after a certain day of the year (April 1). All were asked whether they smoked. The results were clear. Older children in the same grade are more likely to smoke than younger children (30.8 percent versus 22.2 percent). Age had an effect within narrowly defined categories of the "social timetable."

This result, it seems to us, could be predicted from a choice perspective. Age (aging) produces obvious, observable changes in the body of the actor. These changes are *changes in the situation* of the actor. They are most rapid and pronounced in periods of rapid and pronounced change in measures of criminal activity. In contrast, the social variable, grade in school, has no noticeable effect on the body. Grades can be skipped. Students can be held back. They can even drop out. Lacking salience, grade in school has no independent effect on the likelihood of committing criminal acts.

To repeat, in our perspective reality trumps perception. So, to the usual list of external conditions considered by a theory of action (and by the actor) we would add age. The composite it represents influences decision making. The "inexorable aging of the organism," our biological explanation, would now be modified to read: The age effect is due to the inexorable aging of the organism, as such aging is recognized by the actor.

Gender or Sex

Schulz says that our treatment of age is a screen. Iovanni and Miller, the writers of Chapter 9, say essentially the same thing. We do equate age and sex in two respects. First, both are major, persistent causes of crime. Second, as was true with age, "gender differences appear to be invariant over time and space. Men are always and everywhere more likely than women to commit criminal acts" (Gottfredson and Hirschi, 1990, 145).

Contrary to Iovanni and Miller, we believe that the causes of crime are the same for men and women and that this belief is supported by the evidence. We believe that women have higher levels of self-control than men and that this belief too is supported by a wide array of evidence (A. S. Miller and Stark, 2002). We grant that sex differences in crime are more complex than those involving age. In official data the pattern of rise and fall in adolescence and early adulthood holds for at least most crimes. In self-reported data most crimes actually decline during the same age period. In contrast, sex ratios, however measured, tend to be crime specific, ranging in self-report data from 1:1 for drug use to 12:1 for robbery.

Differences in levels of self-control may account for a large or small portion of the overall gender difference, but they alone cannot account for variation in gender differences. The tendency, of course, is to bring in opportunity to fill this explanatory gap. But opportunity, for reasons mentioned, is unsatisfactory. Its "definition of the situation" variant (Zager, 1993) does not square with the utter reliability of crime-to-crime sex differences. Its objective variant (gender is itself an opportunity factor; Zager, 1994) does not satisfy curiosity (Greenberg, Chapter 3). A solution is to "decompose the effects of [gender] on crime into its physiological, psychological, and social components" (Blokland and Nieuwbeerta, 2005, 1233). (Here, we have substituted gender for age.) This solution is more easily proposed than executed. Each offense, it may be assumed, will turn out to have its peculiar set of gender-relevant components. Such detailed "findings" are unlikely to be useful or meaningful, although it could be said in favor of the research producing them that it is likely to be extravagantly expensive.

Better, it seems to us, to accept a choice perspective. From this perspective gender is a situational factor of considerable significance in the actor's decision to commit a criminal act. If we know the crime, it is not difficult to guess (i.e., understand) in an imprecise way its "gender" implications. If it is a crime of force or violence, involves physical risk, or public display, it will tend to be a man's crime. To the extent crimes involve none of these things, gender tends to lose its relevance as a situational factor. If *we* see these connections, individuals in crime-possible situations see them as well or better than we do. After all, their actions produce the crime counts behind our conclusions.

A choice theory puts actors in situations with *observable* elements or features. Self-control theory emphasizes the actor's concern for the implications of the current situation for some future state of affairs, but it does not deny the significance of elements external to the actor. These elements are not seen as exerting a direct causal influence on crime. But they are not "background" factors. On the contrary, they are at the scene, and some of them, notably age and sex, are hard to ignore. The actor consequently takes them into account in deciding whether or not to commit the crime. Put another way, situational factors are causes of crime to the extent that they affect the actor's decision. If the actor cannot see or does not recognize them, their causal effect will be zero. This hypothesis has tautological consequences: *Directly observable features of the actor's situation will tend to account for the effects on crime of indirectly observable factors.* A good example of an indirectly observable cause of crime is tested intelligence, "among the prime discoveries of criminology" (Herrnstein,

1995, 51). A good example of a directly observable feature of the actor's situation is school performance, another prime discovery of criminology. When school performance is controlled, the IQ effect on delinquency disappears (Bellaire and McNulty, 2005, 1154; Hirschi and Hindelang, 1977).

Further examples of risk factors inexplicable without assuming they pass through the actor's awareness are mesomorphy (having a muscular body) and father's "convictions." Obviously, father's convictions cannot pass through the awareness of the adopted child. And of course there is no way to inherit them. If there is a connection between the child's convictions and those of the unknown biological father, the father must have passed on a crime-relevant trait observable to his child. We would expect the list of possible traits to be sufficiently long to satisfy those who wish to emphasize the biological transmission of criminal behavior.

If this scheme explains the effects of salient features of the actor's situation, it also accounts for the lack of effect of truly remote features. We make much of the limited effect of the penalties of the criminal justice system, being as they are far removed from the scene. Equally remote, in the other direction, is social class. As traditionally conceptualized and measured, the actor's place in the stratification system is unlikely to be an important consideration. In consequence, it turns out to be at most a background factor without direct causal significance for crime and delinquency. Of course its visible by-products (e.g., school performance and various aspirations) may affect decision making, but that only serves to reinforce our argument.

Once crime-to-crime gender differences have been accounted for, the question shifts back to the sources and consequences of gender differences in *self*-control. There is nothing we can see in any of this that invalidates self-control theory. The theory does not require that age or sex or, for that matter, any correlate of crime be put behind a screen. It may not advance the theory to deal directly with such factors, but their connection to crime is explicable by resort to the class of theories from which self-control theory derives.

TYPES OF CRIME

White-Collar Crime

None of our critics or explicators has much good to say about our treatment of white-collar crime. Indeed, some of them have mean things to say about it. Schulz (2006), in his exhaustive and otherwise generous analysis of the theory, concludes that it "is of no use in explaining other acts [that] are detrimental to society and therefore have been labelled criminal under the criminal law" (p. 241). The acts in question are, of course, white-collar crimes, and the fault lies with our "material" definition of crime.

The arguments against application of the theory to white-collar crime boil down to three: (1) White-collar offenders do not exhibit low self-control, and the general theory therefore cannot account for their behavior; (2) the theory focuses on relatively trivial acts compared to those it ignores; and (3) white-collar crimes are not crimes within the definition of the theory. The most persuasive argument potentially available to those professing interest in white-collar crime is missing from the essays in this volume. Try as we might, we have been unable to find a counterexplanation of white-collar crime. In their zeal to take down our theory, white-collar "theorists" advance antitheories that undermine their own work as well. Antitheories epitomize the pessimistic view of the possibility of scientific advancement. They apparently cluster around constructionist approaches. As Erich Goode notes in his preface to this volume, it makes no sense to attempt to try to find the causes of behavior not in accord with the whims of legislators or regulatory bodies. Attempts to find such causes are therefore easily ridiculed, giving the antitheory a place of respect in reasoned discourse it does not deserve.

Critics justify the argument that self-control is irrelevant to the actions of white-collar offenders by making self-control an all-or-nothing affair. White-collar workers have high self-control. Offenders have low self-control. Therefore the offenses of white-collar workers cannot result from low self-control. In our view this begs the question. Such a fallacious chain of reasoning has proved useful to antitheorists on many occasions for a good long time. Mention of an individual difference often triggers thoughts of "kinds of people," even visions of Lombroso's atavistic man. What could be plainer than this: "Selection processes inherent in the high end of the occupational structure tend to recruit people with *relatively low propensity to crime*. Our theory therefore predicts *a relatively low rate of offending* among white-collar workers" (Gottfredson and Hirschi, 1990, 191).

These selection processes result in *reduced variation in levels of self-control among white-collar workers* but do not eliminate it. As a result, differences among white-collar workers are sufficient to test the claims of the theory. In this case these claims are that the correlates of white-collar crimes (such as age, sex, and race) should be the same as the correlates of common crimes; that white-collar *offenders* will tend to have committed other crimes and will be relatively likely to continue offending. As we read currently available evidence, these predictions are consistent with research results for embezzlement, tax evasion, fraud in general, insurance fraud, accounting fraud, sex crimes, theft, and insider trading.

At this point, of course, objection 2 comes into play: Our theory ignores the consequential crimes, those committed by elites in the world of business and commerce and those committed by states and corrupt dictators. In the first category are the activities of "high-level corporate executives, acting on behalf of corporations" and the crimes of corporations themselves. As an example, we do not consider the $70 billion in fees collected by mutual fund managers entrusted with the $7 trillion provided them by 100 million investors, as raised by Friedrichs and Schwartz (Chapter 10). In the second category we fail to consider Hitler, Stalin, Crown Prince Abdullah, and ten other names on a "partial" list of persons responsible for horrendous acts of violence and thefts on a monumental scale.

It is easier to consider, first, crimes in the second category: genocides, massacres, and monumental thefts. The theory, it is true, does not consider the consequences of crime for the victim. It focuses, instead, on the consequences for the offender, particularly negative consequences. In our definition a universal condition for crime is an "unrestrained offender." If there are no apparent negative consequences, the unrestrained offender, as Hobbes taught us long ago, is free to do as he pleases. The crime lurking behind such large terms as *genocide* and *massacre* is homicide. If it pleases a dictator to sign off on a plan to shoot, bomb, gas, hack, or starve to death weak and unarmed people, he is free to do so—at least temporarily.

No great skill, planning, or effort on his part is required. And no great skill, planning, or effort is required to execute his plan. The same is true for monumental thefts, where trucks and shipping containers replace purses with false bottoms. We experience no difficulty in calling these acts of force and fraud crimes, and we feel free to speculate about their connection to self-control. At the same time we are confident that the straightforward cures suggested by our perspective are at least as likely to work as those based on the sophisticated view that the multiple factors involved in white-collar crime, "can interact with each other in a virtually infinite number of ways" (Friedrichs and Schwartz, Chapter 10).

Objection 3 focuses on crimes in the world of business and commerce. It asserts that because the theory applies to real crimes, it cannot be applied to acts that are not crimes but are treated as such for the greater good or in the public interest. This frank admission says a great deal about the intellectual foundations of the white-collar crime movement. White-collar crimes, at least those white-collar crimes that our theory does not cover, exist in the world of politics. This accounts for the tone and quality of the argument condemning them, which, as the reader has seen, is often "reminiscent of the preaching of outraged biblical prophets" (J. S. Baker, 2004, quoting Geis and Goff, 1983, xviii). It also accounts for the failure of white-collar criminologists to exhibit more than passing interest in evidence or data and their transparent neglect of trade-offs, the costs of doing what they implicitly or explicitly propose.

So, knowing what we know now, we would agree to this restriction on the range or scope of the theory. It serves no useful purpose to describe governmental regulations or their violations or misuses as crimes. We may feel that it is a crime that fund managers make so much money, that the price of milk is so high in the United States, that the price of rice is so high in South Korea, or that mine workers die in accidents. But there is little evidence that the discipline or the public good is advanced by including phenomenological crimes within the province of criminology. On the contrary, there is good evidence that criminology is not the place to look for expertise in these matters.

Violent Crime

According to Felson and Osgood (Chapter 11), we sometimes use self-control to refer to a loose amalgam that indicates all individual difference factors that might be associated with crime. They say this is mistake, and agree to ignore "all other" individual differences and focus on that part of our work that is most directly a theory of self-control. Their time on this task turns out to be one sentence alluding to a summary of the results of research on the effects of self-control. It is immediately followed by an opaque description of experiments using mirrors said to show that self-control may facilitate as well as inhibit violence. So much for the general theory of crime! Brannigan (2004) points out that such experiments regularly employ smoke as well as mirrors.

Our critique of Felson and Osgood's essay must be correspondingly brief. The means and conditions necessary for rape may differ from those necessary for burglary. Thus a country may have relatively high rates of one crime and relatively low rates of the other. Crime-specific analysis naturally focuses on elements unique to the crime in question and thereby suggests that it is not covered by a general theory. The alternative hypothesis is that a general "propensity" better accounts for the behavior than some crime-specific need or learning history. With regard to rape, specifically, there is reason to believe that the general proclivity explanation is superior to the crime-specific explanation, that rapists are, first of all, offenders (Lussier et al, 2005; cf. Akers, Chapter 6). Until this alternative hypothesis *has at least been considered* with regard to other forms of violence, it seems to us illegitimate to pretend that it has been falsified.

We are not convinced that our theory does not apply to violent acts with negative consequences or that a group of offenders may be said in any useful or meaningful way to specialize in violence. Of course some offenders are more likely than others to bite, kick, punch, threaten, or shoot, but we find the idea of specialization in violence less than enlightening. Toddlers punch, bite, and kick. From then on, violent behavior declines sharply with age. There is no mystery in the relative rarity of violent offenses among adults. Violent careers are self-terminating. Measures interpreted as corroborating specialization too often count the same offense again and again (Deane et al., 2005).

Be that as it may, we only rarely recognize our theory in their discussion. When it does appear, sometimes in pure form, it is not recognized by the writers. Consequently, on more than one occasion, Felson and Osgood use our view of lack of self-control to explain violence and suggest that, in doing so, they are presenting evidence *against* the theory.

THEORETICALLY ORIENTED RESEARCH

Criminology has moved into an age of immense methodological sophistication. Given the expertise of criminologists in measurement, research design, and analysis, all that would seem to be required for a more perfect understanding of crime is better training of students in statistics and the funds required to collect "large quantities of data on large representative samples of individuals" (Nagin and Tremblay, 2005, 918). Nor must we wait for rigorous science to show itself. "Of the 99 articles published" in three volumes of *Criminology* (2001–2004) "82% used statistical analysis of quantitative data, with 32% relying on nonlinear regression approaches including HLM, trajectory analysis, negative binomial and tobit models" (Bushway and Weisburd, 2006, 1).

Our theory attempts to escape substantive positivism, the theories of the disciplines. It attempts to remain true to methodological positivism, science properly understood. Unfortunately, science does not provide unequivocal guidance on all issues. For example, we are not pleased with the widely used measure of self-control described by Piquero in Chapter 2 (Hirschi and Gottfredson, 1993; Hirschi, 2004). Our objection is that it makes of self-control an enduring criminal predisposition, that it leads the unwary to interpret our theory as a species of psychological positivism.

Piquero proposes to referee this "pressing and continually unresolved" dispute. His judgment is quick and final. We had our say in the original statement of the theory. If we gave erroneous or incomplete instructions to researchers, too bad for us. We forced them "to interpret the concept of self-control in their own manner, provide further clarity on the concept, and come up with their own measures of self control." (Marcus [2003], in contrast, has no difficulty interpreting and measuring self-control in a manner perfectly consistent with our understanding of the theory.)

Measurement is the Achilles' heel of theoretically oriented quantitative research. The number of possible measures of an abstract concept may be large. Concepts themselves tend to multiply in the absence of a restraining theory, as Piquero's chapter illustrates. The same measure may be used as an indicator of more than one concept—for example, we interpret a measure of "opportunity" as a measure of "self-control." And as is well known, measures may simply not measure what they are said to measure. Care and thought and analysis are required, and spur-of-the-moment measures risk making a joke of the whole enterprise. As a general rule, the best measure is the measure that produces the best results—that is, best predicts the criterion, best accords with theoretical expectations. We therefore see no ethical deficiency in our preference for supportive measures.

The measure in question has been widely used by researchers. It has helped make "consistent with Gottfredson" and "contrary to Gottfredson" big hitters on Google. We think the ratio of these hits could be more favorable to the theory, but—again—our concern is not with the measure qua measure but with the message it conveys about the theory. From examining its content, personality psychologists conclude that we stumbled into their territory without knowing it, and they have reasons. An alternative interpretation is that we saw an opportunity to undermine personality psychology and almost took advantage of it.

Fortunately, Piquero makes it available again. He and many others reject "behavioral measures" of self-control on the grounds that they are "tautologically" related to crime. This leaves the Grasmick et al. "attitudinal" measure as *the* measure of self-control, and Piquero thus devotes almost a third of his essay to an analysis of its properties and behavior. We believe it is illegitimate to see or treat this scale as the embodiment of the theory. We believe that a priori rejection of behavioral measures (or any class of measures) is also illegitimate—or, perhaps better, nonsense plain and simple.

We grant that attitudes may reflect levels of self-control, that the Grasmick et al. scale has a degree of face validity. What is the source of the attitudes measured by the Grasmick scale? In the first instance, they come from us. We explicitly derive the elements of self-control from our conception of the nature of criminal acts. Grasmick and his colleagues then put together a set of items that explicitly incorporates on a one-to-one basis the conclusions of our logical exercise. So, we directly and the Grasmick team indirectly *derive* the cognitions or attitudes of people from their level of involvement in criminal or analogous acts. It is necessary to assume that those answering the Grasmick questions do the same thing. They report being risk takers because they have taken risks. How else could they reach this conclusion? How then are attitudinal measures of self-control better than behavioral measures? If our theory is correct, it cannot be because attitudes precede acts in the causal chain. On the contrary, in our scheme "personality measures" reflect rather than cause behavior. Behavioral measures are therefore better than attitudinal measures. They are closer to the phenomenon in question, and they save the theory from the taint of a misguided brand of psychological positivism.

We neglected to count the number of times our essayists suggest that self-control is a situational construct—that is, not a trait of individuals. Some of them—for example, Piquero—take this position *after* declaring that behavioral measures of crime are tautologically—that is, logically, necessarily—related to other behavioral measures of crime. The mind, free of all restraints, flies away, and we have the necessary conclusion that situations are enduring properties of individuals. It sometimes appears that those under the sway of the disciplines are strangely undisciplined, that they will say anything to discredit a general theory of crime.

CONCLUSION

Our theory has benefited from disinterested explications. They demonstrate that it is in fact comprehensible, that its claims may be articulated and understood without reference to our hopes and defects. Because they are independent assessments, they provide straight-forward refutation of many of the claims of its critics. We have therefore let them speak for themselves.

The theory is not damaged by weighty pronouncements about the fecklessness of the effort or by ugly insinuations about the character of one or both of its authors. We have therefore ignored them here as we ignored them when they were first published some years ago.

The theory can survive questions about its logical structure. We have devoted space to the tautology issue only because of the frequency with which it is raised. We believe that thought actually requires the tautologies the critics most fear and that the field would be better off with more of them.

The theory *is* threatened by evidence that it leaves unexplained too many important facts about crime. We have therefore tried to locate the theory in a more general theoretical tradition—a tradition that sees actors making choices based on the objective elements of the situation—which importantly include their salient personal characteristics—and their subjective assessment of the likely long-term costs of a particular choice. However successful we have been in this effort, we think it has considerable potential as a guide to research and as a device for protecting the theory against the charge of limited applicability.

The most insidious threats to the theory are the added concepts, the distinctions and false facts that multiply theoretical entities, the qualifications that limit its range and scope. The essays in this volume contain a virtual flood of such theory killers. We have dealt with some. We oppose all of them. How could we do otherwise? That they will keep coming is beyond question. The current mantra of the field is that theories "are generally little more than simple-minded human brain products offered for falsification. Neglecting this reality," the winner of the Sutherland Award and major advocate of group-based trajectory modeling tells us, "is to invite hubris, and hubris is the one sure way to halt the way forward" (Nagin, 2007, 261). Well, humility is a wonderful thing. At the rate statistical modeling is improving our knowledge of crime and criminality, it will be in vogue for a long time. We prefer other virtues, among them, clarity, parsimony, and theoretical power. To those who neglect these virtues, we can only say, enjoy the pebbles, and don't forget to record their colors.

NOTE

1. Available at http://www.medicalnewstoday.com/medicalnewsphp?newsid=57730 (accessed December 20, 2006).

BIBLIOGRAPHY

Abelson, Elaine S. 1989. "The Invention of Kleptomania." *Signs* 15 (1): 123–143.

Adler, Patricia. 1985. *Wheeling and Dealing: An Ethnography of an Upper-Level Drug Dealing and Smuggling Community.* New York: Columbia University Press.

Agence France Presse. 2004. "Indonesia: Suharto Tops List of Embezzling Leaders." *New York Times*, March 26, A7.

Akers, Ronald. 1973. *Deviant Behavior: A Social Learning Approach* (1st ed.). Belmont, CA: Wadsworth.

———. 1977. *Deviant Behavior: A Social Learning Approach* (2nd ed.). Belmont, CA: Wadsworth.

———. 1985. *Deviant Behavior: A Social Learning Approach* (3rd ed). Belmont, CA: Wadsworth.

———. 1991. "Self-Control as a General Theory of Crime." *Journal of Quantitative Criminology* 7 (June): 201–211.

———. 1996. "Is Differential Association/Social Learning Cultural Deviance Theory?" *Criminology* 34 (May): 229–247.

———. 1998. *Social Learning and Social Structure: A General Theory of Crime and Deviance.* Boston: Northeastern University Press.

Akers, Ronald L., Marvin D. Krohn, Lonn Lanza-Kaduce, and Marcia Radosevich. 1979. "Social Learning and Deviant Behavior: A Specific Test of a General Theory." *American Sociological Review* 44: 635–655.

Akers, Ronald L., and Christine S. Sellers. 2004. *Criminological Theories: Introduction, Evaluation, and Application* (4th ed.). Los Angeles: Roxbury.

Amaro, H., and C. Hardy-Fanta. 1995. "Gender Relations in Addiction and Recovery." *Journal of Psychoactive Drugs* 27: 325–337.

Amir, Menachem. 1971. *Patterns in Forcible Rape.* Chicago: University of Chicago Press.

Anderson, Elijah. 1999. *Code of the Street: Decency, Violence, and the Moral Life of the Inner City.* New York: W. W. Norton.

Andrews, D. A., and James Bonta. 2006. *The Psychology of Criminal Conduct* (4th ed.). Cincinnati: Anderson.

Anthony, James C., and Valerie Forman. 2003. "At the Intersection of Public Health and Criminal Justice Research on Drugs and Crime." In *Toward a Drugs and Crime Research Agenda for the 21st Century*. Washington, DC: U.S. Department of Justice, 11–64.

Armstrong, Todd A. 2003. "The Effect of Learning on Crime: Contrasting *A General Theory of Crime* and Social Learning Theory." In Chester L. Britt and Michael R. Gottfredson (eds.), *Control Theories of Crime and Delinquency*. New Brunswick, NJ: Transaction, 39–52.

Arneklev, Bruce J., Harold G. Grasmick, and Robert J. Bursik. 1999. "Evaluating the Dimensionality and Invariance of Low Self-Control." *Journal of Quantitative Criminology* 15: 307–331.

Arneklev, Bruce J., Harold G. Grasmick, Charles R. Tittle, and Robert J. Bursik. 1993. "Low Self-Control and Imprudent Behavior." *Journal of Quantitative Criminology* 9: 225–247.

Aron, Adam R., Tevor W. Robbins, and Russell A. Poldrack. 2004. "Inhibition and the Right Inferior Frontal Cortex." *Trends in Cognitive Sciences* 8: 170–177.

Arrighi, Barbara A., and David J. Maume. 2000. "Workplace Subordination and Men's Avoidance of Housework." *Journal of Family Issues* 21 (May): 464–486.

Asinof, Eliot. 1963. *Eight Men Out: The Black Sox and the 1919 World Series*. New York: Holt, Rinehart & Winston.

Askenasy, Hans. 1984. *Hitler's Secret*. Anaheim, CA: KNI.

Bachman, Jerald G., et al. 2002. *The Decline of Substance Use in Young Adulthood: Changes in Social Activities, Roles, and Beliefs*. Mahway, NJ: Lawrence Erlbaum.

Bakan, Joel. 2004. *The Corporation: The Pathological Pursuit of Profit and Power*. New York: Free Press.

Baker, John S., Jr. 2004. *The Sociological Origins of "White-Collar Crime."* Legal Memorandum 14. Washington, DC: The Heritage Foundation.

Baker, S. P., E. R. Braver, L. H. Chen, J. F. Pantula, and D. Massie. 1998. "Motor Vehicle Occupant Deaths Among Hispanic and Black Children and Teenagers." *Archives of Pediatric Adolescent Medicine* 152: 1209–1212.

Ball, John C., et al. 1981. "The Criminality of Heroin Addicts When Addicted and Off Opiates." In James A. Inciardi (ed.), *The Drugs-Crime Connection*. Newbury Park, CA: Sage, 39–65.

———. 1983. "The Day-to-Day Criminality of Heroin Addicts in Baltimore: A Study in the Continuity of Offense Rates." *Drug and Alcohol Dependence* 12 (October): 119–142.

Barkley, Russell A. 1997. *ADHD and the Nature of Self-Control*. New York: Guilford.

Barkley, Russell A., et al. 2002. "International Consensus Statement on ADHD, January 2002." *Clinical Child and Family Psychology Review* 5: 89–111.

Bartusiak, Marcia. 2000. *Einstein's Unfinished Symphony: Listening to the Sounds of Space Time*. Washington, DC: John Henry Press.

Baskin, Deborah R., and Ira B. Sommers. 1998. *Casualties of Community Disorder: Women's Careers in Violent Crime*. Boulder, CO: Westview.

Baumeister, Roy F., T. F. Heatherton, and D. M. Tice. 1994. *Losing Control: How and Why People Fail at Self-Regulation*. San Diego: Academic Press.

Baumrind, Diana. 1991. "The Influence of Parenting Style on Adolescent Competence and Substance Use." *Journal of Early Adolescence* 11: 56–95.

Bean, Philip. 2002. *Drugs and Crime*. Portland, OR, and Cullompton, U.K.: Willan.

Becker, Howard S. 1953. "Becoming a Marijuana User." *American Journal of Sociology* 59 (November): 235–242.

———. 1963. *Outsiders: Studies in the Sociology of Deviance.* New York: Free Press.

———. 1973. "Labelling Theory Reconsidered." In Howard S. Becker, *Outsiders: Studies in the Sociology of Deviance* (expanded ed.). New York: Free Press, 177–212.

Beckman, Mary. 2004 "Crime, Culpability, and the Adolescent Brain." *Science* 305: 596–599.

Bell, Richard Q., and Lawrence V. Harper. 1977. *Child Effects on Adults.* Hillsdale, NJ: Lawrence Erlbaum.

Bellaire, Paul E., and Thomas L. McNulty. 2005. "Beyond the Bell Curve: Community Disadvantage and the Explanation of Black-White Differences in Adolescent Violence." *Criminology* 43 (November): 1135–1168.

Belsky, Jay, and John Kelly. 1994. *The Transition to Parenthood.* New York: Delacorte Press.

Benson, Michael L. 2002. *Crime and the Life Course: An Introduction.* Los Angeles: Roxbury.

Benson, Michael L., and Elizabeth Moore. 1992. "Are White-Collar and Common Crime the Same? An Empirical and Theoretical Critique of a Recently Proposed General Theory of Crime." *Journal of Research in Crime and Delinquency* 29 (August): 251–272.

Berscheid, Ellen. 2003. "Lessons in 'Greatness' from Kurt Lewin's Life and Works." In Robert J. Sternberg (ed.), *The Anatomy of Impact: What Makes the Great Works of Psychology.* Washington, DC: American Psychological Association, 109–123.

Beveridge, William Ian B. 1950. *The Art of Scientific Investigation.* New York: W. W. Norton.

Birkbeck, C., and G. LaFree. 1993. "The Situational Analysis of Crime and Deviance." *Annual Review of Sociology* 19: 113–137.

Black, Donald. 1983. "Crime as Social Control." *American Sociological Review* 48: 34–45.

Blackwell, Brenda Sims, and Alex R. Piquero. 2005. "On the Relationship Between Gender, Power Control, Self-Control, and Crime." *Journal of Criminal Justice* 33: 1–17.

Blokland, Arjan A. J., and Paul Nieuwbeerta. 2005. "The Effects of Life Circumstances on Longitudinal Trajectories of Offending. *Criminology* 43 (4): 1203–1240.

Blumberg, Paul. 1989. *The Predatory Society: Deception in the American Marketplace.* New York: Oxford University Press.

Blumstein, Alfred. 1995. "Youth Violence, Guns, and the Illicit-Drug Industry." *Journal of Criminal Law and Criminology* 86 (1): 10–35.

Blumstein, Alfred, and Jacqueline Cohen. 1979. "Estimation of Individual Crime Rates from Arrest Records." *Journal of Criminal Law and Criminology* 70: 561–585.

Blumstein, Alfred, Jacqueline Cohen, Jeffrey Roth, and Christy Visher. 1986. *Criminal Careers and "Career Criminals."* Washington, DC: National Academy Press.

Blumstein, Alfred, and Richard Rosenfeld. 1998. "Explaining Recent Trends in U.S. Homicide Rates." *Journal of Criminal Law and Criminology* 88: 1175–1216.

Booth, A., and D. Wayne Osgood. 1993. "The Influence of Testosterone on Deviance in Adulthood." *Criminology* 31: 93–117.

Bottcher, Jean. 2001. "Social Practices of Gender: How Gender Relates to Delinquency in the Lives of High-Risk Youths." *Criminology* 39 (4): 893–931.

Brannigan, Augustine. 2004. *The Rise and Fall of Social Psychology: The Use and Misuse of the Experimental Method.* New York: Aldine de Gruyter.

Brenda, Brent B. 2005. "The Robustness of Self-Control in Relation to Form of Delinquency." *Youth and Society* 36: 418–444.

Briar, Scott, and Irving Piliavin. 1965. "Delinquency, Situational Inducements, and Commitments to Conformity." *Social Problems* 13 (1): 35–45.

Britt, Chester L., and Michael R. Gottfredson (eds.). 2003. *Control Theories of Crime and Delinquency*. New Brunswick, NJ: Transaction.

Browne, John. 1681. *Kidarminister Stuff: A New Piece of Print*. London: Ronald Taylor.

Brownfield, David, and Ann Marie Sorenson. 1993. "Self-Control and Juvenile Delinquency: Theoretical Issues and an Empirical Assessment of Selected Elements of a —General Theory of Crime." *Deviant Behavior* 14 (July-September): 243–264.

Bunge, Mario. 1959. *Causality: The Place of the Causal Principle in Modern Science*. Cambridge, MA: Harvard University Press.

Bureau of Justice Statistics. 2005a. "Prisoner Statistics." Available at http://www.ojp.usdoj.gov/bjs/prisons.htm

———. 2005b. *Sourcebook of Criminal Justice Statistics, 2001*. U.S. Department of Justice. Washington, DC: U.S. Government Printing Office. Available at http://www.albany.edu/sourcebook/

———. 2007. *Sourcebook of Criminal Justice Statistics, 2003*. U.S. Department of Justice. Washington, DC: U.S. Government Printing Office. Available at http://www.albany.edu/sourcebook/

Bureau of Labor Statistics. 2003. "Women at Work: A Visual Essay." *Monthly Labor Review* 126: 45–50. Available at http://www.bls.gov/opub/mlr/2003/10/contents.htm

Burgess, Ernest W. 1925a. "Can Neighborhood Work Have a Scientific Basis?" In Robert E. Park, Ernest W. Burgess, and Roderick D. McKenzie, *The City*. Chicago: University of Chicago Press, 142–155.

———. 1925b. "The Growth of the City: An Introduction to a Research Project." In Robert. E. Park, Ernest W. Burgess, and Roderick D. McKenzie, *The City*. Chicago: University of Chicago Press, 47–62.

Burgess, Robert L., and Ronald L. Akers. 1966. "A Differential Association Reinforcement Theory of Criminal Behavior." *Social Problems* 14: 128–147.

Bursik, Robert J., Jr., and Jim Webb. 1982. "Community Change and Patterns of Delinquency." *American Journal of Sociology* 88 (1): 24–42.

Burt, Collie Harbin, Ronald L. Simons, and Leslie G. Simons. 2006. "A Longitudinal Test of the Effects of Parenting and the Stability of Self-Control: Negative Evidence for the General Theory of Crime." *Criminology* 44 (May): 353–396.

Burton, Velmer S., et al. 1999. "Age, Self-Control, and Adult Offending Behaviors: A Research Note Assessing a General Theory of Crime." *Journal of Criminal Justice* 27: 45–54.

Burton, Velmer S., Jr., Francis T. Cullen, T. David Evans, Leanne Fiftal Alarid, and R. Gregory Dunaway. 1998. "Gender, Self-Control, and Crime." *Journal of Research in Crime and Delinquency* 35 (2): 123–147.

Burton, Velmer S., Francis T. Cullen, T. David Evans, and R. Gregory Dunaway. 1994. "Reconsidering Stain Theory: Operationalization, Rival Theories, and Adult Criminality." *Journal of Quantitative Criminology* 10: 213–239.

Bushway, Shawn, and David Weisburd. 2006. "Acknowledging the Centrality of Quantitative Criminology in Criminology and Criminal Justice." *The Criminologist*, 31 (July-August): 1, 3–4.

Byrnes, James P., David C. Miller, and William D. Schafer. 1999. "Gender Differences in Risk Taking." *Psychological Bulletin* 125: 367–383.

Calavita, Kitty, Henry N. Pontell, and Robert Tillman. 1997. *Big-Money Crime: Fraud and Politics in the Savings and Loan Crisis.* Berkeley: University of California Press.

Callahan, David. 2004. *The Cheating Culture: Why More Americans Are Doing Wrong to Get Ahead.* New York: Harcourt.

Campbell, Anne. 1984. *The Girls in the Gang.* Oxford, U.K.: Basil Blackwell.

Capaldi, D. M., and G. R. Patterson. 1996. "Can Violent Offenders Be Distinguished from Frequent Offenders? Prediction from Childhood to Adolescence." *Journal of Research in Crime and Delinquency* 33: 206–231.

Carver, C. S. 1974. "Physical Aggression as a Function of Objective Self-Awareness and Attitudes Toward Punishment." *Journal of Experimental Social Psychology* 11: 510–519.

Caspi, Avshalom, Glen H. Elder Jr., and Darly J. Bem. 1987. "Moving Against the World: Life-Course Patterns of Explosive Children." *Developmental Psychology* 23: 308–313.

Catalano, Shannan M. 2004. *Criminal Victimization, 2003.* Washington, DC: Bureau of Justice Statistics.

Cauffman, Elizabeth, Laurence Steinberg, and Alex R. Piquero. 2005. "Psychological, Neuropsychological, and Physiological Correlates of Serious Antisocial Behavior." *Criminology* 43: 133–176.

Center for Injury and Violence Prevention. 2004. *Virginia Behavioral Risk Factor Surveillance Survey (BRFSS) Injury-Related Summary, 2002.* Virginia Department of Health, March. Available at http://www.vahealth.org

Centers for Disease Control. 2000. *Tracking the Hidden Epidemics 2000: Trends in STDs in the United States.* Available at http://www.cdc.gov/nchstp/od/news/RevBrochure1pdf closelook.htm

———. 2005. *HIV/AIDS Surveillance Report: HIV Infection and AIDS in the United States.* Available from the CDC National Prevention Information Network at 1-800-458-5231.

Chernkovich, Stephen A., and Peggy C. Giordano. 2001. "Stability and Change in Antisocial Behavior: The Transition from Adolescence to Early Adulthood." *Criminology* 39 (May): 371–410.

Chesney-Lind, Meda, and Lisa Pasko. 2004. *The Female Offender: Girls, Women, and Crime* (2nd ed.). Thousand Oaks, CA: Sage.

Clark, John P., and Richard Hollinger. 1983. *Theft by Employees in Work Situations.* Washington, DC: National Institute of Justice.

Clarke, Ronald V., and Derek B. Cornish. 2001. "Rational Choice." In Raymond Paternoster and Ronet Bachman (eds.), *Explaining Criminals and Crime.* Los Angeles: Roxbury, 23–42.

Clinard, Marshall B. 1964. "Theoretical Implications of Anomie and Deviant Behavior." In Marshall B. Clinard (ed.), *Anomie and Deviant Behavior: A Discussion and Critique.* New York: Free Press, 1–56.

———. 1983. *Corporate Ethics and Crime: The Role of Middle Managers.* Beverly Hills, CA: Sage.

Clinard, Marshall B., and Peter C. Yeager. 1980. *Corporate Crime.* New York: Free Press; New Brunswick, NJ: Transaction.

Cloward, Richard A., and Lloyd E. Ohlin. 1960. *Delinquency and Opportunity: A Theory of Delinquent Gangs.* New York: Free Press.

Cochran, John K., Peter B. Wood, Christine S. Sellers, Wendy Wilkerson, and Mitchell B. Chamlin. 1998. "Academic Dishonesty and Low Self-Control: An Empirical Test of a General Theory of Crime." *Deviant Behavior* 19: 227–255.

Cohen, Albert K. 1955. *Delinquent Boys: The Culture of the Gang.* Glencoe, IL: Free Press.

———. 1965. "The Sociology of the Deviant Act: Anomie Theory and Beyond." *American Sociological Review* 30 (February): 5–14.

Cohen, Lawrence E., and Marcus Felson. 1979. "Social Change and Crime Rate Trends: A Routine Activity Approach." *American Sociological Review* 44: 588–608.

Cohn, Ellen G., and David P. Farrington. 1999. "Changes in the Most-Cited Scholars in Twenty Criminology and Criminal Justice Journals Between 1990 and 1995." *Journal of Criminal Justice* 27 (4): 345–359.

Coleman, James S. 1990. *Foundations of Social Theory.* Cambridge, MA: Harvard University Press.

Coleman, James W. 1987. "Toward an Integrated Theory of White Collar Crime." *American Journal of Sociology* 93 (September): 406–439.

Conklin, John E. 2002. *Why Crime Rates Fell.* Boston: Allyn & Bacon.

Cook, Philip T. 1986. "The Demand and Supply of Criminal Opportunity." *Crime and Justice: An Annual Review of Research* 7: 1–27.

Cressey, Donald R. 1953. *Other People's Money.* Glencoe, IL: Free Press.

———. 1969. *Theft of the Nation.* New York: Harper & Row.

Cullen, Francis T. 1994. "Social Support as an Organizing Concept for Criminology." *Justice Quarterly* 11 (4): 527–559.

Cullen, Francis T., and Karen E. Gilbert. 1982. *Reaffirming Rehabilitation.* Cincinnati, OH: Anderson.

Cullen, Francis T., and John Paul Wright. 1997. "Liberating the Anomie-Strain Paradigm: Implications from Social Support Theory." In Nikos Passas and Robert Agnew (eds.), *The Future of Anomie Theory.* Boston: Northeastern University Press, 187–206.

Cullen, Francis T., John Paul Wright, and Kristie R. Blevins (eds.). 2006. *Taking Stock: The Status of Criminological Theory.* New Brunswick, NJ: Transaction.

Daly, Kathleen, and Meda Chesney-Lind. 1988. "Feminism and Criminology." *Justice Quarterly* 5 (4): 497–538.

D'Antonio, William V. 2004. "Walking the Walk on Family Values." *Boston Globe,* October 31. Available at http://www.boston.com/

Darwin, Charles. 1958 [1869]. *The Autobiography of Charles Darwin, 1809–1882,* Nora Barlow (ed.). London: Collins.

Davis, Clyde Brion. 1956. *Something for Nothing.* Philadelphia: Lippincott.

Davison, S. L., R. Bell, S. Donath, J. G. Montalto, and S. R. Davis. 2005. "Androgen Levels in Adult Females: Changes with Age, Menopause, and Oophorectomy." *Journal of Clinical Endocrinology and Metabolism* 90 (7): 3847–3853.

Deane, Glenn, David Armstrong, and Richard B. Felson. 2005. "An Examination of Offense Specialization Using Marginal Logit Models." *Criminology* 43 (4): 955–988.

DeHart, Dana D. 2004. "Pathways to Prison: Impact of Victimization in the Lives of Incarcerated Women." Columbia, SC: Center for Child and Family Studies, University of

South Carolina. Retrieved September 7, 2005, from http://www.sc.edu/ccfs/research/incarceratedwomen.html

DeLisi, Matt, Andy Hochstetler, and Daniel S. Murphy. 2003. "Self-Control Behind Bars: A Validation Study of the Grasmick et al. Scale." *Justice Quarterly* 20: 241–264.

DeNavas-Walt, Carmen, Bernadette D. Proctor, and Cheryl Hill Lee. 2006. *Income, Poverty, and Health Insurance Coverage in the United States: 2005.* Washington, DC: U.S. Census Bureau.

DiMento, Joseph F. C., and Gilbert Geis. 2006. "The Extraordinary Condition of Extraordinary Rendition: The CIA, the DEA, Kidnapping, Torture, and the Law." *War Crimes, Genocide, and Crimes Against Humanity* 2: 35–64.

Ditton, Jason. 1977. *Part-Time Crime: An Ethnography of Fiddling and Pilferage.* London: Macmillan.

Divorce Magazine. 2005. Available at http://www.divorcemag.com/statistics/statsUS.shtml

Dodge, K.A., and D. R. Somberg. 1987. "Hostile Attributional Biases Among Aggressive Boys Are Exacerbated Under Conditions of Threats to Self." *Child Development* 58: 213–224.

Dohmen, Thomas, Armin Falk, David Huffman, Uwe Sunde, Jürgen Schupp, and Gert G. Wagner. 2005. *Individual Risk Attitudes: New Evidence from a Large, Representative, Experimentally-Validated Survey.* IZA Discussion Paper 1730. Bonn, Germany: Institute for the Study of Labor.

Donohue, John J., and Steven D. Levitt. 2001. "The Impact of Legalized Abortion on Crime." *Quarterly Journal of Economics* 116: 379–420.

Donovan, John E., and Richard Jessor. 1985. "Structure of Problem Behavior in Adolescence and Young Adulthood." *Journal of Consulting and Clinical Psychology* 53: 890–904.

Dowden, Craig, and Don A. Andrews. 1999. "What Works in Young Offender Treatment: A Meta-Analysis." *Forum on Corrections Research* 11: 21–24.

Dubner, Stephen J., and Steven D. Levitt. 2004. "What the Bagel Man Saw." *New York Times Magazine,* June 6, 62–65.

Dugan, Laura, Dean A. Dabney, and Brenda Sims Blackwell. 2001. Paper presented at the Annual Meetings of the American Society of Criminology, Atlanta, November.

Durkheim, Emile. 1966 [1897]. *Suicide: A Study in Sociology.* New York: Free Press.

Elder, Glen H., Jr. 1975. "Age Differentiation and the Life Course." *Annual Review of Sociology* 1: 165–190.

Elliott, Delbert, and Suzanne S. Ageton. 1980. "Reconciling Race and Class Differences in Self-Reporting and Official Explanations of Delinquency." *American Sociological Review* 45: 95–110.

Elliott, Delbert S., David Huizinga, and Suzanne S. Ageton. 1985. *Explaining Delinquency and Drug Use.* Beverly Hills, CA: Sage.

Engel, George L. 1962. *Fainting* (2nd ed.). Springfield, IL: Charles C Thomas.

English, Diana J., Cathy Spatz Widom, and Carol Brandford. 2001. *Childhood Victimization and Delinquency, Adult Criminality, and Violent Criminal Behavior: A Replication and Extension, Final Report.* Washington, DC: U.S. Department of Justice, National Institute of Justice.

Epstein, Joseph. 1997. "Life Sciences." *Wall Street Journal,* October 23, C14.

Erickson, Patricia G., Jennifer Butters, Patti McGillicuddy, and Ase Hallgren. 2000. "Crack and Prostitution: Gender, Myths, and Experiences." *Journal of Drug Issues* 30: 767–789.

Esbensen, Finn-Aage, and David Huizinga. 1993. "Gangs, Drugs, and Delinquency in a Survey of Urban Youth." *Criminology* 4: 565–589.

Evans, T. David, Francis T. Cullen, Velmer S. Burton Jr., R. Gregory Dunaway, and Michael Benson. 1997. "The Social Consequences of Self-Control: Testing the General Theory of Crime." *Criminology* 35: 475–501.

Ezell, Michael, and Lawrence E. Cohen. 2005. *Desisting from Crime: Continuity and Change in Long-Term Crime Patterns of Serious Chronic Offenders.* New York: Oxford University Press.

Faris, Robert E. L. 1955. *Social Disorganization* (2nd ed.). New York: Ronald Press.

Faris, Robert E. L., and H. Warren Dunham. 1939. *Mental Disorders in Urban Areas.* Chicago: University of Chicago Press.

Farrington, David P. 1986. "Age and Crime." *Crime and Justice: An Annual Review of Research* 7: 189–250.

———. 1987. "Implications of Biological Findings for Criminological Research." In S. A. Mednick, T. E. Moffitt, and S. A. Stack (eds.), *The Causes of Crime: New Biological Approaches.* New York: Cambridge University Press, 42–64.

———. 1991. "Childhood Aggression and Adult Violence: Early Precursors and Later Life Outcomes." In Debra J. Pepler and Kenneth H. Rubin (eds.), *The Development and Treatment of Childhood Aggression.* Hillsdale, NJ: Lawrence Erlbaum: 8–30.

———. 2002. "Developmental Criminology and Risk-Focused Prevention." In Mike Maguire, Rod Morgan, and Robert Reiner (eds.), *The Oxford Handbook of Criminology.* New York: Oxford University Press, 657–701.

Faulkner, Robert R., Eric R. Cheney, Gene A. Fisher, and Wayne E. Baker. 2003. "Crime by Committee: Conspirators and Company Men in the Illegal Electrical Industry Cartel, 1954–1959." *Criminology* 41: 511–554.

Federal Bureau of Investigation. 2003. *Crime in the United States, 2002.* U.S. Department of Justice. Washington, DC: U.S. Government Printing Office.

Feingold, Alan. 1994. "Gender Differences in Personality: A Meta-Analysis." *Psychological Bulletin* 116: 429–456.

Feldman, S. Shirley, and Daniel A. Weinberger. 1994. "Self-Restraint as a Mediator of Family Influences on Boys' Delinquent Behavior: A Longitudinal Study." *Child Development* 65: 195–211.

Felson, Marcus. 2006. *Crime and Nature.* Thousand Oaks, CA: Sage.

Felson, Marcus, and R. V. Clarke. 1998. *Opportunity Makes the Thief.* Police Research Series Paper 98. Policing and Reducing Crime Unit, Research, Development, and Statistics Directorate. London: Home Office.

Felson, Richard B. 2002. *Violence and Gender Reexamined.* Washington, DC: American Psychological Association.

Felson, Richard B., G. Deane, and D. A. Armstrong. 2001. "Race and Adolescent Crime and Violence: An Incident-Based Analysis." Paper presented at the annual meetings of the Eastern Sociological Society, Philadelphia.

Felson, Richard B., and Dana Haynie. 2002. "Pubertal Development, Social Factors and Delinquency Among Adolescent Boys." *Criminology* 40: 967–988.

Felson, Richard B., and Allen Liska. 1984. "Explanations of the Sex-Deviance Relationship." *Deviant Behavior* 5 (1): 1–10.

Feynman, Richard. 1985. *"Surely You're Joking, Mr. Feynman?" Adventures of a Curious Character*, Edward Hutchins (ed.). New York: W. W. Norton.

Finley, Nancy J., and Harold G. Grasmick. 1985. "Gender Roles and Social Control." *Sociological Spectrum* 5: 317–330.

Fisher, Bonnie S., Francis T. Cullen, and Michael G. Turner. 2000. *The Sexual Victimization of College Women*. NCJ 182369. Washington, DC: U.S. Department of Justice.

Fitzgerald, F. Scott. 1925. *The Great Gatsby*. New York: Scribner's & Sons.

Forde, David R., and Leslie W. Kennedy. 1997. "Risky Lifestyles, Routine Activities, and the General Theory of Crime." *Justice Quarterly* 14: 265–291.

Fox, Loren. 2003. *Enron: The Rise and Fall*. Hoboken, NJ: Wiley.

Friedrichs, David O. (ed.). 1998. *State Crime*. Aldershot, U.K.: Ashgate.

———. 2007. *Trusted Criminals: White-Collar Crime in Contemporary Society* (3rd ed.). Belmont, CA: Wadsworth/Thomson.

Froming, W. J., G. R. Walker, and K. J. Lopyan. 1982. "Public and Private Self-Awareness: When Personal Attitudes Conflict with Societal Expectations." *Journal of Experimental Social Psychology* 18: 476–487.

Fuerbringer, Jonathan, and William K. Rashbaum. 2003. "Currency Fraud Ran Deep, Officials Say." *New York Times*, November 11, C1.

Gardner, Margo, and Laurence Steinberg. 2005. "Peer Influence on Risk Taking, Risk Preference, and Risky Decision Making in Adolescence and Adulthood: An Experimental Study." *Developmental Psychology* 41: 625–635.

Geis, Gilbert. 2000. "On the Absence of Self-Control as the Basis for a General Theory of Crime: A Critique." *Theoretical Criminology* 4 (1): 35–53.

Geis, Gilbert, and Ivan Bunn. 1997. *A Trial of Witches: A Seventeenth-Century Witchcraft Prosecution*. London: Routledge.

Geis, Gilbert, and Colin Goff. 1983. "Introduction." In Edwin H. Sutherland, *White Collar Crime: The Uncut Version*. New Haven, CT: Yale University Press, ix–xxxiii.

Gendreau, Paul, and Robert R. Ross. 1986. "Effective Correctional Treatment: Bibliotherapy for Cynics." *Crime and Delinquency* 25: 463–489.

Gerstel, Naomi, and Sally K. Gallagher. 2001. "Men's Caregiving: Gender and the Contingent Character of Care." *Gender and Society* 15 (April): 197–217.

Gibbons, Don. 1965. *Changing the Lawbreaker*. Englewood Cliffs, NJ: Prentice Hall.

———. 1994. *Talking About Crime and Criminal Problems and Issues in Theory Development in Criminology*. Englewood, NJ: Prentice Hall.

Gibbs, Jack. 1987. "The State of Criminological Theory." *Criminology* 25 (November): 821–840.

Gibbs, John J., and Dennis Giever. 1995. "Self-Control and Its Manifestation Among University Students: An Empirical Test of Gottfredson and Hirschi's General Theory." *Justice Quarterly* 12 (June): 231–255.

Gibbs, John J., Dennis Giever, and Jamie S. Martin. 1998. "Parental Management and Self-Control: An Empirical Test of Gottfredson and Hirschi's General Theory." *Journal of Research in Crime and Delinquency* 35 (1): 40–70.

Giddens, Anthony. 1976. *New Rules of Sociological Method: A Positive Critique of Interpretative Sociologies.* London: Hutchinson.

Gleick, James. 1993. *Genius: The Life and Science of Richard Feynman.* New York: Viking.

Glueck, Sheldon, and Eleanor Glueck. 1950. *Unraveling Juvenile Delinquency.* Cambridge, MA: Harvard University Press.

———. 1962. *Family Environment and Delinquency.* Boston: Houghton-Mifflin.

Goffman, Erving. 1963. *Stigma: Notes on the Management of Spoiled Identity.* Englewood Cliffs, NJ: Prentice-Hall/Spectrum.

Goldstein, Paul J. 1985. "The Drugs/Violence Nexus: A Tripartite Conceptual Framework." *Journal of Drug Issues* 15 (fall): 493–506.

Goldstein, Paul J., et al. 1989. "Crack in Homicide in New York City, 1988: A Conceptually Based Event Analysis." *Contemporary Drug Problems* 16 (winter): 651–687.

Goldstein, Paul J., Henry H. Brownstein, and Patrick J. Ryan. 1992. "Drug-Related Homicide in New York: 1984 and 1988." *Crime and Delinquency* 38 (October): 459–476.

Goode, Erich. 2005. *Deviant Behavior* (7th ed.). Upper Saddle River, NJ: Prentice Hall.

———. 2008. *Deviant Behavior* (8th ed.). Upper Saddle River, NJ: Prentice Hall.

Gottfredson, Michael R. 2006. "The Empirical Status of Control Theory in Criminology." In Francis T. Cullen, John Paul Wright, and Kristie R. Blevins (eds.), *Taking Stock: The Status of Criminological Theory.* New Brunswick, NJ: Transaction, 77–100.

Gottfredson, Michael R., and Michael J. Hindelang. 1979. "A Study of the Behavior of Law." *American Sociological Review* 44 (1): 3–18.

Gottfredson, Michael R., and Travis Hirschi. 1989. "A Propensity-Event Theory of Crime." In William S. Laufer and Freda Adler (eds.), *Advances in Criminological Theory.* New Brunswick, NJ: Transaction, 57–67.

———. 1990. *A General Theory of Crime.* Stanford, CA: Stanford University Press.

———. 1993. "A Control Theory Interpretation of Psychological Research on Aggression." In Richard B. Felson and James T. Tedeschi (eds.), *Aggression and Violence: Social Interactionist Perspectives.* Washington, DC: American Psychological Association, 47–68.

———. 2003. "Social Control and Opportunity." In Chester L. Britt and Michael R. Gottfredson (eds.), *Control Theories of Crime and Delinquency.* New Brunswick, NJ: Transaction, 5–19.

Gough, Harrison G. 1948. "A Sociological Theory of Psychopathy." *American Journal of Sociology* 53: 359–366.

Gove, Walter. 1985. "The Effect of Age and Gender on Deviant Behavior: A Biopsychosocial Perspective." In Alice Rossi (ed.), *Gender and the Life Course.* New York: Aldine, 115–144.

Grapendaal, Martin, Ed Leuw, and Hans Nelen. 1995. *A World of Opportunities: Life-Style and Economic Behavior of Heroin Addicts in Amsterdam.* Albany: State University of New York Press.

Grasmick, Harold G., Charles R. Tittle, Robert J. Bursik Jr., and Bruce J. Arneklev. 1993. "Testing the Core Empirical Implications of Gottfredson and Hirschi's General Theory of Crime." *Journal of Research in Crime and Delinquency* 30 (1): 5–29.

Green, Penny J., and Tony Ward. 2004. *State Crime.* London: Pluto Press.

Greenberg, David F. 1977a. "The Correctional Effects of Corrections: A Survey of Evaluation Studies." In David F. Greenberg (ed.), *Corrections and Punishment*. Beverly Hills, CA: Sage, 111–148.

———. 1977b. "Delinquency and the Age Structure of Society." *Contemporary Crises* 1 (2): 189–224.

———. 1985. "Age, Crime, and Social Explanation." *American Journal of Sociology* 91 (1): 1–21.

———. 1999. "The Weak Strength of Social Control Theory." *Crime and Delinquency* 45 (1): 66–81.

———. 2004. "Comments on *Criminal Circumstances*." Paper presented to the American Society of Criminology, Nashville, TN.

Greenberg, David F., and Nancy Larkin. 1985. "Age-Cohort Analysis of Arrest Rates." *Journal of Quantitative Criminology* 1: 227–241.

Grey, Stephen, and Don Van Natta. 2005. "13 Within C.I.A. Sought by Italy in Kidnapping." *New York Times*, June 25, A1, A6.

Grunbaum, Jo Anne, et al. 2004. *Youth Risk Behavior Surveillance: United States, 2003*. Atlanta, GA: Centers for Disease Control and Prevention.

Hagan, John. 1989. *Structural Criminology*. New Brunswick, NJ: Rutgers University Press.

Hagan, John, A. R. Gillis, and John Simpson. 1990. "Clarifying and Extending Power-Control Theory." *American Journal of Sociology* 95: 1024–1037.

Hagan, John, John Simpson, and A. R. Gillis. 1987. "Class in the Household: A Power-Control Theory of Gender and Delinquency." *American Journal of Sociology* 92 (4): 788–816.

Hanson, Norwood R. 1972. *Patterns of Discovery: An Inquiry into the Conceptual Foundations of Science*. Cambridge, U.K.: Cambridge University Press.

Harada, Yutaka. 1988. "Age's Impact May Not Be Stable: An Analysis of Age-Crime Relations in Japan." Unpublished.

Hare, Robert D. 1993. *Without Conscience: The Disturbing World of the Psychopaths Among Us*. New York: Pocket Books.

Harris, Judith Rich. 1995. "Where Is the Child's Environment? A Group Socialization Theory of Development." *Psychological Review* 102: 458–489.

———. 1998. *The Nurture Assumption: Why Children Turn Out the Way They Do*. New York: Free Press.

Hart, Jenifer. 1998. *Ask Me No More: An Autobiography*. London: Peter Halban.

Hartshorne, Hugh, and Mark A. May. 1929. *Studies in Deceit*. New York: Macmillan.

Hartsock, Nancy C. M. 1985. *Money, Sex and Power*. Boston: Northeastern University Press.

Hay, Carter. 2001. "Parenting, Self-Control, and Delinquency: A Test of Self-Control Theory." *Criminology* 39: 707–736.

Hay, Carter, and Walter Forrest. 2006. "The Development of Self-Control: Examining Self-Control's Stability Thesis." *Criminology* 44 (November): 739–774.

Haynie, Dana. 2001. "Delinquent Peers Revisited: Does Network Structure Matter?" *American Journal of Sociology* 106: 1013–1057.

Hays, Constance L., and Leslie Eaton. 2004. "Stewart Found Guilty of Lying in Sale of Stock." *New York Times*, March 6, A1f.

Heidenreich, Martin. 2001. "Innovation und Kultur in Europaischer Perspektiv." Accessed July 7, 2006, at http://www.uni-bamberg.de/sowi/europastudien/innovationskulturen .htm

Heiman, Michael K. 1997. "Ours Is Not to Question Why, Ours Is to Quantify." *Journal of Planning Education and Research* 16 (summer): 301–303.

Heitgerd, Janet L., and Robert J. Bursik Jr. 1987. "Extracommunity Dynamics and the Ecology of Delinquency." *American Journal of Sociology* 92: 775–787.

Henry, Stuart, and Mark M. Lanier (eds.). 2001. *What Is Crime? Controversies over the Nature of Crime and What to Do About It.* Lanham, MD: Rowman & Littlefield.

Herrnstein, Richard J. 1995. "Criminogenic Traits." In James Q. Wilson and Joan Petersillia (eds.), *Crime.* San Francisco: ICS Press, 39–63.

Hersch, Joni. 1996. "Smoking, Seat Belts, and Other Risky Consumer Decisions: Differences by Gender and Race." *Managerial and Decision Economics* 17: 471–481.

Heymann, H. G., and Robert Bloom. 1990. *Opportunity Cost in Finance and Accounting.* New York: Quorum.

Higgins, George E. 2004. "Gender and Self-Control Theory: Are There Differences in the Measures and the Theory's Causal Model?" *Criminal Justice Studies* 17: 33–55.

Higgins, George E., and Melissa L. Ricketts. 2004. "Motivation or Opportunity: Which Serves as the Best Mediator in Self-Control Theory?" *Western Criminology Review* 5 (2): 77–96.

Higgins, George E., and Richard Tewksbury. 2006. "Self and Self-Control." *Youth and Society* 37: 479–503.

Hindelang, Michael J. 1979. "Sex Differences in Criminal Activity." *Social Problems* 27: 143–156.

Hindelang, Michael J., Michael R. Gottfredson, and James Garofalo. 1978. *Victims of Personal Crime.* Cambridge, MA: Ballinger.

Hindelang, Michael J., Travis Hirschi, and Joseph G. Weis. 1981. *Measuring Delinquency.* Beverly Hills, CA: Sage.

Hindmarch, Ian, and Rüdiger Brinkmann. 1999. "Trends in the Use of Alcohol and Other Drugs in Cases of Sexual Assault." *Human Psychopharmacology: Clinical and Experimental* 14 (4): 225–231.

Hirschi, Travis. 1969. *Causes of Delinquency.* Berkeley: University of California Press.

———. 1973. "Procedural Rules and the Study of Deviant Behavior." *Social Problems* 21 (2): 169–173.

———. 1979. "Separate and Unequal Is Better." *Journal of Research in Crime and Delinquency* 16: 34–38.

———. 1989. "Exploring Alternatives to Integrated Theory." In Steven F. Messner, Marvin D. Krohn, and Allen E. Liska (eds.), *Theoretical Integration in the Study of Deviance and Crime: Problems and Prospects.* Albany: State University of New York Press, 37–49.

———.1994. "Family." In Travis Hirschi and Michael R. Gottfredson (eds.), *The Generality of Deviance.* New Brunswick, NJ: Transaction, 47–69.

———. 1996. "Theory Without Ideas: Reply to Akers." *Criminology* 34: 249–256.

———. 2002a. *The Craft of Criminology: Selected Papers*, John H. Laub (ed.). New Brunswick, NJ: Transaction.

———. 2002b. "Introduction to the Transaction Edition." In Travis Hirschi, *Causes of Delinquency*. New Brunswick, NJ: Transaction, ix–xx.

———. 2004. "Self-Control and Crime." In Roy F. Baumeister and Kathleen D. Vohs (eds.), *Handbook of Self-Regulation: Research, Theory, and Applications*. New York: Guilford Press, 537–552.

———. 2006a. "Foreword." In Stefan Schulz, *Beyond Self-Control*. Berlin: Duncker & Humboldt, v–vii.

———. 2006b. "Social Control and Self-Control Theory." In Stuart Henry and Mark M. Lanier (eds.), *The Essential Criminology Reader*. Boulder, CO: Westview, 111–128.

Hirschi, Travis, and Michael R. Gottfredson. 1983. "Age and the Explanation of Crime." *American Journal of Sociology* 89: 552–584.

———. 1986. "The Distinction Between Crime and Criminality." In Timothy F. Hartnagel and Robert A. Silverman (eds.), *Critique and Explanation: Essays in Honor of Gwynne Nettler*. New Brunswick, NJ: Transaction, 55–69.

———. 1987. "Causes of White Collar Crime." *Criminology* 25 (1): 949–974.

———. 1990. "Substantive Positivism and the Idea of Crime." *Rationality and Society* 2: 412–428.

———. 1993. "Commentary: Testing the General Theory of Crime." *Journal of Research in Crime and Delinquency* 30 (February): 47–54.

———. 1994a. "The Generality of Deviance." In Travis Hirschi and Michael R. Gottfredson (eds.), *The Generality of Deviance*. New Brunswick, NJ: Transaction, 1–22.

———. 1994b. "Substantive Positivism and the Idea of Crime." In Travis Hirschi and Michael Gottfredson (eds.), *The Generality of Deviance*. New Brunswick, NJ: Transaction, 253–269.

———. 1995. "Control Theory and the Life-Course Perspective." *Studies on Crime and Crime Prevention* 4 (2): 131–142.

———. 2000. "In Defense of Self-Control." *Theoretical Criminology* 4 (1): 55–69.

———. 2001. "Self-Control Theory." In Raymond Paternoster and Ronet Bachman (eds.), *Explaining Criminals and Crime: Essays in Contemporary Criminological Theory*. Los Angeles, CA: Roxbury, 81–96.

———. 2003. "Punishment of Children from the Perspective of Control Theory." In Chester L. Britt and Michael R. Gottfredson (eds.), *Control Theories of Crime and Delinquency*. New Brunswick, NJ: Transaction, 151–160.

———. 2004. "In Defense of Self-Control." *Theoretical Criminology* 4 (1): 55–69.

———. 2006. "Social Control and Self-Control Theory." In Stuart Henry and Mark M. Lanier (eds.), *The Essential Criminology Reader*. Boulder, CO: Westview Press, 111–128.

Hirschi, Travis, and Michael J. Hindelang. 1977. "Intelligence and Delinquency: A Revisionist Review." *American Sociological Review* 42: 571–587.

Hirschman, Albert O. 1992. *Rival Views of Market Society and Other Recent Essays*. Cambridge, MA: Harvard University Press.

Hochstetler, Andy. 2001. "Opportunities and Decisions: Interactional Dynamics in Robbery and Burglary Groups." *Criminology* 39: 737–763.

Hoffman, Bruce. 1998. *Inside Terrorism*. New York: Columbia University Press.

Hooper, Melissa. 1996. "When Domestic Violence Diversion Is No Longer an Option: What to Do with the Female Offender." *Berkeley Women's Law Journal* 6: 168–181.

Hooton, Earnest A. 1939a. *The American Criminal.* Cambridge, MA: Harvard University Press.

———. 1939b. *Crime and the Man.* Cambridge, MA: Harvard University Press.

Hope, Trina L., Harold G. Grasmick, and Laura J. Pointon. 2003. "The Family in Gottfredson and Hirschi's General Theory of Crime: Structure, Parenting, and Self-Control." *Sociological Focus* 36: 291–311.

Horowitz, Ruth. 1983. *Honor and the American Dream.* New Brunswick, NJ: Rutgers University Press.

Hough, Michael. 1987. "Offenders' Choice of Target: Findings from Victim Surveys." *Journal of Quantitative Criminology* 3: 355–369.

Howe, Mark DeWolfe. 1957. *Justice Oliver Wendell Holmes: The Shaping Years, 1841–1870.* Cambridge, MA: Harvard University Press.

Howell, Nancy Lee. 1969. *The Search for an Abortionist.* Chicago: University of Chicago Press.

Hubbard, Robert L., et al. 1989. *Drug Abuse Treatment: A National Study of Effectiveness.* Chapel Hill, NC: University of North Carolina Press.

Hwang, Sunghyun, and Ronald L. Akers. 2003. "Substance Use by Korean Adolescents: A Cross-Cultural Test of Social Learning, Social Bonding, and Self-Control Theories." In Ronald L. Akers and Gary F. Jensen (eds.), *Social Learning Theory and the Explanation of Crime: A Guide for the New Century.* New Brunswick, NJ: Transaction, 39–63.

Inciardi, James A. 1992. *The War on Drugs II: The Continuing Epic of Heroin, Cocaine, AIDS, and Public Policy.* Mountain View, CA: Mayfield.

———. 2002. *The War on Drugs III: The Continuing Saga of the Mysteries and Miseries of Intoxication, Addiction, Crime, and Public Policy.* Boston: Allyn & Bacon.

Inciardi, James A., Dorothy Lockwood, and Anne E. Pottieger. 1993. *Women and Crack-Cocaine.* New York: Macmillan.

Izzo, R. L., and Robert R. Ross (1990). "Meta-Analysis of Rehabilitation Programmes for Juvenile Delinquents." *Criminal Justice and Behavior* 17: 134–142.

Jackall, Robert. 1988. *Moral Mazes: The World of Corporate Managers.* New York: Oxford University Press.

Jenkins, Ann, and John Braithwaite. 1993. "Profits, Pressure, and Corporate Law-Breaking." *Crime, Law, and Social Change* 20: 221–232.

Jianakoplos, Nancy Ammon, and Alexandra Benarsek. 1998. "Are Women More Risk Averse?" *Economic Inquiry* 36: 620–630.

Johnson, Bruce D. 1972. *Marihuana Users and Drug Subcultures.* New York: Wiley.

Johnson, Bruce D., et al. 1985. *Taking Care of Business: The Economics of Crime by Heroin Abusers.* Lexington, MA: Lexington Books.

Johnston, David C. 2003. *Perfectly Legal: The Covert Campaign to Rig Our Tax System to Benefit the Super Rich—and Cheat Everybody Else.* New York: Penguin Books.

Johnston, Lloyd D., Patrick M. O'Malley, Jerald G. Bachman, and J. E. Schlenberg. 2004. *Monitoring the Future: National Survey Results on Drug Use, 1975–2003,* v. 2, *College Students and Adults Ages 19–45.* Bethesda, MD: National Institute on Drug Abuse.

Junger, Marianne. 1994. "Accidents." In Travis Hirschi and Michael Gottfredson (eds.), *The Generality of Deviance.* New Brunswick, NJ: Transaction, 81–112.

Kanin, E. J. 1985. "Date Rapists: Differential Sexual Socialization and Relative Deprivation." *Archives of Sexual Behavior* 6: 67–76.

Katz, Jack. 1988. *Seductions of Crime: Moral and Sensual Attractions in Doing Evil.* New York: Basic Books.

Keane, Carl, Paul S. Maxim, and James J. Teevan. 1993. "Drinking and Driving, Self-Control, and Gender: Testing a General Theory of Crime." *Journal of Research in Crime and Delinquency* 30 (1): 30–46.

Kempf, K. L. 1987. "Specialization and the Criminal Career." *Criminology* 25: 399–420.

Kerr, Peter. 1991. "Vast Amount of Fraud Discovered in Worker's Compensation System." *New York Times*, February 6, A1.

Killias, Martin, and Juan Rabasa. 1997. "Weapons and Athletic Constitution as Factors Linked to Violence Among Male Juveniles: Findings from the Swiss Self-Reported Delinquency Project." *British Journal of Criminology* 37: 446–458.

Kitsuse, John I. 1972. "Deviance, Deviant Behavior, and Deviants: Some Conceptual Problems." In William J. Filstead (ed.), *An Introduction to Deviance: Readings in the Process of Making Deviants.* Chicago: Markham, 233–243.

Klein, Malcolm W. 1995. *The American Street Gang.* New York: Oxford University Press.

Kluger, Richard. 1996. *Ashes to Ashes: America's Hundred-Year Cigarette War—The Public Health and the Unabashed Triumph of Philip Morris.* New York: Alfred Knopf.

Kornhauser, Ruth. 1978. *Social Sources of Delinquency: An Appraisal of Analytic Models.* Chicago: University of Chicago Press.

Koss, Mary P., Christine A. Gidycz, and Nadine Wisniewski. 1987. "The Scope of Rape: Incidence and Prevalence of Sexual Aggression and Victimization in a National Sample of Higher Education Students." *Journal of Consulting and Clinical Psychology* 55 (2): 162–170.

Kreager, Derek A. 2004. "Strangers in the Halls: Isolation and Delinquency in School Networks." *Social Forces* 83: 351–390.

Kruttschnitt, Candace, Christopher Uggen, and Kelly Shelton. 2000. "Predictors of Desistance Among Sex Offenders: The Interaction of Formal and Informal Social Controls." *Justice Quarterly* 17: 61–87.

Ksir, Charles, Carl L. Hart, and Ray Oakley. 2006. *Drugs, Society, and Human Behavior* (11th ed.). New York: McGraw-Hill.

Kurz, Demie. 1997. "Doing Parenting: Mothers, Care Work, and Policy." In Terry Arendell (ed.), *Contemporary Parenting: Challenges and Issues.* Thousand Oaks, CA: Sage, 92–118.

Kuttner, Robert. 1996. *Everything for Sale: The Virtues and Limits of Markets.* New York: Knopf.

Labaton, Stephen. 2003. "Extensive Flaws at Mutual Funds Cited at Hearing." *New York Times*, November 4, A1f.

Labaton, Stephen, and D. Leonhardt. 2002. "Whispers Inside, Thunder Outside." *New York Times*, June 30, C1.

Labrie, Fernand, Alain Bélanger, Lionel Cusan, José-Luis Gomez, and Bernard Candas. 1997. "Marked Decline in Serum Concentrations of Adrenal C19 Sex Steroid Precursors and Conjugated Androgen Metabolites During Aging." *Journal of Clinical Endocrinology and Metabolism* 82 (8): 2396–2402.

LaGrange, Teresa C., and Robert A. Silverman. 1999. "Low Self-Control and Opportunity: Testing the General Theory of Crime as an Explanation for Gender Differences in Delinquency." *Criminology* 37 (February): 41–72.

Lamborn, S. D., N. S. Mounts, Lawrence Steinberg, and Sanford M. Dornbusch. 1991. "Patterns of Competence and Adjustment Among Adolescents from Authoritative, Authoritarian, Indulgent, and Neglectful Families." *Child Development* 62: 1049–1065.

Lattimore, P. K., C. A. Visher, and R. Linster. 1994. "Specialization in Juvenile Careers: Markov Results for a California Cohort." *Journal of Quantitative Criminology* 10: 291–316.

Laub, John H. 2002. "Introduction: The Life and Work of Travis Hirschi." In John H. Laub (ed.), *The Craft of Criminology: Selected Papers—Travis Hirschi*. New Brunswick, NJ: Transaction, xi–xlix.

Laub, John H., and Robert J. Sampson. 2003. *Shared Beginnings, Divergent Lives: Delinquent Boys to Age 70*. Cambridge, MA: Harvard University Press.

Lehti, Martti. 2004a. *Homicides, Homicide Offenders, and Victims in Finland in 1998–2002*. Helsinki, Finland: National Research Institute of Legal Policy.

———. 2004b. *Long-Term Trends in Homicidal Crime in Finland in 1750–2000*. Helsinki, Finland: National Research Institute of Legal Policy.

Levitt, Steven D., and Stephen J. Dubner. 2005. *Freakonomics: A Rogue Economist Explores the Hidden Side of Everything*. New York: William Morrow.

Levitt, Steven D., and Sudhir Alladi Venkatesh. 2000. "An Economic Analysis of a Drug-Selling Gang's Finances." *Quarterly Journal of Economics* 115: 755–789.

Lindesmith, Alfred R. 1938. "A Sociological Theory of Drug Addiction." *American Journal of Sociology* 43 (January): 593–613.

———. 1947. *Opiate Addiction*. Bloomington, IN: Principia Press.

———. 1965. *The Addict and the Law*. Bloomington: Indiana University Press.

Lipsey, Mark W. 1992. "Juvenile Delinquency Treatment: A Meta-Analytic Inquiry into the Variability of Effects." In T. Cook et al. (eds.), *Meta-Analysis for Explanation: A Casebook*. New York: Russell Sage, 83–127.

Lipton, Douglas, Robert Martinson, and Judith Wilks. 1975. *The Effectiveness of Correctional Treatment: A Survey of Treatment Evaluation Studies*. New York: Praeger.

Liska, Allen E. 1975. The *Consistency Controversy*. New York: Wiley.

Liska, Allen, Richard B. Felson, Mitch Chamlin, and William Baccaglini. 1984. "Estimating Attitude-Behavior Relations Within a Theoretical Specification." *Social Psychology Quarterly* 47: 15–23.

Loeber, Rolf, and Marc LeBlanc. 1990. "Toward a Developmental Criminology." *Crime and Justice* 12: 375–473.

———. 1998. "Developmental Criminology Updated." *Crime and Justice* 23: 115–198.

Loeber, Ralph, and Magda Stouthamer-Loeber. 1986. "Family Factors as Correlates and Predictors of Juvenile Conduct Problems and Delinquency." *Crime and Justice: An Annual Review of Research* 7: 29–150.

Long, Thomas. 1697. *A Review of Mr. Baxter's Life*. London: E. Whitlock.

Longshore, Douglas. 1998. "Self-Control and Criminal Opportunity: A Prospective Test of the General Theory of Crime." *Social Problems* 45 (1): 102–113.

Longshore, Douglas, Judith A. Stein, and Susan Turner. 1998. "Reliability and Validity of a Self-Control Measure: Rejoinder." *Criminology* 36: 175–182.

Longshore, Douglas, and Susan Turner. 1998. "Self-Control and Opportunity: Cross-Sectional Test of the General Theory of Crime." *Criminal Justice and Behavior* 25: 81–99.

Longshore, Douglas, Susan Turner, and Judith A. Stein. 1996. "Self-Control in a Criminal

Sample: An Examination of Construct Validity." *Criminology* 34 (May): 209–228.

Lösel, F. (1995). "The Efficacy of Correctional Treatment: A Review and Syntheses of Meta-Evaluations." In J. McGuire (ed.), *What Works: Reducing Reoffending—Guidelines for Research and Practice.* Chichester, U.K.: Wiley, 79–111.

Love, Sharon Redhawk. 2006. "Illicit Sexual Behavior: A Test of Self Control Theory." *Deviant Behavior* 27: 505–536.

Luckenbill, David F., and D. P. Doyle. 1989. "Structural Position and Violence: Developing a Cultural Explanation." *Criminology* 27: 419–436.

Lussier, Patrick, Jean Proulx, and Marc Leblanc. 2005. "Criminal Propensity, Deviant Sexual Interests, and Criminal Activity of Sexual Aggressors Against Women: A Comparison of Explanatory Models." *Criminology* 43 (February): 249–281.

Lynskey, Dana Peterson, L. Thomas Winfree, Finn-Aage Esbensen, and Dennis L. Clason. 2000. "Linking Gender, Minority Group Status, and Family Matter to Self-Control Theory: A Multivariate Analysis of Key Self-Control Concepts in a Youth-Gang Context." *Juvenile and Family Court Journal* 51: 1–19.

Maccoby, Eleanor E., and J. A. Martin. 1983. "Socialization in the Context of the Family: Parent-Child Interaction." In Paul Mussen and E. Mavis Hetherington (eds.), *Handbook of Child Psychology, Socialization, Personality and Social Development* (4th ed.). New York: Wiley, 1–101.

MacCoun, Robert, Beau Kilmer, and Peter Reuter. 2003. "Research on Drugs-Crime Linkages: The Next Generation." In *Toward a Drugs and Crime Research Agenda for the 21st Century.* Washington, DC: National Institute of Justice, 65–95.

MacDonald, John, Andrew Morral, and Alex R. Piquero. 2008. "Assessing the Effects of Social Desirability on Measures of Self-Control." Unpublished.

Maher, Lisa, and Richard Curtis. 1992. "Women on the Edge of Crime: Crack Cocaine and the Changing Contexts of Street-Level Sex Work in New York City." *Crime, Law, and Social Change* 18 (3): 221–258.

Marcus, Bernd. 2003. "An Empirical Examination of the Construct Validity of Two Alternative Self-Control Measures." *Educational and Psychological Measurement* 63: 674–706.

———. 2004a. "Antecedents of Counterproductive Behavior at Work: A General Perspective." *Journal of Applied Psychology* 89 (4): 647–660.

———. 2004b. "Self-Control in the General Theory of Crime: Theoretical Implications of a Measurement Problem." *Theoretical Criminology* 8: 33–55.

Marenin, Otwin, and Michael D. Reisig. 1995. "*A General Theory of Crime*: Patterns of Crime in Nigeria—An Explanation of Methodological Assumptions." *Journal of Criminal Justice* 23 (6): 501–518.

Markowitz, Fred, and Richard B. Felson. 1998. "Social-Demographic Differences in Attitudes and Violence." *Criminology* 36: 117–138.

Markusen, Eric. 1992. "Genocide and Modern War." In M. Dobkowski and I. Wallimann (eds.), *Genocide in Our Time.* Ann Arbor, MI: Pierian Press, 117–148.

Martin, Kimberly R. 2003. "Youths' Opportunities to Experiment Influence Later Use of Illegal Drugs." *NIDA Notes* 17 (January): 1–3.

Massoglia, Michael. 2006. "Desistance or Displacement: The Changing Patterns of Offending from Adolescence to Young Adulthood." *Journal of Quantitative Criminology* 22 (3): 193–215.

Matsueda, Ross. 1988. "The Current State of Differential Association Theory." *Crime and Delinquency* 34: 277–306.

———. 2007. "The Natural History of Social Disorganization Theory: A Critique of Kornhauser and a Research Agenda." Unpublished.

Matsueda, Ross L., and Kathleen Anderson. 1998. "The Dynamics of Peers and Delinquency." *Criminology* 36: 269–308.

Matsueda, Ross L., Kevin Drakulich, and Charis E. Kubrin. 2006. "Race and Neighborhood Codes of the Street." In Ruth D. Peterson, Lauren J. Krivo, and John Hagan (eds.), *The Many Colors of Crime: Inequalities of Race, Ethnicity, and Crime in America*. New York: New York University Press, 334–356.

Matza, David. 1964. *Delinquency and Drift*. New York: Wiley.

Maurois, André. 1957. *The Titans*, Gerard Hopkins (trans.). New York: Harper.

McBride, Duane C., and James A Swartz. 1990. "Drugs and Violence in the Age of Crack Cocaine." In Ralph Weisheit (ed.), *Drugs, Crime, and the Criminal Justice System*. Cincinnati, OH: Anderson, 141–169.

McCarthy, Bill, Diane Felmlee, and John Hagan. 2004. "A Few Good Friends: Gender, Context, and Crime." *Criminology* 42: 805–836.

McClure, S. M., D. I. Laibson, G. Loewenstein, and J. D. Cohen. 2004. "Separate Neural Systems Value Immediate and Delayed Monetary Rewards." *Science* 306: 503–507.

McMullen, John C. 1999. *A Test of Self-Control Theory Using General Patterns of Deviance*. Ph.D. dissertation, Department of Sociology, Virginia Polytechnic Institute and State University, Blacksburg..

Mead, George Herbert. 1934. *Mind, Self, and Society*. Chicago: University of Chicago Press.

Mehrabian, Albert. 1997. "Relations Among Personality Scales of Aggression, Violence, and Empathy: Validational Evidence Bearing on the Risk of Eruptive Violence Scale." *Aggressive Behavior* 23: 433–445.

Menard, Scott, and Delbert S. Elliott. 1994. "Delinquent Bonding, Moral Beliefs, and Illegal Behavior: A Three Wave Panel Model." *Justice Quarterly* 11: 173–188.

Merton, Robert K. 1938. "Social Structure and Anomie." *American Sociological Review* 3 (October): 672–682.

———. 1949. *Social Theory and Social Structure: Toward the Codification of Theory and Research*. Glencoe, IL: Free Press.

———. 1957. *Social Theory and Social Structure* (rev. and enlarged ed.). Glencoe, IL: Free Press.

———. 1964. "Anomie, Anomia, and Social Interaction." In Marshall B. Clinard (ed.), *Anomie and Deviant Behavior*. New York: Free Press, 213–242.

———. 1968. *Social Theory and Social Structure* (rev. ed.). New York: Free Press.

Messerschmidt, James W. 1993. *Masculinities and Crime*. Lanham, MD: Rowman & Littlefield.

Messner, Steven F., and Richard Rosenfeld. 1994. *Crime and the American Dream*. Belmont, CA: Wadsworth.

———. 2001. *Crime and the American Dream* (3rd ed.). Belmont, CA: Wadsworth.

———. 2006. "The Present and Future of Institutional-Anomie Theory." *Advances in Criminological Theory* 15: 127–148.

———. 2007. *Crime and the American Dream* (4th ed.). Belmont, CA: Wadsworth.

Miller, Alan S., and Rodney Stark. 2002. "Gender and Religiousness: Can Socialization Explanations Be Saved?" *American Journal of Sociology* 107: 1399–1423.

Miller, Earl K., and Jonathan D. Cohen. 2001. "An Integrative Theory of Prefrontal Cortex Function." *Annual Review of Neuroscience* 24: 167–202.

Miller, Jody. 2001. *One of the Guys: Girls, Gangs, and Gender.* New York: Oxford University Press.

Miller, Susan L. 2005. *Victims as Offenders: The Paradox of Women's Violence in Relationships.* New Brunswick, NJ: Rutgers University Press.

Miller, Susan L., and Cynthia Burack. 1993. "A Critique of Gottfredson and Hirschi's General Theory of Crime: Selective (In)attention to Gender and Power Positions." *Women and Criminal Justice* 4 (2): 115–134.

Mitchell, Ojmarrh, and Doris L. MacKenzie. 2006. "The Stability and Resiliency of Self-Control in a Sample of Incarcerated Offenders." *Crime and Delinquency* 52: 432–449.

Moffitt, Terrie E., Robert F. Krueger, Avshalom Caspi, and Jeff Fagan. 2000. "Partner Abuse and General Crime: How Are They the Same? How Are They Different?" *Criminology* 38: 199–232.

Monkonnen, Eric. 1975. *The Dangerous Classes: Crime and Poverty in Columbus, Ohio, 1860–1885.* Cambridge, MA: Harvard University Press.

———. 2001. *Murder in New York City.* Berkeley: University of California Press.

Moore, Joan, and John Hagedorn. 2001. *Female Gangs: A Focus on Research.* NCJ 186159. Washington, DC: U.S. Department of Justice.

Morris, Gregory D., Peter B. Wood, and R. Gregory Dunaway. 2006. "Self-Control, Native Traditionalism, and Native American Substance Use: Testing the Cultural Invariance of a General Theory of Crime." *Crime and Delinquency* 52: 572–598.

Morselli, Carlo, and Pierre Tremblay. 2004. "Criminal Achievement, Offender Networks, and the Benefits of Low Self-Control." *Criminology* 42 (August): 773–804.

Mosher, Clayton J., Terance D. Miethe, and Dretha M. Phillips. 2002. *The Mismeasure of Crime.* Thousand Oaks, CA: Sage.

Moss, B. A., C. R. Pitula, J. C. Campbell, and L. Salstead. 1997. "The Experience of Terminating an Abusive Relationship from an Anglo and African American Perspective: A Qualitative Descriptive Study." *Issues in Mental Health Nursing* 18: 433–454.

Mullis, Kary. 1998. *Dancing Naked in the Mind Field.* New York: Pantheon.

Muraven, Mark, R. Lorraine Collins, Saul Shiffman, and Jean A. Paty. 2005. "Daily Fluctuations in Self-Control Demands and Alcohol Intake." *Psychology of Addictive Behaviors* 19: 140–147.

Muraven, Mark, Greg Pogarsky, and Dikla Shmueli. 2006. "Self-Control Depletion and the General Theory of Crime." *Journal of Quantitative Criminology* 22: 263–277.

Nagin, Daniel S. 2007. "Moving Choice to Center Stage in Criminological Research and Theory." *Criminology* 45: 259–272.

Nagin, Daniel S., and Kenneth C. Land. 1993. "Age, Criminal Careers, and Population Heterogeneity: Specification and Estimation of a Nonparametric, Mixed Poisson Model." *Criminology* 31: 327–362.

Nagin, Daniel S., and Raymond Paternoster. 1991. "On the Relationship of Past and Future Participation in Delinquency." *Criminology* 29: 163–190.

Nagin, Daniel, and Richard E. Tremblay. 2005. "From Seduction to Passion: A Response to Sampson and Laub." *Criminology* 43 (4): 915–918.

Nakhaie, M. Reza, Robert A. Silverman, and Teresa C. LaGrange. 2000. "Self-Control and Social Control: An Examination of Gender, Ethnicity, Class, and Delinquency." *Canadian Journal of Sociology* 25 (1): 35–59.

National Highway Traffic Safety Administration. 1991. *Fatal Accidents Reporting System, 1989: A Review of Information on Fatal Traffic Crashes in the United States in 1989.* DOT Publication HS 807–693. Washington, DC: U.S. Government Printing Office.

National Institute on Drug Abuse. 2003. *Drug Use Among Racial/Ethnic Minorities* (rev. ed). Bethesda, MD: U.S. Department of Health and Human Services, National Institutes of Health.

National Marriage Project. 2001. *The State of Our Unions 2001: The Social Health of Marriage in America.* Newark, NJ: Rutgers University. Available at http://marriage.rutgers.edu/Publications/SOOU/NMPAR2001.pdf

Neiderhiser, Jenae M., David Reiss, E. Mavis Hetherington, and Robert Plomin. 1999. "Relationships Between Parenting and Adolescent Adjustment over Time: Genetic and Environmental Contributions." *Developmental Psychology* 35: 680–692.

Newman, Joseph P., C. M. Patterson, and D. S. Kosson. 1987. "Response Perseveration in Psychopaths." *Journal of Abnormal Psychology* 95: 145–148.

Nightingale, Carl Husemoller. 1993. *On the Edge: A History of Poor Black Children and Their American Dreams.* New York: Basic Books.

Nisbett, Richard, and Lee Ross. 1980. *Human Inference: Strategies and Shortcomings of Human Judgment.* Englewood Cliffs, NJ: Prentice-Hall.

Nurco, David N., et al. 1985. "The Criminality of Narcotic Addicts." *Journal of Nervous and Mental Disease* 173 (1): 112–116.

O'Brien, Robert M. 1985. *Crime and Victimization Data.* Beverly Hills, CA: Sage.

Office of Applied Statistics. 2004. *DAWN, 2003: Area Profiles of Drug-Related Mortality.* Rockville, MD: SAMHSA, Drug Abuse Warning Network.

Oppel, Richard A., Jr., and Andrew R. Sorkin. 2001. "Enron Admits to Overstating Its Profits by About $600 Million." *New York Times*, November 1, C1.

Orru, Marco. 1987. *Anomie: History and Meanings.* Boston: Allen & Unwin.

Osgood, D. Wayne, Lloyd D. Johnston, Patrick M. O'Malley, and Jerald G. Bachman. 1988. "The Generality of Deviance in Late Adolescence and Early Adulthood." *American Sociological Review* 53: 81–93.

Osgood, D. W., and Schreck, C. 2007. "A New Method for Studying the Extent, Stability, and Predictors of Individual Specialization in Violence." *Criminology* 45: 273–312.

Ousey, Graham, and Pamela Wilcox. 2007. "The Interaction of Antisocial Propensity and Life Course Varying Predictors of Delinquent Behavior: Differences by Method of Estimation and Implications for Theory." *Criminology* 25 (May): 313–353.

Park, Robert E. 1926. "The Urban Community as a Spatial Pattern and a Moral Order." In Ernest W. Burgess (ed.), *The Urban Community.* Chicago: University of Chicago Press, 3–18.

Parker, Robert Nash. 1995. *Alcohol and Homicide: A Deadly Combination of Two American Traditions.* Albany: State University of New York Press.

Parsons, Talcott. 1949 [1937]. *The Structure of Social Action.* New York: McGraw-Hill/Free Press.

Partnoy, Frank. 2003. *Infectious Greed: How Deceit and Risk Corrupted the Financial Markets.* New York: Times Books.

Passas, Nikos. 1990. "Anomie and Corporate Deviance." *Contemporary Crises* 14: 157–178.

Pastore, A. L., and K. Maguire (eds.). 2002. *Sourcebook of Criminal Statistics: 2001.* Washington, DC: U.S. Government Printing Office.

Paternoster, Raymond, and Robert Brame. 1997. "Multiple Routes to Delinquency? A Test of Developmental and General Theories of Crime." *Criminology* 35 (February): 49–84.

Paternoster, Ray, R. Brame, Alex Piquero, P. Mazerolle, and C. W. Dean. 1998. "The Forward Specialization Coefficient: Distributional Properties and Subgroup Differences." *Journal of Quantitative Criminology* 14: 133–154.

Patterson, Gerald R., and Thomas J. Dishion. 1985. "Contributions of Family and Peers to Delinquency." *Criminology* 23: 63–79.

Patterson, Gerald R., John B. Reid, and Thomas J. Dishion. 1992. *Antisocial Boys.* Eugene, OR: Castalia.

Payne, Brian K., and Randy R. Gainey. 2004. "Ancillary Consequences of Employee Theft." *Journal of Criminal Justice* 32: 63–73.

Pearce, Diana M. 1993. "The Feminization of Poverty: Update." In Allison Jaggar and Paula Rothenberg (eds.), *Feminist Frameworks* (3rd ed.). New York: McGraw Hill, 290–296.

Perrone, Dina, Christopher J. Sullivan, Travis C. Pratt, and Satenik Margaryan. 2004. "Parental Efficacy, Self-Control, and Delinquency: A Test of the General Theory of Crime on a Nationally Representative Sample of Youth." *International Journal of Offender Therapy and Comparative Criminology* 48: 298–312.

Piquero, Alex. 2000. "Frequency, Specialization, and Violence in Offending Careers." *Journal of Research in Crime and Delinquency* 37: 392–418.

Piquero, Alex R., and Jeffrey Bouffard. 2007. "Something Old, Something New: A Preliminary Investigation of Hirschi's Redefined Self-Control." *Justice Quarterly* 24: 1–24.

Piquero, Alex R., John MacDonald, Adam Dobrin, Leah E. Daigle, and Francis T. Cullen. 2005. "Self-Control, Violent Offending, and Homicide Victimization: Assessing the General Theory of Crime." *Journal of Quantitative Criminology* 21: 55–72.

Piquero, Alex R., Randall MacIntosh, and Matthew Hickman. 2000. "Does Self-Control Affect Survey Response? Applying Exploratory, Confirmatory, and Item Response Theory Analysis to Grasmick et al.'s Self-Control Scale." *Criminology* 38: 897–929.

Piquero, Alex R., Terrie E. Moffitt, and Bradley E. Wright. 2007. "Self-Control and Criminal Career Dimensions." *Journal of Contemporary Criminal Justice* 23: 72–89.

Piquero, Alex R., and Andre Rosay. 1998. "The Reliability and Validity of Grasmick et al.'s Self-Control Scale: A Comment on Longshore et al." *Criminology* 36: 157–174.

Piquero, Alex, and Stephen Tibbetts. 1996. "Specifying the Direct and Indirect Effects of Low Self-Control, and Situational Factors in Offenders' Decision Making: Toward a More Complete Model of Rational Offending." *Justice Quarterly* 13: 481–510.

Piquero, Nicole L., M. Lyn Exum, and Sally S. Simpson. 2005. "Integrating the Desire-for-Control and Rational Choice in a Corporate Crime Context." *Justice Quarterly* 22: 252–280.

Piquero, Nicole L., Lynn Langton, and Andrea Schoepfer. 2008. "Completely Out of Control or the Desire to Be in Complete Control? An Examination of Low Self-Control and the Desire-for-Control." Unpublished.

Polakowski, Michael. 1994. "Licking Self- and Social Control with Deviance: Illuminating the Structure Underlying the General Theory of Crime and Its Relation to Deviant Activity." *Journal of Quantitative Criminology* 10 (1): 41–78.

Polatnik, M. Rivka. 1983. "Why Men Don't Rear Children: A Power Analysis." In Joyce Trebilcot (ed.), *Mothering: Essays in Feminist Theory*. Savage, MD: Rowman & Littlefield, 21–40.

Polgar, Steven, and Ellen S. Fried. 1976. "The Bad Old Days: Clandestine Abortions Among the Poor in New York City Before Liberalization of the Abortion Law." *Family Planning Perspectives* 8 (May): 125–127.

Polk, Kenneth. 1991. "Review of *A General Theory of Crime*." *Crime and Delinquency* 37 (October): 575–581.

Pratt, Travis C., Kristie R. Blevins, Leah E. Daigle, Francis T. Cullen, and James D. Unnever. 2002. "The Relationship of ADHD to Crime and Delinquency: A Meta-Analysis." *International Journal of Police Science and Management* 4: 344–360.

Pratt, Travis C., and Francis T. Cullen. 2000. "The Empirical Status of Gottfredson and Hirschi's General Theory of Crime: A Meta-Analysis." *Criminology* 38 (3): 931–964.
———. 2005. "Assessing Macro-Level Predictors and Theories of Crime: A Meta-Analysis." *Crime and Justice: A Review of Research* 32: 373–450.

Pratt, Travis C., Michael G. Turner, and Alex R. Piquero. 2004. "Parental Socialization and Community Context: A Longitudinal Analysis of the Structural Sources of Low Self-Control." *Journal of Research on Crime and Delinquency* 41: 219–243.

President's Commission on Law Enforcement and Administration of Justice. 1967. *Task Force Assessment*. Washington, DC: U.S. Government Printing Office.

Proctor, Bernadette D., and Joseph Dalaker. 2002. *Poverty in the United States: 2001*. Washington, DC: U.S. Census Bureau.

Pyett, P. M., and D. J. Warr. 1999. "Women at Risk in Sex Work: Strategies for Survival." *Journal of Sociology* 35 (2): 183–197.

Rafter, Nicole. 2004. "Earnest A. Hooton and the Biological Tradition in American Criminology." *Criminology* 42 (August): 735– 771.

Raine, Adrian. 2002. "The Biological Basis of Crime." In James Q. Wilson and Joan Petersilia (eds.), *Crime: Public Policies for Crime Control*. Oakland, CA: ICS Press, 43–74.

Raine, Adrian, P. A. Brennan, Donald P. Farrington, and S. A. Mednick. 1997. *Biosocial Bases of Violence*. New York: Plenum Press.

Rand, Michael R., James P. Lynch, and David Cantor. 1997. *Criminal Victimization, 1973–95*. Washington, DC: Bureau of Justice Statistics.

Rathgeber, Bob. 1982. *Lights Out for the Shine Ball: Hod Eller*. Virginia Beach, VA: JCP Corp. of Virginia.

Reagan, Patricia, and Joni Hersch. 2005. "Influence of Race, Gender, and Socioeconomic Status on Binge Eating Frequency in a Population-Based Sample." *International Journal of the Eating Disorders* 38: 252–256.

Reed, Gary E., and Peter Cleary Yeager. 1996. "Organizational Offending and Neoclassical

Criminology: Challenging the Reach of a General Theory of Crime." *Criminology* 34: 357–377.

Richards, Pamela, and Charles R. Tittle. 1981. "Gender and Perceived Chances of Arrest." *Social Forces* 59 (4): 1182–1199.

Richie, Beth. 1996. *Compelled to Crime: The Gender Entrapment of Black Battered Women.* New York: Routledge.

Riesman, David. 1957. "Law and Sociology: Notes on Recruitment, Training, and Colleagueship." *Stanford Law Review* 9 (July): 643–673.

Ritter, Lawrence S. 1966. *The Glory of Their Times: The Story of the Early Days of Baseball Told by the Men Who Played It.* New York: Macmillan.

Robins, Lee, and Kathryn S. Ratcliff. 1978. "Risk Factors in the Continuation of Childhood Antisocial Behavior into Adulthood." *International Journal of Mental Health* 7: 76–116.

Romero, Estrella, Antonio J. Gomez-Fraguela, Angeles M. Luengo, and Jorge Sobral. 2003. "The Self-Control Theory Construct in the General Theory of Crime: An Investigation in Terms of Personality Psychology." *Psychology, Crime, and Law* 9: 61–86.

Rosenfeld, Richard, and Steven F. Messner. 2006. "The Origins, Nature, and Prospects of Institutional-Anomie Theory." In Stuart Henry and Mark Lanier (eds.), *The Essential Criminology Reader.* Boulder, CO: Westview, 164–173.

Rosoff, Stephen M., Henry R. Pontell, and Robert Tillman. 2006. *Profit Without Honor: White-Collar Crime and the Looting of America* (4th ed.). Upper Saddle River, NJ: Prentice Hall.

Rowe, David C. 1994. *The Limits of Family Influence: Genes, Experience, and Behavior.* New York: Guilford.

Rowe, David C., D. Wayne Osgood, and Alan W. Nicewander. 1990. "A Latent Trait Approach to Unifying Criminal Careers." *Criminology* 28: 237–270.

Ruff, Julius R. 1984. *Crime, Justice, and Public Order in Old Regime France: The Sénéchaussée of Libourne and Bazes, 1696–1789.* London: Croom Helm.

Sachs, Susan. 2004. "Hussein's Regime Skimmed Billions from Aid Program." *New York Times*, February 29, A1.

Sampson, Robert J. 2004. "Neighborhood and Community: Collective Efficacy and Community Safety." *New Economy* 11: 106–113.

Sampson, Robert J., and W. Byron Groves. 1989. "Community Structure and Crime: Testing Social-Disorganization Theory." *American Journal of Sociology* 94: 774–802.

Sampson, Robert J., and John H. Laub. 1993. *Crime in the Making: Pathways and Turning Points Through Life.* Cambridge, MA: Harvard University Press.

———. 1994. "Urban Poverty and the Family Context of Delinquency: A New Look at Structure and Process in a Classic Study." *Child Development* 65: 523–540.

———. 1995. "Understanding Variability in Lives Through Time: Contributions of Life-Course Criminology." *Studies on Crime and Crime Prevention* 4: 143–158.

Sampson, Robert J., John H. Laub, and Christopher Wimer. 2006. "Does Marriage Reduce Crime? A Counterfactual Approach to Within-Individual Causal Effects." *Criminology* 44: 465–506.

Sampson, Robert J., Jeffrey Morenoff, and Felton Earls. 1999. "Beyond Social Capital: Spatial Dynamics of Collective Efficacy for Children." *American Sociological Review* 64: 633–660.

Sampson, Robert J., Steven W. Raudenbush, and Felton Earls. 1997. "Neighborhoods and Violent Crime: A Multilevel Study of Collective Efficacy." *Science* 277 (August 15): 918–923.

Sanchez, Lisa. 2001. "Gender Troubles: The Entanglement of Agency, Violence, and Law in the Lives of Women in Prostitution." In Claire M. Renzetti and Lynne Goodstein (eds.), *Women, Crime, and Criminal Justice: Original Feminist Readings.* Los Angeles: Roxbury, 60–76.

Sanday, Peggy Reeves. 1996. *A Woman Scorned: Acquaintance Rape on Trial.* Berkeley: University of California Press.

———. 2007. *Fraternity Gang Rape: Sex, Brotherhood and Privilege on Campus* (2nd ed.). New York: New York University Press.

Scarr, Sandra, and Kathleen McCartney. 1983. "How People Make Their Own Environments: A Theory of Genotype × Environment Effects." *Child Development* 54: 424–435.

Schasre, Robert. 1966. "Cessation Patterns Among Neophyte Heroin Users." *International Journal of the Addictions* 1 (June): 23–32.

Scheier, M. F., A. Fenigstein, and A. H. Buss. 1974. "Self-Awareness and Physical Aggression." *Journal of Experimental Social Psychology* 10: 264–273.

Schichor, A., A. Beck, B. Bernstein, and B. Crabtree. 1990. "Seat Belt Use and Stress in Adolescents." *Adolescence* 25: 773–779.

Schulz, Stefan. 2006. *Beyond Self-Control: Analysis and Critique of Gottfredson and Hirschi's General Theory of Crime.* Berlin: Duncker & Humbolt.

Schur, Edwin M. 1962. *Narcotic Addiction in Britain and America: The Impact of Public Policy.* Bloomington: Indiana University Press.

Schwartz, Mimi, and Sharon Watkins. 2003. *Power Failure: The Inside Story of the Collapse of Enron.* New York: Doubleday.

Scully, Diana. 1990. *Understanding Sexual Violence: A Study of Convicted Rapists.* New York: Routledge.

Sellers, Christine S. 1999. "Self-Control and Intimate Violence: An Examination of the Scope and Specification of the General Theory of Crime." *Criminology* 37 (2): 375–404.

Seltzer, Judith A. 1991. "Relationships Between Fathers and Children Who Live Apart: The Father's Role After Separation." *Journal of Marriage and the Family* 53: 79–101.

Shavit, Yossi, and Aryeh Rattner. 1988. "Age, Crime, and the Early Life Course." *American Journal of Sociology* 93: 1457–1470.

Shaw, Clifford R., and Henry D. McKay. 1929. *Delinquency Areas.* Chicago: University of Chicago Press.

Shaw, Clifford R., and Henry D. McKay. 1931. *Social Factors in Juvenile Delinquency.* Report on the Causes of Crime, v. 2, of the National Commission on Law Observance and Enforcement. Washington, DC: U.S. Government Printing Office.

———. 1942. *Juvenile Delinquency and Urban Areas.* Chicago: University of Chicago Press.

———. 1972. *Juvenile Delinquency and Urban Areas* (rev. ed.). Chicago: University of Chicago Press.

Shaw, Clifford R., Frederick M. Zorbaugh, Henry D. McKay, and Leonard S. Cottrell. 1929. *Delinquency Areas.* Chicago: University of Chicago Press.

Short, James F., Jr., and Fred L. Strodtbeck. 1965. *Group Process and Gang Delinquency.* Chicago: University of Chicago.

Shover, Neal. 1985. *Aging Criminals.* Beverly Hills, CA: Sage.

———. 1996. *Great Pretenders: Pursuits and Careers of Persistent Thieves.* Boulder, CO: Westview.

Shover, Neal, and Kevin M. Bryant. 1993. "Theoretical Explanations of Corporate Crime." In Michael B. Blankenship (ed.), *Understanding Corporate Criminality.* New York: Garland, 141–176.

Simmons, Roberta G., and Dale A. Blyth. 1987. *Moving into Adolescence: The Impact of Pubertal Change and School Context.* New York: Aldine de Gruyter.

Simpson, Sally, and Nicole Leeper Piquero. 2002. "Low Self-Control, Organizational Theory, and Corporate Crime." *Law and Society Review* 36: 509–547.

Sipe, Beth, and Evelyn J. Hall. 1996. *I Am Not Your Victim: Anatomy of Domestic Violence.* Thousand Oaks, CA: Sage.

Siranni, Carmen, and Cynthia Negrey. 2000. "Working Time as Gendered Time." *Feminist Economics* 6 (March): 59–76.

Sloan, Allan. 2001. "Lights Out for Enron." *Newsweek*, December 10, 50–51.

Smith, Dorothy E. 1990. *The Conceptual Practices of Power: A Feminist Sociology of Knowledge.* Boston: Northeastern University Press.

Smith, Douglas A., and Christy A. Visher. 1980. "Sex and Involvement in Deviance/Crime: A Quantitative Review of the Empirical Literature." *American Sociological Review* 45: 691–701.

Smith, Tony R. 2004. "Low Self-Control, Staged Opportunity, and Subsequent Fraudulent Behavior." *Criminal Justice and Behavior* 31: 542–563.

Sorensen, David W. M. 1994. "Motor Vehicle Accidents." In Travis Hirschi and Michael Gottfredson (eds.), *The Generality of Deviance.* New Brunswick, NJ: Transaction, 113–147.

Spahr, Lisa L., and Laurence J. Alison. 2004. "U.S. Savings and Loan Fraud: Implications for General and Criminal Culture Theories of Crime." *Crime, Law, and Social Change* 41: 95–106.

Steffensmeier, Darrell J. 1989. "On the Causes of 'White-Collar' Crime." *Criminology* 27: 359–372.

Steffensmeier, Darrell J., and Emilie Allen. 1991. "Gender, Age, and Crime." In Joseph F. Sheley (ed.), *Criminology: A Contemporary Handbook.* Belmont, CA: Wadsworth, 67–93.

Steffensmeier, Darrell J., Emilie Andersen Allen, Miles D. Harer, and Cathy Streifel. 1989. "Age and the Distribution of Crime." *American Journal of Sociology* 94: 803–831.

Stelzer, Irwin M. 2004. "The Corporate Scandals and American Capitalism." *Public Interest* (Winter): 19–31.

Sullivan, Christopher J., Jean Marie McCloin, Travis C. Pratt, and Alex Piquero. 2006. "Rethinking the 'Norm' of Offender Generality: Investigating Specialization in the Short-Term." *Criminology* 44 (February): 199–233.

Sutherland, Edwin H. 1939. *Principles of Criminology* (3rd ed.). Philadelphia: Lippincott.

———. 1947. *Principles of Criminology* (4th ed.). Philadelphia: Lippincott.

———. 1949. *White-Collar Crime.* New York: Holt, Rinehart & Winston.

———. 1956. "Critique of the Theory: The Swan Song of Differential Association." In Albert Cohen, Alfred Lindesmith, and Karl Schuessler (eds.), *The Sutherland Papers.* Bloomington: Indiana University Press, 30–41.

Sutherland, Edwin H., and Donald R. Cressey. 1978. *Criminology*. Philadelphia: Lippincott.

Sykes, Gresham, and David Matza. 1957. "Techniques of Neutralization: A Theory of Delinquency." *American Sociological Review* 22: 664–670.

Taylor, Ian, Paul Walton, and Jock Young. 1973. *The New Criminology: For a Social Theory of Deviance*. London: Routledge & Kegan Paul.

Tedeschi, James, and Richard B. Felson. 1994. *Violence, Aggression, and Coercive Actions*. Washington, DC: American Psychological Association.

Thomas, Helen S. 1960. *Felix Frankfurter: Scholar on the Bench*. Baltimore: Johns Hopkins University Press.

Thomas, William I. 1923. *The Unadjusted Girl*. Boston: Little, Brown.

Thomas, William I., and Dorothy Swaine Thomas. 1928. *The Child in America*. New York: Knopf.

Thomas, William I., and Florian Znaniecki. 1958 [1927]. *The Polish Peasant in Europe and America*, 2 vols. New York: Dover.

Thornberry, Terence P., Marvin D. Krohn, Alan J. Lizotte, and Deborah J. Chard-Wierschem. 1993. "The Role of Juvenile Gangs in Promoting Delinquent Behavior." *Journal of Research in Crime and Delinquency* 30 (1): 55–87.

Thornberry, Terence P., Marvin D. Krohn, Alan J. Lizotte, Carolyn A. Smith, and Kimberly Tobin. 2003. *Gangs and Delinquency in Developmental Perspective*. Cambridge, U.K.: Cambridge University Press.

Thrasher, Frederic M. 1927. *The Gang*. Chicago: University of Chicago Press.

Tittle, Charles R. 1991. "Review of *A General Theory of Crime*." *American Journal of Sociology* 96 (May): 1609–1611.

———. 1995. *Control Balance: Toward a General Theory of Deviance*. Boulder, CO: Westview.

Tittle, Charles R., and Ekaterina V. Botchkovar. 2005. "Self-Control, Criminal Motivation, and Deterrence: An Investigation Using Russian Respondents." *Criminology* 43 (May): 307–353.

Tittle, Charles R., and Harold G. Grasmick. 1997. "Criminal Behavior and Age: A Test of Three Provocative Hypotheses." *Journal of Criminal Law and Criminology* 88 (Autumn): 309–342.

Tittle, Charles R., David A. Ward, and Harold G. Grasmick. 2003a. "Gender, Age, and Crime/Deviance: A Challenge to Self-Control Theory." *Journal of Research in Crime and Delinquency* 40: 426–453.

———. 2003b. "Self-Control and Crime/Deviance: Cognitive vs. Behavioral Measures." *Journal of Quantitative Criminology* 19: 333–366.

———. 2004. "Capacity for Self-Control and Individuals' Interest in Exercising Self-Control." *Journal of Quantitative Criminology* 20: 143–172.

Tonry, Michael. 1990. "Research on Drugs and Crime." In Michael Tonry and James Q. Wilson (eds.), *Drugs and Crime*. Chicago: University of Chicago Press, 1–8.

Tonry, Michael, and James Q. Wilson (eds.). 1990. *Drugs and Crime*. Chicago: University of Chicago Press.

Torgler, Benno, and Neven T. Valev. 2006. *Women and Illegal Activities: Gender Differences and Women's Willingness to Comply over Time*. Andrew Young School of Public Studies Working Paper 06–56. Atlanta: Georgia State University, Andrew Young School of Public Studies.

Treaster, Joseph B. 2005. "Fraud in Insurance Is Vast, Spitzer Tells a State Panel." *New York Times*, January 8, C2.

Turk, Austin. 1969. *Criminality and the Legal Order*. Chicago: Rand-McNally.

Turner, Michael G., and Alex R. Piquero. 2002. "The Stability of Self-Control." *Journal of Criminal Justice* 30: 457–471.

Uggen, Christopher. 2000. "Work as a Turning Point in the Life Course of Criminals: A Model." *American Sociological Review* 65: 529–546.

Unnever, James D., Mark Colvin, and Francis T. Cullen. 2004. "Crime and Coercion: A Test of Core Theoretical Propositions." *Journal of Research in Crime and Delinquency* 41: 244–268.

Unnever, James D., and Dewey G. Cornell. 2003. "Bullying, Self-Control, and ADHD." *Journal of Interpersonal Violence* 18: 129–147.

Unnever, James D., Francis T. Cullen, and Robert Agnew. 2006. "Why Is 'Bad Parenting' Criminogenic? Implications from Rival Theories." *Youth Violence and Juvenile Justice* 4: 3–33.

Unnever, James D., Francis T. Cullen, and Travis C. Pratt. 2003. "Parental Management, ADHD, and Delinquency Involvement: Reassessing Gottfredson and Hirschi's General Theory." *Justice Quarterly* 20: 471–500.

U.S. Census Bureau. 2007. *Population Estimates: State by Age, Sex, Race, and Hispanic Origin*. Data set available at http://www.census.gov/popest/datasets.html

U.S. Department of Justice, Federal Bureau of Investigation. 2001. *Crime in the United States, 2000*. Washington, DC: U.S. Government Printing Office.

Vaughan, Diane. 1999. "The Dark Side of Organizations: Mistake, Misconduct, and Disaster." *Annual Review of Sociology* 25: 271–305.

Vazsonyi, Alexander T., and Jennifer M. Crosswhite. 2004. "A Test of Gottfredson and Hirschi's General Theory of Crime in African American Adolescents." *Journal of Research in Crime and Delinquency* 41 (4): 407–432.

Vazsonyi, Alexander T., Lloyd E. Pickering, Marianne Junger, and Dick Hessing. 2001. "An Empirical Test of a General Theory of Crime: A Four-Nation Comparative Study of Self-Control and the Prediction of Deviance." *Journal of Research in Crime and Delinquency* 38: 91–131.

Venkatesh, Sudhir. 1997. "The Social Organization of Street Gang Activity in an Urban Ghetto." *American Journal of Sociology* 103: 82–111.

Vold, George B., Thomas Bernard, and Jeffrey B. Snipes. 1998. *Theoretical Criminology* (4th ed.). New York: Oxford University Press.

Von Mises, Ludwig. 1996. *Human Action*. Little Rock, AR: Fox & Wilkes.

Wagner, Fernando, and James C. Anthony. 2002. "From First Drug Use to Drug Dependence: Developmental Periods of Risk for Dependence upon Marijuana, Cocaine, and Alcohol." *Neuropsychopharmacology* 26 (April): 479–488.

Walker, Lenore. 1979. *The Battered Woman*. New York: Harper & Row.

Walsh-Czarnecki, Peggy. 2004. Students on Payroll for Learning. *Detroit Free Press*, November 29. Accessed September 20, 2005, at http://www.freep.com/news/education/pay29e_20041129.htm

Walzer, Susan. 1996. "Thinking About the Baby: Gender and Divisions of Infant Care." *Social Problems* 43 (May): 219–243.

Wang, Gabe T., Hengrui Qiao, Shaowei Hong, and Jie Zhang. 2002. "Adolescent Social Bond, Self-Control, and Deviant Behavior in China." *International Journal of Contemporary Sociology* 39: 52–68.

Warr, Mark. 2002. *Companions in Crime: The Social Aspects of Criminal Conduct.* New York: Cambridge University Press.

Warshaw, Robin. 1988. *I Never Called It Rape.* New York: Harper & Row.

Weisburd, David, and Elin Waring, with Ellen F. Chayet. 2001. *White-Collar Crime and Criminal Careers.* Cambridge, U.K.: Cambridge University Press.

Wellford, Charles F. 1989. "Towards an Integrated Theory of Criminal Behavior." In Steven F. Messner, Marvin D. Krohn, and Allen E. Liska (eds.), *Theoretical Integration in the Study of Deviance and Crime: Problems and Prospects.* Albany: State University of New York Press, 119–127.

West, Carolyn M., and S. Rose. 2000. "Dating Aggression Among Low Income African American Youth: An Examination of Gender Differences and Antagonistic Beliefs." *Violence Against Women* 6 (5): 470–494.

West, D. J., and David P. Farrington. 1977. *The Delinquent Way of Life.* London: Heinemann.

Wheeler, Stanton, David Weisburd, Elin Waring, and Nancy Bode. 1988. "White Crimes and Criminals." *American Criminal Law Review* 25: 331–358.

Wicklund, R. A. 1975. "Objective Self-Awareness." *Advances in Experimental Social Psychology* 8: 233–275.

Widom, Cathy Spatz. 1989. "Does Violence Beget Violence? A Critical Examination of the Literature." *Psychological Bulletin* 106: 3–28.

Widom, Cathy Spatz, and Joseph B. Kuhns. 1996. "Childhood Victimization and Subsequent Risk for Promiscuity, Prostitution, and Teenage Pregnancy: A Prospective Study." *American Journal of Public Health* 86 (11): 1607–1612.

Widom, Cathy Spatz, and Michael G. Maxfield. 2001. *An Update on the "Cycle of Violence."* NCJ 184894. Washington, DC: U.S. Department of Justice, National Institute of Justice.

Wiebe, Richard P. 2003. "Reconciling Psychopathy and Low Self-Control." *Justice Quarterly* 20: 297–336.

Wikström, P.-O. H. 1990. "Age and Crime in a Stockholm Cohort." *Journal of Quantitative Criminology* 6: 61–84.

Wikström, Per-Olof, and Kyle Treiber. 2007. "The Role of Self-Control in Crime Causation: Beyond Gottfredson and Hirschi's General Theory of Crime." *European Journal of Criminology* 48: 237–264.

Wilson, James Q. 1997. *Moral Judgment: Does the Abuse Excuse Threaten Our Legal System?* New York: Basic Books.

Wilson, James Q., and Richard Herrnstein. 1985. *Crime and Human Nature.* New York: Simon & Schuster.

Wilson, William Julius. 1987. *The Truly Disadvantaged: The Inner City, the Underclass, and Public Policy.* Chicago: University of Chicago Press.

———. 1996. *When Work Disappears: The World of the New Urban Poor.* New York: Knopf.

Wright, John Paul, and Kevin M. Beaver. 2005. "Do Parents Matter in Creating Self-Control in Their Children? A Genetically Informed Test of Low Self-Control." *Criminology* 43 (November): 1169–1198.

Wright, John Paul, and Francis Cullen. 2001. "Parental Efficacy and Delinquent Behavior: Do Control and Support Matter?" *Criminology* 39 (August): 677–736.

Wright, Richard T., and Scott Decker. 1994. *Burglars on the Job: Streetlife and Residential Breakins.* Boston: Northeastern University Press.

Wright, Richard, Robert H. Logie, and Scott H. Decker. 1995. "Criminal Expertise and Offender Decision Making: An Experimental Study of the Target Selection Process in Residential Burglary." *Journal of Research in Crime and Delinquency* 32 (March): 39–53.

Wrong, Dennis. 1961. "The Oversocialized Conception of Man in Modern Sociology." *American Sociological Review* 26: 183–193.

Yablonsky, Lewis. 1962. *The Violent Gang.* New York: Macmillan.

Zager, Mary Ann. 1993. *Explicating and Testing a General Theory of Crime.* Ph.D. dissertation, Department of Sociology, University of Arizona, Tempe.

———. 1994. "Gender and Crime." In Travis Hirschi and Michael Gottfredson (eds.), *The Generality of Deviance.* New Brunswick, NJ: Transaction, 71–80.

Zhao, Jihong, and Quint Thurman. 2003. *Funding Community Policing to Reduce Crime: Have COPS Grants Made a Difference from 1994 to 2000?* Technical Report. Omaha: Community Policing Initiative, Department of Criminal Justice, University of Nebraska.

Zimring, Franklin, and Gordon Hawkins. 1997. *Crime Is Not the Problem: Lethal Violence in America.* New York: Oxford University Press.

Zumoff, Barnett, Gladys W. Strain, Lorraine K. Miller, and William Rosner. 1995. "Twenty-Four-Hour Mean Plasma Testosterone Concentration Declines with Age in Normal Premenopausal Women." *Journal of Clinical Endocrinology and Metabolism* 80: 1429–1430.

INDEX

General Theory of Crime, A (Gottfredson and Hirschi), 3, 10–11, 20, 61, 77, 90, 103, 126, 203, 205–7, 209–10, 214; critique of positivism in, 21–24; definition of crime in, 4–9; opportunity in, 54–55, 59–60, 197; self-control in, 12–13, 27–28, 49–50, 104–6
Genetic traits, 65, 72
Genocides, 227
Gratification: delaying, 73
Gratification seeking, 62, 78–79, 104
Group invariance, 29
Gun control policy, 213

Harlem, 193
Hawaii, 135
Health care, 42, 45, 47
Hedonism: short-term, 87
Heredity, 72
Heroin use, 57, 188, 193
High school students, 170, 224; delinquency rates, 47–48
Hispanics. *See* Latina/os
Homicide rates, 39, 40, 45, 47, 53, 59, 168, 169; drug use and, 194–95, 196
Homosexuality, 7–8
Honor: inner-city youth, 119
Hough, Michael, 52
Households, 13, 139, 140, 176, 177, 178
Housing projects: gangs and, 119
Human capital, 98, 116
Human ecology: urban gangs, 107–8
Hungary, 30
Huxley, Thomas, 215

Imitation, 80
Immigrants, 109, 115, 116–17
Impulse control, 3, 15
Impulsivity, 72, 87, 129, 138, 147, 165; vs. planning, 162–63; in psychopathy, 121–22
Incarceration, 214; and decline in crime rate, 183–84
Individuals: criminal trajectories of, 40–41
Industry: and urban growth, 107
Insider trading, 152
Institutional-anomie theory, 92–94; consumer role, 96–97; empirical tests of, 100–101

Insurance industry, 152
Intensification model, 193–94
Interaction: negative reciprocal, 116
Interaction process, 17–18
Intoxication, 6, 27
Investment banking, 148
IRT. *See* Item response theory
Israel, 40
Italy, 207
Item response theory (IRT): self-control attitudinal scale, 31–32

Japan, 30, 31, 40
Johnson, Lyndon B., 174
Junior high school students, 224
Juvenile detention, 108
Juvenile offenders, 32, 45, 178; delinquency, 41–42; larceny-theft, 175–76; property crimes, 180–81. *See also* Adolescents

Koreans, 31
Kornhauser, Ruth, 91; *Social Sources of Delinquency,* 110–13

Labeling theory, 189
Labor force: females in, 183
Labor market, 124; women in, 139–40
Larceny, 40, 45
Larceny-theft, 178, 182; juveniles, 175–76
Latina/os, 39, 119, 135, 140
Laws: criminal, 22
Lay, Ken, 157
Learned behavior: crime as, 145–46
Learning, 100, 120; positive, 62–63; social, 73, 79–81, 85–86
Learning theory, 81, 190–92, 198
Life skills: training in, 98–99
Liquor law violations, 47
Lombroso, Césare, 21; *L'uomo delinquente,* 9–10

Males, 25, 31, 44, 45, 108, 109, 135, 136, 139, 186; masculinity, 132–33; property crimes by, 180–81; self-control theory and, 128–29
Marijuana use, 31, 39, 47, 120, 135, 198
Market culture, 107; education and, 98–100; family and, 97–98